CORPUS RUBENIANUM
LUDWIG BURCHARD

PART XXII (2)
ARCHITECTURE AND SCULPTURE

RUBENS'S HOUSE

IN TWO VOLUMES

I · TEXT

II · APPENDICES & ILLUSTRATIONS

CORPUS RUBENIANUM
LUDWIG BURCHARD

AN ILLUSTRATED CATALOGUE RAISONNÉ
OF THE WORK OF PETER PAUL RUBENS
BASED ON THE MATERIAL ASSEMBLED
BY LUDWIG BURCHARD (1886–1960)
IN TWENTY-NINE PARTS

SPONSORED BY THE CITY OF ANTWERP AND THE RUBENIANUM FUND
AND EDITED BY THE CENTRUM RUBENIANUM

Editorial Board
N. BÜTTNER – F. HEALY – K. JONCKHEERE – G. MARTIN
E. MCGRATH – L. NIJKAMP – N. DE POORTER – B. SCHEPERS
I. VAN TICHELEN – B. VANOPPEN – H. VLIEGHE – J. WOOD

Research Staff
B. SCHEPERS – B. VANOPPEN – I. VAN TICHELEN

UNDER THE PATRONAGE OF HSH PRINCE HANS-ADAM II VON UND ZU LIECHTENSTEIN
AND THE INTERNATIONAL UNION OF ACADEMIES (UAI)

RUBENS

ARCHITECTURE AND SCULPTURE

RUBENS'S HOUSE

BY
NORA DE POORTER AND FRANS BAUDOUIN

VOLUME TWO
APPENDICES & ILLUSTRATIONS

HARVEY MILLER PUBLISHERS

HARVEY MILLER PUBLISHERS
An Imprint of Brepols Publishers
London / Turnhout

Translated from the Dutch by Jantien Black
and
Lee Preedy (Chapters V–VIII)

Edited by Arnout Balis, Brecht Vanoppen, Isabelle Van Tichelen, Marieke D'Hooghe, Joannes van den Maagdenberg and Valerie Herremans (Images)
© 2022 Centrum Rubenianum

British Library Cataloguing in Publication Data
A catalogue record for this book is available from the British Library
ISBN (set) 978-1-912554-64-5
ISBN (volume 1) 978-1-912554-90-4
ISBN (volume 2) 978-1-912554-91-1
D/2022/0095/133

All rights reserved.
No part of this publication may be reproduced,
stored in a retrieval system, or transmitted in any form by
any means, electronic, mechanical, photocopying, recording, or
otherwise, without the prior permission of Harvey Miller Publishers.

Printed in the EU on acid-free paper.

Appendix I: Documents

I.1 – 1610, 1 November. The Amsterdam Sale Contract. Nicolaes Coop, Acting on Behalf of Peter Paul Rubens, Buys a House in Antwerp from Hans Thys

Amsterdam, Stadsarchief, 5075 Inventaris van het Archief van de Notarissen ter Standplaats Amsterdam, Jan Fransen Bruijningh, inv. no. 196 no. 21, fols 33v–34v, under blue no. 595. Published by Bredius, *Rubensdocument*, 1912, pp. 216–218; Devroe, *Rubens' huis*, 2008, I, pp. 133–134.
Also in *Antwerp, Rubenshuis Archive, inv. no. RH.D.054.2.01*. Image in DAMS.

[1] [fol. 33v] Op huyden den eersten Novembris Anno Sestienhondert ende tien, compareerden voor my Jan Fransen Bruyningh etc. ter presentie van de ondergeschreven getuijgen d'eersame Hans Thijsz coopman binnen der voorsz. stede, ter eenre, en Nicolaes Coop, burger der selver stede, uijten name, en van wegen Sr. Pietro Pauli Rubbens, wonende tot Antwerpen, ter andere syden, ende verclaerden, dat sy comparanten in der voorsz. qualiteit geaccordeert en verdragen syn, over de conditien ende voorwaerden van coope hiernae beschreven, te weten, dat de voorn. Hans Thijsz vercocht heeft en vercoopt mits desen aen den voorsz. Nicolaes Coop, dewelcke voor ende ten behoeve van den voorsz. Petro Pauli Rubbens van denselven Hans Thijsz bekendt gecocht te hebben

[2] een huijs ende Bleeckhoff erven ende gronden met eenen vryen gangh aen 't Bleeckvelt, streckende nae de Lammekens raem, in allen schijne 't voorsz. huijs, genaemt de Wapper binnen de stadt van Antwerpen voorsz. op de Wapper gestaen ende gelegen is, beheymt en betimmert staet, met alle de vrydommen ende gerechticheden, daer toe behoorende ende belendt wesende, alles vermogens die schepenbrieven ende bescheyden daervan synde, te leveren tegens kersmisse eerstcomende;

[3] ende dat voor de somme van vijffhondert en tsestich carolus guldens erffelyck tot XL gr. den gulden, bedragende in hoofdsomme (tegens den penninck sestien te reeckenen) achtduijsent negen hondert ende tsestich carolus guldens, welcke cooppenningen de voorsz. Pietro Pauli Rubbens gehouden sal wesen (als hij aenneemt en belooft mits desen) [fol. 34r] aen den voorsz. Hans Thijsz oft sijnder actie hebbende costeloos ende schadeloos binnen Antwerpen voorsz. te voldoen ende te betalen; namentlijck een gerechte derde part gereet, nevens de leveringe ende opdracht, Item een gelycke derdepart een Jaer daernaer, wesende Kersmisse Anno XVJc ende sesstiene, ende 't leste derdepart totter volle ende geheele betalinge toe van de voorsz. cooppenningen kersmisse Anno XVIc ende twaelf, alles vrij, costeloos ende schadeloos gelt, sonder eenige cortinge.

[4] Met dese expresse conditie (alsoo 't voorsz. huys, gronden ende appendentien van dien belast is mette somme van vijff ende tachtentich guldens erffelijck, mede ter losse den penninck sestien, wesende in hoofsomme derthien hondert en tsestich guldens corent,) dat de voorn. cooper alsulcke erffelycke rente t'sijnen laste sal moeten nemen ende den vercooper mitsgaders sijnen erven ende naecomelingen daervan ten eeuwigen daghen [*a word crossed out*] ende bevrijden, dies dat hij de voorsz. hooftsomme van dertienhondert tsestich guldens aen de eerste paije van de voorsz. cooppenningen gereet te betalen, den vercooper sal defalcqueren en afftrecken; voorts vrij huijs en erve, sonder vordere belastinge.

[5] Dies is noch geconditioneert, soo verre den voorn. Petro Pauli Rubbens eenige difficulteijt soude mogen moveren, oft hem beswaert vinden wegen de belastinghe van tsestich guldens erffelijck, oft wat meerder off minder, die op andere panden uijtgaen ende betaelt werden, daervooren dese pant eertijts mede mochte sijn ge(h)ipotequeert ende verbonden, dat hij alsdan vermogen sal ende alleen sijn vrije optie ende keure hebben, omme alsulcke erffelycke renten t'sijnder meerder verseeckeringe ende bewaringe op dit voorsz. vercochte huijs mette gronden ende appendentien van dien te houden, ende in de leste payije van de cooppenninghen die hooftsomme tegens den penninck sestien te defalcqueren,

APPENDIX I

ende de renten daervan alle Jaers aen den voorsz. hr. vercooper oft sijnder actie vercrygende, opleggen ende betalen, costeloos ende schadeloos als voijren.
[6] Is mede geaccordeert, dat de voorsz. hr. Pietro Pauli Rubbens boven de voorgeroerde cooppenningen tot een recognitie ende gedachtenisse van dese [fol. 34v] coope den voors. Hans Thijsz sal toegeven ende leveren een stuck schilderije by syn eygen handt gemaeckt, soo groot ende cleijn als hem Rubbens goetduncken sal, daer hy eere van sal begeren,
[7] ende noch bovendien een soon van den voorsz. Hans Thijsz leeren ende onderwysen sonder daer vooren yets te genieten de conste van schilderen ende voor hem niets secreet houden, volgende sijne belofte, mits dat de Jonghman syn eijgen coste sal doen, alleen de vrije leringe sal hy by de meester genieten, ende daer toe by hem vrij acces hebben.
[8] Eyntelyck zijnter noch bevoirwaert, dat den voorsz. vercooper oft syn commis tot Antwerpen ende den voorn. Petro Paulo Rubbens beyde haer beste ende uijterste vlijt sullen doen, voor ende aleer dese coope voortganck sal hebben, t'voorgeroerde huijs metten appendentien ende de gronden van dien te ontlasten ende te bevrijden van den Exu, ende dat voor soodanigen redelijcken penninck als doenlijck sal wesen. Ende soo sulcx niet en conde geschieden op thoochste ter somme van tien ponden grooten vlaems, die den voorsz. Hans Thysz, soo 't van noode is, daertoe gehouden is te betalen aen den Exumeester, dat in dien gevalle dese coope ende alle de conditien vooren breeder uijtgedruct nul ende van geender waerden sal ende sullen wesen min noch meer, oft desen niet en ware beschreven, ende de coope effect hebbende, sal de leveringe ende opdrachte geschieden binnen Antwerpen voorsz. naer costume aldaer geobserveert soo by den Erentfesten Doctor Andries Backer, raedt ende Medicus van syne F^e D^t van Bruynswyck als by den voorn. Hans Thysz vercooper selffs oft hare respecthive volmachtigers.
[9] Sonder fraude, ende versochten sy comparanten etc. Gedaen binnen der voorsz. stede van Amsterdamme ten huijse van den voorn. Nicolaes Coop ter presentie van Hans Boudaen, Harmen Goris ende Cornelis Velt, getuygen hier toe versocht. Get.: Johan Thys. Nicolaes Coop. Hans Boudaen. Cornelis Feldt. Herman Gooris.

I.2 – 1611, 4 January. The Antwerp Sale Contract. Christoffel Caers, Acting on Behalf of Andries Backer and his Wife, Magdalena Thys, Sells a Property on the Wapper to Peter Paul Rubens

Antwerp, FelixArchief, Schepenregisters 1600–1645, inv. no. SR#494, fols 1r–5r. Published by Génard, *Rubens*, 1877, pp. 442–447; Delen, *Rubens's huis*, 1933, pp. 23–25; Tijs, *Rubens en Jordaens*, 1984, pp. 370–372, repr. (fragment) p. 93; Devroe, Rubens' huis, 2008, I, pp. 135–138.
Also in *Antwerp, Rubenshuis Archive, inv. no. RH.D.054.2.03–11.* Image in DAMS.

[1] Compareerde Christoffel Caers, coopman juwelier, inden name ende als omme, onder andere, tgene nabescreven is te doene volcommelijck gemechticht van Doctor Andreas Backaert ende Jouffrouwe Magdalena Thys, sijne huysvrouwe, bij procuratie gepasseert voor Borgermeesteren, Schepen ende Raedt deser stadt opten xiii den dach Junij anno xvic negen, die wij sagen ende hoorden lesen, ende bekenden ende verlijden inder voors. qualiteyt
[2] dat sij soo midts der sommen van sevenduijsent sessehondert guldens eens die Sr Pietro Paulo Rubbens op heden met eenen anderen brieve, voor ons oock gepasseert, bekent heeft schuldich te sijn den voors. Doctor Andreas Backaert ende Jouffrouwe Magdalena Thys, sijne huysvrouwe, als midts het affdragen vande renten nabescreven, vercocht heeft wel ende wettelijck den voors. Sr Pietro Paulo Rubbens
[3] eene huijsinge met eender grooter poorten, plaetse, gaelderye, coeckene, camers, gronde ende allen den toebehoorten, met noch eenen bleyckhove daarneffens suijtwaert gelegen, oock metten gronde ende allen den toebehoorten, gestaen ende gelegen opden Wapper alhier, [fol. 1v] tusschen derve vande

huijsinge van Henrick Hoons, aen deen sijde noortwaert, ende sekere huijskens toebehoorende […] [sic] aen dander sijde suijtwaert, commende den voors. Bleyckhoff achter, oostwaerts, aenden muer vander gulden vande Coloveriershove,

[4] gelijck ende in alle der manieren ende met alle alsulcke servituijten ende gerechticheden van waterleydingen, lichtscheppinghen ende gemeijnschappen van mueren als wijlen Franchois Gielis deselve huijsen metten raemhove, gronde ende toebehoorten, met diversche andere huijsingen hieraff eertijts gespleten sijnde, opten XIIIe meerte anno XVc sevenendertich, tegens Maria Deckers, weduwe wijlen Peeters Hoon, des lakenbereijders, met heure consorten, gecocht ende gecregen heeft ende gelijck de kinderen ende erffgenamen des voors. wijlen Franchois Gielis bij Heer Lodewijck van Linden, Riddere, Amptman deser stadt, wtten name van sijnder offitie, opten thienden Januarij anno XVc negenentseventich inden voors. raemhoff met gronde ende toebehoorten gegoeijt ende geerft sijn,

[5] ende welcke voors. huijsinghe metten raemhoff den voors. Doc[tor] [fol. 2r] Andreas Backaert ende Jouffrouwe Magdalena Gielis, sijne huysvrouwe, competerende is eensdeels midts der doot ende afflijvicheyt van wijlen Christoffel Thys ende Jouffrouwe Martha Gielis, derselver Magdalena vader ende moeder wijlen, ende eensdeels als wtgecocht hebbende henne medeconsorten ende erffgenamen, volgende de transporten daeraff voor Schepenen deser stadt gepasseert te wetene van Jan Thys, Christoffelssone wijlen, opten vierden Octobris anno XVc vijfentnegentich, van Franchois Thys, voor hem ende als wtgecocht hebbende Anthonis Thys, sijnen broeder, opten elffsten meerte anno XVIc ende twee, […][*a long and detailed listing of the previous owners of the plot is omitted here*]

[6] [fol. 3v] d'welck hij hem met alle de voorgeruerde brieven midts desen overgaff, droech oppe etc., te waerne van allen commere ende calaengien. wtgenomen dryentwintich guldens erffelijck der weduwen Smidt; item, gelijcke XXIII guldenen erffelijck der weduwen Cornelis Pluijm; item, negenthien guldenen derthien stuyvers een ort erffelijck den Capittele tonser Liever Vrouwen alhier ende twintich guldenen erffelijck Doctor Godefridus Verreijcken, daer jaerlijcx wtgaende ende anders nijet, welcken commer, tsamen bedragende vijventachentich guldenen erffelijck,

[7] heeft de voors. Sr PietroPaulo Rubbens (die oock mede voor ons compareerde,) geloeft ende geloeffde, midts desen, voor hem ende sijne nacommelingen van nu voordane eeuwelijck durende jaerlijcx te geldene ende te betalen, sonder des voors. Doctors Andreas Backaerts ende Jouffrouwe Magdalena Thys, sijne huijsvrouwe, henne goeden ende nacommelingen cost, last oft schade, de voors. huijsinge metten raemhove, gronde ende toebehoorten, hem selven ende alle zijne andere goeden, rurende ende onrurende, hoedanich die wesen moghen, die hij nu heeft [fol. 4r] ende noch vercrijgen sal, daervore verbindende ende te pande settende, behoudelijck dat den voors. raemhoff eensdeels medepant is over vijventwintich grooten Brabants erffelijck ten Godtshuijse van Sinte Michiels, die men wt sekere andere huijsen ende erven daerontrent gelegen betalen moet, sonder desselffs raemhoffs cost, last oft schade, oock naer inhoudt der brieven ende anders nijet. Gebraeck ijet aenden voors. coop, opdracht, waernisse ende claernisse, dat geloeffde de voors. comparant dat de voors. Doctor Andreas Backaert ende Jouffrouwe Magdalena Thys, sijne huysvrouwe, midtsgaders Jan Thys, coopman, woonende tot Amstelredamme (die hem comparant daertoe specialijcken gemechticht heeft bij procuratie gepasseert voor Wethouderen van Amstelredamme voors. opten XXIIden dach der voorleder maent Decembris, ons te desen gethoont,) altijt wel ende volcommelijck elck als principael opleggen ende voldoen selen, *unde obligavit* der selver sijner constituanten respective persoonen ende goeden, rurende ende onrurende, present ende toecommende, sonder argelist. [fol. 4v]

[8] De voors. Sr. Pietro Paulo Rubbens bekende schuldich te sijne, van goeder rechtveerdiger schult, Doctor Andreas Backaert ende Jouffrouwe Magdalena Thys, sijnen huysvrouwe, de somme van sevenduijsent seshondert guldenen eens, toecommende ter causer vanden coop vande huijsinghe ende raemhove, metten gronde ende toebehoorten nageruert, daerinne Christoffel Caers, als gemechticht vanden selven Doctor Andreas Backaert ende sijne huysvrouwe, hem comparant op heden date deser, met eenen anderen brieve, voor ons oock gepasseert, gegoeijt ende geerft heeft,

APPENDIX I

[9] welcke voornoemde somme van sevenduijsent seshondert guldenen heeft de voors. comparant geloeft ende geloeffde, midts desen, wel ende volcommelijck opte leggen ende betalen aenden voors. Doctor Andries Backaert ende Jouffrouwe Magdalena Thijs, sijne huijsvrouwe, oft den brenger deser letteren in deser naervolgende manieren, te wetene: eenduijsent seshondert sessentwintich guldens derthien stuijvers eenen grooten brabants eens, soo haest ende schier als hem tvoors. huys ledich gelevert sal wesen; item tweeduijsent negenhondert sessentachtentich guldens derthien stuijvers eenen grooten brabants daeraff [fol. 5r] binnen eenen jaere daerna ende de resterende twee duysent negen hondert sessentachtentich guldens derthien stuijvers eenen grooten brabants eens, binnen eenen anderen jaere daernaest volgende, sonder eenich langer vertreck oft dilaij; verbindende daervore ende te pande settende de voors. huijsinge metten raemhove *ut in praecidenti contractu* ende voordane hem selven ende alle sijne andere goeden, rurende ende onrurende, present ende toecommende, ende dit al op vonnisse ende op parate, reelle ende heerlijcke executie. Sonder argelist.
4 marty […] van spaatgelt xxviij guldens
Quarta Januarij xvicxi.

I.3 – 1611, October – 1614, March. The Account Book of the Guild of the Arquebusiers Mentions Payments Related to Moving the *Triptych of the Descent from the Cross* from 'Rubens's house' to the Cathedral

Antwerp, FelixArchief, Gilden en ambachten, Kolveniersgilde of Gilde van St Christoffel. Rekeningen en bewijs: 1604–1630, inv. no. GA#4665, fols 90v, 103v, 133v. Published by De Reiffenberg, *Rubens*, 1837, pp. 15–16; Max Rooses, *Afdoening*, 1910, pp. 230–231; here quoted as in Van den Nieuwenhuizen, *Descente de croix*, 1962, pp. 40 (docs 3 and 4), 41 (doc. 7).

[1]–1611, between 4 and 12 October (fol. 90v)
Item syn de dekens tot drye distincte reysen gegaen ten huyse van den schilder, soe om de schilderye te doen voorderen, als oyck om het peneel te visiteren ofter egeen speck in en was, ende op de drye reysen soo aen drinckgelt den knechts van den schilder als aldaer in wyn verteert, in alles ix gul. x st.

[2]–1612, between 12 and 17 September (fol. 103v)
Item heeft de rendant noch betaelt aen de arbeyders voor hennen loon gedaen soe int vueren van de stoffen van houtwerck panneel als het affdoen van de schilderye van den solder tot in den vloer, ten huyse van den schilder Rubbens, mede van die te vueren in de cappelle, leveringe van berdt, daertoe verbesicht, ende andere materialen, midsgaeders oyck aen verscheyde gelagen soe in besteden mette aennemers als wercklieden verteert tsamen, nae luyt de particuliere specificatie daer van synde, gesp. nr. 3, de somme van iᶜlxxvii gl. xiiii ¼ st.

[3]–1614, 18 February and March (fol. 133v)
Den 18 february ende 6 meert van de deuren van den aultaer ten huyse van den schilder aff te doene, ende in de kerkcke te draegene. Betaelt met twee guldenen met de arbeyders verteert, vii gl. 1 ist.

I.4 – 1613, 2 March – 13 May. Receipts of Payments from Rubens (Capital and Outstanding Rents) to Redeem Mortgages on his Property

[1] 1613, 2 March – Payment by Rubens of the capital (46 guilders) and all outstanding rents, to Johanna Bredenbach and Godevriet Andriessens.

Antwerp, Rubenshuis Archive, Fonds 'Expropriation 1937', inv. no. RH.D.054.204–11. Image in DAMS.
Also in *Antwerp, FelixArchief, Schepenregister, 1613/ V: Usens & Neesen, SR#506, fol. 295r;* transcription in Büttner – Heinen, eds, *Quellen und Dokumente*, 2011, no. 112 (online publ.).

[2] 1613, 28 March – Payment by Rubens of the capital (19 guilders and 2 stuivers) and all outstanding rents to Canon Godevaert van Santvoirde, acting on behalf of the Cathedral of Our Lady.

Antwerp, Rubenshuis Archive, Fonds 'Expropriation 1937', inv. no. RH.D.054.2.5–11. Image in DAMS.

[3] 1613, 30 May – Payment by Rubens of the capital (20 guilders) and all outstanding rents to Godefridus Verrijcken, 'doctor in medicijnen'.

Antwerp, Rubenshuis Archive, Fonds 'Expropriation 1937', inv. no. RH.D.054.2.6–11. Image in DAMS.
Also in *Antwerp, FelixArchief, Schepenregister 1613/II: Gaverelle & Kieffelt, SR#503, fols 260v–261v;* Büttner – Heinen, eds, *Quellen und Dokumente*, 2011, no. 114 (online publ.).

I.5 – 1615, July and August. Notes from the Account Book of the Guild of the Arquebusiers Concerning the Wall and Privy Bordering Rubens's Garden

Antwerp, FelixArchief, Gilden en ambachten, Kolveniersgilde of Gilde van St Christoffel. Rekeningen en bewijs: 1604–1630, inv. no. GA#4665, fols 150v, 152r.

[1]–1615, 25 July
Den 25 July veraccordeert met Franchoeys de Crayer int opmaecken van den muer tegens den hoff van Sr. Rubbens ende doen verteert metten selven – ix gl. xiiij st.

(fol. 150v: published by Rooses, *Afdoening*, 1910, pp. 232–233; Devroe, *Rubens' huis*, 2008, I, p. 53).

[2]–1615, 13 August
Item den xiiien augusti veraccordeert inden hoff met Franchoeys de Crayere nopens dmaecken van dnieuw huysken ende secret – doen verteert – ix gul. vii st.

(fol. 150v; published by De Poorter, *Kolveniers*, 1988, p. 217, n. 64).

[3]–1615, no date given, on or after 13 August
Item bet[aelt] aen Andries de Vos voer 323 potten biers aldaer gedroncken byde arbeyders int maecken vanden muer ende huysken daer aff Sr. Rubbens de helft van het bier moet gelden in respecte vanden muer ende voorders nyet, tsamen bedragende volgens de twee kerven gesp[ecificeerd]. nr. 33 – xl gl. ij st.

(fol. 152r; published by Rooses, *Afdoening*, 1910, p. 233; Devroe, *Rubens' huis*, 2008, I, p. 53).

[4]–1615, no date given, on or after 13 August
Item Bet[aelt] de erffscheyders voort meten vanden nieuwen gemetsten muer daeraff Rubbens voors. de eene helft moet dragen per quittancie No. 34 – iiij gl.

(fol. 152r; published by Rooses, *Afdoening*, 1910, p. 233).

APPENDIX I

I.6 – 1615. Excerpts from Balthasar Moretus's preface to Seneca, *Opera*, 1615 [not paginated]

[…] opportune Petrus-Paullus Rubenius, aevi nostri Apelles, adiuvit, qui cum huberrimum rei antiquariae thesaurum Roma Antverpiam attulerit, nec eximii Philosophi imaginem […] neglexit.

[…] Alteram quam spectas effigiem, è prototypo marmoreo idem Rubenius expressit: quod Româ allatum, in elegantissimo Muséo suo asservat; […]

Translation[1]:
Peter Paul Rubens, the Apelles of our time, was able to help since he had brought a very rich treasure of antiquities from Rome – and included in it an image of the great Philosopher.

The other image ['portrait'] you see was taken by Rubens from the marble original which he had brought from Rome and kept in his very fine museum.

I.7 – 1616, 17 February. Rubens is Mentioned in the Funeral Roll of Martina Plantin (d. 17 February 1616), as Living in the Neighbourhood of the Arenbergstraat.

Antwerp, Plantin-Moretus Archief, no. 1178, Begrafenisrollen [etc.], no. 2: Begrafenisrol Martina Plantin, weduwe Jan Moretus, 1616 [not paginated]. Mentioned by Rooses, *Rubens*, 1904, p. 146; erroneously dated 1617, see Chapter IV, p. 119, n. 5.

[…] Arenbergstraet […]
Peeter Pauwels Rubbens

I.8 – 1616, September. Rubens appears in the list of members of the Guild of St Luke as living on the Wapper

Antwerp, Plantin-Moretus Archief, no. 184. Published by Rooses, ed., *Boek gehouden*, Antwerp, 1878, p. 5.

[…] Opden Wapper…Peeter Rubbens, pintor

I.9 – 1616, 2 November. Contract between Hans van Mildert (on Behalf of Rubens) and the Joiner Jasper Bulliau Regarding the Construction of a Staircase in Rubens's House

Antwerp, FelixArchief, Notariaat, Kaspar Van der Herstraeten, notaris te Antwerpen, Protocollen en staten, 1615–1616, inv. no. N#3838, fols 267r–267v.
Mentioned (and illustrated) in Tijs, *Rubens en Jordaens*, 1984, p. 96, repr. pp. 98–99; published by Devroe, *Rubens' huis*, 2008, I, pp. 53, 138–139; Maclot, *Rubenssite*, 2016, I, pp. 54–55 (excerpt).

---

1   Sincere thanks to Elizabeth McGrath for the English translation.

[fol. 267r] Op heden de tweede november inde jaren xvi^c ende sesthiene compareerde voer mij Jaspar Vande Herstrate, openbaer wethouder bij de rade van Brabant totter exercitie van tselver offitie geadmitteert alle de getuijghen naergenoempt de eersame Mr Jan van Mildert beltsnyder alhier t'Antwerpen stipuleren voer Mr Sgr. Paulus Rubbens schilder ter eenen ende Jaspar Billeau schrynwercker alhier t'Antwerpen voors. ter anderen welcke voorschrevene comparanten synde ende verclaerde inde voors. hennen qualiteyt metten andere aengegaen te hebben zeker accordt nopende tmaecken stellen ende volmaecken van twee houtte trappen ende laeijnen ende toedoene te staene binnen den woonhuysse ditto Mr Sgr. Paulo Rubbens t'Antwerpen op Wapper alhier ende dat in de voors. manieren te weten dat de voors. Jaspar Billeau de voers. twee trappen ende laeijnen sal maecken ende stellen binnen den voors. huijsse ter plaetse, de gaelderyen [*crossed out*] lainen ende borstweringhe tot al sulcke hooghde ende voors. twee trappen de eenen beneden de voors. gaelderyen ende de anderen daer oppe respective insgelyks tot alsulcker hooghde als hem tweede comparant alle tselven by de voors. Mr Sgr. Paulo gedesigneert ende tusschen hen beijde besproken ende geaccordeert [*in the margin*: volghens de teeckeninge(n?) daer van synde] tot behoudens dat hij tweede comparant totte voors. twee trappen sal moeten leveren alle thout daer toe noodich ende dat drooch ende geheeft naer behoren, dan sal de voors. Mr Sgr. Rubbens leveren thout totte voorschreven leenen ende borstweringhe ende den aennemere over de arbeyt van dien betaelen een hondert ende vyfenseventig gulden eens maer tmaecken vanden trappen sal de aennemere moghen wercken in dachhueren altoos te minste syn tweede sterck tot dat tvoors. werck volmaeckt sal wesen sonder middeler tijt tselver te mogen interromperen by vuijtsplijtinge oft affblijvingen te ware by siecte oft andere merckelycke toevalle die dat souden moghen beletten. Dese heeft sal [*correction*] ditto Sgr. Rubbens den voors. Mr Jaspar metten soo veele gelts contant betaelen als hij mette voors. syne gaste die weken inde voors. wercke soude moghen verdient hebben ende voors. werck alsoo loffelyck ende behoirlyck gestelt ende volmaect syn soo sal de voors. Sgr. Rubbens aen Jaspar Bulliau de voors. belooffde somme al noch schencken een stuck schilderije tsy op doeck oft panneele wesende copije naer eenich stuck van synder hant gemaect ende tselve stellen tsyne Sgr. Rubbens discretie ende midts dezen [fol. 267v] bekende partijen wel eens overcommen ende geaccordeert te synen beloven tselven elck in hennen respectie ende qualiteyt als voren alsoo naer te commende tonderhouden ende volbrenghende over tverbant van henne personen ende goede presentie ende toecommende al sonder argelist. Actum te woonhuysse myns notarius inde Swertsusterstrate binnen deser voors. Stadt van Antwerpen gestaen ten dage maent ende jaere voors. ter presentie van Jaspar Hendrik [*illegible name crossed out*] Everaerts ende Jan Baptista van Male poirtters ende ingesetene ende beyde als getuygen ende tot meerdere vasticheyt soo hebben de contraherende dese ondertekent datum ende in presentie voors.

Hans van Mildert Gaspar Billeau
Quod attestor J. van Herstrate notarius publicus

I.10 – 1618, 12 May. Excerpt from a Letter from Rubens to Sir Dudley Carleton

Kew, The National Archives, Public Record Office, Correspondence and Papers of the Secretary of State: Holland, inv. no. SP 84/125. Transcription as published by Rooses – Ruelens, *Correspondance*, 1887–1909, II, p. 149, doc. CLXVIII. English translation in Magurn, ed., *Letters*, 1955, p. 62, under no. 29.

[…] et io ho speso questo anno qualque migliaia di fiorini nella mia fabrica ne vorrei ecçedere per un capriccio li termini di buon economo […]

APPENDIX I

Translation:
and besides, I have spent this year some thousand florins on my estate, and I should not like, for a whim, to exceed the limits of good economy.

I.11 – 1618, 18 July. Excerpt from a Letter from François Sweerts to Jan de Gruytere, Mentioning the Acquisition of Marble Sculptures

Heidelberg, Universitätsbibliothek Heidelberg, Cod. Pal. Germ. 8, fols 210r–v. Published by Duverger, *Decius Mus*, 1976–78, p. 39; Baumstark – Delmarcel, *Decius Mus (CRLB)*, 2019, II, p. 222; English translation in ibid., p. 223.

[…] Wy van Antwerpen willen allenskens Italiae monumenta incorporeren. Petrus Paulus Rubenius, seculi n[ost]ri Apelles, heeft onlanckx wt Engelant becomen over 100 capita marmorea et statuas. Syn daer comen van Venetiën ex Musaeo Patriarchae Aquileiae. Desen Rubbens windt dagelyckx 100 guldens. Is niet alleen schilder, maer versatissimus in historiis et re politica, heeft alreede over 24 duysent guldens versnoept in syn huys […].

Translation:
In Antwerp, we eventually want to include *Italian monuments*. Petrus Paulus Rubenius, *who is the Apelles of our age*, has recently received from England more than *100 marble heads and statues*, and they arrived via Venice from *the museum of the Patriarch of Aquileia*. This Rubbens earns 100 guilders a day. He is principally a painter, but *well versed in historical and political matters*. He has already squandered over 24 thousand guilders on his house.

I.12 – 1620, 1 October. Excerpt from a Letter from Jan van den Wouwer to Balthasar Moretus. He Praises the City of Antwerp for the Houses of Rubens and Moretus

Antwerp, Plantin-Moretus Archief, inv. no. 94, p. 493. Published by Rooses – Ruelens, *Correspondance*, 1887–1909, II, pp. 254–256 (the excerpt p. 254); Voet, *Golden Compasses*, 1969, pp. 281, n. 3. English translation in Magurn, ed., *Letters*, 1955, p. 13.

Sed o felicem sane quoque nostram Antverpiam duobus praecipue civibus, Rubenio Moretoque! Utriusque aedes spectabunt exteri, admirabuntur advenae […]

Translation:
How fortunate is our city of Antwerp to have as her two leading citizens Rubens and Moretus! Foreigners will gaze at the houses of both, and tourists wil admire them.

I.13 – 1620. Excerpt from the Travel Journal by Wilhelm Neumay(e)r von Ramssla. He Mentions a Visit to the Studios of Rubens and Jan Breughel I in 1614

Neumayr von Ramssla, *Johann Ernst*, 1620, p. 265. Excerpt published by Arents, *Bibliotheek*, 2000, p. 292, no. Q5.

[*In the margin*: Peter Paul Rybent un Brügel zweene berühmbte Mahler]

12

Hierauff sahen sie auch bey den beyden vortrefflichen Mahlern Peter Paul Rybent und Brügeln viel herzliche Gemählde und Kunststück. Rybent Mahlet meistlich grosse Stuck, und alles in rechter natürlicher grosse, aber überauss künstlich schön, und nach dem Leben. Soll alle Wochen auff 100 Gülden arbeiten können, mag leicht ein Stück seyn, er verkauffet solches umb 2. 3. 4. auch 500. Reichsgulden; Brügel aber mahlet kleine Täfflein mit Landschafften, aber alles so subtil und künstlich, dass mans mit Verwunderung ansehen muss.

Translation: [*In the margin*: Peter Paul Rybent and Brügel two famous painters]
Hereafter they also saw many fine paintings and works of art at the houses of those two excellent painters Peter Paul Rybent and Brügeln. Rybent usually paints large pieces, and everything true to the size of the original, but exceptionally beautifully worked, and done from life. He is said to be able to bring in 100 guilders in a normal week from his work, there might be a single piece – he sells such pieces for 2, 3, 4, or even 500 guilders; Brügel, however, paints small panels with landscapes, but everything so subtly and artfully done that one is astounded by what one sees.

I.14 – 1621, 5 January. At the Request of the Slater Abraham van den Bossche, Rubens Testifies against the Carpenters who had Covered his Roof with Boards in 1615, and Failed to Do their Work Correctly. The Slater had Put right the Botched Job

Antwerp, FelixArchief, Gilden en ambachten, Schrijnwerkers en Timmerlieden, Schrijnwerkers. Processen: 1620–1622, inv. no. GA#5701, unnumbered folio. Published by Moortgat, *Rubens Roof Boarding*, online publ. [acc. 18/12/2021]; see also (without transcription): Moortgat, *Rubens's Renovation / Rubenshuis*, 2021, pp. 72–74.

Op heden den vijffden dach der maent van January int iaer onsheeren duijsent sessehondert eenentwintich. Ten versuecke van abraham vanden bossche (schalidecker) compareerden voor mij, peeter van aerdenbodeghem openbaer notaris t' antwerpen residerende ende in presentie vande getuygen naergenoempt, Deersaeme Sr Peeter Paulo Rubbens schilder van haere doorluchtichste hoocheden, ende heeft verclaert ende geattesteert, verclaerde ende attesteerde mits desen voor de gerechte waerheyt waerachtich te syne, hoe dat hij affirmant onder andere aen syne timmerlieden die gemaect hebben syne huysinge inden jare 1615 oock hadden aenbesteet te solderen ende berderen syn dack, dwelck hy heeft doen decken met schalien. Item verclaert oock waerachtich te syne dat alsoo de selve berderinghe by de voorseide timmerlieden was geleet, ende hij attestant bevonden hebbende dat de voorseide timmerlieden de voorseide berderinge licht op hadden geslagen, ende niet genagelt soo dat behoorde, soo heeft hy attestant daernaer deselve berderinge by den requirant sijnen schalidecker wederen doen hernaegelen mits deselve synen schalidecker seyde dat voorseide dack niet en was genagelt soot behoorde (dwelck hy oock heeft bevonden alsoo oock waerachtich te syne) ende dat hy omesulcx schande aen syn werck soude haelen, ende opdat t' werck soude mogen goet wesen soo heeft hy attestant deselve berderinge door den voorseide synen schalidecker doen remedieren sonder dat den selven schalidecker hem attestant daer voren yet geheyscht heeft dan alleenelyck dat hy attestant de nagelen heeft betaelt. Sonder argelist, dit is aldus gedaen ende gepasseert in presentie van ottho vorste[r]man ende maximilian van broeckhen beyde schilders als getuyghen ende heeft den comparant de minute myns notaris geteekent.

      Quod attestor -- P Van Aerdenbodeghem notaris publicus

Translation (based on Justin Davies's translation):
Today the fifth day of the month of January in the year of our Lord one thousand six hundred and twenty one. At the request of Abraham van den Bossche, slater, appeared before me Peeter Van

13

APPENDIX I

Aerdenbodeghem, notary public residing in Antwerp, in the presence of witnesses mentioned below, the honourable gentleman Peeter Paulo Rubens painter to Their Most Serene Highnesses and he has declared and certified, declaring and certifying hereby to be true that he declarant, among other things, asked the same carpenters who constructed his house in 1615 to install a boarding on his roof as support for the slate covering. Also he declared to be true that this same covering had been laid by the above-mentioned carpenters, and he, the witness, having found that the said carpenters had fixed the aforementioned boarding only lightly, and had not nailed it as appropriate, and so the witness afterwards asked the plaintiff, his slater, to renail the same boarding since the same slater had said the aforementioned roof was not nailed as it should be (which he [the witness] had found to be so) and that this would result in harm to his work. And for the job to be well done he, the plaintiff, has had this same covering remedied by the above-mentioned, his slater, for which this slater demanded no more than only that he, the plaintiff, paid for the nails. Without deceit this was done and passed in the presence of Otto Vorsterman and Maximilian van Broeckhen, both painters, as witnesses.

P Van Aerdenbodeghem notary public

I.15 – 1621, 23 December. Rubens Buys Two Houses on the Hopland (one of them Called 'Breda'); Excerpt from the Sale Contract

Antwerp, FelixArchief, Schepenregisters 1600–1645, inv. no. SR#551, fol. 209r. Transcription as published by Büttner – Heinen, eds, *Quellen und Dokumente*, 2011, no. 156 (online publ.).

[…] Peeter Le Roy gesworen procureur alhier… bekende dat hij omme eene somme gelts die hem al ende wel is vergouden vercocht heeft wel ende wettelijck Senior Pietro Paulo Rubbens schilder van hare Hoocheid, twee huysen de welcke nu tertijt een wooninghe is met hove halven borneputte, kelders, coeckene cameren, gronde ende allen den toebehoorten, geheeten, d'een daer aff, Brida, gestaan, ende glegen in't Hoplant alhier tegens over den muer van de lammekensraeme tusschen'thuys van [*left blank*…] aen deen sijde westwaerts ende Huybrechtssens huys ende erve was aen d'ander sijde oostwart commende achter aenden raemhoff van wijlen d'erffgenamen Franchoys Gills met den voorseyden cooper toebehoorende […]

I.16 – 1623, 3 August. Excerpt from a Letter from Rubens to Peiresc, Mentioning a Perpetual Motion Machine that he Keeps in his Private Study

BNF, inv. no. NAF 5173

Transcription as published by Rooses – Ruelens, eds, *Correspondance*, 1887–1909, III, pp. 215–216, under no. CCCXLIII (the excerpt on p. 215). English translation in Magurn, ed., *Letters*, 1955, p. 91, under no. 52.

Ho caro chella habbia ricevuto il dissegno del moto perpetuo fatto con verità […] I forse (che non ardisco daffirmarlo ancora di certo) impetraro dal mio sig^r compadre che mi faccia far qui uno strumento intiero colla cassa i tutto come se fosse per tener appresso di me nel mio studiolo secreto et se posso ottenerlo en farò cordialis^{te} un presente a V S […].

Translation:
I am glad you have received the design of the perpetual motion; it is accurately done […]. Perhaps

(although I dare not yet affirm it with certainty) I shall prevail upon my sponsor to have a complete instrument made here, with a case, as if to be kept in my private study. If I can obtain this, I shall gladly make you a present of it.

I.17 – 1625, 10 July. The Infanta Isabella Visits Rubens at his House. She is Interested in the Egyptian Mummy in his 'Pantheon'

Besançon, Bibliothèque municipale, Collection Chiflet, MS Chiflet 178, fols 47r, 48r. Published by De Maeyer, Albrecht en Isabella, 1955, p. 375, doc. 197.

[…] Après le diner S.A. fut voir le Panthéon de Rubens' et toutses raretez entre lesquelles S.A. admira une mommie fort bien conservée et dit qu'elle se souvenoit de la mention que J.J. Chifflet en faisait dans son livre de Linteis sepulchralibus Christi […]

I.18 – 1627, 18 July. Rubens Buys Six Houses (Three on the Wapper and Three on the Hopland) from Hans Smekens and his Spouse Tanneke Hendrickx; Excerpt from the Contract

Antwerp, FelixArchief, Schepenregisters 1600–1645, inv. no. SR#585, fol. 318r. Transcription as published by Büttner – Heinen, eds, Quellen und Dokumente, 2011, no. 181 (online publ.); see also Tijs, Rubens en Jordaens, 1984, p. 372, repr. (fragment) p. 139; Devroe, Rubens' huis, 2008, I, p. 54, pp. 139–141.

[…] Hans Smekens […] ende Tanneke Hendrickx nu ter tijd zijne wettige huysvrouwe […] bekenden dat zij omme eene somme gelts, die hen al ende wel is vergouden, vercocht hebben wel ende wettelijck Sr. Pietro Paulo Ruebens, Edelman vanden huyse van hare doorlichtichste Hoogheyt, sesse huyskens oft wooninghen elck met een hoffken, gronde ende allen den toebehoorten gestaen ende gelegen de drye daeraff neffen malcanderen opden Wapper alhier, tusschen den naerbescreven Bleyckhoff nu tertyt de voors. coopere toebehoorende aen deen zijde noortwaerts ende de andere drye huysen oft wooningen mitsgaders den hoeckhuyse ghenampt In de Witte Roose die zij vercooperen al noch thenwaerde behoudende blyven aen dander zyde zuytwaerts. Ende dander drye huysen oft wooninghen int Hopland alhier, tegens over de Lammekensraem tusschen den vutganck vanden voor ende naerbescreven bleyckhoff, nu oock de voors. coopere toebehoorende aen dese zijde oostwaerts ende der voors. vercooperen andere twee huysen mitsgaders de voors. hoeckhuyse de Witte roose die zij (als voore) oock tot henwaerdere behoudende blijven aen d'ander zyde westwaert commende alle de voorscreven huysen achter ende ter zyde aenden voors. Bleyckhoff op alzulcken voorwaerden, conditie, lasten ende servituten, te wetene dat de voors. comparanten henne huysen die sij alnoch sijn behoudende tot geene dage en zullen mogen hooger opmetsen, als de zelve nu tertyt ende zijn, noch oock de erve vande zelve achter mogen betimmeren, noch bemetsen om nyet te benemen de sonne van voors. Bleijckhoff […]

I.19 – 1628, 15 June. Rubens Buys another House (on the Hopland) from Hans Smekens and his Spouse; Excerpt from the Contract

Antwerp, FelixArchief, Schepenregisters 1600–1645, inv. no. SR#591, fols 325r–326r. Published by Büttner – Heinen, eds, Quellen und Dokumente, 2011, no. 183 (online publ.). This version has been slightly emended.

APPENDIX I

[fol. 325r] [...] Hans Smekens [...] ende Tanneke Henricx, nu ter tijt zijne wettighe huysvrouwe [...] bekenden dat zij omme eene somme gelts die hen al ende wel is vergouden, vercocht hebben wel ende wettelyck Sr. Pietro Paulo Ruebens, edelman vande huyse van hare doorluchtichste hoocheyt een huysken oft wooninghe metten hofken, gronde ende alle de toebehoorten gestaen ende gelegen int Hoptlandt alhier, tegens over de Lammekens Rame, tusschen de andere dry huyskens oft wooninghen ende erve der voors. coopere van te vooren toebehoorende ende van hen comparanten in de voorleden Jare xvic ende seventwintich oock vercocht aen desen zijde oostwaerts, ende der voors. comparanten vercooperen anderen huyse oft wooninghe, mitsgaders de voors. hoeckhuyse De witte Roose die zij vercooperen alnoch t'henwaerdere behoudende blijven aen d'ander zijde westwaerts, commende achter aen des voors. coopers andere erve op alzulcken voorwaerden, conditien, lasten ende servituten, te wetene dat de voors. comparanten vercooperen, henne huysen die zij alnoch zijn behoudende [fol. 325v] tot geene dagen en sullen moghen hoogher opmetsen oft betimmeren dan de zelve nu tertyt ende zij, noch oock de erve vande zelve achter mogen betimmeren, noch bemetsen, om nyet te benemen de sonne van de hoff ende erve dewelcke eertyts eene Bleyckhoff te wesen plach, nu oock den voors. coopere toebehoorden [...]

I.20 – 1628, 28 August. Excerpts from the Inventory of Isabella Brant's Estate (d. 20 June 1626)

Gaasbeek, Kasteel van Gaasbeek, archief, inv. no. Ae 123 (*Inventaris van de goederen, nagelaten door Isabella Brant, eerste echtgenote van P.P. Rubens, 1626*); transcription as published by Rooses, Sterfhuis Isabella Brant, 1896, pp. 165–183; see also Büttner – Heinen, eds, *Quellen und Dokumente*, 2011, no. 189 (online publ.).

Rooses, *Sterfhuis Isabella Brant*, 1896, p. 166:

[1] Ierst competeert daeraff desen gemeynen sterffhuys een groote huijsinghe metten hove, gronde ende toebehoorten gestaen ende gelegen op den Wapper alhier vry ende onbelast synde bijden voorsch. Heer Petro Paulo Rubens int geheele gebruyckt wordende hier voor ... memorie.
[2] Item een huijs metten gronde ende toebehoorten achter de voorschreven groote huijssinge geleghen vuijtcommende jegens over de Lammekens Raem belast met vyffentwintich guldenen erffelyck competerende de Weduwe Rol [...] daeraff de huere in toecomende rekeninghe verantwoort sal worden hier oyck voor ... memorie.

Ibid., pp. 169–70:

[3] Item competeert daeraff desen gemeynen sterffhuyse een huijs metten gronde ende toebehoorten gestaen ende geleghen op den Wapper alhier neffens de voorsch. groote huijsinghe vry ende onbelast synde by Geeraert Van Hove meulder gebruyckt wordende tot dertich gulden t'siaers.
[4] Item noch competeert desen sterffhuijse een ander huysken daer neffens gestaen oyck onbelast synde by Syke Smits gebruyckt wordende tot zesthien gulden t'siaers.
[5] Item noch een huysken oyck aldaer gestaen oyck ende onbelast synde by Balthasar Peeters gebruyckt wordende tot dertich gulden t'siaers.
[6] Item een huijs gestaen achter der voorschreven huijsinghe vuyttcommende iegens-over de Lammekens Raem onbelast synde by Marcus Huybrechts gebruyckt wordende tot zessentdertich gulden t'siaers.
[7] Item noch een huijs daer neffens oft ontrent gestaen oyck vry ende onbelast sijnde by Michiel De Boeck gebruyckt wordende tot vierentviertich gulden t'siaers.

[8] Item noch een huysken aldaar gestaen oyck onbelast synde by de Weduwe Smits gebruyckt wordende tot tweentwintich gulden.
[9] Item noch een huijsken daerby gestaen insgelycx vry ende onbelast synde bij Fernandt Leenaerts gebruyct wordende tot twintich guldenen t'siaers.

Ibid., p. 182:

[10] Item betaelt aen Hans Smekens over de coop penninghen van zeven huijskens van hem tot behoeff van desen gemeynen sterffhuyse gecocht gestaen by ende omtrent de voorsch. groote huysinghe metten hove byden heer rendant in desen gebruyckt wordende […] de somme van … guld. IIIIm

I.21 – 1638, 17 August. Letter from Rubens (in Elewijt) to Lucas Faydherbe (in Antwerp); Excerpt about the 'schilderhuys'

Present whereabouts unknown, probably lost. F. Jos van den Branden had seen a copy after the original in the possession of a descendant of Faydherbe, in Mechelen. Published by Van den Branden, *Schilderschool*, 1883, p. 576. Transcription as published by Rooses – Ruelens, eds, *Correspondance*, 1887–1909, VI, p. 223, under no. DCCCLXI. English translation in Magurn, ed., *Letters*, 1955, pp. 411, under no. 244.

[…] Siet toch wel toe, als ghij vertrecken sult, dat alles wel opgesloten sij ende datter geene originaelen en blijven staen boven op het schilderhuys oft eenige schetsen. […]
Compt toch over soo haest als ghij cont, opdat het huys mach ghesloten worden, want soo langhe als ghij daer sijt en cont ghij de andere niet buyten sluyten.

Translation:
Take good care, when you leave, that everything is well locked up, and that no originals remain upstairs in the studio, or any sketches. […]
Come here as soon as you can, so the house may be closed; for as long as you are there, you cannot close it to the others.

Note: for the interpretation of 'op het schilderhuys', see Chapter VII, pp. 221–222, n. 63.

I.22 – 1641, 10 October. The Request by Rubens's heirs for Permission to Sell the House and its Annexes is Granted. Excerpts from the Document

Antwerp, FelixArchief, Privilegiekamer, inv. no. PK#743, fols 149r–149v. Transcription as published by Génard, *Nalatenschap*, 1865, pp. 167–168.

[fol. 149r] Verthoont reverentelyck Joncker Albert Rubens, […], Peeter Hanikaert ende Meester Philips Ruebens, […], tsamen als testamentelycke momboirs vande minderjarige kinderen van wylen Heer Petro Paulo Ruebens, riddere, hoe dat UE ghelieft heeft te consenteren by appoinctement collegiael, ghestelt op der supplianten request, hieraene ghehecht, om de huysen van den sterffhuyse, alhier ghelegen, te moghen doen schatten by gesworen schatters ende erffscheyders deser stadt […]; maer ghemerckt de supplianten ende de weduwe vanden voors. heer afflyvigen geraeden vinden de groote huysinge metten hoff gestaen ontrent den Wapper alhier, daerinne deselffve heer afflyvige gewoont ende ghestorven is, met eenighe cleyn huyskens daerby ende int Hoplandt ghestaen, publicquelyck

APPENDIX I

ter Vrydaeghsmerckt deser stadt te vercoopen, doordyen de groote huysinge niet wel cavelbaer en is ende de cleyn huyskens, audt ende caducq syn ende groote reparatien souden behoeven, waerdoore de supplianten ende de bejarde kinderen des voirs. Heer afflyvigens, te meer geraeden vinden te prouven oft sy deselffve [fol. 149v] panden souden connen tot redelycken pryse te vercoopen, om alsoo niet langer in gemeynschap van goeden te blyven; Soo bidden de supplianten dat UE. ghelieven wille hen de voors. vercoopinge te consenteren [...]

Myne Heeren Borgermeesteren ende Schepenen hebben de supplianten geauthoriseert, om, soo vele aengaen hunne weesen in desen gemelt, te moghen vercoopen ter Vrydaeghsmerckt deser stad, in behoorlycker manieren, het groot huys met de cleyne huysen in desen gemelt [...], den cooper oft coopers daerinne te goeden ende erffven ende de cooppenninghen te ontfangen, mits de selffve voor het contingent der voors. Weesen wederom aenleggende aen goede vaste panden binnen dese stadt.

Actum 10 8bris 1641. Onderteeckent: F. Vecquemans

I.23 – 1645, 17 November. Excerpts from the *Staetmasse* (the Inventory of Rubens's Estate)

Antwerp, FelixArchief, Notariaat, Toussaint Guyot, notaris te Antwerpen, Protocollen en staten en rekeningen, 1645–1645, inv. no. N#1894. For a complete transcription of the document, see Génard, *Nalatenschap*, 1865, pp. 69–163. Excerpts in Duverger, *Kunstinventarissen*, 1984–2009, V, pp. 263–284.

Ende ierst aengaende den ontfanck
[1 – *The ivory from 'the tower'*; Génard, *Nalatenschap*, 1865, p. 81]
XXIII. Vuytten thoren [*in the margin*: ten voors. huyse van den afflyvigen] daer de antiquiteyten van den heer afflyvigen stonden, vercocht aen [...] Van Opstal dryentsestich ponden ijvoir tot dryentdertig stuyvers tpont, bedraegt hondert vier guldenen ende derthien stuyvers ... gl. 104–13 [...].

Anderen ontfanck van de onruerend ende erffelycke goeden desen sterffhuyse competerende
[2 – *The house*; Génard, *Nalatenschap*, 1865, p. 97].
I. [...] Soo heeft de voors. afflyvigen achtergelaeten een huyssinge met poorte, pletse, gaelderye, schilderhuys, grooten hove, stallingen, gronde ende allen den toebehoorten, gestaen ende gelegen opden Wapper alhier, commende achter oostwaerts aenden muer vanden Coloveriers hove; ende gemerckt de voors. heer afflyvige deselve huyssinge bewoont ende daerinne gestorven is, soo comt daeraff tot profytte alhier wtgetrocken ... nyet

[3 – *Rent paid by Helena Fourment*; Génard, *Nalatenschap*, 18605, pp. 97–98]
II. Tsedert is de voors. vrouwe Rendante daerinne blyven woonen, ende middeler tyt is de beschryvinge ende inventarisatie van alle goeden daerinne geschiet, de schattinge vande meubelen, mitgaeders de vercoopinge van alle consten, schilderyen ende antiquiteyten; voorts de selve huyssinge, metten hove, naer voorgaende consent van myne eerw. heeren Borgemeesteren ende Schepenen deser stadt te coope gestelt ende geveylt, maer tot nu toe nyemant wtgecommen die weerde daer vore geboden, sulcx dat de voors. Rendante, voor huere vande voors. huyssinge, hier te goet doende tegens vier hondert guldenen tsjaers in gevolch vanden accorde tusschen heur metten voors. heuren man ende de voors. voorkinderen mette momboirs vande minderjaerigen, opden achtentwintichsten dach der maent Augusti lestleden, voor Schepenen deser stadt gepasseert,... voor den tyd van twee jaeren, verschenen te Bamisse xvic ende tweeentviertich; dus comt hier voor de helft, gemerckt dander helft den voorkinderen aengaet ... gl. 400

III. Ende daernaer noch dry jaeren tot Bamis xvi^c ende veyffentviertich; comt voor tgedeelte van desen sterffhuyse ... gl.600

[4 – *The small houses on the Wapper and the Hopland*; Génard, *Nalatenschap*, 1865, pp. 101–102]

XVII. Item naer luyt de brieven gequotteert n° acht soo heeft Hans Smekens ende Tanneken Hendricx syne huysvrouwe op de xxviii july anno 1627 aenden voors. afflyvigen vercocht sesse huyskens oft wooningen elck met een hoffken, gronde ende toebehoorten, gestaen ende gelegen, de dry daeraff neffens malcanderen, opden Wapper alhier neffens denselver vercooperen andere dry huysen metten hoeckhuyse genaemt de Witte Roose aldaer suytwaerts gestaen ende dandere dry huyskens oft wooningen int Hoplant alhier tegen over de Lammekensraeme nu wesende den hoff van Descalsos,

XVIII. Van welcke huysen mitsgaeders van noch eenen anderen huyse neffens de voorgaende int Hoplant gestaen, waeraff de brieven gequoteert syn n° negen ende van noch eenen anderen huyse oft wooningen eertyts twee huyskens geweest synde daerbij oock int Hoplant gestaen [*in the margin*: mitsgaeders vanden huyse genaemt de Sterre inde Jodestraete alhier gestaen] heeft Gielis Princen d'administratie gehadt, die welcke aen haer Rendante syne rekeningen daeraff overgegeven ende gedaen heeft vanden jaere xvi^c viertich, ende haer, by slote van dyen, opgeleegt de somme van dryhondert dertich guldens ende tweelff stuyvers ende gemerckt deselve huysen den voors. voorkinderen voor de helft aengaen, soo heeft sy hen helft daeraff voldaen, dus comt hier voor dander helft van desen sterffhuyse, de somme van ... gl. 165-6

[5 – *The house on the Hopland used by Rubens as his library*; Génard, *Nalatenschap*, 1865, p. 102]

XXI. Het huys int Hoplant geteeckent n° 8, tsedert dat David Ryckaert, lesten huerlinck, te Kerstmisse anno 1639, daer wtgetrocken is, heeft de voors. afflyvighe selver gebruyckt tot syne bibliotheke ende eenighe slechte schilderyen ende copyen daer inne geseth, dienende hier ... p. memorie.

[6 – *The eight small houses*; Génard, *Nalatenschap*, 1865, pp. 102–103]

XXII. Van welcken voors. acht huysen de voorschreven vrouwe Rendante de voorgenoemde voorsonen ende de momboirs vande minderjaerige kinderen naer vermogen van consente collegiaele op den derden dach der maent Aprilis van den voorleden jaer xvi^c eenenviertich op de requeste vande selve momboirs verleent hebben doch schatten ende priseren, by gesworen schatters ende erfscheyders deser stadt; dewelcken geschat ende gepriseert hebben de vijff huysen daeraff te wetene de twee huysen geteeckent n° 4 ende 5 gestaen aenden Wapper tegenover de Lammekensraem op 2200 guldens eens

XXIII de twee andere geteeckent n° 6 ende n° 7 op duysent ende tweehondert guldens eens.

XXIIII. Ende dander huys n° 8 in de selve straete gestaen neffens ende boven de vuytganck vande voors. huyssinge van desen sterffhuyse aldaer, is geestimeert op 2650 guldens eens [...].

Uytgeven ende lasten tegens den ontfanck ende proffyten hiervore gestelt

[7 – '*Grauwen' of the studio*: Génard, *Nalatenschap*, 1865, p. 123]

XXIIII. Aen eenen clatschilder voor het schilderhuys te grauwen ... gl. 2

[8 – *Payments to the slater Bastiaen van den Bosch*; Génard, *Nalatenschap*, 1865, p. 129]

LXXIII. Aen Bastiaen vanden Bosch, schaliedecker, vanden tyt van twee jaeren, verschenen in Augusto anno 1640 ende 1641, de schaliedaecken inde groote huyssinge aenden Wapper gerepareert ende onderhouden te hebben naerluyt de twee quitantien tweentdertich guldenen waeraff de voorkinderen de helft moeten draegen dus comt hier de somme van ... gl. 16

[9 – *Shutters in the studio*; Génard, *Nalatenschap*, 1865, p. 129]

LXXV. Aen Florus gegeven om blaffeturen int schilderhuys te maecken ... gl. 3

[10 – *Paiment to the widow of Hans van Mildert*; Génard, *Nalatenschap*, 1865, p. 141]

CLVII. Aen de weduwe Jans van Milder, by affreckeninge ende liquidatie voor t'gene dat sy tot laste van desen sterffhuyse heeft gepretendeert, van diversche wercken by denselven haeren man, voor den voors. heer afflyvigen, gemaeckt naer luyt der specificatie ende quictancie ... gl. 512

APPENDIX I

I.24 – 1657, 6 December. Excerpt from the Inventory of Albert Rubens's Estate (d. 1 October 1657)

Gaasbeek, Kasteel van Gaasbeek, archief, inv. no. Ad 5; transcription as published by Rooses, *Albertus Rubens*, 1897, p. 53.

[…] *Huysen*. Item competeert desen sterffhuyse een vierendeel midts gaeders een twee-en-dertichste deel in seeckere groote huysinghe gestaen tot Antwerpen op den Wapper alwaer den afflyvighen heere vaeder ghestorven is, midtsgaeders ghelycke ghedeelte in drye cleyne huyskens daer neffens gestaen, waer van het groot huys bewoont wort by den Marquis van Nieuw-Casteel a sess hondert guldens t'sjaers waer van de huere verschenen is t'sedert bamisse sesthien hondert sessenvyfftich volgens den voorschreven boeck folio 117. [memorie….]

I.25 – 1660, 16 September. Excerpt from the Sale Contract of the House to Alderman van Eycke [the Public Sale on the Vrijdagmarkt was on 3 September, 1660]

Antwerp, FelixArchief, Schepenregisters, 1646–1699/1660 II, SR#758, sub Rousseau, fols 59r–60v. Published by Génard, *Rubens*, 1877, pp. 107–111; Büttner – Heinen, eds, *Quellen und Dokumente*, 2011, no. 306 (online publ.). Excerpts published by Tijs, *Rubens en Jordaens*, 1984, p. 147, n. 86, repr. of a page p. 148; Devroe, *Rubens' huis*, 2008, I, pp. 56–57.
Also in *Antwerp, Rubenshuis Archive, inv. no. RH.D.054.3.02–14.* Image in DAMS.

[*Rubens's heirs, represented by 'Philippus Rubens, Guillaume Lunden, Constantia Helman and Franciscus Rubens' declare that they*] […] vercocht hebben wel ende wettelyck aen Sr. Jacomo van Eycke negotiant ter borsen deser stadt, eene groote huysinge metten grooten hove ende schilder-huyse, ende alle tgene daer inne aerd-vast ende nagel-vast is, gronde ende toebehoorten soo deselve tegenwoerdelyck staende ende gelegen is inde strate loopende vande Meir naer den Wapper, tusschen de huysinge ende erve van wijlen Hendrick Moens […], met twee besundere uytgangen den eenen inde selve strate tusschen het voorschreven schilderhuys ende de nabeschreven cleyne huijsen ende den anderen int Hoplandt, ende daertoe noch drye huyskens oft wooningen elck met syn hoffken, gronde ende toebehoorten gestaen ende gelegen neffens malcanderen inde voorscheven strate naer den Wapper tusschen den uijtganck vande voorgemelde groote huysinghe aen d'een zyde noortwaerts, […] voor de somme van twintich duysent guldenen eens, […]

I.26 – 1660s (?). Excerpt from Philip Rubens's unpublished *Vita Petri Pauli Rubenii* (possibly a summary of a text by Albert Rubens)

Original manuscript: whereabouts unknown, probably lost. Several copies are known (see below).
A copy in the KBR (now not to be found) was published, as by G. Gevartius, in De Reiffenberg, *Rubens*, 1937, pp. 3–13 (excerpt p. 7). Latin copies, with slight differences, also as by G. Gevartius, in KBR, inv. nos MS 21740 and MS 5722. Copies with French translations are in the papers of François Mols (same collection, inv. nos II.1329, II.1378); for an early French translation, see Boussard, *Leçons de Rubens*, 1838, pp. 7–12. English translation in Lind, *Latin Life*, 1946, pp. 37–44 (excerpt, p. 39).

[…] In contubernio soceri aliquot annos vixit, quo tempore fecit tabulam magni altaris ecclesiæ parœcialis St^æ. Walburgis Antverpiæ, quæ supplicium Domini nostri exhibet. Interim ædes proprias magnamque juxta aream Antverpiæ emit, ubi diætam² amplissimam romanâ formâ ædificat, picturæ studio aptam, hortumque latissimum omnis generis arboribus conserit. [...]

Translation:
He lived some years in the home of his father-in-law, during this period he painted the picture on the great altar of the parish church of St Walburga at Antwerp which displays the crucifixion of our Lord. In the mean time he purchased his own house and wide grounds in Antwerp, where he built a large summer house in Roman style, adapted for use as a studio, and planted a very extensive garden with all sorts of trees.

I.27 – Between 1664 and 1681. Excerpt from the Autobiography of Otto Sperling (1602–1681). He Visited Rubens's House at the End of May or Beginning of June 1621

KB.DK, Gl. kgl. Samling 3094 4°, pp. 28–29. See also Brieger – Johnson, *Sperlings Studienjahre*, 1920, p. 31; mentioned and cited by numerous authors, e.g.: Rooses, *Reizigers*, 1898, pp. 221–222; Held, *Drawings*, 1959, p. 26, n. 9; Tijs, *Rubens en Jordaens*, 1984, pp. 113, 363, n. 36; Logan, *Rubens as a Teacher*, 2006, pp. 250–251, 254; Van Hout, *Dead colour*, 2010, p. 123, doc. XVII; Büttner, *Hands of Rubens*, 2017, pp. 42, 51, n. 12. For the translation, see ibid., p. 42.

[...] Hernach liess er uns durch einem seiner diener, uberall in seinem herrlichen Palatio herumb führen, und uns zeigen seine antiquiteten und Griechische und Romanische Statuen, die er in grosser Menge hatte. Wir sahen da auch einen grossen Sael, welcher keine fenstern hatte, sondern dass Liecht fiel von oben drein Mitten im Sael durch ein grosses loch. In diesem Sael sassen viel iunge Schilder, welche alle arbeiteten an Unterschiedlichen Stücken, welche zuvor von dem H. Rübbens ihnen mit Kreijde wahren Vorgerissen, und hir und da ein Plack mit Farben hinzugesetzet. Diese Schildereijen musten die jungen gesellen mit Farben vollends aussarbeiten, biss zu lezt der herr Rübbens selber alles mit strichen und farben perfectionirte. So hiess ess dan dass alles Rübbens Werck waer, Wodurch der Mann uberauss grossen reichthumb gesamlet, und von königen und fürsten mit grossen Geschenken und Jowelen ist begabet worden.

Translation:
Afterwards he had a servant take us all around in his splendid 'Palatio' and show us his antiquities and Greek and Roman statues which he had in large quantity. We also saw there a large hall which had no windows, but instead the light come from above from a big opening in the middle of the hall. In this hall sat many young painters who were all working on different pieces which Mr Rubens had previously sketched for them with chalk and on which he had added a blotch of colour here and there. These paintings the young associates had to work up fully in colour until finally Mr Rubens himself perfected everything using brushstrokes and colour to finish everything off. Thus it was all called Rubens's work, through which the man accumulated an enormous fortune and kings and princes showered him with gifts and jewels.

---

2. For the interpretation of the word 'Diaeta', see Chapter II, p. 51, n. 5 and Chapter V, p. 156

APPENDIX I

I.28 – Bellori, *Vite*, 1672. Excerpt from the 'Life' of Rubens Mentioning the House

Bellori, *Vite*, 1672, p. 245. English translation in Bellori, *Lives*, eds Wohl – Wohl, 2005, p. 204.

Haueua egli adunato marmi, e statue, che portò e fece condursi di Roma [...] e fabbricò nella sua casa in Anuersa vna stanza rotonda con vn solo occhio in cima à similitudine della Rotonda di Roma per la perfettione del lume vguale, & in questa collocò il suo pretioso museo, con altre diuerse curiosità peregrine. [...] Era perciò egli visitato, e da gli huomini di lettere, & eruditi, e da gli amatori della pittura; non passando forestiere alcuno in Anuersa che non vedesse il suo Gabinetto, e molto più lui [...]

Translation:
He had amassed a collection of marbles and statues which he brought and had sent from Rome [...] and in his house in Antwerp he built a round room with a single *oculus* at the top, similar to the Rotunda of Rome, for the perfection of even lighting, and in this room he installed his precious museum, with other rare and sundry curiosities. [...] he was visited both by men of letters and scholars and by lovers of painting: no foreigner passed through Antwerp without seeing his cabinet and particularly himself.

I.29 – 1675. Sandrart, *Teutsche Academie*, 1675–80, II. Excerpt from the 'Life' of Rubens Mentioning the House

Sandrart, *Teutsche Academie*, 1675–80, II, p. 292. English translation (of Rubens's *Life*) in Wood, ed., *Lives*, 2005, pp. 45–46.

[...] Auch baute er sich ein sehr bequemes schönes Haus und darein neben dem Garten eine Kunst-Cammer in der Form einer Ritonda, mit einem von oben herab fallendem Liecht so überaus vortheilhaft alle darinnen befindliche und in gute Ordnung gestellte rare Gemälde und statuen so wol von seiner eignen Hand als anderer führnehmsten Künstlere neben mehren versamleten Curiositäten überschiene: Dahin pflöge er die ihn besuchende Liebhabere zu führen [...]

Translation:
He also built himself a very comfortable, beautiful house which contained, next to the garden, a 'Kunstkammer' in the shape of a rotunda with light falling from above, which illuminated to great advantage all the rare and orderly arranged paintings and statues within it, by his own hand as well as by other noble artists, besides several curiosities. It was his habit to take visiting art lovers there.

I.30 – 1680, 18 January. Sale of the House by Cornelia Hillewerve to her Brother Hendrik Hillewerve

a) The sale deed.
Antwerp, FelixArchief, S.R. 885, d.d. 1680, sub Peeters, fol. 119r-v; excerpts published by Rooses, *Maison*, 1888, p. 232, Annexe I; Tijs, *Rubens en Jordaens*, 1984, p. 149, n. 87; Devroe, *Rubens' huis*, 2008, I, pp. 57–58. A legal copy (dated 1726) in *Antwerp, Rubenshuis Archive, inv. nr. RH.D.054.4.01–11*. Image in DAMS.

Wij Adriaen [...] Herman van den Brant [...] ende Philips Rubens [*not Rubens's nephew*] schepenen van Antwerpen maecken cont dat voor ons quamen vrouwe Cornelia Hillewerven weduwe ende geinstitueert erffgenaem van wijlen Jonker Jacobus van Eijcke [...], ende bekende dat sij omme eene somme gelts die haer al ende wel is vergouden vercocht heeft wel ende wettelijcke den Eerw. heere Hendricus Hillewerven priestere haeren broeder, Eerst eene groote huysinge met diversche opper ende neercamers, kelders, solders, groote ende clijne plaetse, grooten hove gronde ende allen den toebehoorten, gestaen ende gelegen in de Wapperstraet loopende vande Meire naer den Wapper tusschen de huysinge ende erve van Hendrick Hoens [...] ende daertoe noch twee andere huijsen eertyts drije huijskens oft wooningen geweest synde elck met syn hoffken gronde ende alle den toebehoorten gestaen neffens malcanderen in de selve strate tusschen den tweeden vuijtganck ofte poorte van de voorgemelde groote huijsinge aen een sijde noortwaerts [...] ende comende achter oostwaerts tegens den hove vande voors. groote huijsinge, [...] met onse segelen gegeven int jaer onse heere als men screef duijsent sesse honderttachentachtich [...] dagen in maent van januarij.

b) A receipt (dated 16 November 1680) is added to the document in the Rubenshuis archive, inv. no. D.054.4.01–11. Image in DAMS.

De weduwe der heer [...] Jacomo van Eijck voor de coope [...] aen heer [...] Henrico van Hillewerve presbiter eene groote huijsinghe ghestaen op den Wapper met ver scheyde cleijne voor de somme van 36000 guldens eens
Pondtgelt 450 guld. / Recepi 16° Nov: 1680 / N° 210: P Bertrijn

I.31 – 1681. De Piles, *Dissertation*, 1681. Excerpt from the 'Life' of Rubens: Description of the House

De Piles, *Dissertation*, 1681, pp. 12–14. English translation in Wood, ed., *Lives*, 2005, pp. 67–68.

[...] il acheta donc une grande maison dans la Ville d'Anvers, il la rebastit à la Romaine, & en embellit les dedans, qu'il rendit commodes pour un grand Peintre & pour un grand Amateur des belles choses. Cette maison estoit accompagnée d'un jardin spatieux, où il fit planter pour sa curiosité des arbres de toutes les especes qu'il peut recouvrer. Entre sa court & son jardin, il a fait bastir une sale de forme ronde comme le Temple du Panteon qui est à Rome, & dont le jour n'entre que par le haut & par une seule ouverture qui est le centre du Dôme. Cette sale estoit pleine de Bustes, de Statuës Antiques, de Tableaux précieux qu'il avoit apportez d'Italie, & d'autres choses fort rares & fort curieuses. Tout y estoit par ordre & en simétrie; & c'est pour cela que tout ce qui méritoit d'y estre, n'y pouvant trouver place, servoit à orner d'autres chambres dans les appartemens de sa maison [...]

Translation:
He therefore bought a large house at Antwerp. He rebuilt it à la romaine and decorated the interior making them suitable for a great painter and a great amateur of beautiful things. This house was graced with a spacious garden in which he planted, for his own interest, all kinds of trees that he was able to collect. Between the courtyard and the garden he had built a rotunda, like the Pantheon in Rome, in which the light enters from a single opening from above in the centre of the dome. This room was filled with busts, antique statues and paintings that he had brought back from Italy, and other rare and very curious things. Everything was placed there according to order and symmetry, which is why anything that merited but could not find a place there was used to decorate the rooms in the apartments of the house.

APPENDIX I

I.32 – 1681. Excerpt from the 'Life' of Rubens by Filippo Baldinucci, Published in 1681

Baldinucci, *Notizie*, 1681–1728, IV, p. 282. English translation in Muller, *Perseus and Andromeda*, 1981–82, p. 131

[...] E maraviglia non fu che egli in Anversa pure si fabbricasse un grande, e nobilissimo Palazzo tutto al moderno modo Italiano con bozzi, ed altri adornamenti per entro di cui dipinse di sua mano una Loggia con Prospettive, Architetture, e con Bassi rilievi di ricca invenzione, e fra l'altre cose finse, che a quelle Architetture fusse stato attaccato un Quadro per asciugarsi al Sole, così bene spiccato del sodo, che dicesi che veduto un dì dalla Sereniss. Clara Eugenia Infanta di Spagna [...], ordinasse, che fusse tolta giù quella Tela, che ella credè vera, e non dipinta [...]

Translation:
[he] built himself a large and most noble palace all in the modern Italian style, with pools and other adornments, inside of which he painted with his hand a loggia with perspectives, architecture, and bas-reliëfs of rich invention, and among other things feigned that a picture had been attached so that architecture to dry in the sun, so well detached from the ground that, it is said, seen one day by the most Serene Clara Eugenia Infanta of Spain [...], she ordered that that canvas should be taken down, because she believed it real and not painted.

I.33 – 1682, 17 June. Hillewerve Donates the House to his Sister Cornelia and her three Children: Joanna, Teresia and Joseph van Eycke. Excerpt from the *Donatio inter vivos* Deed

Legal copy (dated 1726) in *Antwerp, Rubenshuis Archive, RH-D.054.4.04–11*. Image in DAMS (only p. 1).

[1] Inden Jaere ons Heeren duysent sesse hondert tweeentachentigh den seventhiensten dagh der maent junij voor mij Anthoni de Pieters Openbaer notaris [...] compareerden den eerw. Heere Henricus Hillewerven priestere mij notario bekent, ende bekende ende verklaerde, dat hij uijt lieffde ende affectie, die hij is draegende tot vrouwe Cornelia Hillewerve sijne sustere weduwe van wijlen Jon[r] Jacobus van Eijcke in sijnen leven Schepen deser Stadt was, ende haere drije kinderen Jouff[n] Joanna ende Teresia, mitsgaders Jon[r] Joseph van Eijcke aende selve sijne sustere nichten ende neve bij donatie inter vivos gegeven, gecedeert ende getransporteert heeft, sulcx hij doet bij desen,
[2] Eerst eene groote huijsinge met diversche oppercamers ende neercamers, kelders, solders, groote ende cleijne plaetsen grooten hove, gronde ende allen den toebehoorten gestaende ende gelegen inde Wapperstraete loopende vande Meire naer den Wapper, ende daertoe noch twee andere huijsen eertijts drij huijskens ofte wooninghen geweest synde, ook met sijn hoffke, grondt ende alle den toebehoorten gestaen neffens malcanderen inde selve straete, [...] ende tot dien alle de meubelen van de groote Sallette cappelcamer bovencamern ende ciraten van de cappelle, die tot opden dagh van heden inde selve huijsinge sijn berustende en die hij heer comparant gecocht heeft vande selve sijne sustere
[3] op expresse conditie dat de selve sijne Sustere, nichten ende neve de selve panden int geheel off in deel geduerende sijnes Heer donnateurs leven, niet en sullen vercoopen, belasten offe veralinieren, ende dat de selve sijne sustere met haere familie te St Jansmisse naestcomende ende voorts geduerende haer leven sal moeten bewoonen ende gebruijcken met soodaenighe liberteijt de voors. groote huijsinge met den hoff al off sij huerderesse vanden selven pant waeren, behalven het quartier offe slaepcamer, dwelcke hij heer donnateur alsnu gebruijckt met synen knecht, ende sal t'selve altydt tot sijnder dispositie moeten blijven open staen al waert oock soo dat hij absent waere. Item dat hij Heer Donnateur voor cost ende dranck van hem ende synen knecht inden selven grooten huijsinge aen sijne voors. sustere sal betaelen

naer advenant van acht hondert guldens t' siaers, midts dat hij oock naer sijnen staet ende conditie sal worden getracteert, ende ingevalle hij Heer Donnateur gelieffde continuelijck te blijven woonen bij de voors. sijne sustere in sulcken gevalle sal hy volstaen midts betaelende alleenelijck sesse hondert guls. t' siaers,

[4] Item sal de voorschrevenen sijnen Donnateurs sustere oock hebben de dispositie ende innecomen vande voorschrevene twee cleijn huijsen daer nevens gestaen omme de reparatien ende lasten vanden geheelen pant daermede te connen doen ten waere den heer donnateur gelieffde de selve reperatie tot sijnen laste te nemen

[5] ten desen mede compareerde de voorschreve. vrouwe Cornelia Hillewerven, mitsgaders Jouff^e Joanna van Eijcke haere bejaerde dochtere soo voor heur selven als vuijtten naeme ende hen sterckmaeckende voor de voors. Jouff^e Teresia ende Jon^r Joseph van Eijcke alnoch minderjaerigh ende hebben de voors. donnatie overdanckelijck geaccepteert, ende gelooft puntuelijck alle de bovengemelde conditien naer te comen ende te achtervolgen […]

I.34 – 1687, after 19 May. Excerpt from the Travel Notes of Nicodemus Tessin the Younger; he Visited the House and Saw the Wall Paintings

Stockholm, Riksarkivet, inv. no. xxx, p. 71. Cited as published by Laine – Magnussen, eds, *Tessin*, 2002, p. 156; see also Rooses, *Reizigers*, 1898, p. 228; Upmark, *Besuch*, 1900, p. 208; Tessin, *Studieresor*, ed. Sirén, 1914, p. 84.

Rübens hauss darinnen er gewohnt undt seine wercke gemahlt hat, welches al fresco auf ettzliche stellen ausswendig wahr geschillert, haben wir auch gesehen […]

Translation:
We also saw Rubens's house, in which he had lived and made his paintings, and which was painted in fresco in many places on the exterior.

I.35 – 1691, 7 March. Renewal of the Donation by Hillewerve. After the Death of their Mother, Cornelia Hillewerve, and the Calling of their Brother Joseph to the Priesthood, Joanna and Teresia Van Eycke Obtain Possession of the House and its Contents

Antwerp, Archive of the Rubenshuis, inv. no. RH-D.054.4.06–11. Excerpt published by Devroe, *Rubens' huis*, 2008, I, p. 58. Image in DAMS.

[*More or less repeating the text of the 'Donatio' (Appendix I.33), but with an addition at the end*:]
[…] bekende den voors. comparant [Hillewerve] den geheelen inhoudt van de voor geinserreerde acten ende donnatie inter vivos voor ons te vernieuwen ende anderwerven te passeren, versoekende dat de voors. jonckvro.en Joanna ende Tresia van Eijcke mits de doodt van de voors. vrouwe Cornelia Hillewerven henne moedere ende de civile doodt ende proffessie van den voors. Jonker Joseph Van Eycke hennen broeder int cloostervan de Eerw. Paters Carmelieten die men noempt onse Lieve vrouwebroeders binnen dese stadt ten wijckboeken deser stadtsullen worden gesteld als proprietaressen uijt crachte ende in gevolge van de voorghenoemde donnatie van de voorgemelde groote huijsinge metten hove ende de huijsen daer neffens gronde ende toebehoorten gestaen end geleghen […]
den sevensten dagh der maent Meert sesthien hondert eenennegentigh […]

APPENDIX I

I.36 – c. 1695. Excerpt from Desiderius De Sevin's Eulogy of Hendrik Hillewerve (in *Pindus Charitatis*)

De Sevin, *Pindus Charitatis*, s.d., pp. [249]–[250]. More extensive excerpts in Rooses, *Maison*, 1888, pp. 236–237, Annexe V; Devroe, *Rubens' huis*, 2008, I, pp. 41–42 (anonymus Dutch translation), nn. 102 and 104 (Latin excerpt).

[*in the margin*] Amplissima Domus Rubeniana nunc Hilwerveriana.
Haec tua tot titulis fulgens Domus illa RUBENI / Fulget ab HENRICI non minus illa die. / Tectum augustum, ingens, picturis undique clarum, / Et rarae Murus continet Artis opes. / Non ego jam timeam dixisse Palatia Romae / Cedere jam tectis, liminibusque tuis. / Aspicis ut rutilant sublima tecta RUBENI: / Nec micat in tota pulchrior urbe Domus. / Belgicus his (video) tectis regnavit Apelles, / Et Domus haec nostri fertur Apellis honos […]

[*in the margin*] Splendidissimum sacellum variis lypsanothecis decoratum.

[*in the margin*] Oratorium seu conclave devotionis.
Hoc ego conspicio parvi Panthaeonis instar, / Protinus exclamo Gratia quanta loci est! / Marmore, tum mira fulget testudine fornix / Continet hic rari quidquid in Arte fuit […] / Ars ea Romana est, & gloria tota sacelli: / Splendor & exuviis, Relliquiisque micat. / Et quacumque animum, gressumque, oculosque reflectis, / Textilibus sertis ossa sacrata vides.

Translation[3]:
[*in the margin*] The Grand House of Rubens, now of Hillewerve
This house of yours, illustrious on so many counts as that of Rubens, is no less lustrous since the day it became Hendrik's. A distinguished building, large, full of brilliant pictures – the [outside] wall[4] too holds remarkable artistic riches. I might venture to say that the palaces of Rome give place to your halls and doorways. You see how they glow, Rubens's lofty rooms. No house in the all the city is more strikingly beautiful. In this building (I can see) the Belgic[5] Apelles ruled supreme, and this house is considered the honour of our Apelles.

[*in the margin*] The very splendid chapel distinguished by a number of reliquaries.

[*in the margin*] The oratory, or room of private devotion.
This I perceive as a sort of small Pantheon, and straightaway exclaim 'What Grace is in the place!'. The vault gleams in its marble and wonderful arches; and here is contained all that was rare in art […]. That art is Roman, and the glory of the whole chapel: it glistens splendidly with relics and reliquaries. And wherever you turn your mind, your step, or your eyes, you will see the sacred bones wrapped in their woven cloths.

---

3. Sincere thanks to Elizabeth McGrath for the English translation and interpretation of this excerpt (see following notes).
4. I think it is clear that *murus* means the external wall(s).
5. I use this term to avoid the unhistorical 'Belgian'.

I.37 – 1696, 8 December. Sale Contract: Michiel van Steencruyse Sells the Large House to Thomas de Letter, but Keeps the two Small Houses on the Wapper. Excerpt from the Contract

Antwerp, FelixArchief, Schepenregisters 1646–1699, inv. no. SR#971, fols 141r–143v. Published (a shorter excerpt) in Devroe, *Rubens' huis*, 2008, I, p. 59; Maclot, *Rubenssite*, 2016, I, pp. 87–88.

[*Michiel van Steencruyse sells to Thomas de Letter* – fol. 141r] […] eene groote huysinge metten grooten hove, groote salette, met noch diversche neercameren, diversche oppercameren, solders, kelders, groote ende [fol. 141v] cleijne plaetse, metten stalle inden selven hove, ita mitsgaders steenen en marmeren beelden vasen ende pedestaelen ende oock mette meublen ende stoffatien vande groote salette, spiegels ende schilderijen vuijter sonderen aff mitsgaders alle de ornementen ende verciersel vande capelle voor soo wel deselve meublen, statuten ende vercierselen des comparanten constituanten syn aengande, Item metten wagenhuyse, coetshuyse ita est waschuyse oock metten gronde ende toebehoorten van onder tot boven neffens de voorschreven groote huysinge suytwarts gestaen ende met eender groote poorte daer neffens vuijtcommende, met noch eenen anderen particulieren vuytganck int Hoplant, […] ende alsoo het verschreven coetshuys wagenhuijs inden scheydemuur ter erven warts, vanden eerten der voorscheven tsee huysen neffens het selve coetshuys gestaen ende op nu als voren van gespleten erf is hebbenden seven vensteren wardoer het selve coetshuys zyn licht schept van den hoff of pletse vant selve cleyn huys, welcke vensteren beseth syn met ijzere garden soo op condaitie dat de selve vernsteren alsoo sullen moeten blyven ende sal den veoorschreven proprietaris van dit groot huys inde selve vensters moeten stellen vaststande gelasen, die alsoo ten eeuwigen dage sullen moeten blyven sonder dat tselve llicht vant voorschreven coetshuis wagenhuys ita est washuijse lancx oft vanden cant vant voorschreven cleyn huys dar neffens als voorschreven suytsaerts gestaen oyt en sal mogen becommrt, beleth oft met enighe bauw moghen geblint oft verdonckert worden ita behoudelijk dat het tegenwoordelyck inden hof van cleyn huys omtrant dan voorschreven vensters staende aldaar zal mogen inlyve staen ende het gootken liggende onder het dack van voorschreven wasshuyss oft wagenhuys ter sydewarts vant voorschreven cleyn huis, tselven sal byden proprietaris van desen huyse altyt moeten onderhouden worden […]

I.38 – 1701, 7 April. Thomas de Letter Exchanges the Property for Two Rural Estates. Excerpt from the Contract

Antwerp, FelixArchief, Schepenregisters, SR#993, fols 34r–35v. Excerpts published by Rooses, *Maison*, 1888, pp. 20–21, Annexe II; Tijs, *Rubens en Jordaens*, 1984, p. 157; Devroe, *Rubens' huis*, 2008, I, 59–60; see also Maclot, *Rubenssite*, 2016, I, pp. 88–89.

[*Description follows that of the sale deed of 1696, but also mentioning a gilt leather decoration*]
[…] eene groote huijsinge met grooten hove, grooten salette, met noch diversche neercameren, diversche oppercameren, solders, kelders, groote ende cleyne plaetse, metten stalle inden selven hove, mitsgaders de steene ende marmeren belden, vasen ende pedestaelen, oock mette meubelen ende stoffatien vande groote ende cleyne saletten, spiegels, goude leiren ende schilderyen, [fol. 34v] mitsgaders alle de ornementen ende verciersel vande capellen item metten wagenhuijse, coetshuijse oft waschuijse, […].

APPENDIX I

I.39 – 1707, 22 July. The House is Rented to Justus Forchondt. Excerpt from the Lease Contract

Antwerp, FelixArchief. Published by Denucé, *Kunstuitvoer*, 1931, pp. 265–266.

Notitie vant goet int huys van de heer Thomas de Letter Saliger op de Wapper:
[*selection from the items*]
op de solder […]12 eyseren bogen die van de waegen uyt den hof afgenomen syn.
3 gevlochten raemen van eijserdraet om voor de glasen vant salet te setten vant groodt quartier.
3 lossen beelties int huys.
in den hof 3 losse beelden
een koopere vaes int blomparck.
int koetshuys 2 leeren 1 hage banck.
inde capel de oude goudt leeren.
4 vergulden candelaers 2 kleyne engelties op den autaer.
op het voorcamer vant kleyn quartier 1 boecken cas.

I.40 – 1755, 26 December. Announcement of the Public Sale of the House (9 January 1756) in the *Gazette van Antwerpen*

Gazette van Antwerpen, Friday 26 December 1755, no. 103 (last page); published by Tijs, *Rubens en Jordaens*, 1984, p. 157.

Men sal publieck verkoopen ter Vrydaghs-merckt binnen Antwerpen, door den gesworen Roeper Petrus Domenicus Mooson, eene schoone groote Huysinge met Hove, groote Sallette, diversche neer en boven-Camers, Capelle, Solders, Kelders, groote en kleyne Plaetse, Stallinge, Wagen-huys, Koets, of Was-huys, neffens de voorsz. groote Huysinge gestaen, en met eender Poorte daer neffens uytkomende, met nogh eenen particulieren uytganck in't Hoplant, gestaen de voorsz. Huysinge in de Wapper straet alhier, eertydts toebehoort hebbende den fameusen Schilder Rubbens, en waer inne hy oock gewoont heeft, en dit met de Figueren, Pedestaelen, Copere Vasen in den Hof &c. Alle de opgaende Boomen, Haegen en Palmen, oock de Tapyten hangende in de groote Sallette, den Schouwdoeck beneden in de Schouw, met alle de Ciraeten van de Capelle, de vergulde Reliquair-kaskens en eenige kleynigheden in de selve Capelle staende. De Conditien berusten onder de voorsz. Roeper en den Notaris Corvers in de lange Gast-huys straet. Men sal den absolueten Palm-slagh geven op den 9. January 1756.

I.41 – 1767. Excerpt from the Life of Rubens in Basan, *Estampes*, 1767

Basan, *Estampes*, 1767, pp. xx–xxi.

[…] Quelque-temps après son mariage Rubens fit bâtir une Maison magnifique, dont il orna la façade de Peintures à fresque. Entre la cour & le jardin de cette Maison il fit élever [p. xxi] un salon en rotonde, qu'il enrichit de Statues, de Bustes & de Vases antiques, de Tableaux exquis, & d'un Médaillier précieux. Tout y étoit en ordre & en symmétrie: ce qui ne pouvoit y trouver place décoroit les autres appartements de la Maison […].

Translation:
Some time after his marriage Rubens had a magnificent house built, the façade of which he decorated with fresco paintings. Between the courtyard and the garden of this house he had a circular salon built, which he enriched with statues, busts and antique vases, exquisite paintings and a precious coin cabinet. Everything there was ordered and symmetrical: objects that could not be placed there were used to decorate other rooms of the house.

I.42 – 1660s. Jacobus Van der Sanden Gives Information about Rubens's house in his MS *Oud Konst-Tooneel van Antwerpen*, volume II. Excerpts Concerning the House, which he had Visited before its Transformation c. 1766

Antwerp, FelixArchief, Privilegiekamer, inv. no. PK#172. Transcription from the unpublished manuscript by Jacobus van der Sanden. For the date of the manuscript, see Chapter II, p. 78, n. 84.
Excerpt published by Devroe, *Rubens' huis*, 2008, I, p. 47.

[1] [II, p. 205] *main text, in verse*:
Tot dat hij had bij koop een eigen huijs verkregen,
Bij de Antwerpsche Meir en 't Hert der Stad gelegen;
     Waer hij als een Palijs, van den grond tot het Zop,
     Na de Romijnsche konst met stalling bouwde op;
Met Camers, Gehijm-zael, School, de Boek- en Konstzaelen;
Waer bij een in het rond gaf door een Koupel Straelen,
     Bequaem tot Oeffening van Pictur en 't Verstand,
     Waer toe den ruijmsten Hof al lustbaer was beplant. […]
[…] Hij in Italien deed 't allen kant opkoopen
Pronkbelden van 't Antik, Konstperels met heel hoopen,
     En Penningen aloud, vergaerd in groot getal,
     Tot luijster van zijn Huijs, School en Konstzaelen al.

[2] *footnote, beginning with a Latin citation from Philip Rubens's Vita (see Appendix I.26), and additional footnote*:

'Interim Aedes proprias magnamque juxta aream Antverpiae emit, ubi diaetam amplissimam Romanâ formâ aedificat, Picturae Studio aptam, Hortumque latissimum omnis generis arboribus conserit'.
Dit Hotel van Rubens is in de Topographische Caert van Antwerpen door J.Th. Lucas bezonderlijk aengeteekend in de Voortstraet [sic], loopende van de plaets de Meir na het Clooster der EE. PP. Discalsen en na de Brabandsche Koremerkt; maer zedert dat die Heerlyke Wooning daer, als een Romijns Gebouw, is gestist, blijft die straet voeren den Roemrugtigen naem van Rubens Straet. Boven de eerste verdieping van dit Hotel was het Cabinet en de groote Schilders-camer in 't rond en verlicht, als een koupel, bij meer andere Camers, dienende voor konstgallerijen en zijn school, tegen de schoone Hoving en Binneplijn, waar de balustrade of afschutzel, als ook het Zomerhuys tegen den Colveniers Hof groots was gebouwd met uytgehouwen Steen en toepassende Beldwerken, gelijk ik ook de muren van buijten heb beschilderd gezien in fresco met colossale en klyndere Belden; want Jonker de Bosschaert eijgenaer geworden zynde van dit vermaerd Hotel, is den bouw zedert het jaer 1766 maer veranderd.

[3] [II, p. 532] *footnote to the entry on the painter Jan-Baptist Floris*:
'Het Cabinet van den Ridder Rubens, in sijn zoogenaemd Hotel, heden herbouwd door den edelen Heer De Bosschaert, was rond om verlicht, als een kouppel, gelyk ik die ruijme en heerlycke bovenplaetzen

APPENDIX I

heb gezien, de welke in syn leven waeren verciered met de alderkeurelijkste vazen van Porphir en Agaet, met antike en nieuwtydsche Borstbelden, op't konstigste Gevrogt; met een ryke Boekzael en verzameling van Medaillen of oude Gedenkpenningen, en met de Dierbaerste schilderijen van allen de Scholen [...].

I.43 – 1770s. Manuscript Notes on Rubens by François Mols. Excerpts with Information about the House, which he Visited Several Times (in 1763 and on Other Occasions)

KBR, MS 5724 (Vie de Rubens, Notes et remarques), fols 11r–12r; MS 5726 (Rubeniana, tome 2), fols 10r–11r. Some of these excerpts are published by numerous authors; see, e.g., Rooses, *Maison*, 1888, pp. 235–236; Rooses, *Œuvre*, 1886–92, III, p. 145; Tijs, *Rubens en Jordaens*, 1984, p. 159; Devroe, *Rubens' huis*, 2008, pp. 44–45, n. 109; Maclot , pp. 91–93, 182

I. Excerpts from Ms. 5724

[1] *Excerpt by Mols from* Basan, *Estampes*, 1767 (see Appendix I.41)
[fol. 11r] 46. [...] quelque tems après son mariage, Rubens fit batir une
[fol. 12r] maison magnifique dont il ornait la façade des Peintures à fresque (*footnote* 'o') Entre la Cour et le Jardin de cette maison il fit elever un salon a la rotonde qu'il enrichit de statues [...].
[2] [fol. 12r] *Footnote 'o'*: C'etoit principalement sur les murailles du coté de la Cour et du Jardin, entre le premier et Second Etage, qu'on voioit ces peintures; qui ont subsistées longtemps, et qui auroient subsistées encore si elles n'eussent pas été négligées. Elles representoient plusieurs Sujets de fable en différents compartiments de la largeur des fenêtres. Une entre autres à subistée le plus longtems, c'etoit l'Andromède peint en couleurs naturelles. Elle etoit debout vers la droite du tableau, toute nue; Persée après avoir vaincu le monstre, s'approche d'elle pour la detacher du rocher, aidé par quelques Amours, le pegase vers la gauche etoit retenu par d'autres génies qui badinoient avec lui, en voulant monter sur sa croupe; et l'orison etoit terminé de ce coté par la mer, et au bout de Ciel, au bord du tableau, etoit le monstre se vautrant dans son sang.[*footnote* 'x']

[3] [fol. 11v] *Footnote 'x'*: Le sujet de l'Andromede peint sur les murailles de la Bassecourt de Rubens n'etoit pas celui que represente l'Estampe du Cabinet du Comte de Bruhl, mais celui décrit sans la note ('o'). Je ne scais d'ou Harrewijn peut dérivé la sienne. Car je puis attester que le sujet gravé par Harrewijn ne se trouvoit nullement sur cette muraille à la vente de cette maison où je l'ai examiné nombre de fois.
[*Supplementary note*:] La composition de l'histoire d'Andromède qu'Harrewijn a gravé, sur la façade la la Maison de Rubens, est exactement le même de l'Andromède du Comte de Bruhl que Tardieu a gravé et que se trouve actuellement dan le cabinet de l'Imperateur de Russie. Mais, les objets sont du coté opposé.

II. Excerpts from Ms. 5726

[4] [fol. 10r] 75. Il est assez surprenant que Rubens, qui etait un si habile homme, a bati sa maison d'une forme si singuliere en apparence, si irreguliere et si peu commode, surtout en la voyant en dedans. Mais certainement qu'il avait eu ses raisons de la batir de cette façon, car c'est le moins qu'on doit soupçonner de son habilité.
[5] 76. En achetant cette maison, il eut de la difficulté avec la Confrérie ou Serment des Arquebusiers, pour un [fol. 10v] emplacement au bout de son Jardin qu'on dit qu'une partie de ces messieurs lui avait cédé sans le consentement de l'autre. Cela aurait occasionné un procés tres vif et des fraix plus honereux encore, mais par l'entremise du bourgemaitre Rockox (qui en cette qualité est le chef de cette confrerie)

APPENDIX I

l'affaire fut assoupie par accord; Rubens leur peignit leur tableau de la Decente de Croix moyennant 2400 florins. Comme cet oeuvre porte la date de 1611 et qu'en 1612 le tableau et ses volets fut délivré, on croit inferré de ca que cet achat de sa maison a été enterieur.

[6] [Fol. 10v] **Drawn plan of Rubens's house with comments** (see Appendix III.4; Fig. 3; Text ill. 21;)

Comment referring to parts of the plan:

[*left of the chapel*] a. Cette Chapelle, bâtie en octogone, dépasse de tout son diamètre les limites de la maison.
1. Galerie servant d'antichambre. 2. Cabinet. 3. Salon en rotonde. 4. Chambre à coucher. 5. Alcove. 6. Genier au dessus de la Remise
[7] [*General comment on the plan*] Ce plan, de la distribution de l'ancienne maison de Rubens, n'est fait que de memoire, et se reduit, à peu près, a ce que l'on voit ici, pour le gros de la distribution, tant du plein pied ou ré de Chaussée, que pour le permier Etage de l'aile droite, où il y avoit son atelier, (*footnote: crossed 'o'*) 1.; Le petit cabinet 2., au dessus de la porte de la remise; la rotonde 3.; et le cabinet à Alcôve 4. et 5.; avec le grenier 6. au dessus de la remise, mais qui n'avoit aucune communiquation avec les appartements; de même que son ré de chaussée, par ou on entrait du côté du jardin, et du côté de la rue. L'aile gauche servoit de logement à la famille, ou il y avoit deux chambres sur la rue; ensuite la cuisine; une place à manger; un escalier et
[8] [fol. 11r] La chapelle bâtie en octogone, montant de fond avec son antichambre qui étoit dans le retour. Celle, au-dessus de celle-ci, avoit une tribune ou l'on pouvait entendre messe; cette chapelle avoit eu, autre fois, un nombre assez considerable de reliques dans des Chasses placées de bas en haut dans des niches pratiquées dans les Angles. Je crois même que le retable avoit renfermé un Tableau, mais je n'en suis pas assuré.
[9] Au fond du jardin, il y a un pavillon ouvert de trois cotés, ornéz de colonnes et de Cariatides, qui subsistent encore en partie, ainsi que le portique ouvert à trois arcades grillées qui separe le jardin de la basse court. Ce portique, le pavillon, la Chapelle avec son Antichambre est tout ce qui reste de l'ancien bâtiment, ainsi que quelque partie de l'aile gauche; encore le portique a souffert une alteration assez considerable, en ce qu'on y a adossé un coridor pour communiquer d'une aile à l'autre, ce qui ferme deux de ses arcades, n'y ayant plus que celle du milieu qui est restée ouverte pour l'entrée du jardin. Pour la face du portique du coté de la cour, elle subsiste encore en son entier, on en voit l'élévation dans les Estampes qu'en a gravées Harrewijn, tant de celui-ci que du reste du bâtiment.
[10] L'aile droite, ainsi que la façade du côté de la rue, ont été entièrement rebaties de neuf depuis les fondements. Les plans particuliers a coté droit de celui de la Maison de Rubens sont immaginaires et denotent seulement ceux qui sont de ce coté la jusqu'au coin de la rue, qui retourne en equerrez jusqu'au Jardin des Arquebusiers le quel lui même forme celui de l'autre côté.
[11] *In the margin of fol. 10v: footnote crossed 'o'*: A côté de la grande maison, il y en a 2 petites, marquées I. II. Ces maisons ont toujours appartenu au même fond; il est probable que, du temps de Rubens, elles étoient occupées par sa famille plustôt que l'aile gauche, qui était trop petite pour cela; cecy est d'autant plus probable que l'on voit par la distribution de ce Bâtiment qu'il étoit plustôt fait pour l'ostentation que pour l'habiter, et d'ailleurs, je ne vois pas trop bien comment Rubens pouvait travailler tranquillement dans son atelier qui étoit près de l'Escalier et par conséquent trop bruiant! [*In de margin of fol. 11r*] Je croirais plustôt qu'il l'avoit placé dans un des appartements de ces maisons a coté de la grande où il était plus tranquille pour vaquer à son travail.

Appendix II: Timeline

Information about the houses in Antwerp where Rubens lived and worked; the acquisition of the property on the Wapper; construction of the house; extension of the property; the house after Rubens's death; sources providing information on the house.

1589, Spring
Maria Pypelinckx leaves Cologne and returns to Antwerp with her three children Blandina, Philip and Peter Paul. With her sister Susanna, she owns a house on the Meir ('Sint-Arnout'; now no. 54) (Text ills 1–2), but this may have been occupied by tenants at the time, and there is no certainty that they moved into the house.

1600, early May
Rubens departs for Italy, and will remain there for more than eight years. He leaves some of his possessions (including paintings) with his mother.

1601, 31 October
Maria Pypelinckx and her sister sell the house 'Sint-Arnout' on the Meir (Text ills 1–2) to the merchant Hendrik Hoons.

1608, 19 October
Death of Maria Pypelinckx at her home in the Sint-Michielsstraat (in a house which she rented from the Norbertines of St Michael's Abbey, and which adjoined the abbey).

1608, November or December
Rubens returns to Antwerp. He probably stays for a while (with his brother Philip?) at the house where his mother had lived, in the Sint-Michielsstraat, opposite Jan Brant's house. The whereabouts of his studio is unknown.

1608
Publication of Philip Rubens's book: Rubenius, *Electorum Libri II*, 1608.

1609, 9 April
The 'Twelve Years' Truce' is concluded in Antwerp. The prospect of peace probably played a part in Rubens's decision to settle in the Netherlands.

1609, 3 October
Rubens marries Isabella Brant; the couple move in with Isabella's parents, the lawyer and municipal secretary Jan Brant and Clara de Moy, in their house on the Sint-Michielsstraat, opposite St Michael's Abbey (Appendix I.26). It is unlikely that he had a large studio in this house.

1610, June
Rubens paints the large panels of the *Triptych of the Elevation of the Cross*, not in a studio, but in the choir of St Walburga's Church.

1610, 22 September
Death of Jan Moretus I; the funeral roll states that Rubens is residing in the Sint-Michielsstraat.

APPENDIX II

1610, 1 November
Acquisition by Rubens of the property on the Wapper: a sale contract drawn up in Amsterdam registers an agreement between Rubens and Hans Thys (Appendix I.1).

1610, Christmas
First payment of 2986 guilders etc. to Hans Thys; handover of the property.

1611, 4 January
Acquisition by Rubens of the property on the Wapper; a second sale contract, drawn up in Antwerp, registers the agreement between Rubens and Andries Backer (Appendix I.2).

1611, 21 March
Baptism of Clara Serena Rubens at St Andrew's Church, parish church for residents of the Sint-Michielsstraat.

1611, 11 May
Letter from Rubens to Jacques de Bie: Rubens is attracting large numbers of aspiring artists who are hoping for an apprenticeship in his studio, and has been obliged to turn down more than one hundred applicants. The whereabouts of this very busy studio is unknown.

1611, 7 September
Agreement between the arquebusiers (kolveniers) and Rubens to paint the *Triptych of the Descent from the Cross* (Text ill. 55) for their altar in the Cathedral of Our Lady.

October 1611–March 1614
The Account Book of the Guild of the Arquebusiers includes several references to panels of the *Triptych of the Descent from the Cross* which are 'at the house of the painter' (Appendix I.3). The location of this house is a matter of debate; we can probably rule out the house of Jan Brant in the Sint-Michielsstraat.

1611, September
Death of Hans Thys (accident during a boat trip on the Zuiderzee).

1611, Christmas
Second payment of 2986 guilders, etc. to the family of Hans Thys.

1612, between 12 and 16 September
The Guild of the Arquebusiers (kolveniers) pays workers for 'bringing down' the central panel of the *Triptych of the Descent from the Cross* from the attic to the ground floor at 'the house of the painter Rubens', and transporting it to the Cathedral (Appendix I.3: [2]). The location of this house is a matter of discussion.

1612, Christmas
Third (and final) payment of 2986 guilders, etc. to the family of Hans Thys.

1613, 2 March–13 May
Mortgages (hereditary rents) on the property on the Wapper are paid off by Rubens (Appendix I.4).

1614, between 31 January and 6 February
A group of German noblemen visit Rubens's studio (mentioned in an account of their journey across

various European countries by Wilhelm Neumayr von Ramssla, in 1620: Appendix I.13). It cannot be ascertained if the workshop was already established in the property on the Wapper.

1614, 18 February and March
The wings of the *Triptych of the Descent from the Cross* (Text ill. 55) are brought down in 'the house of the painter' and carried to the Cathedral (Appendix I.3: [3]).

1614, 5 June
Baptism of Albert Rubens at St Andrew's Church, parish church for residents of the Sint-Michielsstraat. This suggests that the family were still living in Jan Brant's house.

1615, 2 February
Rubens acquires from the Officina Plantiniana two editions of Vitruvius's *De architectura libri decem*.

1615, 7 March
Laying of the first stone for the Church of St Augustine in Antwerp, designed by Wenzel Cobergher. It was consecrated on 2 September 1618. The façade incorporates several 'Rubensian' architectural motifs.

1615, July and August
Notes from the account book of the Guild of the Arquebusiers concerning the wall and privy bordering Rubens's garden (Appendix I.5). An agreement (concerning the wall) between the arquebusiers and Franchoys De Crayer is signed on 25 July.

1615, 13–17 August
The Archdukes Albert and Isabella are in Antwerp. Given the indications that Rubens's studio on the Wapper was still under construction at this point, it seems unlikely that the couple came to visit him there.

1615
The roof of the house is constructed by carpenters and slaters, as is clear from Rubens's testimony in 1621 (Appendix I.14).

1615
Balthasar Moretus I mentions Rubens's 'museum' (Appendix I.6). It is not certain if this room (a study?) is already situated in the house on the Wapper.

1616, 17 February
Death of Martina Plantin; the funeral roll lists Rubens as living near the Arenbergstraat (Appendix I.7), in the same neighbourhood as the Wapper.

1616, 2 May
Mention of a folio edition of Sebastiano Serlio's treatises, which Rubens had bound by the Officina Plantiniana.

1616, September
Rubens is listed in the 'Liggeren' of the Guild of St Luke as living on the Wapper (Appendix I.8). This is the first explicit record of Rubens residing in his new house on the Wapper.

1616, 2 November
Contract between Rubens, represented by Hans van Mildert, and Jasper Bulliau for the installation of a staircase in the house (Appendix I.9).

1616, 9 November
An agreement is signed for the production of the *Decius Mus* tapestry series. The parties are: the Brussels tapestry weaver Jan Raes I with the Antwerp tapestry dealer and humanist François Sweerts (Sweertius), and the Genoese merchant Franco Cattaneo.

1616, 30 December
Letter from Tobie Matthew to Sir Dudley Carleton mentioning an exceptionally large *Wolf Hunt* made by Rubens.

1617
The canvases for the *Decius Mus* series (Text ill. 56), covering an area of some seventy square metres, were completed within the twelve months of 1617.

1618, 23 March
Baptism of Nicolaas Rubens at St James's Church, parish church for residents of the Wapper.

1618, 12 May
Letter from Rubens to Sir Dudley Carleton concerning the acquisition of antique sculptures; Rubens mentions having spent 'some thousand florins' that year on his estate (Appendix I.10).

1618, 20 May
Rubens acquires an important collection of antique sculptures and objects from Sir Dudley Carleton; the collection arrives in Antwerp on 1 June; most of it is exhibited in the 'antiquarium' (until August 1627).

1618, 18 July
In a letter to Jan de Gruytere, François Sweerts mentions that Rubens has already squandered 24,000 guilders on his house (Appendix I.11).

1620, 1 October
Letter from Jan van den Wouwer to Balthasar Moretus, praising the houses of Moretus and Rubens (Appendix I.12).

1621, 5 January
Rubens testifies against the carpenters who constructed the roof of his house in 1615 (Appendix I.14).

1621, late May–early June
Otto Sperling, a German medical student at Leiden University, together with a friend visits Rubens at his house; they see the master at work, as well as the studio with many assistants. Much later, Sperling writes about it in his autobiography (a manuscript composed during his captivity in Copenhagen (1664–1681). He gives a unique, but probably not wholly reliable account of what he witnessed (Appendix I.27).

1621, 13 September
Letter from Rubens to William Trumbull, expressing his predilection for painting large-format compositions.

APPENDIX II

1621, October
Anthony van Dyck, in several of whose early works (first Antwerp period) the portico is depicted, leaves for Italy.

1621, 23 December
Rubens buys two houses (one of them called 'Breda') on the Hopland, adjoining his property (Appendix I.15).

1622
Publication of *Palazzi di Genova* (with an introduction by Rubens).

1623, 3 August
Letter from Rubens to Nicolas Claude Fabri de Peiresc, in which he mentions a private study ('studiolo secreto') in his house (Appendix I.16).

1624, end (?)–beginning of 1625 (?)
Georg Petel possibly in Antwerp.

1625, 10 July
The Infanta Isabella visits Rubens at his house; she admires the Egyptian mummy in the 'Pantheon' (Appendix I.17).

1626, beginning–1630, June
Willem Panneels is active in Rubens's house as assistant and caretaker during Rubens's absence (1628–1630).

1626, 20 June
Death of Isabella Brant.

1627, 29 May
Rubens buys a country estate in Ekeren, the Hof van Ursele.

1627, 28 July
Rubens buys six houses (adjoining his property): three on the Hopland and three on the Wapper (Appendix I.18).

1627, August
Rubens sells his collection of antique sculptures (exhibited in his 'antiquarium') to the Duke of Buckingham.

1627 (?)
Publication of an addendum to the *Palazzi di Genova*: *Palazzi Moderni di Genova*.

1628, 15 June
Rubens buys another house (on the Hopland) adjoining his property (Appendix I.19).

1628, 28 August
Estate inventory of Isabella Brant (Appendix I.20). The inventory listing the objects found in the house (with details of the rooms, etc.) has not been preserved.

1628, shortly after 28 August
Rubens departs on a diplomatic mission to Madrid. He will stay abroad for eighteen months (in Spain, France and England), with the exception of a few days in Antwerp in May 1629. Willem Panneels acts as caretaker of the house and closed studio. He copies many works from Rubens's collection of drawings that were kept in his so-called Cantoor.

1630, beginning of April
Rubens is back in Antwerp after an eighteen-month absence.

1630, 1 June
Rubens testifies that Willem Panneels trained under him for five and a half years, and that he was entrusted with managing the house during Rubens's diplomatic missions.

1630, 6 December
Rubens marries Helena Fourment.

1630s
Rubens and studio, *The Walk in the Garden* (Munich), showing the garden and the garden pavilion (Figs 25 and 182).

1630s
Rubens, *Hélène Fourment au Carrosse* (Paris), showing an idealised image of the house on the Wapper in the background (Fig. 21).

c. 1630
Willem van Haecht, *The Studio of Apelles* (The Hague), showing a variant of Rubens's 'antiquarium' in the background (Text ill. 100).

1631, between 4 September and 2 October
The exiled Queen-Mother Maria de' Medici and the Infanta Isabella stay in Antwerp; the queen goes to Rubens's workshop (accompanied by the Infanta?) to admire his paintings.

1635, 12 May
Rubens buys the manor of Het Steen in Elewijt.

1636–1640
Lucas Faydherbe lives and works in Rubens's house for at least three years, before returning to settle in his native town of Mechelen.

1637, 1 August
Letter from Rubens to Franciscus Junius about the art of painting of the ancients (especially on long-lost Greek masterpieces).

17 August 1638
Letter from Rubens (staying in Elewijt) to Lucas Faydherbe, who is at the house on the Wapper and about to join Rubens at Elewijt. He mentions the studio (Appendix I.21).

1638, 21 September
Death of Hans van Mildert.

APPENDIX II

1639, 25 December
The painter David Ryckaert II leaves one of Rubens's houses on the Hopland, which he had been renting. Rubens installs his library here, and also uses the house to store less valuable paintings (Appendix I.23: [5]).

1640, 5 April
Rubens writes a favourable reference for Lucas Faydherbe.

1640, 30 May
Death of Rubens in his house on the Wapper. The property passes to Albert and Nicolaas Rubens, Helena Fourment and her five children.

1640, 8 June and following days
An inventory is drawn up of the contents of the house (now lost).

1640, 2 August
Constantijn Huygens drafts a letter intended for Rubens, answering a lost letter by Rubens about architecture and discussing Huygens's house in The Hague.

1640 until 1645, 1 October
Helena Fourment (with her children) lives on at the house for five years, as a tenant paying rent (Appendix I.23: [3]); she also remains there for a while after her marriage (in 1644) to Jan-Baptist van Broechoven van Bergeyck; eventually the family moves to Brussels.

1641, 10 October
The guardians of Rubens's underage children request the sale of the house and its annexes (Appendix I.22). The request is granted but no buyer can be found.

1645, 17 November
Estate inventory of Rubens, the so-called *Staetmasse* (Appendix I.23). The inventory of the contents of the house, drawn up in June 1640, is lost.

1645
Govaert Flinck builds a studio (with light falling from above) in his house in Amsterdam, probably inspired by a room in Rubens's house.

1648, July (?)–1660
William Cavendish and his wife Margaret (née Lucas) rent the house. It becomes the site of Cavendish's famous riding school; his book on dressage, *La méthode nouvelle*, is published in Antwerp in 1658. An illustration in one of Margaret Cavendish's books shows a scene with an interior of the house (Cavendish, *Natures Pictures*, 1656); Appendix III.28b.

c. 1655
Anonymous, *Portrait of a Couple in a Garden* (Berlin), showing the garden pavilion in the background (Appendix III.10; Fig. 22).

1657, 1 October
Death of Albert Rubens (living in Brussels).

APPENDIX II

1657, 6 December
Estate inventory of Albert Rubens, mentioning the house, which is let to Cavendish (Appendix I.24).

1658, February
Charles II, accompanied by his sister Mary (widow of the Prince of Orange) and his brothers James and Henry, visit William and Margaret Cavendish in Antwerp. In honour of their visit the Cavendishes organise a royal entertainment at the house (with a banquet and ball).

1660, May
Cavendish returns to England, leaving Margaret behind in Antwerp as pawn for his debts.

1660, 3 September
Public sale of the property on the Vrijdagmarkt; it is sold to the alderman Jacomo van Eycke the Younger for 20,000 guilders. The deed of sale is drawn up on 16 September 1660 (Appendix I.25).

1660s
Philip Rubens mentions the house in his MS *Vita* of Rubens (Appendix I.26).

1660s (?)
Anonymous, *View of the Courtyard of Rubens's House* (Aylesbury) (Appendix III.3; Fig. 16).

1672
Giovan Pietro Bellori mentions the house in his *Life* of Rubens (Appendix I.28).

1673, 15 July
Death in Brussels of Helena Fourment, Baroness van Broechoven van Bergeyck.

c. 1675
Gonzales Coques, *Portrait of Maria Agnes van Eycke as St Agnes* (London), showing the portico in the background (Appendix III.11; Text ills 20, 95 and 123).

1675–1680
Joachim von Sandrart mentions the house in his *Life* of Rubens (Appendix I.29).

1679, 2 October
Death of Jacomo Van Eycke; the house passes to his widow Cornelia Hillewerve.

1680, 18 January
Cornelia Hillewerve sells the house to her brother, Canon Hendrik Hillewerve (Appendix I.30).

1681
Roger De Piles mentions the house in his *Life of Rubens* (Appendix I.31).

1682, 17 June
Hendrik Hillewerve gives the property as 'donatio inter vivos' to his sister Cornelia and her three children (Joanna, Teresia and Joseph van Eycke). He continues to live in the house, retaining the use of the chapel and a number of rooms (Appendix I.33).

APPENDIX II

1684
First print by Jacob Harrewijn (Appendix III.1; Fig. 17).

1686, 27 March
Death of Cornelia Hillewerve.

1687, after 19 May
Nicodemus Tessin visits the house; he mentions the wall paintings in his travel notes (Appendix I.34).

1691, 7 March
Renewal of the donation by Hillewerve, to his nephew and nieces (Appendix I.35).

1692
Second print by Jacob Harrewijn (Appendix III.2; Fig. 18).

1694, 22 February
Death of Hendrik Hillewerve. The property is inherited by his two nieces (who had left Antwerp to live in Brussels); in 1695 they sell it to Michiel van Steencruyse.

c. 1695
Desiderius de Sevin praises the house in his ode to Hillewerve in his collection titled *Pindus charitatis* (Appendix I.36).

1696, 8 December
Sale contract between Michiel van Steencruyse and Thomas de Letter (Appendix I.37).

1701, 7 April
Thomas de Letter exchanges the property for two rural estates (Appendix I.38).

1707, 22 July
The house is rented by the banker Justus Forchondt (Appendix I.39).

1681–1728
Fillippo Baldinucci mentions the house and its mural paintings in his *Life* of Rubens (Appendix I.32).

1755, 25 December
Announcement of the sale of Rubens's house in the *Gazette van Antwerpen* (Appendix I.40).

1760s
The house is visited by Jacob van der Sanden and François Mols (see Appendix I.42–43).

1763
The property is acquired by Charles-Nicolas de Bosschaert de Pret, and subsequently passes to his son Charles-Jean.

1766 and following years
Major changes are made to the house (Appendix I.42). Extensions are added to the garden side of the portico and its top; the wall paintings disappear.

1767

François Basan mentions the house and its (former) wall paintings in his *Life* of Rubens (Appendix I.41).

1760s

Jacob Van der Sanden, in his manuscript *Oud Konst-Tooneel van Antwerpen*, praises the house in verse, describing what he had seen during his visit (Appendix I.42).

1770s

In his extensive notes on Rubens, François Mols gives information about the house which he visited on several occasions; he includes an annotated plan sketched from memory (Appendices I.43 and III.4; Figs 3, 125 and 126; Text ill. 21).

APPENDIX III

Appendix III:
Images of Rubens's House. Fact and Fiction

If the work has already been shown elsewhere, the size of the photo in this appendix is smaller.

A. Providing Essential Information on the House – in its Entirety, and Lay-out

III.1. Jacob Harrewijn after Jacob van Croes, *View of the Courtyard of Rubens's House*, 1684 (Fig. 17; details: passim).

Etching and engraving, 291 × 356 mm; lettered: *J. van Croes Deli.* (on the plinth, left); titled: *Maison Hilwerve a Anvers dit l hostel Rubens 1684.* (centrally on the plinth); *Harrewijn Fecit.* (on the plinth, right).

LIT.: *V.S.*, p. 226, no. 28; Van Heurck, *Harrewijn*, 1920, p. 10, no. 4; Hollstein et al., *Dutch and Flemish*, 1949–2010, VIII, p. 220 (as 'Frans Harrewijn'); Uppenkamp – Van Beneden, *Palazzo Rubens*, 2011, no. 41.
Note: there are two states of this print: before the portrait of Hillewerve (in a roundel at the top) (Museum Plantin-Moretus, Stedelijk Prentenkabinet, inv. no. PK.OP.17876), and a later state with portrait.
Impressions consulted: Antwerp, Rubenshuis, inv. no. P.1113; Antwerp, Museum Plantin-Moretus, Stedelijk Prentenkabinet, inv. no. PK.OP.17877.
For a full description, see Chapter III, passim.

APPENDIX III

III.2. Jacob Harrewijn after Jacob van Croes, *View of Rubens's House and Garden*, **1692 (Fig. 18; details: passim).**

Etching and engraving, 330 × 435 mm; lettered on banderole floating in the sky above the garden: *Parties de la maison* HILWERVE *A anvers 1692*.

LIT.: *V.S.*, p. 226, no. 28; Rooses, *Oeuvre*, 1886–92, V, no. 1362; Van Heurck, *Harrewijn*, 1920, no. 5; Hollstein et al., *Dutch and Flemish*, 1949–2010, VIII, p. 220 (as 'Frans Harrewijn'); Diels, *Schaduw van Rubens*, 2009, pp. 22–23, no. 4; Uppenkamp – Van Beneden, *Palazzo Rubens*, 2011, no. 42.
Impressions consulted: Antwerp, Rubenshuis, inv. no. P.1114; Antwerp, Museum Plantin-Moretus, Stedelijk Prentenkabinet, inv. no. PK.OP. 17875.
For a full description, see Chapter III, passim.

III.3. Anonymous seventeenth-century artist, *View of the Courtyard of Rubens's House*, **1660s (?) (Fig. 16; details: passim).**

Aylesbury, Discover Bucks Museum (formerly Buckinghamshire County Museum), inv. no. AYBCM:2007.58.5.; oil on canvas, 109.3 × 140.2 cm.

PROV.: possibly the painting referred to in *L.*, 10198: sale, London (Collection Richard Cosway), 9 May 1822, lot 94 (as 'Rubens, a view of his Palace at Antwerp, with Portraits of Himself, his Wife and Child'); Denham Court, Uxbridge, Buckinghamshire (as 'set into the wall panelling'); transferred to the Museum, 1986.
LIT.: Van Beneden, *Revealed*, 2009; Uppenkamp – Van Beneden, *Palazzo Rubens*, 2011, pp. 17, 44, 158, no. 1, figs 7, 45, 148; Uppenkamp, *Palazzetto*, 2018, p. 220, fig. 3.
See also Chapter II, p. 62.

APPENDIX III

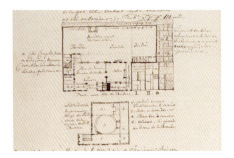

III.4. François Mols, *Plan of Rubens's House*, c. 1770 (Fig. 3, Text ill. 21; details: Figs 125–126).

KBR, MS 5726 (see Appendix I.43: [II.6]).

LIT.: Tijs, *Rubens en Jordaens*, 1984, pp. 158–159; Uppenkamp – Van Beneden, *Palazzo Rubens*, 2011, p. 17.

B. Providing Essential Information about the Portico, the Garden Pavilion and 'Antiquarium'

III.5. Anthony van Dyck, *Portrait of Isabella Brant*, 1620s (Fig. 19; detail: Fig. 232).

The background contains an image of the portico (in reverse), with a statue on a balustrade to the left. Washington, National Gallery of Art, Andrew W. Mellon Collection, inv. no. 1937.1.47; oil on canvas, 153 × 120 cm.

LIT.: S. Barnes in Wheelock et al., *Van Dyck*, 1990, no. 23; Brown et al., *Van Dyck*, 1999, no. 27; N. De Poorter in Barnes et al., *Van Dyck*, 2004, no. I.100; K. Belkin in Belkin – Healy, *House of Art*, 2004, no. 56; Uppenkamp – Van Beneden, *Palazzo Rubens*, 2011, pp. 20, 102, no. 57, figs 129, 157 (details: frontispiece). Note: The dating of c. 1620, which is often given (and used as *terminus ante quem*), is not certain. The portrait is possibly posthumous, and so is more likely to date from after 1627 (see N. De Poorter, ibid.).

APPENDIX III

III.6. ? Rubens and Studio, *Peter Paul Rubens with his Wife Helena Fourment and his Son Nicolaas Rubens (The Walk in the Garden)*, **after 1630 (Fig. 25; details: Figs 182, 196, 205, 210, 218).**

Relevant for the garden pavilion and the fountain with dolphin and Cupid.
Munich, Bayerische Staatsgemäldesammlungen, Alte Pinakothek, inv. no. 313; oil on canvas, 98 × 130.5 cm.

LIT.: Vlieghe, *Portraits (CRLB)*, 1987, pp. 165–167, no. 139, fig. 192; Renger – Denk, *Cat. Munich (Flämische Malerei)*, 2002, no. 313, pp. 284–287; Neumeister, ed., *Cat. Munich, Pinakothek (Flämische Malerei)*, 2009, p. 368.
See also Chapter X, pp. 301–303.

III.7. Rubens, *Helena Fourment with her Son Frans (?) Rubens (Hélène Fourment au carrosse)*, **1630s (Fig. 21; details: Figs 31, 55).**

The background contains a variant of the studio (west and south façade).
Paris, Musée du Louvre, inv. no. RF1977-13; oil on canvas, 195 × 132 cm.

LIT.: Foucart, *Nouveau Rubens*, 1977, pp. 343–353; Vlieghe, *Portraits (CRLB)*, 1987, pp. 103–105, no. 100, figs 103–104 (as 'Helena Fourment and Frans Rubens'); Foucart, *Cat. Paris, Louvre*, 2009, p. 244 (as 'Hélène Fourment et son jeune fils Frans'); Van der Stighelen – Vlieghe, *Portraits Unidentified Sitters (CRLB)*, 2021, pp. 58–59, 63, 185, 186 (n. 9), 207 (nn. 29, 36) (as 'Helena Fourment with her Son Frans Rubens'). Note: the dating of this portrait remains a matter of debate because we cannot be certain which of Rubens's sons accompanies Helena Fourment: the boy is usually seen as Frans (b. 1633), but sometimes – more likely in our view – as Nicolaas (b. 1618).
See Chapter V, esp. pp. 159–161.

APPENDIX III

III.8. Willem van Haecht, *The Studio of Apelles (Apelles Painting Campaspe)*, **c. 1630 (Text ill. 100; details: Text ill. 103 and Figs 128, 130, 135).**

The background includes a variant of Rubens's 'antiquarium'. The doorway is crowned with festoons and a Hercules bust in a niche, possibly deriving from a similar arrangement in Rubens's house.
The Hague, Mauritshuis, inv. no. 266; oil on panel, 104.9 × 148.7 cm.

LIT.: Speth-Holterhoff, *Cabinets*, 1957, pp. 104–107, fig. 38; Tijs, *Rubens en Jordaens*, 1984, p. 236, repr. p. 115; Broos, *Historiestukken*, 1993, pp. 136–146, no. 15, repr. detail opposite p. 140; Muller, *House of Art*, 2004, p. 47, fig. 5; Van Suchtelen – Van Beneden, *Room for Art*, 2009, p. 123, no. 11, fig. 1, figs pp. 11–16, 19); Van Beneden, *Van Haecht*, 2009, pp. 77–83, figs 48, 56; Uppenkamp – Van Beneden, *Palazzo Rubens*, 2011, pp. 18, 104, figs 12, 133.
See Chapter VIII, pp. 238–239.

III.9. Jacques Jordaens, *Cupid and Psyche*, **c. 1640–1650 (Fig. 20; details: Figs 159, 179, 220).**

Relevant for variants of the portico (represented twice), the pavilion, and fountain with Cupid and dolphin.
Madrid, Museo Nacional del Prado, inv. no. P01548; oil on canvas (pasted on panel), 131 × 127 cm. (including later addition at the top).

LIT.: d'Hulst, *Jordaens*, 1982, p. 208, p. 336, n. 25; Tijs, *Rubens en Jordaens*, 1984, p. 123; Díaz Padrón, *Cat. Madrid, Prado (Pintura Flamenca)*, 1995, I, pp. 626–627, no. 1548; Uppenkamp – Van Beneden, *Palazzo Rubens*, 2011, pp. 20, 91, 102, 167, no. 58. figs 16, 128 (as 'c. 1640–1645'); U. Heinen in Vander Auwera et al., eds, *Jordaens*, 2012, p. 161, no. 62 (as 'c. 1640–1650').

APPENDIX III

III.10. Anonymous 17th-century artist, *Portrait of a Couple in a Garden***, c. 1655**
(Fig. 22; details: Figs 167, 181, 208, 212, 230).

The background contains an image of the garden pavilion with statues, and a simplified variant of the portico with statue.
Berlin, Staatliche Museen zu Berlin, Gemäldegalerie Alte Meister, inv. no. 858; oil on canvas, 239.8 × 173.8 cm.

LIT.: Härting, *Cavendish*, 2002, pp. 15–28, fig. 1 (as '*William and Margaret Cavendish* and by Conzales Coques'); Lisken-Pruss, *Coques*, 2013, pp. 175–176, no. U3 (as 'not by Gonzales Coques').
Note: the sitters are certainly not William and Margaret Cavendish.

III.11. Gonzales Coques, *Portrait of Maria Agnes van Eycke as St Agnes***, c. 1675**
(Text ill. 20; details: Text ills 95, 123).

The portico appears in the background.
Oil sketch, London, The National Gallery, inv. no. NG1011; oil on silver, 18.3 × 14.4 cm.

LIT.: Martin, *Cat. London, NG (Flemish School)*, 1970, pp. 19–21, no. 1011 (as 'It is possible that the sitter is a member of the Hillewerve family. None has been traced with the name Agnes.'); Uppenkamp – Van Beneden, *Palazzo Rubens*, 2011, pp. 25 (n. 38), 167, no. 59, fig. 17 (as 'a young woman as St Agnes'); Lisken-Pruss, *Coques*, 2013, no. 56 (as 'a young woman as St Agnes').
Note: For the identification of the sitter as Maria Agnes Van Eycke, the daughter of the residents of the house c. 1750, see Chapter II (pp. 73–74, n. 74).

APPENDIX III

C. Elements of the House Reflected in Works by Rubens and Van Dyck

III.12. Rubens, *Susanna and the Elders*, c. 1610 (Detail: Fig. 222).

Relevant for a variant of the fountain with Cupid and dolphin.
Madrid, Real Academia de Bellas Artes de San Fernando, inv. no. 688; oil on panel, 190 × 223 cm.

LIT.: d'Hulst – Vandenven, *Old Testament (CRLB)*, 1989, pp. 202–204, no. 59, fig. 153.

III.13. Rubens with Frans Snijders, *Homage to Ceres*, c. 1612–1615 (Fig. 23; detail: Fig. 121).

The architecture of the niche is related to the portico; on top of the pediments are quoins and oil lamps, related to the façades of the south wing can be seen.
Oil sketch, St Petersburg, The State Hermitage Museum, inv. no. ГЭ-504; oil on panel, 90.3 × 65.5 cm.

LIT.: Uppenkamp – Van Beneden, *Palazzo Rubens*, 2011, pp. 96, 160, no. 13, figs 121–122; Büttner, *Allegories (CRLB)*, 2018, I, pp. 103–111, no. 5; II, fig. 23.

APPENDIX III

III.14. Rubens, *St Ambrose and Theodosius*, **c. 1618.**

The gateway in the background is a variant of the central section of the portico.
Vienna, Kunsthistorisches Museum, inv. no. 524; oil on canvas, 362 × 246 cm.

LIT.: McGrath, *History (CRLB)*, 1997, I, fig. 204; II, no. 55, pp. 297–308; W. Prohaska in Kräftner *et al.*, *Rubens in Wien*, 2004, pp. 114–118, no. 25.

III.15. Anthony van Dyck, *St Ambrose and Theodosius*, **c. 1619–1620.**

The gateway in the background is a variant of the central section of the portico.
London, The National Gallery, inv. no. NG50; oil on canvas, 149 × 113.2 cm.

LIT.: McGrath, *History (CRLB)*, 1997, II, p. 302, no. 55, copy, fig. 205; N. De Poorter, in Barnes et al., *Van Dyck*, 2004, no. I.87.

49

APPENDIX III

III.16. Anthony van Dyck, *St John the Evangelist and St John the Baptist,* **1618–1619.**

The columns either side of the two saints correspond to the central section of the portico.
Berlin, Kaiser-Friedrich-Museum (lost); oil on canvas, 261 × 212 cm.

LIT.: N. De Poorter, in Barnes et al., *Van Dyck*, 2004, no. I.37.

III.17. Studio of Peter Paul Rubens and Frans Snijders, *The Fish Market (The Emperor's Mullet),* **c. 1620.**

The background contains a variant of the portico.
Vienna, Kunsthistorisches Museum, inv. no. 383; oil on canvas, 253 × 375 cm.

LIT: Balis et al, *Vlaamse schilderkunst*, 1987, pp. 200–201, no. 85; McGrath, *Emperor's Mullet*, 2020, pp. 349 ff..

APPENDIX III

III.18. Rubens, *Henri IV Consigns the Regency to Maria de' Medici*, 1622–1625 (Fig. 24).

The backdrop is a variant of the central section of the portico; through the archway appears a variant of the garden pavilion.
Paris, Musée du Louvre, inv. no. 1777; oil on canvas, 394 × 295 cm.

LIT.: Thuillier – Foucart, *Médicis*, 1969, pp. 84–86, pl. XVIII; Millen – Wolf, *Maria de' Medici*, 1989, pp. 96–106, figs 30–33; Baudouin, *Motieven*, 2006, pp. 199–203; Foucart, *Cat. Paris, Louvre*, 2009, p. 231; The painting will be discussed by Nils Büttner in his forthcoming volume on *The Maria de' Medici Series (CRLB, XIV.1)*.
See also Chapter IX, p. 289 (esp. n. 115) and Chapter X, p. 300.

III.19. Rubens, *Henri IV Consigns the Regency to Maria de' Medici*, 1622 (Text ill. 135).

The backdrop is a variant of the central section of the portico; through the archway appears a variant of the garden pavilion.
Oil sketch, Munich, Bayerische Staatsgemäldesammlungen, Alte Pinakothek, inv. no. 98; oil on panel, 47.8 × 35.7 cm.

LIT.: Held, *Sketches*, 1980, pp. 107–108, no. 66; Renger – Denk, *Cat. Munich (Flämische Malerei)*, 2002, pp. 409, 412, no. 98; Uppenkamp – Van Beneden, *Palazzo Rubens*, 2011, pp. 139–140, figs 14, 168.

APPENDIX III

III.20. Rubens, *The Flight [of Maria de' Medici] from the Chateau of Blois*, 1622–1625.

The gateway in the background is a variant of the central section of the portico.
Paris, Musée du Louvre, inv. no. 1785; oil on canvas, 394 × 295 cm.

LIT.: Thuillier – Foucart, *Médicis*, 1969, p. 91, pl. XLIV; Millen – Wolf, *Maria de' Medici*, 1989, pp. 178–181, figs 55–56; Foucart, *Cat. Paris, Louvre*, 2009, p. 234.
Note: for the sketch, see Munich, Bayerische Staatsgemäldesammlungen, Alte Pinakothek, inv. no. 106.
LIT.: Held, *Sketches*, 1980, pp. 119–120, no. 77; Renger – Denk, *Cat. Munich (Flämische Malerei)*, 2002, p. 436, no. 106; The sketch will be discussed by Nils Büttner in his forthcoming volume on *The Maria de' Medici Series (CRLB, XIV.1)*.

III.21. Rubens, *The Flight of Lot and his Family from Sodom*, dated 1625.

The gateway in the background is a variant of the central section of the portico.
Paris, Musée du Louvre, inv. no. 1760; oil on panel, 74 × 118 cm.

LIT.: d'Hulst – Vandenven, *Old Testament (CRLB)*, 1989, pp. 44–47, no. 6, fig. 13; Foucart, *Cat. Paris, Louvre*, 2009, p. 223.

APPENDIX III

III.22. After Rubens, *Susanna and the Elders*, 1620s.

Relevant for a variant of the fountain with Cupid and dolphin.
St Petersburg, The State Hermitage Museum, inv. no. GE496; oil on canvas, 178.5 × 220 cm.

LIT.: d'Hulst – Vandenven, *Old Testament (CRLB)*, 1989, p. 215, no. 64, copy 1, fig. 167.
Note: woodcut (in reverse) by Christoffel Jegher, between 1633 and 1636 (detail: Fig. 225); LIT.: d'Hulst – Vandenven, *Old Testament (CRLB)*, 1989, p. 216, no. 64, copy 5, fig. 168.

III.23. Rubens, *The Discovery of Erichthonius by the Daughters of Cecrops*, 1631–1632 (Text ill. 138; detail: Fig. 226).

Variant of the fountain with Cupid and dolphin, and of a *serliana* from the pavilion.
Stockholm, Nationalmuseum, inv. no. NM 607; oil on panel, 31 × 33 cm.

LIT.: F. Healy in McGrath et al., *Mythological Subjects I (CRLB)*, 2016, I, pp. 431–434, no. 42a; II, fig. 370.

APPENDIX III

III.24. Rubens, *The Garden of Love*, 1630–1635 (Detail: Text ill. 134).

The background contains a variant of the portico.
Madrid, Museo Nacional del Prado, inv. no. P001690; oil on canvas, 199 × 286 cm.

LIT.: Uppenkamp – Van Beneden, *Palazzo Rubens*, 2011, pp. 121, 140, figs 28, 155; Büttner, *Genre (CRLB)*, 2019, pp. 64–96, no. 1, fig. 1.

III.25. Rubens, *The Supper at Emmaus*, c. 1638.

The figures are sitting in a loggia which resembles the garden pavilion.
Madrid, Museo Nacional del Prado, inv. no. P001643; oil on canvas, 144 × 157 cm.

LIT.: Freedberg, *Christ after the Passion (CRLB)*, 1984, pp. 48–52, no. 9, fig. 16; Díaz Padrón, *Cat. Madrid, Prado (Pintura flamenca)*, 1995, II, pp. 876–877, no. 1643; Baudouin, *Motieven*, 2006, pp. 206–210.

D. Other Portraits with Variants of Architectural Elements

III.26. Philip Fruytiers, *The Four Eldest Children of Rubens and Helena Fourment, with a Maid and Helena Fourment (?)*, 1640.

The background contains a variant of the garden pavilion.
London, The Royal Collection Trust, inv. RCIN 452433; watercolour and bodycolour on vellum, laid down on oak panel, 246 × 336 cm.

LIT.: Baudouin, *Fruytiers*, 1967, pp. 173–174, no. 2, fig. 9; B. Watteeuw in Van Beneden, ed., *Rubens in Private*, 2015, no. 35.
Note: the woman on the far right is probably Helena Fourment and not a maid.

III.27. Anonymus, *Rubens and his Son (Albert?)*, ? 1620s.

Probably intended as an image of Rubens in his study.
St Petersburg, The State Hermitage Museum, inv. GE 7728; oil on canvas, 133.5 × 112.2 cm.

LIT.: Bastet, *Oudheden*, 1980, p. 76; Gritsai – Babina, *Hermitage*, 2008, pp. 297–299, no. 342 (as 'Rubens school'); Gritsay, *Rubens and his Workshop*, 2011, p. 58, no. 17 (as 'Rubens school'); T. Esposito in Van Beneden, ed., *Rubens in Private*, 2015, no. 24; Esposito, *Occult Knowledge*, 2016, pp. 211–234.
Note: there is a copy in the Kunstsammlung of the Universität Göttingen (on loan to the Rubenshuis since 2004). LIT.: F. Healy in Belkin – Healy, *House of Art*, 2004, pp. 241–243, no. 57.

APPENDIX III

III.28a   III.28b

III.28a. Abraham van Diepenbeeck, *William Cavendish and his Family Seated in Front of a Fireplace [in Rubens's House]*, drawing (Text ill. 19; Fig. III.28a).

The family is represented in an (imaginary?) room in Rubens's house; chimneypiece with herms. Drawing, London, The British Museum, inv. no. 1858-4-17-1629; pen and brown ink, with brown and grey wash, heightened with white, 182 × 160 mm.

LIT: Hind, *Cat. British Museum (Flemish Drawubgs)*, 1923, pp. 103–104, no. 14; U. Härting in Van Beneden – De Poorter, eds, *Royalist Refugees*, 2006, p. 170, no. 43.
Note: Engraving (Fig. III.28b) by Petrus Clouwet (1629–1670) after Abraham van Diepenbeeck in Cavendish, *Natures Pictures*, 1656. LIT: Hollstein et al., *Dutch and Flemish*, 1949–2010, IV, p. 174, no. 15; M. Keblusek in Van Beneden – De Poorter, eds, *Royalist Refugees*, 2006, p. 188, no. 53. See also URL: https://projectvox.org/cavendish-1623-1673/

III.29. Abraham van Diepenbeeck, *William Cavendish and Family Seated in Front of a Fireplace [in Rubens's House]*.

The family is represented in an (imaginary?) room in Rubens's house; chimneypiece with herms. Berlin, Staatliche Museen zu Berlin, Kupferstichkabinett, inv. no. 3365; pen and brown ink, brush and grey (or black) ink, brown wash and white heightening, framing line with pen and black ink.
PROV.: Acquired in 1874 from Barthold Suermondt (see *L.*, 415, recto lower left corner).

LIT: Van Beneden – De Poorter, eds, *Royalist Refugees*, 2006, repr. as frontispiece.

APPENDIX III

E. Art Galleries

III.30. Willem van Haecht, *The Picture Gallery of Cornelis Van der Geest* (Details: Figs 199, 224).

Statue of Venus; Seneca bust; fountain visible through doorway.
Antwerp, Rubenshuis, inv. no. RH.S.171; oil on panel, 102.5 × 137.5 cm.

LIT.: Speth-Holterhoff, *Cabinets*, 1957, pp. 100–104, fig. I, 32–37; Held, *Artis Pictoriae Amator*, 1957, pp. 53–84; Healy, *Vive l'Esprit*, 2006, pp. 423–441; Van Suchtelen – Van Beneden, *Room for Art*, 2009, no. 10, ills 51–56; Van Beneden, *Willem van Haecht*, 2009, pp. 67–77, fig. 35.

III.31. Willem van Haecht, *A Picture Gallery*, c. 1630 (Detail: Text ill. 151).

Overdoor decoration: Seneca bust with scallop-shell niche and garlands.
Isle of Bute (Scotland), Mount Stuart, Collection of the Marquess of Bute; oil on panel, 73 × 104 cm.

LIT.: Van Beneden, *Willem van Haecht*, 2009, pp. 83–88, 212, 213 (n. 138), no. 12, figs 60–61.

APPENDIX III

III.32. Cornelis de Baellieur, *Collector's Cabinet with the Figure of Pictura,* **c. 1635–1640 (Detail: Text ill. 88).**

In the background is a painter's studio inspired by that of Rubens.
Rohrau (Lower Austria), Schloss Rohrau, Graf Harrach'schen Familienstiftung, inv. no. W.F. 180; oil on panel, 48 × 74.6 cm.

LIT.: Speth-Holtherhoff, *Cabinets*, 1957, pp. 86–87, fig. 25 (as 'Frans Francken I'); Hartung, *Francken*, 1983, no. B 279 (as not Frans Francken II); J. Lange in Lange – Schnackenburg, eds, *Pan & Syrinx*, 2004, pp. 113–114, no. 5 (as 'Cornelis de Baellieur', 'um 1640'); G. Martin and E. McGrath in McGrath et al., *Mythological Subjects I (CRLB)*, 2016, I, p. 267, under copy 10; II, fig. 193 (as 'perhaps Cornelis de Baellieur and collaborators'); Van Mulders, *Collaborations Brueghel (CRLB)*, 2017, pp. 128, 134, fig. 184; Baumstark – Delmarcel, *Decius Mus (CRLB)*, 2019, I, pp. 156–157, text ill. 42.
See also Chapter VII, pp. 210–211.

III.33. Jan Brueghel II, *Allegory of Painting / Allegory of Pictura,* **c. 1625–1630 (Detail: Text ill. 89).**

In the background is a painter's studio inspired by that of Rubens.
The Netherlands, Private Collection; oil on copper, 45 × 75 cm.

PROV.: Private Collection in Russia (until 1914); Private Collection France; Private Collection England; Gallery Johnny van Haeften, London, 1992 (No. 8).
LIT.: Mai – Wettengl, eds, *Wettstreit*, 2002, pp. 382–383, no. 165; Van Suchtelen – Van Beneden, *Room for Art*, 2009, pp. 33–34, no. 1, fig. 14.
Note: there is a second version, probably by the same hand, with a number of differences; Private Collection; oil on panel, 48 × 75 cm. PROV.: formerly in the collection of Count Yturbe, Paris. LIT: S. Speth-Holterhoff, *Cabinets*, 1957, pp. 87–88; Brenninkmeyer-de Rooij, *Zeldzame bloemen*, 1990, pp. 240 (n. 38), 224 (fig. 9).
See also Chapter VII, pp. 210–211.

F. Gardens and Palaces

III.34. David Teniers II, *Elegant Company in a Garden***, 1651 (Detail: Fig. 190).**

The background contains a variant of the garden pavilion.
Antwerp, The Phoebus Foundation: oil on copper, 71.5 × 88.5 cm, signed and dated: DAVID·TENIERS·FEC·/*1651*.

LIT.: Klinge – Lüdke, eds, *Teniers*, 2005, no. 85; Kelchtermans, *Portret*, 2019, repr. pp. 46–47; Van Cauteren, ed., *Blind Date*, 2020, p. 368, repr. pp. 160–161.
Note: there is also an anonymous copy (with two herms instead of statues, and two vases instead of putti); oil on canvas, 64 × 77.5 cm; sale, London (Christie's), 20 July 1990, lot 114.

APPENDIX III

III.35. Attributed to Jan van Balen, *Bathing Women*, c. 1640.

The background contains a variant of the portico.
Amersfoort, Rijksdienst voor het cultureel erfgoed, inv. no. R3192; oil on canvas, 141 × 110 cm.

LIT.: De Heer et al., *Old Master Paintings*, 1992, p. 259, no. 2262, repr. (as 'Manner of Pieter Paul Rubens').
Note: the painting was attributed to Jan van Balen (1611–1654) by Bert Schepers (personal communication).

III.36a   III.36b

III.36a. Anonymous, *Elegant Company in a Garden*, c. 1640 (Fig. III.36a).

In the background a variant of the garden pavilion.
Whereabouts unknown; oil on canvas, 86 × 95 cm.

LIT.: Tijs, *Rubens en Jordaens*, 1984, p. 141, detail repr. on p. 145 (as 'Hiëronymus Janssens').
Note: there is a second version (Fig. III.36b), with Cupid hovering above the lovers (painting on the right): whereabouts unknown; oil on panel, 71 × 94 cm. LIT.: Tijs, *Rubens en Jordaens*, 1984, p. 141, repr. on p. 146 (as 'Hiëronymus Janssens').

APPENDIX III

III.37. Anonymous seventeenth-century artist, *Elegant Company in a Garden (with a Statue of Diana)*, **c. 1640.**

The background contains a variant of the garden pavilion.
Whereabouts unknown; oil on panel, 49.5 × 74.5 cm.

PROV.: sale, Monaco (Sotheby's), 17 June 1988, lot 846 (as 'Simon de Vos').

III.38. Anonymous seventeenth-century artist, *Bathsheba Bathing*, **c. 1660.**

The architectural structure in the background incorporates a version of the portico; variant of the fountain.
Spain, Private Collection; oil on canvas, 54.6 × 81.9 cm.

PROV: sale, New York (Christie's), 12 January 1996, lot 173 (as 'David Teniers II').
LIT.: Díaz Padrón, *Betsabé*, 2018, pp. 86–88 (as 'David Teniers II').

61

APPENDIX III

III.39. Frans Wouters, *The Discovery of Callisto's Pregnancy*, c. 1641–1644.

Variant of the portico, and of the fountain.
Kroměříž, Olomouc Archbishopric / Archdiocesan Museum, inv. no. KE2797/O186; oil on panel, 112 × 149 cm, signed: *F.Wouters f.*

LIT.: Daniel – Togner, *Cat. Kroměříž*, 1999a, pp. 376–379, no. 373, repr.

G. Nineteenth Century: Romantic Re-imagining and Archaeological Curiosity

a) Nineteenth Century: Paintings and Drawings

III.40. Philippe van Brée, *The Farewell of Van Dyck in the Courtyard of Rubens's House*, 1814.

The architecture is copied literally from the Harrewijn print of 1684 (see Appendix III.1 and Fig. 17).
Antwerp, Rubenshuis, inv. no. RH-S.115; oil on canvas, 127 × 162 cm, signed and dated: *P 'J'. Van Brée / D'Anvers. / Paris 1814.*

LIT.: Tijs, *Rubens en Jordaens*, 1984, afb. p. 162; Verbraeken et al., *Na en Naar Van Dyck*, 1999, no. 72, repr. p. 168.

APPENDIX III

III.41. Mathieu Ignace van Bree, *Rubens Surrounded by his Colleagues in the Garden Pavilion*, 1825.

Garden pavilion (variant) with statue of Hercules and table; the earliest nineteenth-century image of part of the house.
Weimar, Klassik Stiftung, inv. no. G.178; oil on wood, 96.2 × 74.6 cm (without frame); 114.50 × 94,00 cm (with frame); signed (on the foot of the table) *M: I: Van Brée* and dated *1825* (below on the right).

LIT.: Coekelberghs – Loze, *Neo-Classicisme*, 1985, p. 83, repr.; Verbraeken et al., *Na en Naar Van Dyck*, 1999, no. 47, repr. p. 143.

III.42. Philippe van Brée, *Rubens Painting in his Garden*, 1833 (Detail: Fig. 236).

Garden pavilion with statues and table.

Brussels, Musées royaux des Beaux-Arts de Belgique, inv. no. 1188; oil on panel, 75 × 98.5 cm, signed and dated: *P. Van Brée / Bruxelles 1833*.

LIT.: Van Kalck, *Rubens and the Brussels Museum*, 2007, p. 22, fig. 33.

APPENDIX III

III.43. Nicaise de Keyser, *Drawn Studies of Details of the Portico*, ? 1840.

Elements of the portico: the satyrs with inscribed tablets; three busts.
Drawing, Antwerp, Koninklijk Museum voor Schone Kunsten Antwerpen, inv. no. 2138(II)/79; pencil on paper, 231 × 167 mm.

LIT.: Schoonbaert – Cardyn-Oomen, eds, *Cat. Antwerpen (19th and 20th Cent.)*, 1981, p. 307 (as 'Sculptures on the Inner Colonnade in the Rubenshuis in Antwerp'). This collection catalogue also states that the sketches might have been studies for illustrations [of the portico] in Buschmann, *Rubens*, 1840.

b) Nineteenth-Century Prints (a Selection)

III.44. Erin Corr after Nicaise de Keyser, *The Courtyard of Rubens's House*, **1840.**

Combination of elements taken from Harrewijn, and later alterations (raised portico).
Impression consulted: Antwerp, Rubenshuis, inv. no. RH.P.1108; copper engraving, 502 × 660 mm.

LIT.: Tijs, *Rubens en Jordaens*, 1984, repr. p. 166; Tijs, *Hirtengrotte*, 2002, fig. 1; Maclot, *Rubenssite*, 2016, p. 107, repr..

APPENDIX III

III.45. Erin Corr after Nicaise de Keyser and J. Stordiau, *The Portico of Rubens's House***, 1840.**

Impression consulted: Antwerp, Rubenshuis, inv. no. RH.P.0186; copper engraving, 364 × 469 mm.

LIT: Devroe, *Rubens' huis*, 2008, II, no. 20.

III.46. Erin Corr and Jozef Linnig after Nicaise de Keyser and J. Stordiau, *The Garden Pavilion of Rubens's House***, 1840.**

Impression consulted: Antwerp, Rubenshuis, inv. no. RH.P.0187; copper engraving, 511 × 344 mm.

LIT: Devroe, *Rubens' huis*, 2008, II, no. 21.
See also pp. 80, 82.

APPENDIX III

III.47. Jozef Linnig, *The Courtyard of Rubens's House*, 1840–1891.

Copied literally from the Harrewijn print of 1684.
Impression consulted: Antwerp, Museum Plantin-Moretus, Stedelijk Prentenkabinet, inv. no. AV.3359.018.43–66; etching, 164 × 249 to plate edge (142 mm × 191 mm to page edge).

III.48. Louis Haghe, *The Visit of Maria de' Medici to Rubens*, 1840.

Portico based on its nineteenth-century appearance with raised top, two of the arches closed off, and reclining dog to the left.
Hand-coloured tinted lithograph, 368.3 × 590.5 mm. From the series *Sketches in Belgium and Germany*, London, Henry Graves & Co, 1840–1850.

LIT.: Tijs, *Rubens en Jordaens*, 1984, repr. p. 165; Maclot, *Rubenssite*, 2016, p. 108, repr..

APPENDIX III

III.49. Adrien Canelle, *Rubens, his Family and Visitors in the Courtyard of his House*, 1847–1874.

Raised portico (with various alterations).
Ex.: Antwerp, Rubenshuis, inv. no. RH.P.0180; colour lithograph, 254 × 347 mm.

LIT.: Tijs, *Rubens en Jordaens*, 1984, repr. p. 164; Maclot, *Rubenssite*, 2016, p. 107, repr..

c) *The Earliest Photographs*

III.50. Louis Schweig, *Rubens's Garden Pavilion*, 1856–1857.

Stereophotograph, Antwerp, MAS | Museum aan de Stroom, inv. no. MAS.0062.010.

A photographic print (not cropped at the right, and not rounded at the top) is in the collection of the Bibliothèque nationale de France, Paris (illustrated in: Van Goethem, *Fotografie en realisme*, 1999, p. 390, no. SL2; De Clercq, *Tuinpaviljoen*, 2012, p. [12]).
See also Chapter II, p. 82, n. 97.

APPENDIX III

III.51. Edmond Fierlants, *Rubens's Garden Pavilion*, 1860 (Text ill. 22; details: Fig. 189).

Antwerp, FelixArchief, inv. no. FOTO-GF#974.

LIT:. Joseph – Schwilden, *Fierlants*, 1988, pp. 107, 211, no. 594; Ceuleers, *Verloren Stad*, 2016, no. 96. See also Chapter II, p. 82, n. 97.

III.52. Edmond Fierlants, *The Portico of Rubens's House*, 1860 (Text ill. 23; details: Text ills 53, 125).

The earliest known photograph of the portico.
Antwerp, FelixArchief, inv. no. FOTO-GF#973.

LIT:. Joseph – Schwilden, *Fierlants*, 1988, p. 211, no. 593; Ceuleers, *Verloren Stad*, 2016, no. 95. See also Chapter II, p. 82, n. 97.

III.53. Adolphe Braun, *The Garden Pavilion of Rubens's House*, 1864 (Detail: Text ill. 140).

Lit: Ceuleers, *Verloren Stad*, 2016, no. and fig. 95.

LIST OF TEXT ILLUSTRATIONS

Text ill. 1. 'Maison de Rubens' (Antwerp, Meir 54), picture postcard (c. 1900).

Text ill. 2. Detail of the house represented in Text ill. 1: Bust of Peter Paul Rubens on top of the façade.

Text ill. 3. Joris Snaet, *Reconstruction of a Protestant Temple in Ghent*, drawing. Private Collection.

Text ill. 4. Hieronymus Cock, *Bird's-eye View of Antwerp* (1557), engraving, detail. Antwerp, Museum Plantin-Moretus.

Text ill. 5. Petrus (Pieter) Van der Heyden after Lambert van Noort, *View on the City of Antwerp* (1569), engraving, detail. Antwerp, Museum Plantin-Moretus.

Text ill. 6. Frans Hogenberg, *Map of Antwerp with the Citadel and the Head* (1572), etching, detail. Antwerp, Museum Plantin-Moretus.

Text ill. 7. Joris Hoefnagel, *Panoramic View of Antwerp* (1574), detail of engraving in Braun – Hogenberg, *Civitates*, 1575.

Text ill. 8. Plan of the cellars of the Rubenshuis, blueprint. Antwerp, Rubenshuis Archive.

Text ill. 9. Detail of the 1692 Harrewijn print (Fig. 18): the remodelled houses on the right of Rubens's house on the Wapper.

Text ill. 10. Pieter Verbiest, *The Siege of Antwerp by Prince Maurice of Orange in 1605* (1628), engraving, detail.

Text ill. 11. Theodoor van Thulden, *Map of Antwerp with the Joyous Entry of Cardinal-Infante Ferdinand*, etching and engraving, detail.

Text ill. 12. Joan Blaeu, *Map of Antwerp* (1649), engraving, detail. Antwerp, Museum Plantin-Moretus.

Text ill. 13. Pieter Verbiest, *Bird's-eye View of Antwerp from the West* (c. 1650), engraving, detail. Antwerp, Felixarchief.

Text ill. 14. After Abraham van Diepenbeeck, *William and Margaret Cavendish Watching while William's Sons Charles and Henry are Demonstrating a Courbette and a Ballotade*, engraving.

Text ill. 15. The Riding House in Bolsover Castle (UK).

Text ill. 16. View of the open gallery in the studio of the restored Rubenshuis.

Text ill. 17. Detail of the 1692 Harrewijn print (Fig. 18): the dressage pole in the garden.

Text ill. 18. Lucas Vorsterman II after Abraham van Diepenbeeck, *Courbette de côté à gauche*, engraving.

Text ill. 19. Petrus Clouwet after Abraham van Diepenbeeck, *William Cavendish and his Family Seated in Front of a Fireplace [in Rubens's House]* (Appendix III.28b), engraving.

Text ill. 20. Gonzales Coques, *Portrait of Maria Agnes van Eycke as St Agnes*. London, The National Gallery.

Text ill. 21. Page including the plan of Rubens's House in the Notes of François Mols. Brussels, KBR, MS 5726.

Text ill. 22. Edmond Fierlants, *The Garden Pavilion of the Rubens House* (1860), photograph. Antwerp, FelixArchief.

Text ill. 23. Edmond Fierlants, *The Portico of the Rubens House* (1860), photograph. Antwerp, FelixArchief.

Text ill. 24. Detail of the 1692 Harrewijn print (Fig. 18): the portrait of Canon Hendrik Hillewerve in a tondo.

Text ill. 25. Detail of the 1684 Harrewijn print (Fig. 17): two scenes of the frieze on the north façade of the studio wing.

Text ill. 26. Detail of the 1692 Harrewijn print (Fig. 18): the same scenes as in Text ill. 25, in reverse.

Text ill. 27. Detail of the 1684 Harrewijn print (Fig. 17): the light falling from the left (the north) in the garden.

Text ill. 28. Detail of the 1692 Harrewijn print (Fig. 18): the footprint of the omitted portico.

Text ill. 29. Detail of the 1684 Harrewijn print (Fig. 17): the coat of arms of Canon Hendrik Hillewerve.

Text ill. 30. Detail of the 1692 Harrewijn print (Fig. 18): the trees on the Wapper.

Text ill. 31. Detail of the 1692 Harrewijn print (Fig. 18): the latticed pergola and walkway at the south side of the garden.

Text ill. 32. Detail of the 1692 Harrewijn print (Fig. 18): the roof of the Church of the Discalced Carmelites.

Text ill. 33. Detail of the 1692 Harrewijn print (Fig. 18): a dolphin (a sculpture ?) at the bottom left of the print.

Text ill. 34. Detail of the 1684 Harrewijn print (Fig. 17): a part of the south façade of the north wing.

Text ill. 35. Detail of the 1692 Harrewijn print (Fig. 18): the old part (at the left) of west façade.

LIST OF TEXT ILLUSTRATIONS

Text ill. 36. Detail of the 1692 Harrewijn print (Fig. 18): the entrance gate to the courtyard.

Text ill. 37. Detail of the 1692 Harrewijn print (Fig. 18): the stables (at the left) and (at the right) the gateway used as a coach house.

Text ill. 38. The recreated open passageway from the Wapper to the garden in the Rubenshuis.

Text ill. 39. Detail of the 1692 Harrewijn print (Fig. 18): the walkway with 'windows' and busts at the south side of the garden.

Text ill. 40. Detail of the 1692 Harrewijn print (Fig. 18): the pergola at the south side of the garden.

Text ill. 41. Detail of the 1692 Harrewijn print (Fig. 18): the parterres 'de broderie'.

Text ill. 42. Detail of the 1692 Harrewijn print (Fig. 18): the caryatids on the north façade of the stables.

Text ill. 43. The reconstructed so-called gardener's lodge (previously stables) in the garden of the Rubenshuis.

Text ill. 44. Detail of the 1684 Harrewijn print (Fig. 17): the open door (in the courtyard), giving a view into the former studio.

Text ill. 45. Detail of the 1684 Harrewijn print (Fig. 17): the view through the windows of the north façade of the studio wing.

Text ill. 46. Detail of the 1692 Harrewijn print (Fig. 18): the open door on the garden side of the south or 'Italian' wing.

Text ill. 47. Detail of the 1692 Harrewijn print (Fig. 18): Hillewerve's bedroom.

Text ill. 48. Detail of the 1684 Harrewijn print (Fig. 17): the water pump against the façade of the north wing.

Text ill. 49. The water pump in the courtyard of the Rubenshuis.

Text ill. 50. Detail of the 1684 Harrewijn print (Fig. 17): the fountain with bagpiper in the corner between the portico and the former studio.

Text ill. 51. Detail of the 1684 Harrewijn print (Fig. 17): the dog on the doorstep of the former studio.

Text ill. 52. Detail of the 1692 Harrewijn print (Fig. 18): the dog (in reverse) on the doorstep of the former studio.

Text ill. 53. Detail of Text ill. 23: A marble dog on top of a store in the courtyard.

Text ill. 54. *A Marble Dog*, sculpture. Belgium, Private Collection.

Text ill. 55. View on Rubens's *Triptych of the Descent of the Cross*. Antwerp, Cathedral of Our Lady.

Text ill. 56. *Decius Mus* series in Vienna, Gartenpalais Liechtenstein.

Text ill. 57. Detail of the 1692 Harrewijn print (Fig. 18): the roof of the L-shaped studio wing.

Text ill. 58. Detail of the 1684 Harrewijn print (Fig. 17): the eaves cornice of the studio wing.

Text ill. 59. The north façade of the studio wing before the restoration.

Text ill. 60. The north façade of the studio wing during the restoration.

Text ill. 61. Detail of the 1692 Harrewijn print (Fig. 18): two windows at the upper level of the garden façade (with a smoking oil lamp at the right).

Text ill. 62. Theodoor van Thulden after Rubens, *The Portico of the Emperors*, etching, detail of *Frederick III and Albert II, with Mars Ultor and Ceres*.

Text ill. 63. Cornelis Galle I after Rubens, *The Bust of Seneca*, engraving.

Text ill. 64. Roman, the so-called *Bust of 'Seneca'*, sculpture. Antwerp, Rubenshuis.

Text ill. 65. The so-called *Bust of Seneca*, sculpture in the reconstructed north façade.

Text ill. 66. Detail of the 1692 Harrewijn print (Fig. 18): the quoins at a corner of the studio wing.

Text ill. 67. The studio wing with the demolished apocryph garden or east façade.

Text ill. 68. Detail of the 1692 Harrewijn print (Fig. 18): two windows of the lower section of the west façade.

Text ill. 69. The street façade in 1930.

Text ill. 70. Façade of Giulio Romano's house, Mantua.

Text ill. 71. Façade in the first courtyard of the Palazzo Mattei di Giove, Rome.

Text ill. 72. Garden façade of the Villa Medici, Rome.

Text ill. 73. Detail of a façade in the courtyard of the Palazzo Farnese, Rome.

Text ill. 74. Giovanni Antonio Pordenone, *Design for the Façade of Palazzo d'Anna, Venice*, drawing. London, Victoria and Albert Museum.

Text ill. 75. Giovanni Maria Falconetto, *Frescoes on the Façade of the Casa Trevisani-Lonardi, Verona* (before 1908), photograph.

Text ill. 76. Perino del Vaga, *Design for the North Façade of the Palazzo Doria, Genoa*, drawing. Amsterdam, Rijksmuseum.

Text ill. 77. Nicolaes Ryckmans, *Façade of the Palazzo Interiano Pallavicino (Palazzo G)*, engraving in *Palazzi di Genova* (*Palazzi Antichi*), 1st series, 1622.

Text ill. 78. Palazzo Interiano Pallavicino, Genoa.

Text ill. 79. Nicolaes Ryckmans, *Façade of the Palazzo Gambaro* (without the painted decorations), engraving in *Palazzi di Genova (Palazzi Moderni)*, 2nd series, after1622.

Text ill. 80. Hans Holbein II, Design for a façade (Tanzgässlein) of the House 'Zum Tanz', Basel, drawing. Basel, Kunstmuseum Basel.

Text ill. 81. Jacques van Croes, *Façade of Frans Floris's House*, drawing. Brussels, KBR.

Text ill. 82. Émile Van Averbeke, Design for the reconstruction of the house: intersection of the studio wing, blueprint. Antwerp, FelixArchief.

Text ill. 83. View of the studio in the Rubenshuis.

Text ill. 84. The temporary reconstruction of a window with round arch in the south façade of the studio wing (c. 1940).

Text ill. 85. Émile Van Averbeke, Design for the south façade of the studio wing (1939), blueprint. Antwerp, FelixArchief.

Text ill. 86. Passageway from the Wapper to the garden (seen from the garden side).

Text ill. 87. Cornelis de Vos, *A Young Painter Behind a Balustrade*, detail with the window with light-diffuser in the background. Whereabouts unknown.

Text ill. 88. Cornelis de Baellieur, *A Collector's Cabinet with the Figure of Pictura* (Appendix III.32), detail of the studio in the background. Rohrau, Schloss Rohrau.

Text ill. 89. Jan Brueghel II, *Allegory of Painting* (Appendix III.33), detail of the studio in the background. The Netherlands, Private Collection.

Text ill. 90. Detail of the 1692 Harrewijn print (Fig. 18): the location of Hillewerve's bedroom.

Text ill. 91. The so-called 'Pupils' studio' in the Rubenshuis.

Text ill. 92. Pieter Post after Jacob van Campen, *North-South Cross-Section of the Mauritshuis, The Hague* (1652), drawing, detail. The Hague, Koninklijke Bibliotheek / Nationale Bibliotheek van Nederland.

Text ill. 93. The wooden windlass with ropes in the attic of the studio wing (1938).

Text ill. 94. Detail of the 1684 Harrewijn print (Fig. 17): a strip of wall (left of the portico) of the east or garden wing.

Text ill. 95. Detail of Text ill. 20: a section of the east wing seen through the portico.

Text ill. 96. The reconstructed east wing (south and east façade).

Text ill. 97. The 'Art Gallery' in the Rubenshuis.

Text ill. 98. Émile Van Averbeke, Design for the reconstruction of the east wing (intersection south-north), detail of a blueprint. Antwerp, FelixArchief.

Text ill. 99. Foundation for the pilasters of the 'antiquarium' discovered in the 1930's.

Text ill. 100. Willem van Haecht, *Apelles Painting Campaspe*. The Hague, Mauritshuis (Appendix III.8).

Text ill. 101. The reconstructed 'antiquarium' in the Rubenshuis.

Text ill. 102. Detail of the 1692 Harrewijn print (Fig. 18): decoration of Hillewerve's chapel (oval niches and rectangular scenes).

Text ill. 103. Detail of Text ill. 100: decoration of the 'antiquarium' (oval niches and rectangular scenes).

Text ill. 104. The portico with a raised structure (a corridor and a roof), 1937. Antwerp, FelixArchief.

Text ill. 105. The garden with the partition wall (at the left), 1906.

Text ill. 106. The garden after the partition wall has been taken down, 1938.

Text ill. 107. The rear of the dismantled portico and (at the right) the reconstructed east wing, during the restoration (c. 1938).

Text ill. 108. The reconstructed rear of the portico.

Text ill. 109. The portico seen from the rear, showing the vertical 'seams' on the jambs of the three arches.

Text ill. 110. M. Bonte, *Cross-sections of the Portico*, blueprint, detail. Antwerp, FelixArchief.

Text ill. 111. Anonymous 17th-century artist, *Palazzetto Viewed from the Garden*, drawing. Antwerp, Museum Plantin-Moretus, Stedelijk Prentenkabinet.

Text ill. 112. *Guttae* (detail of the portico).

Text ill. 113. Bartolomeo Ammanati, Garden portal with inscribed tablets. Rome, Villa Medici.

Text ill. 114. One of the courtyard façades of Jacques Jordaens's house (detail), Antwerp.

Text ill. 115. Wenzel Cobergher, The façade of the Church of St Augustine, Antwerp, detail.

LIST OF TEXT ILLUSTRATIONS

Text ill. 116. Jacques Jordaens, *Design for a Wall Decoration*, drawing. Washington, National Gallery of Art.

Text ill. 117. Portal of the former Jesuit college, La Flèche (Fr.).

Text ill. 118. Attributed to Willem Paneels after Rubens, *The Assumption of the Virgin*, drawing. Budapest, Szépművészeti Múzeum, Print Room.

Text ill. 119. Anonymous, *Portrait of a Young Man*, 1636. London, The National Gallery.

Text ill. 120. Anonymous after ? Rubens, Sheet from the 'Architectural Sketchbook', drawing. St Petersburg, The State Hermitage Museum.

Text ill. 121. Anonymous after ? Rubens, Sheet from the 'Architectural Sketchbook', drawing. St Petersburg, The State Hermitage Museum.

Text ill. 122. Detail of the 1684 Harrewijn print (Fig. 17): a sphere and a two-headed eagle in front of the balustrade.

Text ill. 123. Detail of Text ill. 20: the bust of a bearded man in the central niche of the portico.

Text ill. 124. Detail of the 1684 Harrewijn print (Fig. 17): the busts in the rectangular niches of the portico.

Text ill. 125. Detail of Text ill. 23: the bust of Minerva.

Text ill. 126. Michelangelo, *Porta Pia*, Rome.

Text ill. 127. Michelangelo, *Porta Pia*, detail, engraving in Vignola, *Regola delli Cinque ordini d'architettura*, 1602.

Text ill. 128. Michelangelo, Study for the *Porta Pia*, drawing. Florence, Casa Buonarotti.

Text ill. 129. A courtyard of the Palazzo Te, Mantua.

Text ill. 130. Giulio Romano, *Study for the Palazzo Te*, drawing. Vienna, Albertina.

Text ill. 131. Bartolomeo Ammanati, Courtyard of the Palazzo Pitti, Florence.

Text ill. 132. Central part of the front façade of the Palais du Luxembourg, Paris.

Text ill. 133. *The Five Orders*, engraving in Serlio, *Regole generali di Architettura*, Book IV, 1537.

Text ill. 134. Rubens, *The Garden of Love*, detail with the architecture in the background. Madrid, Museo Nacional del Prado.

Text ill. 135. Rubens, *Henri IV Consigns the Regency to Maria de' Medici*, oil sketch (Appendix III.19). Munich, Bayerische Staatsgemäldesammlungen, Alte Pinakothek.

Text ill. 136. Theodoor van Thulden, *The Stage of Isabella (Front Face)*, etching, detail of the lower storey.

Text ill. 137. Detail of Fig. 177: the black bricks.

Text ill. 138. Rubens, *The Discovery of Erichtonius*, oil sketch. Stockholm, Nationalmuseum (Appendix III.23).

Text ill. 139. Detail of the 1692 Harrewijn print (Fig. 18): the putti on the volutes of the garden pavilion.

Text ill. 140. The busts in the niches of the garden pavilion before the restoration, detail of Appendix III.53.

Text ill. 141. Anonymous artist, *Bust of Cicero*, plaster. Antwerp, Rubenshuis.

Text ill. 142. Anonymous artist, *Head of a Woman (Niobe?)*, plaster. Antwerp, Rubenshuis.

Text ill. 143. Sebastiano Serlio, *A Façade* ('with Serliana's') in the 4th volume of his *Regole generali di architettura*, 1537.

Text ill. 144. Palladio, Basilica, Vicenza, detail.

Text ill. 145. Giulio Romano, *Design for a Loggia with Rustic Portal*, drawing. Vienna, Albertina, Grafische Sammlung.

Text ill. 146. Rubens, *Dancing Peasants and Mythological Figures*, detail. Madrid, Museo Nacional del Prado.

Text ill. 147. Rome, Villa Medici, Loggia di Cleopatra.

Text ill. 148. Rome, Villa Giulia, detail: upper part of the Nymphaeum.

Text ill. 149. The so-called Rubens Chimney piece. Mentmore (Buckinghamshire), Mentmore Towers.

Text ill. 150. ? Willem Paneels after Rubens, *Niche with Scallop and Bust*, drawing. Copenhagen, Statens Museum for Kunst, Kongelige Kobberstiksamling.

Text ill. 151. Detail of Appendix III.31: a niche with the bust of the pseudo-Seneca.

Text ill. 152. ? Hans van Mildert, *Honos*, sculpture. Antwerp, Museum Plantin-Moretus.

Text ill. 153. Artus Quellinus I, *Mercury*, sculpture. Amsterdam, Paleis op de Dam (formerly Town Hall).

Text ill. 154. ? Artus Quellinus I after Rubens, *Mercury*, statuette. St Petersburg, The State Hermitage Museum.

Text ill. 155. Artus Quellinus I, *Labore et Constantia*, relief above the entrance to the Plantin Press. Antwerp, Museum Plantin-Moretus.

LIST OF FIGURES

1. Virgilius Bononiensis, *Map of Antwerp (1565)*, woodcut, detail. Antwerp, Museum Plantin-Moretus.

2. François Antoine Losson, *Cadastral Map of Antwerp* (1846), print, detail. Antwerp, FelixArchief.

3. François Mols, *Plan of Rubens's House* (c. 1763). Brussels, KBR (Appendix III.4).

4. Detail of the groundplan of 1932, showing the dividing wall through the courtyard and the garden, blueprint.

5. Émile Van Averbeke, Detail of the plan of the first floor, showing the corridor on top of the portico (1936), blueprint.

6. Components of the property in Rubens's time, drawing (partly based on a blueprint

7. Alternative denominations of the wings of the Rubenshuis.

8. Parts of the building and garden visible in the Harrewijn prints (Figs XXX and XXX).

9. Plan of the roofs of the restored house.

10. The reconstructed north façade of the Italian wing.

11. The reconstructed east façade of the Italian wing facing the courtyard with a 'real' loggia.

12. The reconstructed east or garden façade of the Italian wing.

13. The reconstructed street (west) façade.

14. The reconstructed east façade of the east (or garden) wing.

15. The reconstructed east façade of the (Flemish) west wing and the reconstructed south façade of the (Flemish) north wing facing the courtyard.

16. Anonymous seventeenth-century artist, *View of the Courtyard of Rubens's House*. Aylesbury, Discover Bucks Museum (Appendix III.3).

17. Jacob Harrewijn after Jacques van Croes, *View of Rubens's Courtyard* (1684), etching (Appendix III.1).

18. Jacob Harrewijn after Jacques van Croes, *View of Rubens's House and Garden* (1692), etching (Appendix III.2).

19. Anthony van Dyck, *Portrait of Isabella Brant*. Washington, DC, National Gallery of Art (Appendix III.5).

20. Jacques Jordaens, *Cupid and Psyche*. Madrid, Museo Nacional del Prado (Appendix III.9).

21. Rubens, *Helena Fourment with her Son Frans (?) Rubens (Hélène Fourment au carrosse)*. Paris, Musée du Louvre (Appendix III.7).

22. Anonymous seventeenth-century artist, *Portrait of a Couple in a Garden*. Berlin, Staatliche Museen zu Berlin, Gemäldegalerie Alte Meister (Appendix III.10).

23. Rubens with Frans Snijders, *Homage to Ceres*. St Petersburg, The State Hermitage Museum (Appendix III.13).

24. Rubens, *Henri IV Consigns the Regency to Maria de' Medici*. Paris, Musée du Louvre (Appendix III.18).

25. ? Rubens and Studio, *Peter Paul Rubens with his Wife Helena Fourment and his Son Nicolaas Rubens (The Walk in the Garden)*. Munich, Bayerische

26. Detail of the 1692 Harrewijn print (Fig. 18): west façade of Rubens's House.

27. Detail of the Aylesbury Painting (Fig. 16): north façade of the Italian wing.

28. Detail of the 1684 Harrewijn print (Fig. 17): north façade of the Italian wing.

29. Detail of the 1692 Harrewijn print (Fig. 18): large east façade (garden side) of the Italian wing.

30. Detail of the 1692 Harrewijn print (Fig. 18): small east façade (courtyard) of the Italian wing.

31. Detail of Fig. 21: The house in the background.

32. Detail of the 1692 Harrewijn print (Fig. 18): west façade of Rubens's studio (Italian wing).

33. Detail of the 1684 Harrewijn print (Fig. 17): *Busts in Niches, with amongst others a Faun* (No. 1).

34. Detail of the 1684 Harrewijn print (Fig. 17): Bust of a Faun in a niche.

35. *Bust of a Faun*, plaster cast (No. 1, Copy). Antwerp, Rubenshuis.

36. Detail of the 1684 Harrewijn print (Fig. 17): *Bust in a Niche with a Scallop* (No. 2).

37. Detail of the Aylesbury Painting (Fig. 16): *Bust in a Niche with a Scallop, Flanked by Cornucopias* (Appendix III.3).

LIST OF FIGURES

38. Detail of the 1684 Harrewijn print (Fig. 17): *Four Unidentified Herm Busts* (No. 3).

39. Detail of the 1692 Harrewijn print (Fig. 18): *Herm Bust*.

40. Paulus Pontius after Rubens, *Herm Bust of Sophocles*, engraving.

41. Detail of the 1692 Harrewijn print (Fig. 18): *Six Herms* (No. 4).

42. Detail of the Aylesbury Painting (Fig. 16): herms in relief?

43. Detail of the 1684 Harrewijn print (Fig. 17): quoins terminating the north façade.

44. Detail of the 1692 Harrewijn print (Fig. 18): *Hermes Belvedere* (No. 5).

45. Roman, *Hermes Belvedere*, statue. Rome, Musei Vaticani.

46. Willem Panneels after Rubens, *Study of the Hermes Belvedere*, drawing. Copenhagen, Statens Museum for Kunst, Kongelige Kobberstiksamling.

47. Detail of the 1692 Harrewijn print (Fig. 18): *Flora Farnese* (No. 6).

48. Roman, *Flora Farnese*, statue. Naples, Museo Archeologico Nazionale di Napoli.

49. Cornelis Galle I after Rubens, *Iconismus duplicis statuae tunicatae (Illustration of a Pair of Statues with Tunics)*, engraving.

50. Theodoor van Thulden after Rubens, *The Stage of Welcome*, etching, detail of the statue of *Good Hope (Spes)*.

51. Detail of the 1692 Harrewijn print (Fig. 18): two types of window framing (No. 7).

52. Detail of the Aylesbury Painting (Fig. 16): two types of window framing (No. 7).

53. Detail of the 1684 Harrewijn print (Fig. 17): window with (remodelled ?) grids (No. 7).

54. Rubens, *Architectural Study of a Window Framing and Other Elements*, drawing (No. 7a). Antwerp, Museum Plantin-Moretus.

55. Detail of Figs 21 and 31: the window on the upper floor of the house in the background.

56. Detail of the Villa Medici garden façade: window with an open-topped pediment and a sphere on a pedestal. Rome, Villa Medici.

57. Detail of the 1692 Harrewijn print (Fig. 18): frieze panel with *A Chariot Race (The Lowering of the Cloth)* (No. 8).

58. Roman, *The Lowering of the Cloth*, relief. Rome, Musei Vaticani.

59. Cornelis Galle I after Rubens, *Iconismus circensium et missionis mappae (Illustration of Circus Racing and the Lowering of the Cloth)*, engraving.

60. Detail of the 1692 Harrewijn print (Fig. 18): frieze panel with *The Triumph of Apollo* (No. 9).

61. Rubens, *Centaur Tormented by Cupid*, drawing. Cologne, Wallraf-Richartz-Museum & Fondation Corboud, Graphische Sammlung.

62. Rubens, *Sketches for a Figure of Victory*, drawing, detail: *Crowning Victory*. Darmstadt, Hessisches Landesmuseum.

63. Verso of Fig. 62: two variants of a winged figure, drawing, detail: *Victory Crowning Apollo*.

64. Detail of the 1692 Harrewijn print (Fig. 18): frieze panel with *The Sacrifice of an Ox* (No. 10).

65. Rubens, *The Sacrifice of an Ox*, drawing, 24.9 × 38.4 cm (No. 10a). Private Collection, on loan to the Wallraf-Richartz-Museum & Fondation Corboud, Graphische Sammlung, Cologne.

66. Roman, *A Roman Sacrifice*, sarcophagus relief, detail. Mantua, Palazzo Ducale.

67. Roman, *A Roman Sacrifice*, relief. Rome, Villa Medici.

68. *A Roman Sacrifice*, woodcut in Du Choul, *Discours*, 1581.

69. Detail of the 1684 Harrewijn print (Fig. 17): frieze panel with *The Sacrifice of Iphigenia* (No. 11).

70. Detail the Aylesbury Painting (Fig. 16): frieze panel with *The Sacrifice of Iphigenia*.

71. Willem Panneels after Rubens, *The Sacrifice of Iphigenia*, drawing (No. 11, Copy 1). Copenhagen, Statens Museum for Kunst, Kongelige Kobberstiksamling.

72. After Rubens, *The Sacrifice of Iphigenia*, drawing (No. 11, Copy 2). Budapest, Szépművészeti Múzeum.

73. After Rubens, *The Sacrifice of Iphigenia*, drawing (No. 11, Copy 3). Whereabouts unknown.

74. Rubens, *The Lamentation with St Francis*, detail with Mary Magdelen. Brussels, Musées royaux des Beaux-Arts de Belgique.

75. Detail of Fig. 71.

76. Roman, *Marcus Aurelius Sacrificing before the Capitoline Temple*, detail with *tibicen* and *camillus*, relief. Rome, Palazzo dei Conservatori.

77. Detail of Fig. 71.

LIST OF FIGURES

78. Rubens, *The Interpretation of the Victim*, detail. Vaduz – Vienna, Liechtenstein, The Princely Collections.

79. Giorgio Vasari, *Timanthes Painting the Sacrifice of Iphigenia*, fresco. Arezzo, Casa Vasari.

80. Roman, Candelabrum Base. Chantilly, Musée Condé.

81. Roman, *Ara of Cleomenes*, view of Agamemnon wrapped in his cloak. Florence, Museo Archeologico

82. Detail of the 1684 Harrewijn print (Fig. 17): frieze panel with *Alexander with the Thunderbolt* (No. 12).

83. Detail of the Aylesbury Painting (Fig. 16): frieze panel with *Alexander with the Thunderbolt*.

84. Willem Panneels after Rubens, *Alexander with the Thunderbolt*, drawing (No. 12, Copy). Copenhagen, Statens Museum for Kunst, Kongelige Kobberstiksamling.

85. Roman, *The Sacrifice to Apollo*, relief, detail. Rome, Arch of Constantine.

86. Roman, *Proserpina sarcophagus* relief, detail with Pluto and Cerberus. Mantua, Palazzo Ducale.

87. Jacques de Bie, *Imago Iovis cum fulmine*, engraving in Hemelaer – de Bie, *Numismata Aurea*, 1615.

88. Roman, *Barbarian King*, statue. Rome, Palazzo dei Conservatori.

89. After Nicolas Béatrizet, *Roma victrix*, engraving in Antonio Lafreri, *Speculum Romanae Magnificentiae*, c. 1550.

90. Detail of the 1684 Harrewijn print (Fig. 17): frieze panel with *The Calumny of Apelles* (No. 13).

91. Detail of the Aylesbury Painting (Fig. 16): frieze panel with *The Calumny of Apelles*.

92. Cornelis Cort after Federico Zuccari, *The Calumny of Apelles*, engraving.

93. Rubens, *The Departure of Maria de' Medici from Paris*, oil sketch, detail with a monster personifying Deceit. Munich, Bayerische Staatsgemäldesammlungen, Alte Pinakothek.

94. *Imagine del Furore & dell'Ira*, woodcut in Vincenzo Cartari, *Imagini*, 1615.

95. Rubens after Adam Elsheimer, *The Sacrifice to Venus*, detail with the statue of Venus.

96. Rubens, *The Calumny of Apelles*, drawing, 30.6 × 38.5 mm (No. 13a). London, The Courtauld Gallery.

97. Verso of Fig. 96: *Architectural Studies and Figure Studies for an Entombment* (No. 13b).

98. Detail of the 1684 Harrewijn print (Fig. 17): frieze panel with *Zeuxis and the Maidens of Croton* (No. 14).

99. Otto van Veen, *Zeuxis and the Maidens of Croton*, oil sketch. Whereabouts unknown.

100. *Pudicitia Mattei*, statue, Copenhagen, Statens Museum for Kunst. Plaster cast after the Roman original in Rome, Musei Vaticani.

101. Detail of the 1684 Harrewijn print (Fig. 17): frieze panel with *The Drunken Hercules* (No. 15).

102. The *Borghese Vase*, view of a flute-playing faun. Paris, Musée du Louvre.

103. The *Borghese Vase*, view of a dancing bacchante. Paris, Musée du Louvre.

104. *The Drunken Hercules*, engraving in Venuti – Amaduzzi, *Vetera Monumenta*, 1774–1779.

105. Rubens, *The Drunken Hercules*. Dresden, Staatliche Kunstsammlungen, Gemäldegalerie Alte Meister.

106. Detail of the 1692 Harrewijn print (Fig. 18): frieze panel with *A Youthful Hero with a Lance and Chariot* (No. 16).

107. Detail of the 1692 Harrewijn print (Fig. 18): the first floor of the small east façade with *The Loggia with a Figure and Animals* (No. 17).

108. Paolo Veronese, *Loggia with a Lady and her Maid*, fresco, detail. Maser, Villa Barbaro.

109. Jacques Jordaens, *A Company making Music in a Loggia*, drawing. Cambridge, Fitzwilliam Museum.

110. Detail of the 1692 Harrewijn print (Fig. 18): *Andromeda Liberated by Perseus* (No. 18).

111. Rubens, *Andromeda Liberated by Perseus*. St Petersburg, The State Hermitage Museum.

112. Attributed to Willem Panneels after Rubens, *Andromeda Liberated by Perseus*, drawing. Copenhagen, Statens Museum for Kunst, Kongelige Kobberstiksamling.

113. Rubens, *Andromeda Liberated by Perseus*. Berlin, Staatliche Museen zu Berlin.

114. Pierre François Tardieu after Rubens, *Andromeda Liberated by Perseus*, etching and engraving.

115. *Andromeda Liberated by Cupid*, engraving, detail, in Philostratus, *Les images*, 1614.

116. Detail of Fig. 111: Andromeda.

117. Rubens, *The Discovery of Erichthonius*, detail. Vienna – Vaduz, Liechtenstein, The Princely Collections.

118. Detail of Fig. 111: Perseus.

119. Rubens, *Abraham and Melchizedek*, detail with Abraham. Caen, Musée des Beaux-Arts.

LIST OF FIGURES

120. Detail of Fig. 111: a putto disrobing Andromeda.

121. Detail of Fig. 23: two putti.

122. Detail of the 1692 Harrewijn print (Figs 18 and 110): boy holding the horse.

123. Roman, *Horse Tamer*, statue, detail. Rome, Quirinal.

124. Detail of the 1692 Harrewijn print (Fig. 18): *Staircase* (No. 19).

125. Detail of Fig. 3: the staircase on the ground floor c. 1763.

126. Detail of Fig. 3: the staircase on the second floor c. 1763.

127. Detail of the 1692 Harrewijn print (Fig. 18): Rubens's 'antiquarium' transformed into Canon Hillewerve's chapel (Nos 20–22).

128. Detail of Text ill. 100; the 'antiquarium' in the background.

129. The cupola of the Antwerp Jesuit Church (now Church of St Carolus Borromeus).

130. Detail of Text ill. 100: the cupola of the 'antiquarium'.

131. Photograph taken in April 1938: door with a *Head of Hercules under a Scallop, and Garlands* (No. 23). Antwerp, FelixArchief.

132. Detail of Fig. 4: location of the door with *Head of Hercules under a Scallop and Garlands* in 1932.

133. Head of Hercules (original or later copy), plaster, 54 cm (No. 23). Antwerp, Rubenshuis.

134. Rubens, *The Four Philosophers*, detail with the bust of Seneca in a niche with a scallop. Florence, Palazzo Pitti.

135. Detail of Text ill. 100: bust of Hercules in a niche, and garlands, above the

136. Scallop (original or later copy), plaster (No. 23). Antwerp, Centraal Depot Musea – Stad Antwerpen.

137. Rubens, *The Discovery of Erichthonius*, detail: fountain with a scallop and 'Nature' holding dolphins. Vienna – Vaduz, Liechtenstein, The Princely Collections.

138. The portico, frontside, 810 × 1213 cm (No. 24). Antwerp, Rubenshuis.

139. Anthony van Dyck, *Architectural Study of Rubens's Portico* (No. 24, Copy), drawing. Paris, Fondation Custodia.

140. Combination of two types of arch with columns of different dimensions.

141. Detail of the Aylesbury Painting (Fig. 16): the portico.

142. Detail of the 1684 Harrewijn print (Fig. 17): the portico.

143. The portico with later additions, before the restoration (c. 1938).

144. ? Hans van Mildert after Rubens, *Keystone with the Head of Medusa and a Thunderbolt,* architectural sculpture, approx. 72 × 52 × 30 cm (No. 25). Antwerp, Rubenshuis, portico.

145. Plaster cast of the *Keystone with the Head of Medusa and a Thunderbolt* (No. 25, Copy). Antwerp, Centraal Depot Musea – Stad Antwerpen.

146. Keystone of the central arch of the garden façade of the Villa Medici, Rome.

147. Rubens, *Head of Medusa*, drawing. New York, The Morgan Library & Museum.

148. Rubens, *The Obsequies of Decius Mus*, painting, detail: a shield with the Head of Medusa and a Thunderbolt. Vaduz – Vienna, Liechtenstein, The Princely Collections.

149. 20th-century sculptor after Rubens, *Dolphin*, relief, approx. 72 cm (No. 26). Antwerp, Rubenshuis, portico.

150. ? Hans van Mildert after Rubens, *Dolphin*, approx. 72 cm (No. 26). Antwerp, Rubenshuis, portico.

151. Detail of the 1684 Harrewijn print (Fig. 17): dolphins in the spandrels of the windows on the façade of the studio.

152. Detail of a relief with sea monsters on the lantern of the bell tower of the Jesuit Church of Antwerp (now Church of St Carolus Borromeus).

153. ? Hans van Mildert after Rubens, *Pediment with a Niche Surrounded by Two Eagles Holding a Fruit Garland*, architectural sculpture, approx. 200 × 310 cm (No. 27). Antwerp, Rubenshuis, above the central arch of the portico.

154. Jacopo Barozzi da Vignola, *Garden Portal of the Villa Carpi in Rome*, engraving, detail, in *Regola delli cinque ordini d'architettura*, 1635.

155. Antonio Lombardo, *Relief with Inscription and Eagles*, relief. Vaduz – Vienna, Liechtenstein, The Princely Collections.

156. Rubens, *Ganymede Welcomed into Heaven*, detail. Vaduz, Fürstlich

157. Detail of Fig. 153: the right eagle with feathers underneath its beak.

158. ? Hans van Mildert after Rubens, *Ram's Head Ending in a Volute and a Snake's Head*, relief, 121 cm (No. 28; left). Antwerp, Rubenshuis, portico.

78

LIST OF FIGURES

159. Detail of Fig. 20: ram's head ending in volute and a snake's head.

160. Detail of Fig. 143.

161. ? Hans van Mildert after Rubens, *Ram's Head Ending in a Volute and a Snake's Head*, relief, 121 cm (No. 28; right). Antwerp, Rubenshuis, portico.

162. Detail of Fig. 129: ornamental banderole ending in a snake's head.

163. Rubens, *Upper Part of an Altar Dedicated to the Virgin Mary*, oil sketch, detail: pedestal with ram's heads. Antwerp, Rubenshuis.

164. Theodoor van Thulden after Rubens, *The Stage of Welcome*, etching, detail of a pedestal with rams' heads.

165. ? Hans van Mildert after Rubens, *Left Bucranium*, relief, 63 cm (No. 29). Antwerp, Rubenshuis, portico.

166. ? Hans van Mildert after Rubens, *Right Bucranium*, relief, 63 cm (No. 29). Antwerp, Rubenshuis, portico.

167. Detail of Fig. 22; ram's head motif in the form of a skull (*aegicranium*) in the frieze of the garden pavilion.

168. Detail of the 1684 Harrewijn print (Fig. 17): a bucranium beneath the cornice.

169. Bucranium in the metopes of the Doric frieze in Cornelis Galle I after Rubens, *Iconismus apicis in lapide clivi capitolini* ('Illustration of the Pointed Helmet on the Relief on the Capitoline Hill'), engraving.

170. Bucrania in the metopes of the Doric frieze in Vignola, *Regola delli cinque ordini d'architettura*, 1563.

171. ? Hans van Mildert after Rubens, *Male Satyr Facing Right*, relief, approx. 150 × 100 cm (No. 30). Antwerp, Rubenshuis, left spandrel of the left arch of the portico.

172. Photograph taken c. 1940 with the right hand of the satyr still visible.

173. ? Hans van Mildert after Rubens *Female Satyr Seen from Behind, Facing Left*, relief, approx. 150 × 100 cm (No. 31). Antwerp, Rubenshuis, right spandrel of the left arch of the portico.

174. Willem Panneels after Rubens, *Female Satyr Seen from Behind, Facing Left*, drawing. Copenhagen, Statens Museum for Kunst, Kongelige Kobberstiksamling.

175. ? Hans van Mildert after Rubens, *Male Satyr Facing Left*, relief, approx. 150 × 100 cm (No. 32). Antwerp, Rubenshuis, left spandrel of the right arch of the portico.

176. ? Hans van Mildert after Rubens, *Female Satyr Facing Left*, relief, approx. 150 × 100 cm (No. 33). Antwerp, Rubenshuis, right sprandrel of the right arch of the portico.

177. Garden pavilion (Front face) (No. 34). Antwerp, Rubenshuis.

178. Garden pavilion (seen from the North) (No. 34). Antwerp, Rubenshuis.

179. Detail of Fig. 20: the garden pavilion.

180. Detail of the 1684 Harrewijn print (Fig. 17): the garden pavilion.

181. Detail of Fig. 22: the garden pavilion.

182. Detail of Fig. 25: the garden pavilion and fountain.

183. Detail of the 1692 Harrewijn print (Fig. 18): the garden pavilion.

184. Frans Claessens after? Hans van Mildert after Rubens, *Left Caryatid (Sphinx?)*, sculpture (No. 35). Antwerp, Rubenshuis, garden pavilion.

185. Frans Claessens after? Hans van Mildert after Rubens, *Right Caryatid (Sphinx?)*, sculpture (No. 35). Antwerp, Rubenshuis, garden pavilion.

186. ? Rubens or retouched by him, *Head of a Sphinx*, drawing. Mougins, Musée d'Art Classique de Mougins.

187. ? Hans van Mildert after Rubens, *Youth with a Cornucopia (Genius Loci ?)*, statue (No. 36). Antwerp, Rubenshuis, garden pavilion.

188. Detail of the 1692 Harrewijn print (Fig. 18): *Youth with a Cornucopia* in the garden pavilion.

189. Detail of Appendix III.51: *Youth with a Cornucopia* in the garden pavilion.

190. Detail of Appendix III.34: *Youth with a Cornucopia* in the garden pavilion.

191. Rubens, *Virtus and Honos*, drawing. Antwerp, Museum Plantin-Moretus.

192. Theodoor van Thulden after Rubens, *The Stage of Welcome*, etching, detail of the *Genius of the City of Antwerp*.

193. Roman, *Genius*, statue. Naples, Museo Archeologico Nazionale.

194. *Genio buono*, woodcut engraving in Cartari, *Imagini*, 1608.

195. Detail of the 1692 Harrewijn print (Figs 18, 183): the statue of Venus and Cupid in the garden pavilion (No. 37).

196. Detail of Figs 25, 182: statue of Venus in the garden pavilion.

197. Georg Petel, *Venus and Cupid*, ivory statuette. Oxford, Ashmolean Museum.

79

LIST OF FIGURES

198. Georg Petel, *Venus and Cupid*, ivory statuette. Oxford, Ashmolean Museum.

199. Detail of Appendix III.30: statue of Venus and Cupid.

200. Willem Panneels, *Venus and Cupid*, drawing. Copenhagen, Statens Museum for Kunst, Kongelige Kobberstiksamling.

201. Willem Panneels, *Venus and Cupid*, drawing. Copenhagen, Statens Museum for Kunst, Kongelige Kobberstiksamling.

202. Anonymous artist, *Bacchus*, statue (No. 38). Antwerp, Rubenshuis, garden pavilion.

203. Idem seen from the statue's left side.

204. Idem seen from the statue's right side.

205. (Left) Detail of Fig. 25: the statue of Bacchus in the garden pavilion.

206. Detail of the 1692 Harrewijn print (Fig. 18): the statue of Bacchus in the garden pavilion.

207. (Left) Roman, *Resting Faun*, statue. Rome, Fondazione Torlonia.

208. Detail of Fig. 22: the statue of Bacchus in the garden pavilion.

209. Attributed to Rubens after an unidentified (16th-century?) model, *Head of Hercules with a Snub Nose*, drawing. London, The British Museum.

210. Detail of Fig. 25: the *Bust of Hercules* (No. 39).

211. Anonymous seventeenth-century artist, *Hercules*, statue, approx. 240 × 125 cm (No. 40). Antwerp, Rubenshuis, garden pavilion.

212. Detail of Fig. 22; the statue of Hercules in the garden pavilion.

213. Lucas Faydherbe, *Hercules*, statue. Lost.

214. After ? Hans van Mildert after Rubens, *Hercules*, plaster cast (No. 40, Copy). Antwerp, Rubenshuis.

215. Anonymous seventeenth-century artist after Rubens, *Right Hand of Hercules*, original fragment of No. 40 (Fig. 211). Antwerp, Rubenshuis.

216. Roman, *Hercules Farnese*, statue. Naples, Museo Archeologico Nazionale di Napoli.

217. Roman, *Hercules ('Commodus')*, statue. Rome, Musei Vaticani, Museo Chiaramonti.

218. Detail of Fig. 25: fountain with a putto (Cupid) riding a dolphin (No. 41).

219. Roman, '*The Gatchina Venus*', marble statue, detail with dolphin and Cupid. St Petersburg, The State Hermitage Museum.

220. Detail of Fig. 20: fountain with a putto (Cupid) riding a Dolphin.

221. Roman, *Amor Riding a Dolphin*, statue. Naples, Museo Archeologico di Napoli.

222. Rubens, *Susanna and the Elders*, detail. Madrid, Real Academia de Bellas Artes de San Fernando.

223. Rubens, *Cimon and Iphigenia*, detail. Longniddry (Scotland), Gosford House, Collection of the Earl of Wemyss and March.

224. Detail of Appendix III.30: fountain with a putto (Cupid) riding a Dolphin.

225. Christoffel Jegher after Rubens, *Susanna and the Elders*, woodcut, detail.

226. Rubens, *The Discovery of Erichthonius*, detail. Stockholm. Nationalmuseum.

227. Detail of the 1684 Harrewijn print (Fig. 17): *The Statues of Pictura (?) and Minerva* on top of the portico (Nos R1 and R2).

228. Detail of the 1684 Harrewijn print (Figs 17 and 227): *The Statue of Pictura (?)* (No. R1).

229. Antonio Palomino, title-page to part II of his *Museo Pictórico*, 1715–24, engraving, detail with Pictura.

230. Detail of Fig. 22: the statue of Mercury.

231. Detail of the 1684 Harrewijn print (Figs 17 and 227): *The Statue of Minerva* (No. R2).

232. Detail of Fig. 19: unidentified statue.

233. Detail of the 1692 Harrewijn print (Fig. 18): *Bundle of Attributes* (No. R3).

234. Hubertus Quellinus after Artus Quellinus I, *Decorative Elements (bundles of attributes) after the Sculptural Decoration of the Town Hall of Amsterdam*, engraving.

235. Photograph taken in the late 1930s: *The Statue of Ceres* in the garden pavilion (No. R4).

236. Detail of Appendix III.42: the statue of Ceres in the garden pavilion.

FIGURES

GENERAL FIGURES

Fig. 1. Virgilius Bononiensis, *Map of Antwerp (1565)*, woodcut, detail. Antwerp, Museum Plantin-Moretus.

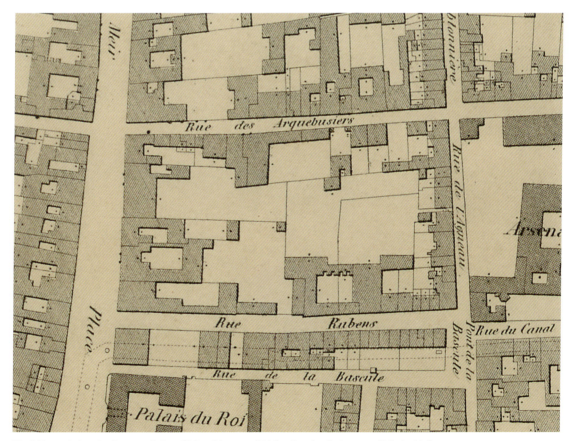

Fig. 2. François Antoine Losson, *Cadastral Map of Antwerp* (1846), print, detail. Antwerp, FelixArchief.

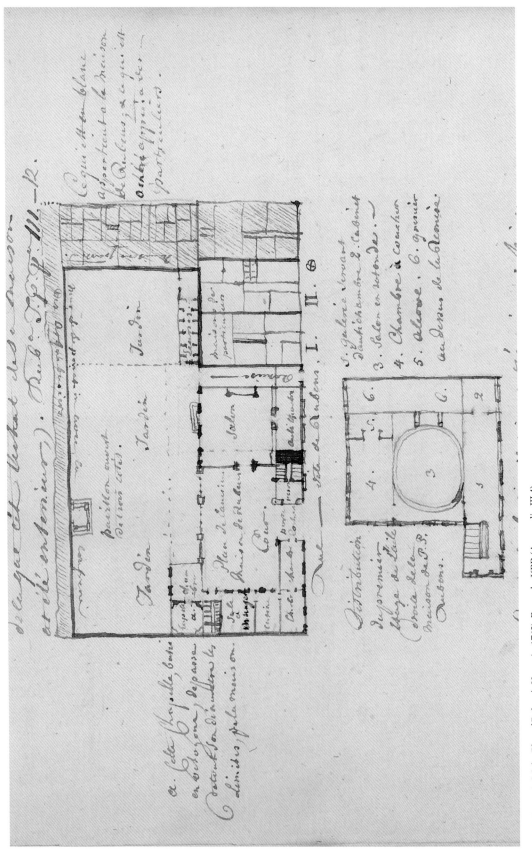

Fig. 3. François Mols, *Plan of Rubens's House* (c. 1763). Brussels, KBR (Appendix III.4).

GENERAL FIGURES

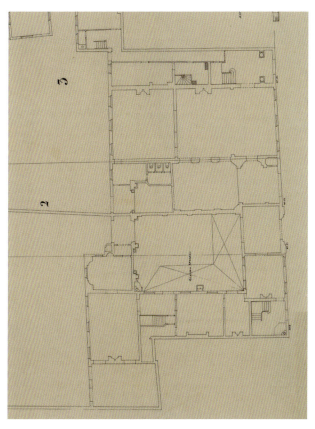

Fig. 5. Émile Van Averbeke, Detail of the plan of the first floor, showing the corridor on top of the portico (1936), blueprint.

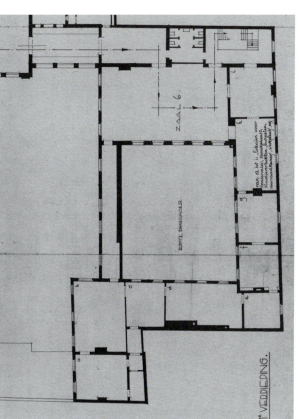

Fig. 4. Detail of the groundplan of 1932, showing the dividing wall through the courtyard and the garden, blueprint.

GENERAL FIGURES

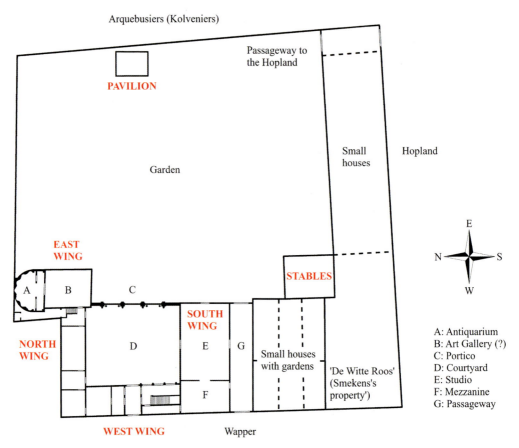

Fig. 6. Components of the property in Rubens's time, drawing (partly based on a blueprint

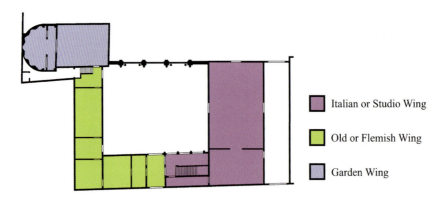

Fig. 7. Alternative denominations of the wings of the Rubenshuis.

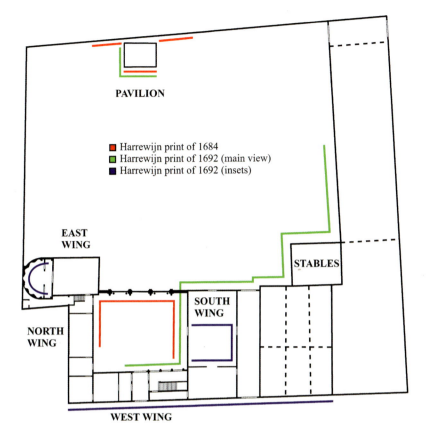

Fig. 8. Parts of the building and garden visible in the Harrewijn prints (Figs XXX and XXX).

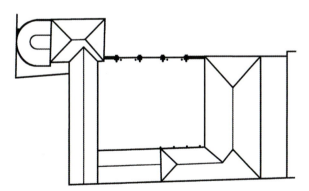

Fig. 9. Plan of the roofs of the restored house.

Fig. 10. The reconstructed north façade of the Italian wing.

Fig. 11. The reconstructed east façade of the Italian wing facing the courtyard with a 'real' loggia.

Fig. 12. The reconstructed east or garden façade of the Italian wing.

Fig. 13. The reconstructed street (west) façade.

Fig. 14. The reconstructed east façade of the east (or garden) wing.

GENERAL FIGURES

Fig. 15. The reconstructed east façade of the (Flemish) west wing and the reconstructed south façade of the (Flemish) north wing facing the courtyard.

GENERAL FIGURES

Fig. 16. Anonymous seventeenth-century artist, *View of the Courtyard of Rubens's House*. Aylesbury, Discover Bucks Museum (Appendix III.3).

GENERAL FIGURES

Fig. 17. Jacob Harrewijn after Jacques van Croes, *View of Rubens's Courtyard* (1684), etching (Appendix III.1).

Fig. 18. Jacob Harrewijn after Jacques van Croes, *View of Rubens's House and Garden* (1692), etching (Appendix III.2).

Fig. 19. Anthony van Dyck, *Portrait of Isabella Brant*. Washington, DC, National Gallery of Art (Appendix III.5).

Fig. 20. Jacques Jordaens, *Cupid and Psyche*. Madrid, Museo Nacional del Prado (Appendix III.9).

Fig. 21. Rubens, *Helena Fourment with her Son Frans (?) Rubens (Hélène Fourment au carrosse)*. Paris, Musée du Louvre (Appendix III.7).

Fig. 22. Anonymous seventeenth-century artist, *Portrait of a Couple in a Garden*. Berlin, Staatliche Museen zu Berlin, Gemäldegalerie Alte Meister (Appendix III.10).

Fig. 23. Rubens with Frans Snijders, *Homage to Ceres*. St Petersburg, The State Hermitage Museum (Appendix III.13).

Fig. 24. Rubens, *Henri IV Consigns the Regency to Maria de' Medici*. Paris, Musée du Louvre (Appendix III.18).

GENERAL FIGURES

Fig. 25. ? Rubens and Studio, *Peter Paul Rubens with his Wife Helena Fourment and his Son Nicolaas Rubens (The Walk in the Garden)*. Munich, Bayerische

GENERAL FIGURES

Fig. 26. Detail of the 1692 Harrewijn print (Fig. 18): west façade of Rubens's House.

Fig. 27. Detail of the Aylesbury Painting (Fig. 16): north façade of the Italian wing.

GENERAL FIGURES

Fig. 28. Detail of the 1684 Harrewijn print (Fig. 17): north façade of the Italian wing.

GENERAL FIGURES

Fig. 29. Detail of the 1692 Harrewijn print (Fig. 18): large east façade (garden side) of the Italian wing.

GENERAL FIGURES

Fig. 30. Detail of the 1692 Harrewijn print (Fig. 18): small east façade (courtyard) of the Italian wing.

GENERAL FIGURES

Fig. 31. Detail of Fig. 21: The house in the background.

GENERAL FIGURES

Fig. 32. Detail of the 1692 Harrewijn print (Fig. 18): west façade of Rubens's studio (Italian wing).

Fig. 33. Detail of the 1684 Harrewijn print (Fig. 17): *Busts in Niches, with amongst others a Faun* (No. 1).

Fig. 34. Detail of the 1684 Harrewijn print (Fig. 17): Bust of a Faun in a niche.

Fig. 35. *Bust of a Faun,* plaster cast (No. 1, Copy). Antwerp, Rubenshuis.

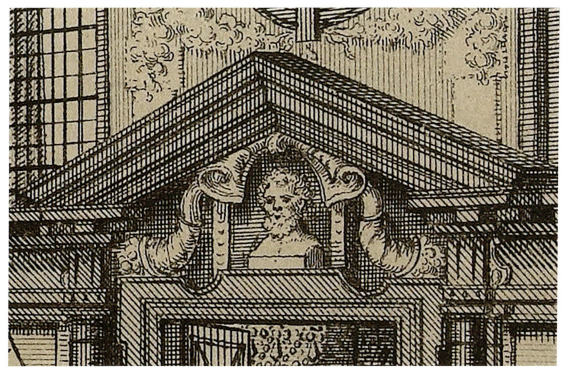

Fig. 36. Detail of the 1684 Harrewijn print (Fig. 17): *Bust in a Niche with a Scallop* (No. 2).

Fig. 37. Detail of the Aylesbury Painting (Fig. 16): *Bust in a Niche with a Scallop, Flanked by Cornucopias* (Appendix III.3).

Fig. 38. Detail of the 1684 Harrewijn print (Fig. 17): *Four Unidentified Herm Busts* (No. 3).

Fig. 39. Detail of the 1692 Harrewijn print (Fig. 18): *Herm Bust*.

Fig. 40. Paulus Pontius after Rubens, *Herm Bust of Sophocles*, engraving.

Fig. 41. Detail of the 1692 Harrewijn print (Fig. 18): *Six Herms* (No. 4).

Fig. 42. Detail of the Aylesbury Painting (Fig. 16): herms in relief?

Fig. 43. Detail of the 1684 Harrewijn print (Fig. 17): quoins terminating the north façade.

FIGURES No. 5

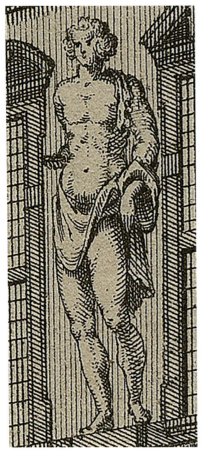

Fig. 44. Detail of the 1692 Harrewijn print (Fig. 18): *Hermes Belvedere* (No. 5).

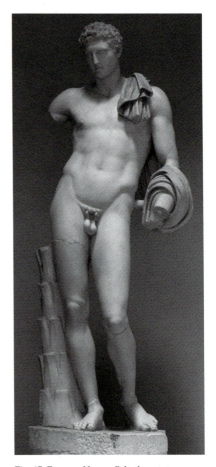

Fig. 45. Roman, *Hermes Belvedere*, statue. Rome, Musei Vaticani.

Fig. 46. Willem Panneels after Rubens, *Study of the Hermes Belvedere*, drawing. Copenhagen, Statens Museum for Kunst, Kongelige Kobberstiksamling.

FIGURES No. 6

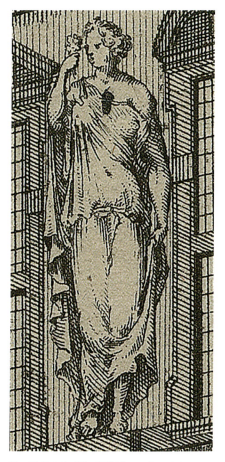

Fig. 47. Detail of the 1692 Harrewijn print (Fig. 18): *Flora Farnese* (No. 6).

Fig. 48. Roman, *Flora Farnese*, statue. Naples, Museo Archeologico Nazionale di Napoli.

Fig. 49. Cornelis Galle I after Rubens, *Iconismus duplicis statuae tunicatae (Illustration of a Pair of Statues with Tunics)*, engraving.

Fig. 50. Theodoor van Thulden after Rubens, *The Stage of Welcome*, etching, detail of the statue of *Good Hope (Spes)*.

Fig. 51. Detail of the 1692 Harrewijn print (Fig. 18): two types of window framing (No. 7).

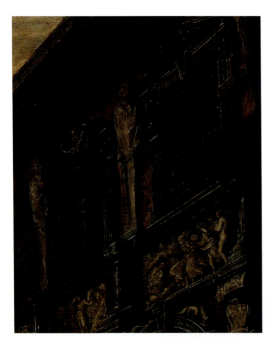

Fig. 52. Detail of the Aylesbury Painting (Fig. 16): two types of window framing (No. 7).

Fig. 53. Detail of the 1684 Harrewijn print (Fig. 17): window with (remodelled ?) grids (No. 7).

FIGURES No. 7a

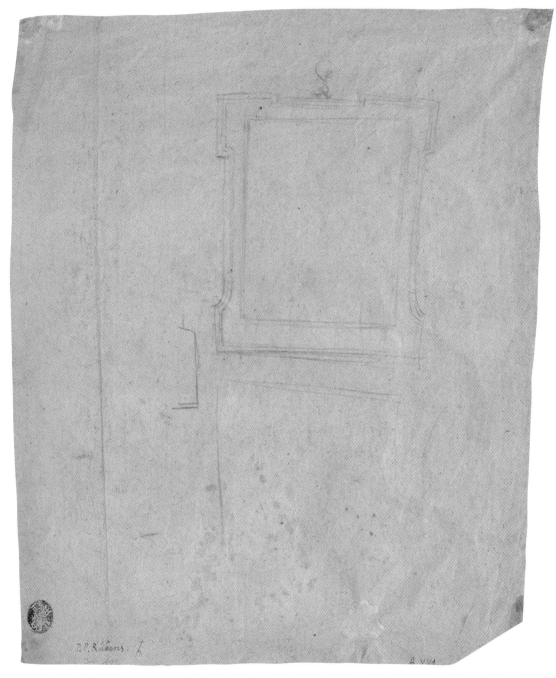

Fig. 54. Rubens, *Architectural Study of a Window Framing and Other Elements*, drawing (No. 7a). Antwerp, Museum Plantin-Moretus.

Fig. 55. Detail of Figs 21 and 31: the window on the upper floor of the house in the background.

Fig. 56. Detail of the Villa Medici garden façade: window with an open-topped pediment and a sphere on a pedestal. Rome, Villa Medici.

Fig. 57. Detail of the 1692 Harrewijn print (Fig. 18): frieze panel with *A Chariot Race (The Lowering of the Cloth)* (No. 8).

Fig. 58. Roman, *The Lowering of the Cloth*, relief. Rome, Musei Vaticani.

Fig. 59. Cornelis Galle I after Rubens, *Iconismus circensium et missionis mappae (Illustration of Circus Racing and the Lowering of the Cloth)*, engraving.

FIGURES No. 9

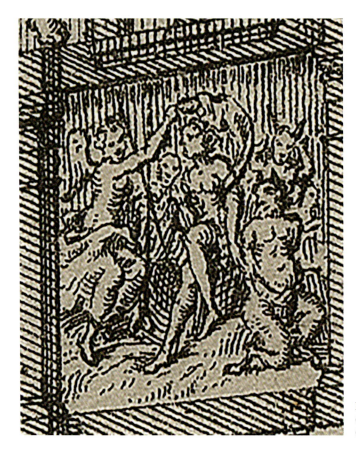

Fig. 60. Detail of the 1692 Harrewijn print (Fig. 18): frieze panel with *The Triumph of Apollo* (No. 9).

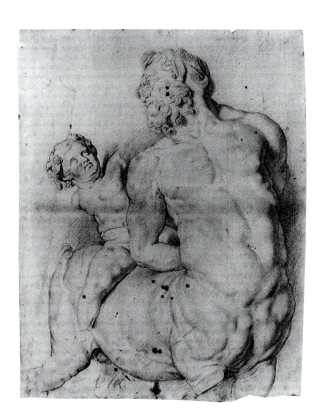

Fig. 61. Rubens, *Centaur Tormented by Cupid*, drawing. Cologne, Wallraf-Richartz-Museum & Fondation Corboud, Graphische Sammlung.

Fig. 62. Rubens, *Sketches for a Figure of Victory*, drawing, detail: *Crowning Victory*. Darmstadt, Hessisches Landesmuseum.

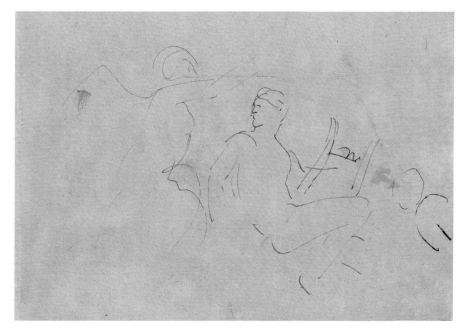

Fig. 63. Verso of Fig. 62: two variants of a winged figure, drawing, detail: *Victory Crowning Apollo*.

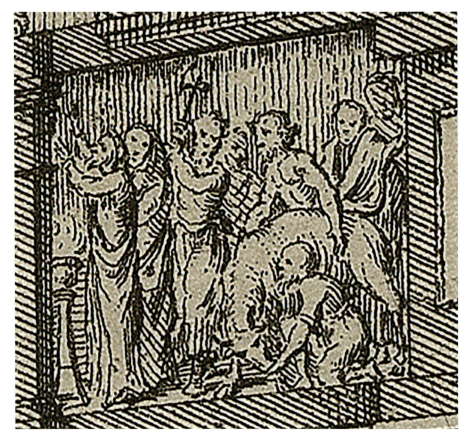

Fig. 64. Detail of the 1692 Harrewijn print (Fig. 18): frieze panel with *The Sacrifice of an Ox* (No. 10).

Fig. 65. Rubens, *The Sacrifice of an Ox*, drawing, 24.9 × 38.4 cm (No. 10a). Private Collection, on loan to the Wallraf-ichartz-Museum & Fondation Corboud, Graphische Sammlung, Cologne.

FIGURES No. 10

Fig. 66. Roman, *A Roman Sacrifice*, sarcophagus relief, detail. Mantua, Palazzo Ducale.

Fig. 67. Roman, *A Roman Sacrifice*, relief. Rome, Villa Medici.

Fig. 68. *A Roman Sacrifice*, woodcut in Du Choul, *Discours*, 1581.

Fig. 69. Detail of the 1684 Harrewijn print (Fig. 17): frieze panel with *The Sacrifice of Iphigenia* (No. 11).

Fig. 70. Detail the Aylesbury Painting (Fig. 16): frieze panel with *The Sacrifice of Iphigenia*.

Fig. 71. Willem Panneels after Rubens, *The Sacrifice of Iphigenia*, drawing (No. 11, Copy 1). Copenhagen, Statens Museum for Kunst, Kongelige Kobberstiksamling.

Fig. 72. After Rubens, *The Sacrifice of Iphigenia*, drawing (No. 11, Copy 2). Budapest, Szépművészeti Múzeum.

Fig. 73. After Rubens, *The Sacrifice of Iphigenia*, drawing (No. 11, Copy 3). Whereabouts unknown.

Fig. 74. Rubens, *The Lamentation with St Francis*, detail with Mary Magdelen. Brussels, Musées royaux des Beaux-Arts de Belgique.

Fig. 75. Detail of Fig. 71.

Fig. 76. Roman, *Marcus Aurelius Sacrificing before the Capitoline Temple*, detail with *tibicen* and *camillus*, relief. Rome, Palazzo dei Conservatori.

Fig. 77. Detail of Fig. 71.

Fig. 78. Rubens, *The Interpretation of the Victim*, detail. Vaduz – Vienna, Liechtenstein, The Princely Collections.

Fig. 79. Giorgio Vasari, *Timanthes Painting the Sacrifice of Iphigenia*, fresco. Arezzo, Casa Vasari.

Fig. 80. Roman, Candelabrum Base. Chantilly, Musée Condé.

Fig. 81. Roman, *Ara of Cleomenes*, view of Agamemnon wrapped in his cloak. Florence, Museo Archeologico

FIGURES No. 12

Fig. 82. Detail of the 1684 Harrewijn print (Fig. 17): frieze panel with *Alexander with the Thunderbolt* (No. 12).

Fig. 83. Detail of the Aylesbury Painting (Fig. 16): frieze panel with *Alexander with the Thunderbolt*.

Fig. 84. Willem Panneels after Rubens, *Alexander with the Thunderbolt*, drawing (No. 12, Copy). Copenhagen, Statens Museum for Kunst, Kongelige Kobberstiksamling.

Fig. 85. Roman, *The Sacrifice to Apollo*, relief, detail. Rome, Arch of Constantine.

Fig. 86. Roman, *Proserpina sarcophagus* relief, detail with Pluto and Cerberus. Mantua, Palazzo Ducale.

Fig. 87. Jacques de Bie, *Imago Iovis cum fulmine*, engraving in Hemelaer – de Bie, *Numismata Aurea*, 1615.

FIGURES No. 12

Fig. 88. Roman, *Barbarian King*, statue. Rome, Palazzo dei Conservatori.

Fig. 89. After Nicolas Béatrizet, *Roma victrix*, engraving in Antonio Lafreri, *Speculum Romanae Magnificentiae*, c. 1550.

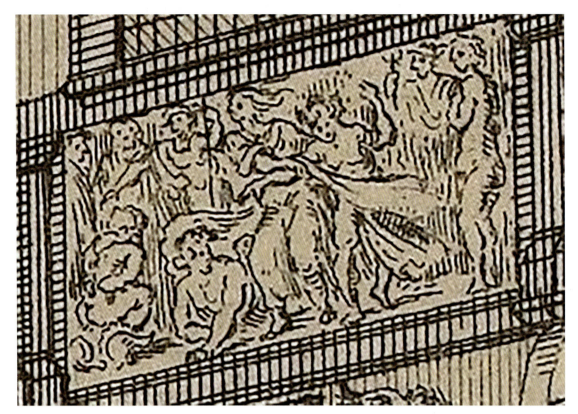

Fig. 90. Detail of the 1684 Harrewijn print (Fig. 17): frieze panel with *The Calumny of Apelles* (No. 13).

Fig. 91. Detail of the Aylesbury Painting (Fig. 16): frieze panel with *The Calumny of Apelles*.

FIGURES No. 13

Fig. 92. Cornelis Cort after Federico Zuccari, *The Calumny of Apelles*, engraving.

Fig. 93. Rubens, *The Departure of Maria de' Medici from Paris*, oil sketch, detail with a monster personifying Deceit. Munich, Bayerische Staatsgemäldesammlungen, Alte Pinakothek.

Fig. 94. *Imagine del Furore & dell'Ira*, woodcut in Vincenzo Cartari, *Imagini*, 1615.

Fig. 95. Rubens after Adam Elsheimer, *The Sacrifice to Venus*, detail with the statue of Venus.

FIGURES No. 13a

Fig. 96. Rubens, *The Calumny of Apelles*, drawing, 30.6 × 38.5 mm (No. 13a). London, The Courtauld Gallery.

FIGURES No. 13b

Fig. 97. Verso of Fig. 96: *Architectural Studies and Figure Studies for an Entombment* (No. 13b).

FIGURES No. 14

Fig. 98. Detail of the 1684 Harrewijn print (Fig. 17): frieze panel with *Zeuxis and the Maidens of Croton* (No. 14).

FIGURES No. 14

Fig. 99. Otto van Veen, *Zeuxis and the Maidens of Croton*, oil sketch. Whereabouts unknown.

Fig. 100. *Pudicitia Mattei*, statue, Copenhagen, Statens Museum for Kunst. Plaster cast after the Roman original in Rome, Musei Vaticani.

FIGURES No. 15

Fig. 101. Detail of the 1684 Harrewijn print (Fig. 17): frieze panel with *The Drunken Hercules* (No. 15).

Fig. 102. The *Borghese Vase*, view of a flute-playing faun. Paris, Musée du Louvre.

Fig. 103. The *Borghese Vase*, view of a dancing bacchante. Paris, Musée du Louvre.

Fig. 104. *The Drunken Hercules*, engraving in Venuti – Amaduzzi, *Vetera Monumenta*, 1774–1779.

Fig. 105. Rubens, *The Drunken Hercules*. Dresden, Staatliche Kunstsammlungen, Gemäldegalerie Alte Meister.

Fig. 106. Detail of the 1692 Harrewijn print (Fig. 18): frieze panel with *A Youthful Hero with a Lance and Chariot* (No. 16).

Fig. 107. Detail of the 1692 Harrewijn print (Fig. 18): the first floor of the small east façade with *The Loggia with a Figure and Animals* (No. 17).

Fig. 108. Paolo Veronese, *Loggia with a Lady and her Maid*, fresco, detail. Maser, Villa Barbaro.

Fig. 109. Jacques Jordaens, *A Company making Music in a Loggia*, drawing. Cambridge, Fitzwilliam Museum.

Fig. 110. Detail of the 1692 Harrewijn print (Fig. 18): *Andromeda Liberated by Perseus* (No. 18).

Fig. 111. Rubens, *Andromeda Liberated by Perseus*. St Petersburg, The State Hermitage Museum.

Fig. 112. Attributed to Willem Panneels after Rubens, *Andromeda Liberated by Perseus*, drawing. Copenhagen, Statens Museum for Kunst, Kongelige Kobberstiksamling.

Fig. 113. Rubens, *Andromeda Liberated by Perseus*. Berlin, Staatliche Museen zu Berlin.

FIGURES No. 18

Fig. 114. Pierre François Tardieu after Rubens, *Andromeda Liberated by Perseus*, etching and engraving.

Fig. 115. *Andromeda Liberated by Cupid*, engraving, detail, in Philostratus, *Les images*, 1614.

FIGURES No. 18

Fig. 116. Detail of Fig. 111: Andromeda.

Fig. 117. Rubens, *The Discovery of Erichthonius*, detail. Vienna – Vaduz, Liechtenstein, The Princely Collections.

Fig. 118. Detail of Fig. 110: Perseus.

Fig. 119. Rubens, *Abraham and Melchizedek*, detail with Abraham. Caen, Musée des Beaux-Arts.

Fig. 120. Detail of Fig. 18–2: a putto disrobing Andromeda.

Fig. 121. Detail of Fig. 23: two putti.

Fig. 122. Detail of the 1692 Harrewijn print (Figs 18 and 18–1): boy holding the horse.

Fig. 123. Roman, *Horse Tamer*, statue, detail. Rome, Quirinal.

Fig. 124. Detail of the 1692 Harrewijn print (Fig. 18): *Staircase* (No. 19).

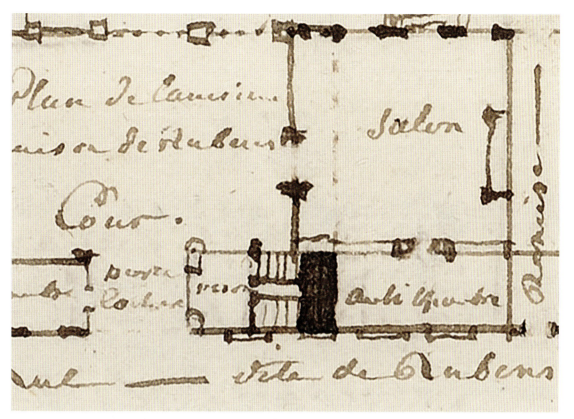

Fig. 125. Detail of Fig. 3: the staircase on the ground floor c. 1763.

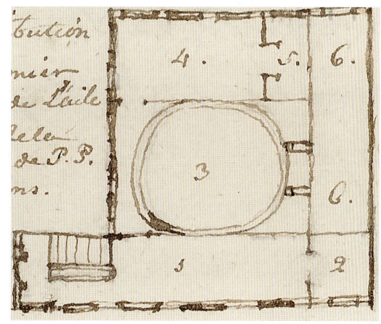

Fig. 126. Detail of Fig. 3: the staircase on the second floor c. 1763.

Fig. 127. Detail of the 1692 Harrewijn print (Fig. 18): Rubens's 'antiquarium' transformed into Canon Hillewerve's chapel (Nos 20–22).

FIGURES Nos 21–22

Fig. 128. Detail of Text ill. 100; the 'antiquarium' in the background.

Fig. 129. The cupola of the Antwerp Jesuit Church (now Church of St Carolus Borromeus).

Fig. 130. Detail of Text ill. 100: the cupola of the 'antiquarium'.

FIGURES No. 23

Fig. 131. Photograph taken in April 1938: door with a *Head of Hercules under a Scallop, and Garlands* (No. 23), Antwerp, FelixArchief.

Fig. 132. Detail of Fig. 4: location of the door with *Head of Hercules under a Scallop and Garlands* in 1932.

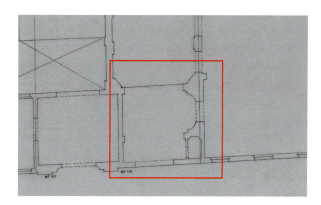

Fig. 133. Head of Hercules (original or later copy), plaster, 54 cm (No. 23). Antwerp, Rubenshuis.

Fig. 134. Rubens, *The Four Philosophers*, detail with the bust of Seneca in a niche with a scallop. Florence, Palazzo Pitti.

Fig. 135. Detail of Text ill. 100: bust of Hercules in a niche, and garlands, above the

FIGURES No. 23

Fig. 136. Scallop (original or later copy), plaster (No. 23). Antwerp, Centraal Depot Musea – Stad Antwerpen.

Fig. 137. Rubens, *The Discovery of Erichthonius*, detail: fountain with a scallop and 'Nature' holding dolphins. Vienna – Vaduz, Liechtenstein, The Princely Collections.

Fig. 138. The portico, frontside, 810 × 1213 cm (No. 24). Antwerp, Rubenshuis.

FIGURES No. 24

Fig. 140. Combination of two types of arch with columns of different dimensions.

Fig. 139. Anthony van Dyck, *Architectural Study of Rubens's Portico* (No. 24, Copy), drawing. Paris, Fondation Custodia.

FIGURES No. 24

Fig. 141. Detail of the Aylesbury Painting (Fig. 16): the portico.

Fig. 142. Detail of the 1684 Harrewijn print (Fig. 17): the portico.

FIGURES No. 24

Fig. 143. The portico with later additions, before the restoration (c. 1938).

Fig. 144. ? Hans van Mildert after Rubens, *Keystone with the Head of Medusa and a Thunderbolt*, architectural sculpture, approx. 72 × 52 × 30 cm (No. 25). Antwerp, Rubenshuis, portico.

FIGURES No. 25

Fig. 145. Plaster cast of the *Keystone with the Head of Medusa and a Thunderbolt* (No. 25, Copy). Antwerp, Centraal Depot Musea – Stad Antwerpen.

Fig. 146. Keystone of the central arch of the garden façade of the Villa Medici, Rome.

Fig. 147. Rubens, *Head of Medusa*, drawing. New York, The Morgan Library & Museum.

Fig. 148. Rubens, *The Obsequies of Decius Mus*, painting, detail: a shield with the Head of Medusa and a Thunderbolt. Vaduz – Vienna, Liechtenstein, The Princely Collections.

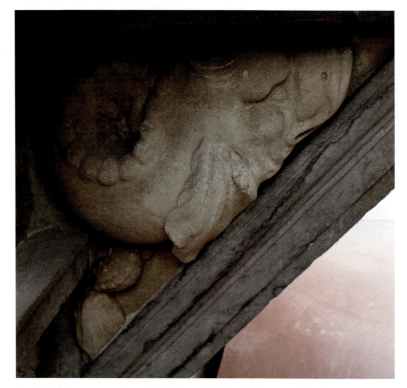

Fig. 149. 20th-century sculptor after Rubens, *Dolphin*, relief, approx. 72 cm (No. 26). Antwerp, Rubenshuis, portico.

Fig. 150. ? Hans van Mildert after Rubens, *Dolphin*, approx. 72 cm (No. 26). Antwerp, Rubenshuis, portico.

Fig. 151. Detail of the 1684 Harrewijn print (Fig. 17): dolphins in the spandrels of the windows on the façade of the studio.

Fig. 152. Detail of a relief with sea monsters on the lantern of the bell tower of the Jesuit Church of Antwerp (now Church of St Carolus Borromeus).

Fig. 153. ? Hans van Mildert after Rubens, *Pediment with a Niche Surrounded by Two Eagles Holding a Fruit Garland*, architectural sculpture, approx. 200 × 310 cm (No. 27). Antwerp, Rubenshuis, above the central arch of the portico.

Fig. 154. Jacopo Barozzi da Vignola, *Garden Portal of the Villa Carpi in Rome*, engraving, detail, in *Regola delli cinque ordini d'architettura*, 1635.

Fig. 155. Antonio Lombardo, *Relief with Inscription and Eagles*, relief. Vaduz – Vienna, Liechtenstein, The Princely Collections.

Fig. 156. Rubens, *Ganymede Welcomed into Heaven*, detail. Vaduz, Fürstlich

Fig. 157. Detail of Fig. 153: the right eagle with feathers underneath its beak.

Fig. 158. ? Hans van Mildert after Rubens, *Ram's Head Ending in a Volute and a Snake's Head*, relief, 121 cm (No. 28; left). Antwerp, Rubenshuis, portico.

Fig. 159. Detail of Fig. 20: ram's head ending in volute and a snake's head.

Fig. 160. Detail of Fig. 143.

Fig. 161. ? Hans van Mildert after Rubens, *Ram's Head Ending in a Volute and a Snake's Head*, relief, 121 cm (No. 28; right). Antwerp, Rubenshuis, portico.

Fig. 162. Detail of Fig. 129: ornamental banderole ending in a snake's head.

Fig. 163. Rubens, *Upper Part of an Altar Dedicated to the Virgin Mary*, oil sketch, detail: pedestal with ram's heads. Antwerp, Rubenshuis.

Fig. 164. Theodoor van Thulden after Rubens, *The Stage of Welcome*, etching, detail of a pedestal with rams' heads.

FIGURES No. 29

Fig. 165. ? Hans van Mildert after Rubens, *Left Bucranium*, relief, 63 cm (No. 29). Antwerp, Rubenshuis, portico.

Fig. 166. ? Hans van Mildert after Rubens, *Right Bucranium*, relief , 63 cm (No. 29). Antwerp, Rubenshuis, portico.

Fig. 167. Detail of Fig. 22; ram's head motif in the form of a skull (*aegicranium*) in the frieze of the garden pavilion.

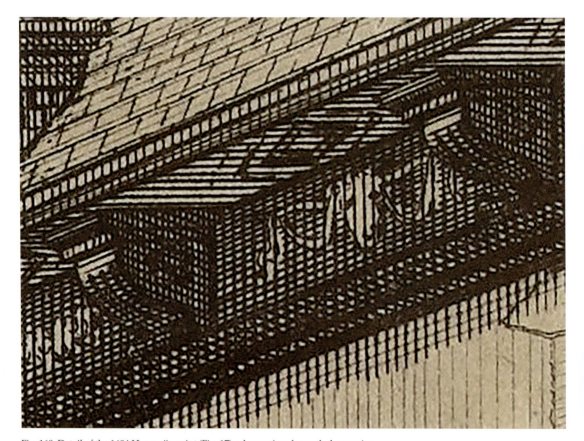

Fig. 168. Detail of the 1684 Harrewijn print (Fig. 17): a bucranium beneath the cornice.

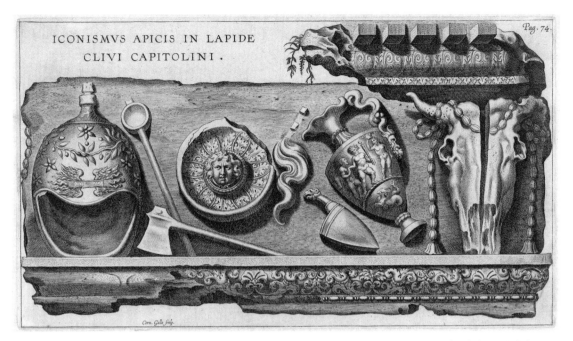

Fig. 169. Bucranium in the metopes of the Doric frieze in Cornelis Galle I after Rubens, *Iconismus apicis in lapide clivi capitolini* ('*Illustration of the Pointed Helmet on the Relief on the Capitoline Hill*'), engraving.

Fig. 170. Bucrania in the metopes of the Doric frieze in Vignola, *Regola delli cinque ordini d'architettura*, 1563.

Fig. 171. ? Hans van Mildert after Rubens, *Male Satyr Facing Right*, relief, approx. 150 × 100 cm (No. 30). Antwerp, Rubenshuis, left spandrel of the left arch of the portico.

Fig. 172. Photograph taken c. 1940 with the right hand of the satyr still visible.

FIGURES No. 31

Fig. 173. ? Hans van Mildert after Rubens *Female Satyr Seen from Behind, Facing Left*, relief, approx. 150 × 100 cm (No. 31). Antwerp, Rubenshuis, right spandrel of the left arch of the portico.

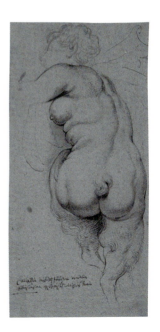

Fig. 174. Willem Panneels after Rubens, *Female Satyr Seen from Behind, Facing Left*, drawing. Copenhagen, Statens Museum for Kunst, Kongelige Kobberstiksamling.

Fig. 175. ? Hans van Mildert after Rubens, *Male Satyr Facing Left*, relief, approx. 150 × 100 cm (No. 32). Antwerp, Rubenshuis, left spandrel of the right arch of the portico.

Fig. 176. ? Hans van Mildert after Rubens, *Female Satyr Facing Left*, relief, approx. 150 × 100 cm (No. 33). Antwerp, Rubenshuis, right sprandrel of the right arch of the portico.

Fig. 177. Garden pavilion (Front face) (No. 34). Antwerp, Rubenshuis.

Fig. 178. Garden pavilion (seen from the North) (No. 34). Antwerp, Rubenshuis.

Fig. 179. Detail of Fig. 20: the garden pavilion.

Fig. 180. Detail of the 1684 Harrewijn print (Fig. 17): the garden pavilion.

Fig. 181. Detail of Fig. 22: the garden pavilion.

Fig. 182. Detail of Fig. 25: the garden pavilion and fountain.

Fig. 183. Detail of the 1692 Harrewijn print (Fig. 18): the garden pavilion.

FIGURES No. 35

Fig. 184. Frans Claessens after? Hans van Mildert after Rubens, *Left Caryatid (Sphinx?)*, sculpture (No. 35). Antwerp, Rubenshuis, garden pavilion.

Fig. 185. Frans Claessens after? Hans van Mildert after Rubens, *Right Caryatid (Sphinx?)*, sculpture (No. 35). Antwerp, Rubenshuis, garden pavilion.

Fig. 186. ? Rubens or retouched by him, *Head of a Sphinx*, drawing. Mougins, Musée d'Art Classique de Mougins.

Fig. 187. ? Hans van Mildert after Rubens, *Youth with a Cornucopia (Genius Loci ?)*, statue (No. 36). Antwerp, Rubenshuis, garden pavilion.

Fig. 188. Detail of the 1692 Harrewijn print (Fig. 18): *Youth with a Cornucopia* in the garden pavilion.

Fig. 189. Detail of Appendix III.51: *Youth with a Cornucopia* in the garden pavilion.

Fig. 190. Detail of Appendix III.34: *Youth with a Cornucopia* in the garden pavilion.

Fig. 191. Rubens, *Virtus and Honos*, drawing. Antwerp, Museum Plantin-Moretus.

Fig. 192. Theodoor van Thulden after Rubens, *The Stage of Welcome*, etching, detail of the *Genius of the City of Antwerp*.

Fig. 193. Roman, *Genius*, statue. Naples, Museo Archeologico Nazionale.

Fig. 194. *Genio buono*, woodcut engraving in Cartari, *Imagini*, 1608.

FIGURES No. 37

Fig. 195. Detail of the 1692 Harrewijn print (Figs 18, 183): the statue of Venus and Cupid in the garden pavilion (No. 37).

Fig. 196. Detail of Figs 25, 182: statue of Venus in the garden pavilion.

Fig. 197. Georg Petel, *Venus and Cupid*, ivory statuette. Oxford, Ashmolean Museum.

FIGURES No. 37

Fig. 198. Georg Petel, *Venus and Cupid*, ivory statuette. Oxford, Ashmolean Museum.

Fig. 199. Detail of Appendix III.30: statue of Venus and Cupid.

Fig. 200. Willem Panneels, *Venus and Cupid*, drawing. Copenhagen, Statens Museum for Kunst, Kongelige Kobberstiksamling.

Fig. 201. Willem Panneels, *Venus and Cupid*, drawing. Copenhagen, Statens Museum for Kunst, Kongelige Kobberstiksamling.

Fig. 202. Anonymous artist, *Bacchus*, statue (No. 38). Antwerp, Rubenshuis, garden pavilion.

FIGURES No. 38

Fig. 203. Idem seen from the statue's left side.

Fig. 204. Idem seen from the statue's right side.

FIGURES No. 38

Fig. 205. (Left) Detail of Fig. 25: the statue of Bacchus in the garden pavilion.

Fig. 206. Detail of the 1692 Harrewijn print (Fig. 18): the statue of Bacchus in the garden pavilion.

Fig. 207. (Left) Roman, *Resting Faun*, statue. Rome, Fondazione Torlonia.

Fig. 208. Detail of Fig. 22: the statue of Bacchus in the garden pavilion.

Fig. 209. Attributed to Rubens after an unidentified (16th-century?) model, *Head of Hercules with a Snub Nose*, drawing. London, The British Museum.

Fig. 210. Detail of Fig. 25: the *Bust of Hercules* (No. 39).

Fig. 211. Anonymous seventeenth-century artist, *Hercules*, statue, approx. 240 × 125 cm (No. 40). Antwerp, Rubenshuis, garden pavilion.

FIGURES No. 40

Fig. 212. Detail of Fig. 22; the statue of Hercules in the garden pavilion.

Fig. 213. Lucas Faydherbe, *Hercules*, statue. Lost.

Fig. 214. After ? Hans van Mildert after Rubens, *Hercules*, plaster cast (No. 40, Copy). Antwerp, Rubenshuis.

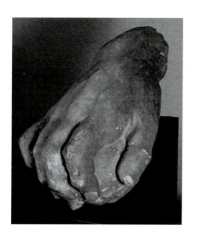

Fig. 215. Anonymous seventeenth-century artist after Rubens, *Right Hand of Hercules*, original fragment of No. 40 (Fig. 211). Antwerp, Rubenshuis.

Fig. 216. Roman, *Hercules Farnese*, statue. Naples, Museo Archeologico Nazionale di Napoli.

Fig. 217. Roman, *Hercules ('Commodus')*, statue. Rome, Musei Vaticani, Museo Chiaramonti.

Fig. 218. Detail of Fig. 25: fountain with a putto (Cupid) riding a dolphin (No. 41).

Fig. 219. Roman, '*The Gatchina Venus*', marble statue, detail with dolphin and Cupid. St Petersburg, The State Hermitage Museum.

Fig. 220. Detail of Fig. 20: fountain with a putto (Cupid) riding a Dolphin.

Fig. 221. Roman, *Amor Riding a Dolphin*, statue. Naples, Museo Archeologico di Napoli.

FIGURES No. 41

Fig. 222. Rubens, *Susanna and the Elders*, detail. Madrid, Real Academia de Bellas Artes de San Fernando.

Fig. 223. Rubens, *Cimon and Iphigenia*, detail. Longniddry (Scotland), Gosford House, Collection of the Earl of Wemyss and March.

Fig. 224. Detail of Appendix III.30: fountain with a putto (Cupid) riding a Dolphin.

Fig. 225. Christoffel Jegher after Rubens, *Susanna and the Elders*, woodcut, detail.

Fig. 226. Rubens, *The Discovery of Erichthonius*, detail. Stockholm. Nationalmuseum.

Fig. 227. Detail of the 1684 Harrewijn print (Fig. 17): *The Statues of Pictura (?) and Minerva* on top of the portico (Nos R1 and R2).

Fig. 228. Detail of the 1684 Harrewijn print (Figs 17 and 227): *The Statue of Pictura (?)* (No. R1).

Fig. 229. Antonio Palomino, title-page to part II of his *Museo Pictórico*, 1715–24, engraving, detail with Pictura.

Fig. 230. Detail of Fig. 22: the statue of Mercury.

FIGURES No. R2

Fig. 231. Detail of the 1684 Harrewijn print (Figs 17 and 227): *The Statue of Minerva* (No. R2).

Fig. 232. Detail of Fig. 19: unidentified statue.

FIGURES Nos R3–R4

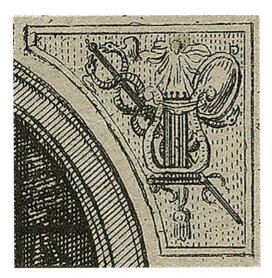

Fig. 234. Hubertus Quellinus after Artus Quellinus I, *Decorative Elements (bundles of attributes) after the Sculptural Decoration of the Town Hall of Amsterdam*, engraving.

Fig. 233. Detail of the 1692 Harrewijn print (Fig. 18): *Bundle of Attributes* (No. R3).

Fig. 235. Photograph taken in the late 1930s: *The Statue of Ceres* in the garden pavilion (No. R4).

Fig. 236. Detail of Appendix III.42: the statue of Ceres in the garden pavilion.

BIBLIOGRAPHY

Achilles Tatius, *Leucippe and Clitophon,* **trans. S. Gaselee, 1969**
Achilles Tatius, *Leucippe and Clitophon*, trans. S. Gaselee (*Loeb Classical Library*), London – Cambridge, MA, 1969 (1st revised edn).

Ackerman, *Architecture of Michelangelo,* **1961**
J.S. Ackerman, *The Architecture of Michelangelo*, London, 1961.

Ackerman, *Tuscan/Rustic Order,* **1994**
J.S. Ackerman, 'The Tuscan/Rustic Order, A Study in the Metaphorical Language of Archicture', in J.S. Ackerman, *Distance Points, Essays in Theory and Renaissance Art and Architecture*, Cambridge, MA – London, 1994, pp. 495–545.

Adler, *Landscapes (CRLB),* **1982**
W. Adler, *Landscapes* (*Corpus Rubenianum Ludwig Burchard*, XVIII.1), London – Oxford – New York, 1982.

Adriaenssens, *Steenhouwersmerken,* **1976**
R. Adriaenssens, 'Steenhouwersmerken in het Kolveniershof te Antwerpen', *Antwerpen, Tijdschrift der Stad Antwerpen*, XXI, 2, 1976, pp. 81–84.

Van Aerschot, ed., *Bouwen / Antwerpen,* **1979**
S. Van Aerschot, ed., *Bouwen door de eeuwen heen. Inventaris van het cultuurbezit in België. Architectuur.3nb: Stad Antwerpen*, Brussels – Ghent, 1979.

Aerts et al., *Meir,* **1983**
W. Aerts et al., [Exh. Cat.] *De Meir te Antwerpen, Monumentenzorg in historisch perspectief* (ICC-Antwerpen, Antwerp, 1983), Antwerp, 1983.

Akkerman – Corporaal, *Margaret Cavendisch,* **2010**
N. Akkerman and M. Corporaal, 'Margaret Cavendish, Constantijn Huygens en de Bataafse tranen', in E. Kloek et al., eds, *Vrouwen rondom Huygens*, Hilversum, 2010, pp. 224–239.

Alberti, *De Pictura,* **ed. Venatorius, 1540**
L.B. Alberti, *De Pictura [...]* [Florence,1435], ed. T. Venatorius, Basel, 1540.

Albrecht, *Häuser von Giorgio Vasari,* **1985**
J. Albrecht, 'Die Häuser von Giorgio Vasari in Arezzo und Florenz', in E. Hüttinger, ed., *Künstlerhäuser von der Renaissance bis zur Gegenwart*, Zürich, 1985, pp. 83–100.

Alen, *Rubenstuin,* **2021**
K. Alen, *'Oft iets anders treffelijck uit den hoff'. Een verkennend archief- en literatuuronderzoek voor een historisch verantwoorde beplanting en een museale omkadering van de Rubenstuin* (onuitgegeven rapport Rubenssite Antwerpen), Antwerp, 2021.

Alpers, *Torre (CRLB),* **1971**
S. Alpers, *The Decoration of the Torre de la Parada* (*Corpus Rubenianum Ludwig Burchard*, IX), Brussels – London – New York, 1971.

Arents, *Bibliotheek,* **2001**
P. Arents, *De Bibliotheek van Pieter Pauwel Rubens: een reconstructie* (*De Gulden Passer*, LXXVIII–LXXIX, 2000–2001), ed. A.K.L. Thijs et al., Antwerp, 2001.

Vander Auwera – van Sprang, eds, *Rubens,* **2007**
J. Vander Auwera and S. van Sprang, eds, [Exh. Cat.] *Rubens: A Genius at Work. The Works of Peter Paul Rubens in the Royal Museums of Fine Arts of Belgium Reconsidered / Rubens: l'atelier du génie. Autour des oeuvres du maître aux Musées royaux des Beaux-Arts de Belgique / Rubens: een genie aan het werk. Rondom de Rubenswerken in de Koninklijke Musea voor Schone Kunsten van België* (Musées royaux des Beaux-Arts de Belgique, Brussels, 2007–2008), Tielt, 2007.

Vander Auwera et al., eds, *Jordaens,* **2012**
J. Vander Auwera, I. Schaudies and J. Lange, eds, [Exh. Cat.] *Jordaens and the Antique / Jordaens et l'Antiquité / Jordaens en de antieken / Jordaens und die Antike* (Musées royaux des Beaux-Arts de Belgique, Brussels; Museum Fridericianum, Kassel, 2012-2013), Brussels – Kassel – New Haven, CT, 2012.

Van Averbeke, *Eerste bevindingen,* **1938**
E. Van Averbeke, 'De eerste bevindingen, Het plan van Blomme, De dwalingen van Mols, wat er dient gedaan te worden', *Het Huis van Rubens. Periodisch Bulletin*, I, 1938, pp. 27–45.

Van Averbeke, *Rubenshuis, restauratie I,* **1938**
E. Van Averbeke, *Rubenshuis. Restauratie [Eerste reeks nota's]*, unpublished report, Rubenshuis, Antwerp, 30 April 1938.

Van Averbeke, *Rubenshuis, restauratie II,* **1938**
E. Van Averbeke, *Rubenshuis. Restauratie [Tweede verslag]*, unpublished report, Rubenshuis, Antwerp, 23 July 1938.

Avery, *Dolphins,* **2009**
C. Avery, *A School of Dolphins*, London, 2009.

Babina – Gritsay, *Cat. St Petersburg, Hermitage (Flemish Painting),* **2005**
N. Babina and N. Gritsay, *The State Hermitage Museum. Flemish Painting 17th–18th Centuries. The Catalogue of the Collection*, St Petersburg, 2005.

Baisier, ed., *Divine Interiors,* **2016**
C. Baisier, ed., [Exh. Cat.] *Divine Interiors. Experience Churches in the Age of Rubens* (Museum Mayer van den Bergh, Antwerp, 2016), Kontich, 2016.

Baldinucci, *Notizie,* **1702**
F. Baldinucci, *Notizie de' professori del disegno da Cimabue in qua. Che contengono tre Decennali, dal 1580. al 1610. Opera posthuma*, Florence, 1702.

Balis, *Hunting Scenes (CRLB),* **1986**
A. Balis, *Rubens, Hunting Scenes* (*Corpus Rubenianum Ludwig Burchard*, XVIII, 2), London – Oxford, 1986.

Balis, *Panneels,* **2020**
A. Balis, 'A painting by Willem Panneels, an Intriguing Pupil of Rubens', *The Rubenianum Quarterly*, 2020, 3, pp. 3–6.

Balis, *Rubens and his Studio,* **2007**
A. Balis, 'Rubens and his Studio: Defining the Problem', in J. Vander Auwera and S. van Sprang, eds, [Exh. Cat.] *Rubens: A Genius at Work. The Works of Peter Paul Rubens in the Royal Museums of Fine Arts of Belgium Reconsidered / Rubens: l'atelier du génie. Autour des œuvres du maître aux Musées royaux des Beaux-Arts de Belgique / Rubens: een genie aan het werk. Rondom de Rubenswerken in de Koninklijke Musea voor Schone Kunsten van België* (Musées royaux des Beaux-Arts de Belgique, Brussels, 2007–2008), Tielt, 2007, pp. 30–51.

BIBLIOGRAPHY

Balis, *Rubens und Inventio*, 2001
A. Balis, 'Rubens und Inventio: Der Beitrag seines theoretischen Studienbuches', in U. Heinen and A. Thielemann, eds, *Rubens Passioni: Kultur der Leidenschaften im Barock*, Göttingen, 2001, pp. 11–40.

Balis, *Studio Practices*, 1994
A. Balis, '"Fatto da un mio discepolo". Rubens's Studio Practices Reviewed', in T. Nakamura, ed., *Rubens and his Workshop. The Flight of Lot and his Family from Sodom*, Tokyo, 1994, pp. 97–127.

Balis et al., *Vlaamse schilderkunst*, 1987
A. Balis et al., *De Vlaamse schilderkunst in het Kunsthistorisches Museum te Wenen* (*Flandria extra muros*), Antwerp, 1987.

Banz-Heinhold, *Fassadenmalerei*, 1952
M. Banz-Heinhold, *Süddeutsche Fassadenmalerei vom Mittelalter bis zum Gegenwart*, Munich, 1952.

Barnes et al., *Van Dyck*, 2004
S.J. Barnes, N. De Poorter, O. Millar and H. Vey, *Van Dyck, A Complete Catalogue of the Paintings*, New Haven, CT – London, 2004.

Barolsky, *Trick of Art*, 1998
P. Barolsky, 'The Trick of Art', in P. Jacks, ed., *Vasari's Florence, Artists and Literati at the Medicean Court*, Cambridge, MA, 1998, pp. 23–29.

Basan, *Estampes*, 1767
[P-]F. Basan, *Catalogue des estampes gravées d'après P.P. Rubens, avec une méthode pour blanchir les estampes les plus rousses, & en ôter les taches d'huile. Nouvelle édition, corrigée, considérablement augmentée, & précédée de la vie de Rubens. Troisième partie faisant suite au dictionnaire des graveurs anciens & modernes*, Paris, 1767.

Bastet, *Oudheden*, 1980
F.L. Bastet, 'Oudheden uit Rubens' verzameling te Leiden', in A.W.A. Boschloo et al., eds, 'Nederlandse kunstnijverheid en interieurkunst, opgedragen aan professor Th.H. Lunsingh Scheurleer', *Nederlands Kunsthistorisch Jaarboek*, XXXI, 1980, pp. 72–85.

Baticle – Georgel, *Technique*, 1976
J. Baticle and P. Georgel, *Technique de la peinture, l'atelier* (*Les dossiers du département des peintures*, XII), Paris, 1976.

Baudouin, *Altaartuinen*, 1985
F. Baudouin, 'Rubens en de altaartuinen "van metaal" te 's-Hertogenbosch, 1616–1617', in A. Balis, F. Baudouin, N. De Poorter et al., eds, *Rubens and his World, Bijdragen – Études – Studies – Beiträge, Opgedragen aan Prof. Dr. Ir. R.-A. d'Hulst [...]*, Antwerp, 1985, pp. 163–169.

Baudouin, *Altaren / Sint-Elisabethgasthuis*, 1993
F. Baudouin, 'Twee altaren in de kapel van Sint-Elisabethgasthuis te Antwerpen', in *In verscheidenheid. Liber amicorum Prof. Dr. Em. Robert Van Passen*, Aartrijke, 1993, pp. 45–55.

Baudouin, *Altars*, 1972
F. Baudouin, 'Altars and Altarpieces before 1620', in J.R. Martin, ed., [Exh. Cat.] *Rubens before 1620* [Conference proceedings and Exh. Cat. Princeton University Art Museum, Princeton, 1971], Princeton, NJ, 1972, pp. 45–92.

Baudouin, *Architecturale Motieven*, 2006
F. Baudouin, 'Architecturale motieven op schilderijen van Rubens: enkele voorbeelden', in K. Van der Stighelen, ed., *Munuscula Amicorum. Contributions on Rubens and his Colleagues in Honour of Hans Vlieghe* (Pictura Nova: Studies in 16th- and 17th-Century Flemish Painting and Drawing, X), I–II, Turnhout, 2006, I, pp. 199–212.

Baudouin, *Barok*, 1982
F. Baudouin, 'De Barok in de Zuidelijke Nederlanden', *Openbaar Kunstbezit in Vlaanderen*, XX.3, 1982, pp. 83–120.

Baudouin, *Cat. Antwerp, Rubenshuis*, 1974
F. Baudouin, *Kunstwerken tentoongesteld in het Rubenshuis: dertig afbeeldingen met commentaar*, Antwerp, 1974.

Baudouin, *Charles Van Herck*, 2000
F. Baudouin, 'Charles Van Herck and his Collection of Drawings and Terracottas', in F. Baudouin and D. Allard, eds, [Exh. Cat.] *Drawings from the 17th and 18th Century: the Charles Van Herck Collection / Tekeningen uit de 17de en 18de eeuw: de verzameling Van Herck / Dessins des XVIIe et XVIIIe siècles: la collection Van Herck* (Museum Plantin-Moretus / Prentenkabinet, Antwerp, 2000), Brussels, 2000, pp. 15–21.

Baudouin, *Drawings in Budapest*, 2004
F. Baudouin, 'Notes about Four Drawings in the Budapest Fine Arts Museum', in C. Van de Velde, ed., *Flemish Art in Hungary* (Conference, Budapest, 12–13 May 2000), Brussels, 2004, pp. 9–16.

Baudouin, *Fresco's*, 1998
F. Baudouin, *De fresco's op de gevels van Rubens' werkplaats: enkele addenda*, Academiae Analecta, Mededelingen van de Koninklijke Academie voor Wetenschappen, Letteren en Schone Kunsten van België, Klasse der Schone Kunsten, LVII.1, 1998, pp. 1–24.

Baudouin, *Fruytiers*, 1967
F. Baudouin, 'Een Antwerps schilder uit Rubens' omgeving, Philips Fruytiers, de monogrammist PHF', *Jaarboek Koninklijk Museum voor Schone Kunsten Antwerpen*, 1967, pp. 151–186.

Baudouin, *Herinneringen*, 1958
F. Baudouin, [Exh. Cat.] *Herinneringen aan P.P.Rubens* (Antwerp, Rubenshuis, 1958), Antwerp, 1958.

Baudouin, *Intervention*, 2000
F. Baudouin, 'Concept, Design and Execution. The Intervention of the Patron', in H. Vlieghe, A. Balis and C. Van de Velde, eds, *Concept, Design and Execution in Flemish Painting (1530–1700)*, Turnhout, 2000, pp. 1–26.

Baudouin, *Keizersbeelden*, 2005
F. Baudouin, '*Rubens en de keizersbeelden in de galerij van het paleis op de Coudenberg te Brussel*', in A. Balis et al., eds, *Florissant. Bijdragen tot de kunstgeschiedenis der Nederlanden (15de–17de eeuw), opgedragen aan Prof. Carl Van de Velde*, Brussels, 2005, pp. 335–346.

Baudouin, *Kolveniershof*, 1975
F. Baudouin, 'De ontwerper van het Kolveniershof te Antwerpen en de datering van dit gebouw', *Gentse Bijdragen tot de Kunstgeschiedenis*, XXIII, 1973–1975, pp. 183–198.

Baudouin, *Nota's*, 1953
F. Baudouin, 'Nota's bij de tentoonstelling "Schetsen en tekeningen van P.P. Rubens"', *Bulletin Koninklijke Musea voor Schone Kunsten*, II, 1953, pp. 46–54.

Baudouin, *Painter-Architect*, 2002
F. Baudouin, 'Peter Paul Rubens and the Notion "Painter-Architect"', in P. Lombaerde, ed., *The Reception of P.P. Rubens's Palazzi di Genova During the 17th Century in Europe: Questions and Problems* (Architectura Moderna, I), Turnhout, 2002, pp. 15–36 (reprinted in: F. Baudouin, *Rubens in Context: Selected Studies, Liber Memorialis*, Schoten, 2005, pp. 153–173).

Baudouin, *Pictor doctus*, 2001
F. Baudouin, 'Rubens *pictor doctus*, zijn bibliotheek en zijn lectuur', in P. Arents, *De Bibliotheek van Pieter Pauwel Rubens: een reconstructie* (*De Gulden Passer*, LXXVIII–LXXIX), ed. A.K.L. Thijs et al., Antwerp, 2001, pp. 47–75.

Baudouin, *Rubens en zijn tijd*, 1971
F. Baudouin, [Exh. Cat.] *Rubens en zijn tijd: Tekeningen uit Belgische verzamelingen: tentoonstelling naar aanleiding van het 25-jarig bestaan van het Rubenshuis als Museum* (Rubenshuis, Antwerp, 1971), Antwerp, 1971.

Baudouin, *Rubenshuis*, 1951
F. Baudouin, 'Bewoners en bezoekers van het Rubenshuis in de XVIIde eeuw', *Kroniek, orgaan van Stabuco*, October 1951, pp. 97–104.

Baudouin, *Rubenshuis*, 1955
F. Baudouin, *Het Rubenshuis, beknopte gids*, Antwerp, 1955.

Baudouin, *Rubenshuis*, 1977
F. Baudouin, *Het Rubenshuis, beknopte gids*, Antwerp, 1977.

Baudouin, *Rubens House*, 1977
F. Baudouin, 'The Rubens House at Antwerp and the Château de Steen at Elewijt', *Apollo*, CV, 1977, pp. 181–188 (reprinted in: F. Baudouin, *Rubens in Context: Selected Studies, Liber Memorialis*, Schoten, 2005, pp. 175–189).

Baudouin, *Rubens House*, 2005
F. Baudouin, 'The Rubens House at Antwerp and the Château de Steen at Elewijt', in F. Baudouin, *Rubens in Context: Selected Studies, Liber Memorialis*, Schoten, 2005, pp. 175–189.

Baudouin, *Rubens' kinderjaren*, 1991
F. Baudouin, 'Rubens' kinderjaren in Keulen en in Antwerpen', *Jaarboek Provinciale Commissie voor Geschiedenis en Volkskunde*, 1990–1991, pp. 133–159 (reprinted in: F. Baudouin, *Rubens in Context: Selected Studies, Liber Memorialis*, Schoten, 2005, pp. 45–65).

Baudouin, *Rubens's House*, 1955
F. Baudouin, *Rubens's House, a Summary Guide*, Antwerp, 1955.

Baudouin, *Selected Studies*, 2005
F. Baudouin, *Rubens in Context: Selected Studies, Liber Memorialis*, Antwerp – Schoten, 2005.

Baudouin, *Summary Guide*, 1977
F. Baudouin, *Rubens House, a Summary Guide*, Antwerp, 1977.

Baudouin, *Toren*, 1983
F. Baudouin, 'De toren van de Sint-Carolus Borromeuskerk te Antwerpen', *Academiae Analecta. Mededelingen van de Koninklijke Academie voor Wetenschappen, Letteren en Schone Kunsten van België. Klasse der Schone Kunsten*, XLIV.3, 1983, pp. 15–56.

Baudouin, *Willem van Ehrenberg*, 1981
F. Baudouin, 'Het interieur van de Sint-Carolus Borromeuskerk te Antwerpen. Een schilderij op marmer van Willem van Ehrenberg', *Antwerpen, Tijdschrift van de stad Antwerpen*, XXVII, 1, 1981, pp. 7–14.

Baudouin – Allard, eds, *Cat. Van Herck (Drawings)*, 2000
F. Baudouin and D. Allard, eds, [Exh. Cat.] *Drawings from the 17th and 18th Century: the Charles Van Herck collection / Tekeningen uit de 17de en 18de eeuw: de verzameling Van Herck / Dessins des XVIIe et XVIIIe siècles: la collection Van Herck* (Museum Plantin-Moretus / Prentenkabinet, Antwerp, 2000), Brussels, 2000.

Baudouin – Allard, eds, *Cat. Van Herck (Terracottas)*, 2000
F. Baudouin and D. Allard, eds, [Exh. Cat.] *17th and 18th Century Terracottas: The Charles Van Herck Collection / Terracotta's uit de 17de en 18de eeuw: de verzameling Van Herck / Terres cuites des 17e et 18e siècles: la collection Van Herck* (Koninklijk Museum voor Schone Kunsten, Antwerp, 2000), Brussels, 2000.

Bauer – Delmarcel, eds, *Tapisseries bruxelloises*, 1977
R. Bauer and G. Delmarcel, eds, [Exh. Cat.] *Tapisseries bruxelloises au siècle de Rubens, du Kunsthistorisches Museum, Vienne, et des Musées royaux d'Art et d'Histoire, Bruxelles / Brusselse Wandtapijten in Rubens' eeuw, uit het Kunsthistorisches Museum, Wenen, en de Koninklijke Musea voor Kunst en Geschiedenis, Brussel* (Musées royaux d'Art et d'Histoire, Brussels, 1977), Brussels, 1977.

Baumstark, *Decius Mus*, 1988
R. Baumstark, *Peter Paul Rubens: Tod und Sieg des römischen Konsuls Decius Mus*, Vaduz, 1988.

Baumstark – Delmarcel, *Decius Mus (CRLB)*, 2019
R. Baumstark and G. Delmarcel, *The Decius Mus Series* (*Corpus Rubenianum Ludwig Burchard*, XIII.2), I–II, Turnhout – London, 2019.

Baumstark et al., *Liechtenstein*, 1985
R. Baumstark, G.C. Bauman, K. Christiansen et al., [Exh. Cat.] *Liechtenstein: The Princely Collections* (The Metropolitan Museum of Art, New York, 1985–1986), New York, 1985.

Becker, *Altarbau*, 1990
U. Becker, *Studien zum flämischen Altarbau im 17. und 18. Jahrhundert* (Verhandelingen van de Koninklijke Academie voor Wetenschappen, Letteren en Schone Kunsten van België, Klasse der Schone Kunsten, LII, 49), Brussels, 1990.

Bedeer – Janssens, *Steden in beeld*, 1993
G. Bedeer and L. Janssens, [Exh. Cat .] *Steden in beeld. Antwerpen, 1200–1800* (Hof van Liere, Antwerp, 1993), Brussels – Antwerp, 1993.

Belkin, *Copies (CRLB)*, 2009
K. Lohse Belkin, *Copies and Adaptations from Renaissance and later Artists. German and Netherlandish Artists* (*Corpus Rubenianum Ludwig Burchard*, XXVI.1), I–II, London – Turnhout, 2009.

Belkin – Healy, *House of Art*, 2004
K. Lohse Belkin and F. Healy, [Exh. Cat.] *A House of Art. Rubens as a Collector / Een luis vol kunst: Rubens als verzamelaar* (Rubenshuis, Antwerp, 2004), Antwerp – Schoten, 2004.

Van Belle, *Signes lapidaires*, 1994
J.-L. van Belle, *Signes lapidaires, nouveau dictionnaire, Belgique et Nord de la France*, Louvain-la-Neuve, 1994.

Bellori, *Vite*, 1672
G.P. Bellori, *Le Vite de' Pittori, Scultori et Architetti moderni*, I, Rome, 1672.

Bellori, *Lives*, eds Wohl – Wohl, 2005
A.S. Wohl and H. Wohl, eds, *Giovanni Pietro Bellori. The Lives of the Modern Painters, Sculptors and Architects. A New Translation and Critical Edition*, Cambridge, 2005.

Bellori, *Rubens und Van Dyck*, ed. Healy, 2020
G.P. Bellori, *Vita di Pietro Paolo Rubens & Vita di Antonio Van Dyck / Das Leben des Peter Paul Rubens & Das Leben des Anthonis van Dyck* (Giovan Pietro Bellori. *Le vite de' pittori, scultori e architetti moderni / Die Lebensbeschreibungen der modernen Maler, Bildhauer und Architekten*, VI), ed. F. Healy, trans. A. Brug, Göttingen, 2020.

Van Beneden, *Portiek en tuinpaviljoen*, 2019
B. van Beneden, 'De portiek en het tuinpaviljoen van het Rubenshuis: Italië als model', *M & L, Monumenten, Landschappen en Archeologie*, XXXVIII.4, 2019, pp. 13–19.

BIBLIOGRAPHY

Van Beneden, *Rubens and Architecture*, 2011
B. van Beneden, 'Introduction: Rubens and Architecture', in B. Uppenkamp and B. van Beneden, [Exh. Cat.] *Palazzo Rubens: The Master as Architect / Palazzo Rubens: de meester als architect / Palazzo Rubens: le maître et l'architecture* (Rubenshuis, Antwerp, 2011), Antwerp, 2011, pp. 8–32.

Van Beneden, *Rubens's House*, 2008
B. van Beneden, *The Rubens's House: Highlights* [vistor's guide], Antwerp, 2008.

Van Beneden, *Rubens's House Revealed*, 2009
B. van Beneden, 'Rubens's House Revealed', *Apollo*, CLXIX, 2009, pp. 102–108.

Van Beneden, ed., *Rubens in Private*, 2015
B. van Beneden, ed., [Exh. Cat.] *Rubens in Private: The Master Portrays his Family / Rubens privé: de meester portretteert zijn familie* (Rubenshuis, Antwerp, 2015), Brussels, 2015.

Van Beneden, *Van Haecht*, 2009
B. van Beneden 'Willem van Haecht. An Erudite and Talented Copyist', in A. van Suchtelen and B. van Beneden, [Exh. Cat.] *Room for Art in Seventeenth-Century Antwerp / Kamers vol Kunst in zeventiende-eeuws Antwerpen* (Rubenshuis, Antwerp, 2009–2010; Mauritshuis, The Hague, 2010), Zwolle, 2009, pp. 56–92.

Van Beneden – De Poorter, eds, *Royalist Refugees*, 2006
B. van Beneden and N. De Poorter, eds, [Exh. Cat.] *Royalist Refugees, William and Margaret Cavendish in the Rubens House, 1648–1660* (Rubenshuis, Antwerp, 2006), Antwerp – Schoten, 2006.

Bezemer Sellers, *Tuinen*, 1997
V. Bezemer Sellers, 'Condet Aurea Saecula. De tuinen van Frederik Hendrik', in M. Keblusek and J. Zijlmans, eds, [Exh. Cat.] *Vorstelijk vertoon. Aan het hof van Frederik Hendrik en Amalia* (Haags Historisch Museum, The Hague, 1997–1998), The Hague – Zwolle, 1997, pp. 126–142.

Bieber, *Ancient Copies*, 1977
M. Bieber, *Ancient Copies. Contributions to the History of Greek and Roman Art*, New York, 1977.

Birke – Kertész, *Albertina*, 1997
V. Birke and J. Kertész, *Die italienischen Zeichnungen der Albertina* (Generalverzeichnis, IV), Vienna, 1997.

Blockmans, *Krijgstekening*, 1962
F. Blockmans, 'Een krijgstekening, een muurschildering en een schilderij van Hans Vredeman de Vries te Antwerpen (1577–1586)', *Antwerpen, Tijdschrift der Stad Antwerpen*, VIII, 1, pp. 20–42.

Blommaert, *Barokarchitectuur*, 1982
V. Blommaert, 'Barokarchitectuur in de eerste helft van de 17e eeuw te Antwerpen', *Hades: Periodiek tijdschrift van de Antwerpse Vereniging voor Bodem- en Grotonderzoek*, 9–10, 1982, pp. 156–164.

Blommaert, *Woonhuis*, 1980
V. Blommaert, 'Onderzoek naar de typologische ontwikkeling van het woonhuis in de zes cultuurhistorische perioden', in [Exh. Cat.] *500 Jaar woonhuizen te Antwerpen XVe – XIXe eeuw* (Generale Bankmaatschappij, Antwerp, 1980), Antwerp, 1980, pp. 9–30, 51.

Blomme, *Huis van Rubens*, 1910
H. Blomme, *Het huis van Rubens: heropbouwing door Henri Blomme, paviljoen der stad Antwerpen in de Wereldtentoonstelling van Brussel in 1910*, Antwerp, 1910.

Blunt, *Borromini*, 1979
A. Blunt, *Borromini*, Cambridge, MA, 1979.

Blunt, *Rubens and Architecture*, 1977
A. Blunt, 'Rubens and Architecture', *The Burlington Magazine*, CXIX, 1977, pp. 609–621.

Bober – Rubinstein, *Antique Sculpture*, 2010
P.P. Bober and R.O. Rubinstein, *Renaissance Artists and Antique Sculpture: A Handbook of Sources* (Studies in Medieval and Early Renaissance Art History, LXII), London – Turnhout, 2010 (2nd rev. edn).

Boccardo et al., eds, *Genua Picta*, 1982
P. Boccardo et al., eds, [Exh. Cat.] *Genua picta. Proposte per la scoperta e il recupero delle facciate dipinte* (Commenda di S. Giovanni di Prè, Genoa, 1982), Genoa, 1982.

Bochius, *Historica narratio*, 1602
J. Bochius, *Historica narratio profectionis et inaugurationis serenissimorum Belgii principum Alberti & Isabellae, Austriae Archiducum*, Antwerp, 1602.

Boele et al., eds, *Liefde*, 2002
V. Boele et al., eds, [Exh. Cat.] *Liefde uit de Hermitage* (Nieuwe Kerk, Amsterdam, 2002–2003), Zwolle – Amsterdam, 2002.

Boeykens, *Reflections*, 2014
S. Boeykens, 'Reflections on the Digital Reconstruction of the Portico and Garden Paviljon of the Rubens House', in P. Lombaerde, ed., *The Notion of the Painter-Architect in Italy and the Southern Low Countries* (Architectura Moderna, XI), Turnhout, 2014, pp. 223–236.

Borggrefe et al., eds, *Vredeman de Vries*, 2002
H. Borggrefe, T. Fusenig and B. Uppenkamp, eds, [Exh. Cat.] *Tussen stadspaleizen en luchtkastelen: Hans Vredeman de Vries en de Renaissance* (Weserrenaissance-Museum Schloss Brake, Lemgo; Koninklijk Museum voor Schone Kunsten, Antwerp, 2002), Ghent – Amsterdam, 2002.

Van Bos – Hayen, *Verborgen polychromie*, 2019
M. Van Bos and R. Hayen, 'De verborgen polychromie van Hercules en de guirlande', *M & L, Monumenten, Landschappen en Archeologie*, XXXVIII.4, 2019, pp. 78–80.

Bosman, *Rembrandts plan*, 2019
M. Bosman, *Rembrandts plan. De ware geschiedenis van zijn faillissement*, Amsterdam, 2019.

Boussard, *Leçons de Rubens*, 1838
J.F. Boussard, *Les Leçons de Rubens*, Brussels, 1838

De Brabander, *Na-Kaarten*, 1988
G. De Brabander, *Na-Kaarten over Antwerpen*, Bruges, 1988.

Braham, *Rubens*, 1988
H. Braham, [Exh. Cat.] *Rubens: Paintings – Drawings – Prints in the Princes Gate Collection* (The Courtauld Gallery, London, 1988–1989), London, 1988.

Van den Branden, *Schilderschool*, 1883
F.J. Van den Branden, *Geschiedenis der Antwerpsche schilderschool*, Antwerp, 1883.

Braun – Hogenberg, *Civitates*, 1572–1617
G. Braun and F. Hogenberg, *Civitates orbis terrarum*, I–VI, Cologne, 1572–1617.

Bredius, *Rubens-document*, 1912
A. Bredius, 'Een onbekend Rubens-document', *Oud-Holland*, XXX, 1912, pp. 215–218.

Brendel, *Immolatio Boum*, 1930
O. Brendel, 'Immolatio Boum', *Mitteilungen des Deutschen Archäologischen Instituts: Römische Abteilung*, XLV, 1930, pp. 196–226.

Brenninkmeyer-de Rooij, *Jan Brueghel I,* **1990**
B. Brenninkmeyer-de Rooij, 'Zeldzame bloemen, "Fatta tutti del natturel" door Jan Brueghel I', *Oud Holland*, CIV, 1990, pp. 218–248.

Bresseleers – Kanora, *Rubens te Ekeren,* **1957**
F. Bresseleers and H. Kanora, *P.P. Rubens te Ekeren*, Ekeren, 1957.

Brieger – Johnson, *Sperlings Studienjahre,* **1920**
W. G. Brieger and J. W.S. Johnson, *Otto Sperlings Studienjahre nach dem Manuskript der Kgl. Bibliothek zu Kopenhagen herausgegeben*, Copenhague, 1920.

Brink – Hornbostel, eds, *Pegasus,* **1993**
C. Brink and W. Hornbostel, eds, [Exh. Cat.] *Pegasus und die Künste* (Museum für Kunst und Gewerbe, Hamburg, 1993), Munich, 1993.

Briquet, 1923
C.M. Briquet, *Les filigrans: Dictionnaire historique des marques du papier des leur apparition vers 1282 jusqu'en 1600*, I–IV, Leipzig, 1923.

Broos, *Historiestukken,* **1993**
B. Broos, *Liefde, list en lijden. Historiestukken in het Mauritshuis*, The Hague – Ghent, 1993.

Brown, Vlieghe, et al., *Van Dyck,* **1999**
C. Brown, H. Vlieghe et al., [Exh. Cat.] *Antoon Van Dyck:1599– 1641/ Anthony van Dyck: 1599–1641 / Antoine van Dyck: 1599– 1641* (Koninklijk Museum voor Schone Kunsten, Antwerp; Royal Academy of Arts, London, 1999), London – Antwerp, 1999.

De Bruyn, *Quelllinus,* **1988**
J.-P. De Bruyn, *Erasmus II Quellinus (1607–1678). De schilderijen met catalogue raisonné* (*Vlaamse schilders uit de tijd van de grote meesters*, IV), Freren, 1988.

De Bruyn, *Rubens,* **2006**
N. de Bruyn, *Peter Paul Rubens: een 'self-made man'? De familiale invloeden op het leven en de carrière van een Antwerpse schilder en diplomaat*, unpublished master thesis, Universiteit Antwerpen, Antwerp, 2005–2006.

Bulckens, *Rubens and Workshop,* **2019**
K. Bulckens, 'The Bigger Picture: Rubens and his Workshop during the Twelve Years' Truce', in S. Suda and K. Nickel, eds, [Exh. Cat.] *Early Rubens* (Fine Arts Museums of San Francisco: de Young / Legion of Honor, San Francisco, CA, 2019; Art Gallery of Ontario, Toronto, 2019–2020), Munich – London – New York, 2019, pp. 84–101.

Burchard, *Wildenstein,* **1950**
L. Burchard, [Exh. Cat.] *A Loan Exhibition of Works by Peter Paul Rubens* (Wildenstein & Co, London, 1950), London, 1950.

Burchard – d'Hulst, *Drawings,* **1963**
L. Burchard and R.-A. d'Hulst, *Rubens Drawings* (*Monographs of the Nationaal Centrum voor de Plastische Kunsten van de XVIde en de XVIIde Eeuw*, II), I–II, Brussels, 1963.

Buschmann, *Huis-Rubens,* **1938**
P. Buschmann, 'Over herstelling en bestemming van het Huis-Rubens', *Het Huis van P.P. Rubens, Periodisch Bulletin*, II, 1938, pp. 51–81.

Buschmann, *Rubens,* **1840.**
E. Buschmann, *Pierre Paul Rubens* (Société royale des Sciences, Lettres, et Arts d'Anvers, Antwerp, 1840), Antwerp, 1840.

Busken Huet, *Land van Rubens,* **1881**
C. Busken Huet, *Het land van Rubens, Belgische Reisherinneringen*, Amsterdam, 1881 [2d ed.].

Bussers, *Faydherbe,* **1986**
H. Bussers, 'Faydherbe onderschat of een verkeken kans voor de Koninklijke Musea voor Schone Kunsten', *Bulletin van de Koninklijke Musea voor Kunst en Geschiedenis Brussel*, LVII, 1986, pp. 81–103.

Büttner, *Allegories (CRLB),* **2018**
N. Büttner, *Allegories and Subjects from Literature* (*Corpus Rubenianum Ludwig Burchard*, XII), I–II, London – Turnhout, 2018.

Büttner, *Genre Scenes (CRLB),* **2019**
N. Büttner, *Genre Scenes* (*Corpus Rubenianum Ludwig Burchard*, XVIII), London – Turnhout, 2019.

Büttner, *Hands of Rubens,* **2017**
N. Büttner, 'The Hands of Rubens: On Copies and their Reception', in T. Nakamura, ed., *Appreciating the Traces of an Artist's Hand* (*Kyoto Studies in Art History*, II), Kyoto, 2017, pp. 41–53.

Büttner, *Rubens,* **2015**
N. Büttner, *Pietro Paulo Rubens. Eine Biographie* (*Regensburger Studien zur Kunstgeschichte*, XXV), Regensburg, 2015.

Büttner, *Rubens berühmt,* **2006**
N. Büttner, *Herr P.P. Rubens. Von der Kunst, berühmt zu werden* (*Rekonstruktion der Künste*, VII), Göttingen, 2006.

Büttner, *Rubens und Junius,* **2011**
N. Büttner, 'Peter Paul Rubens und Franciscus Junius. Aemulatio in Praxis und Theorie', in J.-D. Müller, ed., *Aemulatio. Kulturen des Wettstreits in Text und Bild (1450–1620)*, Berlin, 2011, pp. 319–367.

Büttner, *Rubenshaus,* **2020**
N. Büttner, 'Rubens und das Rubenshaus: Eine deutschbelgische Geschichte nationaler Vereinnahmungen', in S. Schmitz and H. Kamp, eds., *Erinnerungsorte in Belgien: Instrumente lokaler, regionaler und nationaler Sinnstiftung*, Bielefeld, 2020, pp. 137–156.

Büttner – Heinen, *Leidenschaften,* **2004**
N. Büttner and U. Heinen, [Exh. Cat.] *Peter Paul Rubens. Barocke Leidenschaften* (Herzog Anton Ulrich-Museum, Braunschweig, 2004), Munich, 2004.

Büttner – Heinen, eds, *Quellen und Dokumente,* **2011**
N. Büttner and U. Heinen, eds, *Quellen und Dokumente zu Leben, Werk und literarischen Bezüge des Malers, Unternehmers und Diplomaten Peter Paul Rubens (1577–1640)*, published online Wolfenbüttel, Herzog August Bibliothek, 2011: <URL: http://diglib.hab.de/wdb.php?distype = toc&dir = edoc%2Fed000083 [accessed 7/04/2021]

Buys, *Maria en Martha,* **1989**
H. Buys, 'Voorstellingen van Christus in het huis van Maria en Martha in het zestiende-eeuwse keukenstuk', *Nederlands Kunsthistorisch Jaarboek*, XL, 1989, pp. 93–128.

Van Calster et al., *Flemish Painting,* **1988**
P. Van Calster, A. Balis, W. Laureyssens et al., [Exh. Cat.] *The Golden Age of Flemish Painting* (Taiwan Museum of Art, Taichung, 1988), Taichung, 1988.

Carpeggiani – Tellini Perina, *Giulio Romano,* **1987**
P. Carpeggiani and C. Tellini Perina, *Giulio Romano a Mantova: "…una nuova e stravagante maniera"*, Mantua, 1987.

Cartari, *Images,* **trans. Mulryan, 2012**
V. Cartari, *Images of the Gods of the Ancients, The First Italian Mythography*, trans. J. Mulryan (*Medieval and Renaissance Texts and Studies*, CCCXCVI), Tempe, 2012.

BIBLIOGRAPHY

Cartari, *Imagini*, 1608
 V. Cartari, *Le imagini delli dei degli Antichi* [...], Padua, 1608 (1st edn Venice, 1556).

Cartari, *Imagini*, 1615
 V. Cartari, *Le vere e nove imagini de gli dei delli antichi* […], ed. L. Pignoria, Padua, 1615 (1st edn Venice, 1556).

Cast, *Calumny*, 1981
 D. Cast, *The Calumny of Apelles. A Study in the Humanist Tradition*, New Haven, CT – London, 1981.

Casteels, *Cardon*, 1964
 M. Casteels,'Cardon, Forci (...), bijgenaamd "den Wale", beeldhouwer', in *Nationaal Biografisch Woordenboek*, I, Brussels, 1964, cols 298–299.

Casteels, *De Nole*, 1961
 M. Casteels, *De beeldhouwers de Nole te Kamerijk, te Utrecht en te Antwerpen* (Verhandelingen van de Koninklijke Vlaamse Academie voor Wetenschappen, Letteren en Schone Kunsten van België, Klasse der Schone Kunsten, XVI), Brussels, 1961.

Van de Castyne, *Architecture*, 1934
 O. Van de Castyne, *L'architecture privée en Belgique dans les centres urbains aux XVIe et XVIIe siècles* (Académie royale de Belgique. Classe des Beaux-Arts, Mémoires, IV), Brussels, 1934.

Van de Castyne, *Rubens*, 1931
 O. Van de Castyne, 'La question Rubens dans l'histoire de l'architecture', *Revue belge d'Archéologie et d'Histoire de l'Art*, I, 1931, pp. 103–119.

Van Cauteren, ed., *Blind Date*, 2020
 K. Van Cauteren, ed., [Exh. Cat.] *Blind Date: portretten met blikken en blozen* (Snijders&Rockoxhuis Museum and Keizerskapel, Antwerp, 2020), Lichtervelde, 2020.

Van Cauteren, *Zalig tot zot*, 2020
 K. Van Cauteren, *Wij: van zalig tot zot*, Antwerp – Veurne, 2020.

Cavalli-Björkman, ed., *Rubens i Sverige*, 1977a
 G. Cavalli-Björkman, ed., *Rubens i Sverige* (Årsbok for Svenska statens kontsamlingar, XXIV), Stockholm, 1977.

Cavalli-Björkman et al., *Cat. Stockholm (Flemish Paintings)*, 2010
 G. Cavalli-Björkman, C. Fryklund and K. Sidén, *Dutch and Flemish Paintings, III, Flemish Paintings c. 1600–c. 1800*, Stockholm, 2010.

Cavendish, *Natures Pictures*, 1656
 M. Cavendish, *Natures Pictures drawn by Fancies Pencil to the Life* [...], London, 1656.

Cavendish, *Méthode nouvelle*, 1658
 W. Cavendish, *La méthode nouvelle et invention extraordinaire de dresser les chevaux* […], Antwerp, 1658.

Cavendish, *New Method*, 1667
 W. Cavendish, *A New Method, and Extraordinary Invention to Dress Horses*, London, 1667.

Cavendish, *Sociable Letters*, 2004
 M. Cavendish, *Sociable Letters*, ed. J. Fitzmaurice, Peterborough, 2004.

Ceuleers, *Verloren Stad*, 2016
 J. Ceuleers, *Antwerpen, Verloren Stad, 1860–1880*, Antwerp, 2016.

Chapman, *Cornelis Ketel*, 2009
 H.P. Chapman, 'Cornelis Ketel, Fingerpainter and Poet-Painter', in H.P. Chapman and J. Woodall, eds, 'Envisioning the Artist in the Early Modern Netherlands / Het beeld van de kunstenaar in de vroegmoderne Nederlanden', *Netherlands Yearbook for History of Art / Nederlands Kunsthistorisch Jaarboek*, LIX, 2009, pp. 249–273.

Chifflet, *De linteis*, 1624
 J.-J. Chifflet, *De linteis sepulchralibus Christi* [...], Antwerp, 1624.

Cicero, *De Inventione* etc., trans. Hubbel, 1949
 Cicero, *De Inventione; De optimo genere oratorum; Topica*, trans. H.M. Hubbel (*Loeb Classical Library*), Cambridge, MA – London, 1949 (repr. 1960).

De Clercq, *Conservatie*, 2019
 J. De Clercq, 'De conservatie- en restauratiebehandeling van Rubens' portiek en paviljoen', *M & L, Monumenten, Landschappen en Archeologie*, XXXVIII.4, 2019, pp. 73–77, 81–88.

De Clercq, *Materieel-technisch onderzoek*, 1997
 L. De Clercq, *Rubenshuis Tuinportiek Antwerpen, Aanvulling op het materieel-technisch onderzoek en restauratie-advies in opdracht van het stadsbestuur van Antwerpen*, unpublished report (Studiebureau L. De Clercq), Antwerp, 1997.

De Clercq, *Moulages*, 2012
 L. De Clercq, 'Rubenshuis Moulages', in *Rubens' portiek en tuinpaviljoen*, unpublished report (Studiebureau L. De Clercq / Maat_werk architecten), Antwerp, 2012, pp. 1–29.

De Clercq, *Portiek Rubenshuis*, 1991
 L. De Clercq, *Vooronderzoek Portiek Rubenshuis Antwerpen*, unpublished report (Studiebureau L. De Clercq), Antwerp, 1991.

De Clercq, *Rubens schilderend*, 2019
 L. De Clercq, 'Rubens schilderend in zijn tuin [...]', *M & L, Monumenten, Landschappen en Archeologie*, XXXVIII.4, 2019, p. 54.

De Clercq, *Tuinpaviljoen*, 2012
 L. De Clercq, 'Bouwhistorische gegevens tuinpaviljoen', in: *Rubens' portiek en tuinpaviljoen*, unpublished report (Studiebureau L. De Clercq / Maat_werk architecten), Antwerp, 2012. [22 pp., non paginated].

De Clercq – Hayen, *Historische schets*, 2019
 L. De Clercq and R. Hayen, 'Historische schets van de portiek en het tuinpaviljoen in de periode 1946–2012', *M & L, Monumenten, Landschappen en Archeologie*, XXXVIII.4, 2019, pp. 39–51.

De Clercq – Van Deyck, *Letterkundigen*, 1952
 C. De Clercq and C. Van Deyck, 'Letterkundigen en schrijvers', in *Antwerpen in de XVIIIe eeuw*, Antwerp, 1952, pp. 248–274.

De Clercq et al., *Conservatie–restauratie*, 2020
 L. De Clercq et al., *Behandelingsrapport conservatie-restauratie te Rubenshuis, Antwerpen*, unpublished report (Studiebureau L. De Clercq / Maat_werk architecten), I-V, Antwerp, 2020.

De Clercq et al., *Rubens' tuinportiek en tuinpaviljoen*, 2014
 J. De Clercq et al., *Rubens' tuinportiek en tuinpaviljoen, Als zeldzame bewaard gebleven, materiële getuigen [...], Restauratienota*, unpublished report (Maat_werk architecten), Antwerp, 2014.

Clijmans, *Wederopbouw Rubenshuis*, 1941
 F. Clijmans, *Rondom den wederopbouw van het Rubenshuis*, Antwerp, 1941.

Clijmans, *Wederopbouw Rubenshuis*, 1946
 F. Clijmans, *Wederopbouw van Rubens' woon- en werkhuis*, Antwerp, 1946.

Coekelberghs, *Review Palazzo Rubens*, 2012
 D. Coekelberghs, [Review] B. Uppenkamp and B. van Beneden, 'À propos d'un livre sur Rubens et l'architecture: Palazzo Rubens, le maître et l'architecture (Rubenshuis, Antwerp, 2011)', *La tribune de l'art*, published online, 29 March

2012: <URL: https://www.latribunedelart.com/a-propos-d-un-livre-sur-rubens-et-l-architecture [accessed 7/04/2021]

Coekelberghs – Loze, eds, *Néo-Classicisme*, 1985
D. Coekelberghs and P. Loze, eds, [Exh. Cat.] *Autour du néo-classicisme en Belgique, 1770–1830 / Om en rond het neo-classicisme in België, 1770–1830* (Musée d'Ixelles, Ixelles, 1985), Brussels, 1985.

Coffin, *Villa*, 1988
D.R. Coffin, *The Villa in the Life of Renaissance Rome* (Princeton Monographs in Art and Archeology, XLIII), Princeton, NJ, 1988.

Cohen, *Drawings*, 1980
C.E. Cohen, *The Drawings of Giovanni Andrea da Pordenone* (Corpus Graphicum, III), Florence, 1980.

Cohen, *Pordenone*, 1996
C.E. Cohen, *The Art of Giovanni Antonio da Pordenone. Between Dialect and Language*, I–II, Cambridge, 1996.

Coope, *Salomon de Brosse*, 1972
R. Coope, *Salomon de Brosse and the Development of the Classical Style in French Architecture from 1565 to 1630*, London, 1972.

Cornet, ed., *Na en Naar Van Dyck*, 1999
P. Cornet, ed., [Exh. Cat.] *Na en Naar Van Dyck, De romantische recuperatie in de 19de eeuw* (Hessenhuis et al., Antwerp, 1999), Antwerp, 1999.

Coulon, *L'Ulysse*, 1643
[L.] Coulon, *L'Ulysse François ou le voyage de France, de Flandre et de Savoye* [...], Paris, 1643.

Couvreur, *Iconografie*, 1975
W. Couvreur, [Iconografie] in *Antwerpen in de zestiende eeuw*, Antwerp, 1975, pp. 559–568.

Couvreur, *Ikonografie*, 1989
W. Couvreur, 'Ikonografie', in *Antwerpen in de XVII^{de} eeuw*, Antwerp, 1989, pp. 487–499.

Couvreur, *Stadsplattegronden*, 1985
W. Couvreur, 'Galle en Hoefnagels stadsplattegronden en de Antwerpse verdedigingswerken van september 1577 tot februari 1581', in F. de Nave, ed., 'Liber Amicorum Leon Voet', *De Gulden Passer*, LXI–LXIII, 1985, pp. 519–545.

Cresti – Rendina, *Palazzi*, 1998
C. Cresti and C. Rendina, *Palazzi of Rome*, Cologne, 1998.

Dacosta-Kauffman, *L'école de Prague*, 1985
T. Dacosta-Kauffman, *L'école de Prague. La peinture à la cour de Rodolphe II*, Paris, 1985.

Daniel – Togner, *Cat. Kroměříž*, 1999a
L. Daniel and M. Togner, *Kroměříž Picture Gallery: Catalogue of the Painting Collection of the Archbishop's Palace in Kroměříž*, Kroměříž, 1999.

Davies, *Rubens's Roof*, 2017
J. Davies, 'The Botched Job on Rubens's Roof', *Jordaens Van Dyck Panel Paintings Project*, 17 September 2017, published online: <URL: http://jordaensvandyck.org/rubens-had-problems-with-his-roof/> [accessed 2/03/2020].

Degueldre, *Kadastrale ligger*, 2011
G. Degueldre, *Kadastrale ligger van Antwerpen (1584–1585), proeve van reconstructie op de vooravond van de scheiding der Nederlanden*, Antwerp, 2011.

Deknop et al., *Van 't stadt*, 2007
A. Deknop et al., [Exh. Cat.] *Van 't stadt en schoone buytens. Een kijk op Brussel en omgeving in de 18de eeuw / De la ville et ses plaisantes campagnes. Regard sur Bruxelles et ses environs au 18e siècle* (Fontes Bruxellae, IV) (Town Hall, Brussels, 2007–2008), Brussels, 2007.

Delen, *Geschiedenis Rubenshuis*, 1938
A.J.J. Delen, 'De geschiedenis van het huis van Rubens', *Het huis van P.P. Rubens. Periodisch Bulletin*, I, 1938, pp. 7–21.

Delen, *Rubens' huis*, 1933
A.J.J. Delen, *Het huis van Pieter Pauwel Rubens, Wat het was, wat het werd, wat het worden kan*, Brussels, 1933.

Delen, *Rubens' huis*, 1940
A.J.J. Delen, *Het huis van P.P. Rubens. De invloed van Rubens op de Vlaamsche Barokarchitectuur*, Diest, 1940.

Dempsey, *Prometheus Bound*, 1967
C. Dempsey, 'Euanthes Redivivus: Rubens's Prometheus Bound', *Journal of the Warburg and Courtauld Institutes*, XXX, 1967, pp. 420–425.

Denucé, *Konstkamers*, 1932
J. Denucé, *De Antwerpsche 'Konstkamers'. Inventarissen van de kunstverzamelingen te Antwerpen in de 16de en 17de eeuwen* (Bronnen voor de geschiedenis van de Vlaamsche Kunst, II), Antwerp, 1932.

Denucé, *Kunstuitvoer*, 1931
J. Denucé, *Kunstuitvoer in de 17e eeuw te Antwerpen. De firma Forchoudt* (Bronnen voor de geschiedenis van de Vlaamsche Kunst, I), Antwerp – Amsterdam, 1931.

Denucé, *Musson*, 1949
J. Denucé, *Na Peter Pauwel Rubens: documenten uit den kunsthandel te Antwerpen in de XVIIe eeuw van Matthijs Musson* (Bronnen voor de geschiedenis van de Vlaamsche Kunst, V), Antwerp – The Hague, 1949.

Derycke et al., *Mercator-Orteliushuis*, 2002
I. Derycke et al, 'Het Mercator-Orteliushuis te Antwerpen', *Brabom*, V, 2002, pp. 139–225.

Descamps, *Vie*, 1753–64
J.B. Descamps, *La vie des peintres flamands, allemands et hollandois, avec des portraits gravés en taille-douce, une indication de leurs principaux ouvrages, & des réflexions sur leurs différentes manieres*, I–IV, Paris, 1753–1764.

Devisscher – De Poorter, eds, *Jordaens*, 1993
H. Devisscher and N. De Poorter, eds, [Exh. Cat.] *Jacob Jordaens (1593–1678)* (Koninklijk Museum voor Schone Kunsten, Antwerp, 1993), I–II, Antwerp, 1993.

Devisscher – Vlieghe, *Youth of Christ (CRLB)*, 2014
H. Devisscher and H. Vlieghe, *The Life of Christ Before the Passion: The Youth of Christ* (Corpus Rubenianum Ludwig Burchard, V.1), I–II, London – Turnhout, 2014.

Devroe, *Rubens' huis*, 2008
A. Devroe, *Van Rubens' huis tot Rubenshuis, een bouwhistorische studie*, unpublished bachelor's thesis, Hogeschool Antwerpen (Hoger Instituut voor architectuurwetenschappen Henry van de Velde), I–II, Antwerp, 2007–2008.

Díaz Padrón, *Betsabé*, 2018
M. Díaz Padrón, 'El baño de Betsabé, Un lienzo de David Teniers II en el coleccionismo madrileño', *Tendencias del Mercado del Arte*, CX, 2018, pp. 86–88.

Díaz Padrón, *Cat. Madrid, Prado (Pintura flamenca)*, 1995
M. Díaz Padrón, *El Siglo de Rubens en el Museo del Prado: catálogo razonado de pintura flamenca del siglo XVII*, I–II, Barcelona – Madrid, 1995.

Diels, *Ombre de Rubens*, 2009
A. Diels, [Exh. Cat.] *'Uit de schaduw van Rubens': prentkunst naar Antwerpse historieschilders / 'Sortant de l'ombre de Rubens': gravures d'après des peintres d'histoire anversois* (Bibliothèque royale de Belgique, Brussels, 2009–2010), Brussels, 2009.

BIBLIOGRAPHY

Dionysius, *Opera*, ed. Reiske, 1774–77
Dionysius of Halicarnassus, *Opera*, ed. F. F. Reiske, I–VI, Leipzig, 1774–1777.

Docquier et al., *Mythologie*, 2016
G. Docquier et al., *La mythologie au fil de la collection Van Herck / Mythologie in de collectie Van Herck*, Brussels, 2016.

De Dominico, *Vite*, 1742
B. de Dominico, *Vite de' pittori, scultori ed architetti Napoletani [...]*, III, Naples, 1742.

Douxchamps et al., *Rubens*, 1977
H. Douxchamps et al., *Rubens et ses descendants*, I, Brussels, 1977.

Van Driessche, *Herschepping*, 2009
T. Van Driessche, *De herschepping van Rubens' huis. Over de restauratie van het Rubenshuis door Emiel van Averbeke (1939–1946)*, unedited research report, Brussels, 2009.

Van Driessche, *Herschepping*, 2013
T. Van Driessche, '"Teneinde de historische werkelijkheid op een zo volmaakt mogelijke wijze te benaderen". Emiel van Averbeke en de "herschepping" van het Rubenshuis', *M & L, Monumenten, Landschappen en Archeologie*, XXXII.2, 2013, pp. 12–43.

Van Driessche, *Herschepping*, 2019
T. Van Driessche, 'De 'Herschepping' van het Rubenshuis in 1937–1946 en de eerste restauratie van de portiek en het paviljoen', *M & L, Monumenten, Landschappen en Archeologie*, XXXVIII.4, 2019, pp. 34–38.

Du Choul, *Discours*, 1581
G. Du Choul, *Discours de la Religion des Anciens Romains. De la Castrametation & discipline militaire d'iceux. Des Bains & Antiques exercitations Greques & Romaines*, Lyon, 1581.

Dubois, *Grands tableaux de Rubens*, 2007
H. Dubois, '"Come s'usa di fare non volendo ingannarsi": l'exécution des grands tableaux d'autel sur toile dans l'atelier de Rubens', in J. Vander Auwera and S. van Sprang, eds, [Exh. Cat.] *Rubens: A Genius at Work. The Works of Peter Paul Rubens in the Royal Museums of Fine Arts of Belgium Reconsidered / Rubens: l'atelier du génie. Autour des oeuvres du maître aux Musées royaux des Beaux-Arts de Belgique / Rubens: een genie aan het werk. Rondom de Rubenswerken in de Koninklijke Musea voor Schone Kunsten van België* (Musées royaux des Beaux-Arts de Belgique, Brussels, 2007–2008), Tielt, 2007, pp. 160–162.

Dudok van Heel, *Het Schilderhuis*, 1982
S.A.C. Dudok van Heel, 'Het "Schilderhuis" van Govert Flinck en de Kunsthandel van Uylenburgh aan de Lauriergracht te Amsterdam', *Jaarboek Amstelodamum*, L74, 1982, pp. 70–90.

Duverger, *Decius Mus*, 1976–78
J. Duverger, 'Aantekeningen betreffende de patronen van P.P. Rubens en de tapijten met de Geschiedenis van Decius Mus', *Gentse bijdragen tot de kunstgeschiedenis*, XXIV, 1976–1978, pp. 15–42.

Duverger, *Getuigschrift*, 1977
E. Duverger, 'Het Getuigschrift van Rubens voor Lucas Faydherbe', *Jaarboek Koninklijk Museum voor Schone Kunsten Antwerpen*, 1977, pp. 259–279.

Duverger, *Kunstinventarissen*, 1984–2009
E. Duverger, *Antwerpse kunstinventarissen uit de zeventiende eeuw* (Fontes Historiae Artis Neerlandicae. Bronnen voor de kunstgeschiedenis van de Nederlanden, I), I–XIV, Brussels, 1984–2009.

Duverger, *Musson*, 1968
E. Duverger, 'Nieuwe gegevens betreffende de kunsthandel van Matthijs Musson en Maria Fourmenois te Antwerpen tussen 1633 en 1681', *Gentse bijdragen tot de kunstgeschiedenis en de oudheidkunde*, XXI, 1968, pp. 5–273.

Duverger, *Panneels*, 1993
E. Duverger, 'Enige biografische gegevens over Willem Panneels / Some biographical details about Willem Panneels', in P. Huvenne and I. Kockelbergh, eds, [Exh. Cat.] *Rubens Cantoor. Een verzameling tekeningen ontstaan in Rubens' atelier* (Rubenshuis, Antwerp, 1993), Ghent, 1993, pp. 38–46.

Duverger, *Waeyens*, 1989
E. Duverger, 'Inventaris van het sterfhuis van Elizabeth Waeyens († 1657), weduwe van Hans van Mildert', *Jaarboek Koninklijk Museum voor Schone Kunsten Antwerpen*, 1989, pp. 387–414.

Duverger – Maufort, *Decius Mus*, 1996
E. Duverger and D. Maufort, 'Giovanni Battista van Eycke en de patronen met de Historie van Decius Mus van Antoon van Dyck naar inventies van Peter Paul Rubens', *Gentse Bijdragen tot de Kunstgeschiedenis en Oudheidkunde*, XXXI, 1996, pp. 97–119.

Ebert-Schifferer et al., *Trompe l'Oeil*, 2002
S. Ebert-Schifferer et al., [Exh. Cat.] *Deceptions and Illusions, Five Centuries of Trompe l'Oeil Painting* (National Gallery of Art, Washington, 2002–2003), Washington, 2002.

Van Eck, *Jezuïeten*, 1998
X. van Eck, 'De Jezuïeten en het wervende wisselaltaarstuk', *De zeventiende eeuw: cultuur in de Nederlanden in interdisciplinair perspectief*, XIV, 1, 1998, pp. 81–94.

Van Eck, *Medusa*, 2016
C. van Eck, 'The Petrifying Gaze of Medusa: Ambivalence, *Explesis*, and the Sublime', *Journal of Historians of Netherlandish Art (JHNA)*, VIII.2, 2016, pp. 1–22. URL: https://jhna.org/articles/petrifying-gaze-medusa-ambivalence-explexis-sublime/

Van Eeghen, *Rubens en Rembrandt*, 1977
I.H. van Eeghen, 'Rubens en Rembrandt kopen van de familie Thijs', *Amstelodamum. Maandblad voor de kennis van Amsterdam, orgaan van het genootschap Amstelodamum*, LXIV, 1977, pp. 59–62.

Van Eikema Hommes, *Painters' Methods*, 1998
M. van Eikema Hommes, 'Painters' Methods to Prevent Colour Changes Described in Sixteenth to Early Eighteenth Century Sources on Oil Painting Techniques', in E. Hermens et al., eds, 'Looking through Paintings', *Leids Kunsthistorisch Jaarboek*, XI, 1998, pp. 91–131.

Van Eikema Hommes – Kolfin, *Oranjezaal*, 2013
M. van Eikema Hommes and E. Kolfin, *De Oranjezaal in Huis ten Bosch. Een zaal uit loutere liefde*, Zwolle, 2013.

Erftemeijer, *Kunstenaarsanekdotes*, 2000
A. Erftemeijer, *De aap van Rembrandt: Kunstenaarsanekdotes van de klassieke oudheid tot heden*, Haarlem, 2000.

Esposito, *Antique Shields*, 2018
T. Esposito, 'Ignis artificiosus: Images of God and the Universe in Rubens's Depiction of Antique Shields', *Early Modern Low Countries*, II, 2, 2018, pp. 244–277.

Esposito, *Occult Knowlegde*, 2016
T. Esposito, 'Occult Knowledge and Sacred Geometry. A New Interpretation of a Portrait of Rubens and his Son from the Hermitage Museum', *De Zeventiende Eeuw. Cultuur in*

de Nederlanden in interdisciplinair perspectief, XXXII.2, 2016, pp. 211–234.

Esposito, *Portret van Rubens,* **2010**
T. Esposito, *Het portret van Rubens met zijn zoon Albert voor een beeld van "Hecate Triformis"*, unpublished master's thesis, K.U.Leuven, Leuven, 2009–2010.

Evers, *Neue Forschungen,* **1943**
H.G. Evers, *Rubens und sein Werk. Neue Forschungen* (Arbeiten und Forschungen des Deutschen Instituts in Brüssel, I), Brussels, 1943.

Evers, *Perseus und Andromeda,* **1941–42**
H.G. Evers, 'Perseus und Andromeda von Rubens', in *Das Werk des Künstlers*, II, Berlin, 1941–1942, pp. 200–218.

Evers, *Rubens,* **1942**
H.G. Evers, *Peter Paul Rubens*, Munich, 1942.

Fabri – Lombaerde, *Jesuit Church (CRLB),* **2018**
R. Fabri and P. Lombaerde, *Rubens, The Jesuit Church of Antwerp* (Corpus Rubenianum Ludwig Burchard, XXII, 3), Turnhout, 2018.

Falck, *Rubenselevs Tegninger,* **1918**
G. Falck, 'En Rubenselevs Tegninger, *Kunstmuseets Aarsskrift*, 1918, pp. 64–77.

Fermor, *Raphael Cartoons,* **1996**
S. Fermor, *The Raphael Tapestry Cartoons: Narrative, Decoration, Design*, London, 1996.

Feuchtmayr – Schädler, *Petel,* **1973**
K. Feuchtmayr and A. Schädler, *Georg Petel, 1601/2–1634*, Berlin, 1973.

Filippi, *Van Heemskerck,* **1990**
E. Filippi, *Maarten van Heemskerck, Inventio Urbis*, Milan, 1990.

Van Fornenbergh, *Protheus,* **1658**
[A. van Fornenbergh], *Den Antwerpschen Protheus ofte Cyclopschen Apelles, dat is; Het leven, ende Konst-rijcke Daden des Uyt-nemenden, ende Hoogh-beroemden mr. Quinten Matsys [...]*, Antwerp, 1658.

Forssman, *Säulenordnungen,* **1984**
E. Forssman, *Dorisch, Jonisch, Korintisch, Studien über den Gebrauch der Säulenordnungen in der Architektur des 16.–18. Jahrhunderts*, Stockholm, 1961 (reprint Braunschweig – Wiesbaden, 1984).

Foucart, *Cat. Paris, Louvre,* **2009**
J. Foucart, *Catalogue des peintures flamandes et hollandaises du Musée du Louvre*, Paris, 2009.

Foucart, *Nouveau Rubens,* **1977**
J. Foucart, 'Un nouveau Rubens au Louvre: « Hélène Fourment au carrosse »', *La Revue du Louvre et des Musées de France*, V–VI, 1977, pp. 343–347.

Fransolet, *Du Quesnoy,* **1942**
M. Fransolet, *François du Quesnoy, sculpteur d'Urbain VIII, 1597–1643*, Brussels, 1942.

Fredlund, *Arkitektur,* **1974**
B. Fredlund, *Arkitektur i Rubens Måleri. Form och funktion* (With an English summary), Göteborg, 1974.

Freedberg, *Christ after the Passion (CRLB),* **1984**
D. Freedberg, *The Life of Christ after the Passion* (Corpus Rubenianum Ludwig Burchard, VII), London – Oxford, 1984.

Freedberg, *Fornenbergh and Gerbier,* **1983**
D. Freedberg, 'Fame, Convention and Insight: On the Relevance of Fornenbergh and Gerbier', *The Ringling Museum of Art Journal*, I, 1983, pp. 236–259.

Fremantle, *Town Hall of Amsterdam,* **1959**
K. Fremantle, *The Baroque Town Hall of Amsterdam*, Utrecht, 1959.

Fremantle – Halsema-Kubes, *Beelden kijken,* **1977**
K. Fremantle and W. Halsema-Kubes, [Exh. Cat.] *Beelden kijken, de kunst van Quellien in het paleis op de Dam / Focus on Sculpture, Quellien's Art in the Palace on the Dam* (Royal Palace, Amsterdam, 1977), Amsterdam, 1977.

Fuhring, *Rubens' zilveren sierstel,* **2001**
P. Fuhring, *Theodoor I Rogiers: Met glans verworven, Rubens' zilveren sierstel, Gift van Pierre en Colette Bauchau*, Brussels, 2001.

Gabriëls, *Erasmus Quellien I,* **1925**
J. Gabriels, 'De "antycksnyder" Erasmus Quellien I', *Vlaamsche Arbeid*, XV, 1925, pp. 326–331.

Gabriëls, *Quellien,* **1930**
J. Gabriëls, *Artus Quellien, de oude "Kunstryck belthouwer"*, Antwerp, 1930.

Gage, *Color,* **1993**
J. Gage, *Color and Culture: Practice and Meaning from Antiquity to Abstraction*, Berkeley, CA – Los Angeles, CA – London, 1993.

Garff – de la Fuente Pedersen, *Panneels,* **1988**
J. Garff and E. de la Fuente Pedersen, *Rubens Cantoor. The Drawings of Willem Panneels*, I–II, Copenhagen, 1988.

Gelderblom, *Kooplieden,* **2000**
O. Gelderblom, *Zuid-Nederlandse kooplieden en de opkomst van de Amsterdamse stapelmarkt (1578–1630)*, Hilversum, 2000.

Génard, *Intrede,* **1869–76**
P. Génard, 'Intrede van den Prins-Kardinaal Ferdinand van Spanje te Antwerpen, op 17 April 1635', *Antwerpsch Archievenblad*, VI, 1869, pp. 400–472; VII, 1870, pp. 1–113; XIII, 1876, pp. 215–345.

Génard, *Nalatenschap,* **1865**
[P. Génard], 'De nalatenschap van P.P. Rubens / La succesion de P.P. Rubens', *Antwerpsch Archievenblad*, II, 1865, pp. 69–179.

Génard, *Rubens,* **1877**
P. Génard, *P.P. Rubens, Aanteekeningen over den grooten meester en zijne bloedverwanten*, Antwerp, 1877.

Génard et al., *Inscriptions funéraires,* **1856–1903**
P. Génard et al., *Inscriptions funéraires et monumentales de la Province d'Anvers / Verzameling der Graf- en Gedenkschriften van de Provincie Antwerpen*, I–XI, Antwerp, 1856–1903.

Gevartius, *Pompa Introitus,* **1642**
C. Gevartius, *Pompa Introitus honori Serenissimi Principis Ferdinandi Austriaci Hispaniarum Infantis … a S.P.Q. Antverp. decreta et adornata …*, Antwerp, 1641 [1642].

Van Ginhoven, *Forchondt,* **2011**
S. van Ginhoven, 'Exports of Flemish Imagery to the New World: Guilliam Forchondt and his Commercial Network in the Iberian Peninsula and New Spain, 1644–1678', *Jaarboek Koninklijk Museum voor Schone Kunsten Antwerpen*, 2011, pp. 119–144.

Goeree, *Teyken-Konst,* **1705**
W. Goeree, *Inleydinge tot de algemeene Teyken-Konst; waar in de gronden en eygenschappen, die tot onfeylbaar en verstandig begryp van de Teyken-Konst noodig te weten zyn [...]*, Amsterdam, 1705 (4th edn).

Van Goethem, *Fotografie en Realisme,* **1999**
H. Van Goethem, *Fotografie en realisme in de 19de eeuw, Antwerpen: de oudste foto's, 1847–1880*, Antwerp, 1999.

Golnitzius, *Ulysses,* **1631**
A. Golnitzius, *Ulysses Belgico-Gallicus*, Leiden, 1631.

BIBLIOGRAPHY

Gombrich, *Art and Illusion*, 1977
E.H. Gombrich, *Art and Illusion, a Study in the Psychology of Pictorial Representation*, London, 1977.

Goodman, *Garden of Love*, 1992
E. Goodman, *The Garden of Love as Conversatie à la Mode*, Amsterdam – Philadelphia, PA, 1992.

Goossens, *Amsterdamse stadhuis*, 1996
E.-J. Goossens, *Schat van beitel en penseel. Het Amsterdamse stadhuis uit de gouden eeuw*, Amsterdam – Zwolle, 1996.

Gordon, *Whitehall*, 1975
D.J. Gordon, 'Rubens and the Whitehall Ceiling', in S. Orgel, ed., *The Renaissance Imagination*, Berkeley, CA – London, 1975, pp. 24–50.

Goris, *Lof van Antwerpen*, 1940
J.-A. Goris, *Lof van Antwerpen. Hoe reizigers Antwerpen zagen, van de XVe tot de XXe Eeuw*, Brussels, 1940.

Grimal, *Mythologie grecque et romaine*, 1988
P. Grimal, *Dictionnaire de la mythologie grecque et romaine*, Paris, 1988 (9th edn).

Van Grimbergen, *Rubens*, 1840
V.C. Van Grimbergen, *Historische Levensbeschryving van P.P. Rubens. Ridder, Heer van Steen enz. Benevens eene naeuwkeurige opgave zyner schilderyen, berustende in hoven, kerken en verdere openbaere gebouwen van Europa, met aenwyzing welke van de zelve in het koper zyn gebracht*, Rotterdam, 1840.

Grimmett, *Drunken Hercules*, 2020
K. Grimmett, 'Stumbling along the Virtuous Path with Rubens's *Drunken Hercules*', *Jaarboek De Zeventiende Eeuw*, 2020, pp. 41–66.

Gritsay, *Rubens and his Workshop*, 2011
N. Gritsay, 'Rubens and his Workshop' in [Exh. Cat.] *Rubens, Van Dyck & Jordaens: Flemish Painters from the Hermitage* (Hermitage Amsterdam, 2011–2012), Amsterdam, 2011, pp. 23–59.

Gritsay – Babina, *Cat. St Petersburg, Hermitage (Flemish Painting)*, 2008
N. Gritsay and N. Babina, *State Hermitage Museum Catalogue. Seventeenth- and Eighteenth-Century Flemish Painting*, New Haven, CT – London, 2008.

Gruber, *Medusenhaupt*, 2018
G. Gruber, 'Albtraumhaft Schön: Rubens' Wiener Medusenhaupt trifft auf die Brünner Fassung', in G. Gruber and P. Tomášek, [Exh. Cat.] *Albtraumhaft Schön: Rubens' Wiener Medusenhaupt trifft auf die Brünner Fassung* (Kunsthistorisches Museum, Vienna, 2018–19), Vienna, 2018, pp. 10–19.

Gruber – Tomášek, *Medusa*, 2018
G. Gruber and P. Tomášek, [Exh. Cat.] *Albtraumhaft Schön: Rubens' Wiener Medusenhaupt trifft auf die Brünner Fassung* (Kunsthistorisches Museum, Vienna, 2018–19), Vienna, 2018. URL: https://www.khm.at/fileadmin/user_upload/Ansichtssachen23.pdf

De Gruyter, *Lichtinval*, 2012
S. de Gruyter, *Studierapport: lichtinval in Rubens' leerlingenatelier en museum*, unpublished research paper, University of Antwerp, Faculty of Design Sciences, Antwerp, 2012.

Hairs, *Sillage*, 1977
M.-L. Hairs, *Dans le sillage de Rubens*, Liège, 1977.

Hart – Hicks, *Serlio*, 1996
V. Hart and P. Hicks, *Sebastiano Serlio on Architecture*, I, Books I–V, New Haven, CT – London, 1996.

Härting, *Cavendish*, 2002
U. Härting, 'Lord William Cavendish und Duchess Margaret Cavendish im Rubensgarten in Antwerpen', *Jahrbuch der Berliner Museen*, XLIV, 2002, pp. 15–28.

Härting, *Entertainment*, 2006
U. Härting, "A Small Entertainment" für König Karl II im Rubenshaus', in K. van der Stighelen, ed., *Munuscula Amicorum. Contributions on Rubens and his Colleagues in Honour of Hans Vlieghe* (Pictura Nova: Studies in 16th- and 17th-Century Flemish Painting and Drawing, X), Turnhout, 2006, I, pp. 331–339.

Härting, *Francken*, 1983
U. Härting, *Studien zur Kabinettbildmalerei des Frans II Francken (1581–1642). Ein repräsentativer Werkkatalog* (Studien zur Kunstgeschichte, XXI), Hildesheim – Zürich – New York, 1983.

Härting, *Prestige and Magnificenza*, 2004
U. Härting, 'Prestige and Magnificenza – On the Function and Purpose of Painted Gardens in 16th and 17th-Century Belgium Illustrated by the Example of the Rubens Garden' / 'Prestige und Magnificenza – Zu Funktion und Zweck gemalter Gärten in Belgien im 16. und 17. Jahrhundert am Beispiel des Rubensgartens', in M. Rohde and R. Schomann, eds, *Historic Gardens Today*, Leipzig, 2004, pp. 120–125.

Härting, *Rubens' Garten*, 2000
U. Härting, 'Rubens' Garten in Antwerpen', in U. Härting, ed., [Exh. Cat.] *Gärten und Höfe der Rubenszeit im Spiegel der Malerfamilie Breughel und der Künstler um Peter Paul Rubens* (Gustav-Lübcke-Museum, Hamm; Landesmuseum, Mainz, 2000–2001), Munich, 2000, pp. 59–66.

Hartt, *Giulio Romano*, 1958
F. Hartt, *Giulio Romano*, I–II, New Haven, CT, 1958 (reissued 1981).

Haskell – Penny, *Antique*, 1982
F. Haskell and N. Penny, *Taste and the Antique. The Lure of Classical Sculpture, 1500–1900*, 2nd ed., New Haven, CT – London, 1982.

Hautecoeur, *Architecture classique*, 1967
L. Hautecoeur, *Histoire de l'architecure classique en France*, I–II, 1967.

Haverkamp Begemann, *Achilles (CRLB)*, 1975
E. Haverkamp Begemann, *The Achilles Series* (Corpus Rubenianum Ludwig Burchard, X), Brussels – New York – London, 1975.

Hayen – De Clercq, *Rubenshuis / Tuinpaviljoen*, 2010
R. Hayen and H. De Clercq, *Antwerpen, Rubenshuis, Tuinpaviljoen, Bouwtechnisch en bouwhistorisch onderzoek [...]*, Appendix 3, unpublished report, Rubenshuis, Antwerp, 2010.

Healy, *Judgement of Paris*, 1997
F. Healy, *Rubens and the Judgement of Paris. A Question of Choice* (Pictura Nova: Studies in 16th- and 17th- Century Flemish Painting and Drawing, III), Turnhout, 1997.

Healy, *Vive l'Esprit*, 2006
F. Healy, 'Vive l'Esprit. Sculpture as the Bearer of Meaning in Willem van Haecht's Art Cabinet of Cornelis van der Geest', in K. Van der Stighelen, ed., *Munuscula Amicorum. Contributions on Rubens and his Colleagues in Honour of Hans Vlieghe* (Pictura Nova: Studies in 16th- and 17th- Century Flemish Painting and Drawing, X), Turnhout, 2006, II, pp. 423–441.

Hecht, *Onbekende voorbeeld*, 1999
P. Hecht, 'Het onbekende voorbeeld. Op zoek naar de antieke schilderkunst', *Kunstschrift*, V, 1999, pp. 8–21.

Hedley, *Van Dyck*, 1999
  J. Hedley, *Van Dyck at the Wallace Collection*, London, 1999.
De Heer et al., *Cat. The Netherlands Office for Fine Arts The Hague*, 1992
  E. de Heer et al., *Rijksdienst beeldende kunst, The Netherlands Office for Fine Arts The Hague. Old Master Paintings, an Illustrated Summary Catalogue*, Zwolle, 1992.
Heijnen, *Familie Thys(ius)*, 1984
  W.M.M. Heijnen, 'De familie Thys(ius) alias Keynooge te Amsterdam en Leiden', *Handelingen van de Koninklijke Kring voor Oudheidkunde, Letteren en Kunst van Mechelen*, LXXXVIII, 1984 (1985), pp. 111–116.
Heinen, *Auctores*, 2009
  U. Heinen, '"Auctores generis Venerem Martemque fatemur": Peter Paul Rubens' Konzepte von Erotik und Gewalt', *Simpliciana*, XXXI, 2009, pp. 27–74.
Heinen, *Garten*, 2002
  U. Heinen, 'Rubens' lipsianischer Garten', in U. Härting and E. Schwinzer, eds, *Gärten und Höfe der Rubenszeit. Internationales Symposium im Gustav-Lübcke-Museum der Stadt Hamm, 12.–14.1. 2001*, Worms, 2002, pp. 1–8.
Heinen, *Gesundheit*, 2004
  U. Heinen, 'Rubens' Garten und die Gesundheit des Künstlers', *Wallraf-Richartz-Jahrbuch*, LXV, 2004, pp. 71–182.
Heinen, *Immolatio boum*, 2010
  U. Heinen, 'Immolatio boum: Eine unpublizierte Zeichnung für ein Scheinrelief an Rubens' haus', *Wallraf–Richartz–Jahrbuch*, LXXI, 2010, pp. 197–232.
Heinen, *Medusa*, 2010
  U. Heinen, 'Huyghens, Rubens and Medusa: Reflecting the Passions in Paintings, with some Considerations of Neuroscience in Art History', *Nederlands Kunsthistorisch Jaarboek*, LX, 2010, pp. 151–178.
Heinen, *Text- und Bild-Formen*, 2008
  U. Heinen, 'Text- und Bild-Formen neostoischen Wissens von den Leidenschaften', in W. Oechslin, ed., *Wissensformen*, Zürich, 2008, pp. 194–219.
Heinen, *Versatissimus*, 2002
  U. Heinen, '"Versatissimus in historiis et re politica": Rubens' Anfänge als Diplomat', *Wallraf-Richartz-Jahrbuch*, LXIII, 2002, pp. 283–318.
Heirman – Staes, *Stadhuis van Leuven*, 1997
  M. Heirman and J. Staes, *Het Stadhuis van Leuven*, Tielt, 1997.
Held, *Artis Pictoriae Amator*, 1957
  J.S. Held, '*Artis Pictoriae Amator*. An Antwerp Art Patron and His Collection', *Gazette des Beaux-Arts*, XCIX, 1957, pp. 53–84.
Held, *Drawings*, 1959
  J.S. Held, *Rubens, Selected Drawings, with an Introduction and a Critical Catalogue*, I–II, London, 1959.
Held, *Drawings*, 1986
  J.S. Held, *Rubens, Selected Drawings, with an Introduction and a Critical Catalogue*, rev. ed., Oxford – Mount Kisco, NY, 1986.
Held, *Drawings Unknown*, 1974
  J.S. Held, 'Some Rubens Drawings – Unknown or Neglected', *Master Drawings*, XII, 1974, pp. 249–260.
Held, *Review Garff – de la Fuente Pedersen*, 1991
  J.S. Held, [Review] 'J. Garff and E. de la Fuente Pedersen, *Rubens Cantoor: The Drawings of Willem Panneels* (Copenhagen,1988)', *Master Drawings*, XXIX, 1991, pp. 416–430.

Held, *Rubens*, 1982
  Rubens and his Circle. Studies by Julius S. Held, eds. A.W. Lowenthal et al., Princeton, NJ, 1982.
Held, *Sketches*, 1980
  J.S. Held, *The Oil Sketches of Peter Paul Rubens. A Critical Catalogue* (National Gallery of Art, Kress Foundation Studies in the History of Art, 7), I–II, Princeton, NJ, 1980.
Helmstutler Di Dio, *Leoni*, 2011
  K. Helmstutler Di Dio, *Leone Lioni and the Status of the Artist at the End of the Renaissance*, Farnham, 2011.
Hemelaers – de Bie, *Numismata aurea*, 1615
  J. Hemelaers and J. de Bie, *Imperatorum Romanorum Numismata Aurea a Julio Caesare ad Heraclium usque numismata aurea excellentissimi nuper dum viveret Caroli ducis Croyi et Arschotani & magno & sumptuoso studio collecta / nec minore fide atque arte Iacobi de Bye ex archetypis in aes incisa. Opera autem atque industria Ioannis Hemelarii*, Antwerp, 1615.
Henkel – Schöne, *Emblemata*, 1967–76
  A. Henkel and A. Schöne, *Emblemata. Handbuch zur Sinnbildkunst des XVI. und XVII. Jahrhundert*, I–II, Stuttgart, 1967–1976.
Henrard, *Marie de Médicis*, 1876
  P. Henrard, 'Maria de Médicis dans les Pays-Bas, 1631–1638', *Annales de l'Académie d'Archéologie de Belgique*, XXXI, 3me série, I, 1876.
Herremans, *Architectural Sculpture (CRLB)*, 2019
  V. Herremans, *Architectural Sculpture* (*Corpus Rubenianum Ludwig Burchard*, XXII, 4), Turnhout, 2019.
Herremans, *Rubens Unveiled*, 2013
  V. Herremans, *Rubens doorgelicht. Schilderijen uit verdwenen Antwerpse kerken / Rubens Unveiled. Paintings from Lost Antwerp Churches*, Antwerp, 2013.
Herremans et al., *Heads on Shoulders*, 2008
  V. Herremans et al., [Exh. Cat] *Heads on Shoulders. Portrait Busts in the Low Countries, 1600–1800 / Voorbeeldige Busten. Het borstbeeld in de Nederlanden, 1600–1800* (Koninklijk Museum voor Schone Kunsten Antwerpen, Antwerp, 2008), Ghent, 2008.
Van Heurck, *Harrewijn*, 1920
  E. Van Heurck, *Les Harrewijn: Jacques, Jacques-Gérard, François, Jean-Baptiste et leurs descendants*, Antwerp, 1920.
Heydenreich – Lotz, *Architecture*, 1974
  L. H. Heydenreich and W. Lotz, *Architecture in Italy, 1400 to 1600* (The Pelican History of Art), Harmondsworth, 1974.
Hill – Bracken, *Carleton*, 2014
  R. Hill and S. Bracken, 'Sir Dudley Carleton's Relationship with Peter Paul Rubens: Connoisseurship and Art Collecting at the Court of the Early Stuarts', *Journal of the History of Collections*, XXVI, 2014, pp. 171–191.
Hind, *Cat. British Museum (Flemish Drawings)*, 1923
  A.M. Hind, *Catalogue of Drawings by Dutch and Flemish Artists preserved in the Department of Prints and Drawings in the British Museum, II: Drawings by Rubens, Van Dyck and other artists of the Flemish School of the XVII Century*, London, 1923.
Hollstein et al., *Dutch and Flemish*, 1949–2010
  F.W.H. Hollstein et al., *Dutch and Flemish Etchings, Engravings and Woodcuts, ca. 1450–1700*, I–LXXII, Amsterdam, 1949–2010.
Horst, *Metafoor*, 2006
  D.R. Horst, 'De Metafoor als cliché. Het beeld van Willem van Oranje in propagandaprenten uit de eerste decennia van de Nederlandse Opstand', in J.de Kruif et al., eds, *Het lange*

leven van het pamflet. Boekhistorische, iconografische, literaire en politieke aspecten van pamfletten 1600–1900, Hilversum, 2006, pp. 192–201.

Houbraken, *Konstschilders*, 1718–21
A. Houbraken, *De Groote Schouburgh der Nederlantsche Konstschilders en schilderessen*, I–III, Amsterdam, 1718–1721.

Van Hout, *Dead colour*, 2010
N. Van Hout, 'On Dead Colour', *Jaarboek van het Koninklijk Museum voor Schone Kunsten Antwerpen*, 2008 (2010), pp. 1–191.

Hoven, *De Constantia*, 1997
R. Hoven, 'De Constantia', in [Exh. Cat.] *Justus Lipsius (1547–1606) en het Plantijnse Huis* (Museum Plantin-Moretus, Antwerp, 1997–1998), Antwerp, 1997, pp. 75–81.

Howard, *Jacopo Sansovino*, 1975
D. Howard, *Jacopo Sansovino, Architecture and Patronage in Renaissance Venice*, New Haven, CT – London, 1975.

Huemer, *Portraits* (*CRLB*), 1977
F. Huemer, *Portraits Painted in Foreign Countries* (*Corpus Rubenianum Ludwig Burchard*, XIX.1), Brussels – London, 1977.

Huet, *La mise à mort*, 2005
V. Huet, 'La mise à mort sacrificielle sur les reliefs romains: une image banalisée et ritualisée de la violence ?', in J.-M. Bertrand, ed., *La Violence dans les mondes Grec et Romain* (*Histoire ancienne et médiévale*, LXXX), Paris, 2005, pp. 91–119.

Huisken et al., eds, *Van Campen*, 1995
J. Huisken et al. eds, *Jacob van Campen, Het klassieke ideaal in de Gouden Eeuw*, Amsterdam, 1995.

d'Hulst, *Jordaens*, 1974
R.-A. d'Hulst, *Jordaens Drawings*, I–IV, Brussels, 1974.

d'Hulst, *Jordaens*, 1982
R.-A. d'Hulst, *Jacob Jordaens*, Antwerp, 1982.

d'Hulst, *Supplement I*, 1980
R.-A. d'Hulst, 'Jordaens Drawings: Supplement I', *Master Drawings*, XVIII, 1980, pp. 360–370.

d'Hulst – Vandenven, *Old Testament* (*CRLB*), 1989
R.-A. d'Hulst and M. Vandenven, *Rubens. The Old Testament* (*Corpus Rubenianum Ludwig Burchard*, III), London – Oxford – New York, 1989.

d'Hulst et al., *Kruisoprichting*, 1992
R. d'Hulst et al., *De Kruisoprichting van Peter Paul Rubens*, Brussels, 1992.

Hüttinger, ed., *Künstlerhaüser*, 1985
E. Hüttinger, ed., *Künstlerhäuser von der Renaissance bis zur Gegenwart*, Zürich, 1985.

Huvenne, *Rubens' Cantoor*, 1993
P. Huvenne, 'Over Rubens' Cantoor, Panneels en de Kopenhaagse Cantoor-tekeningen / On Rubens' *Cantoor*, Panneels and the Copenhagen *Cantoor* drawings' in P. Huvenne and I. Kockelbergh, eds, [Exh. Cat.] *Rubens Cantoor: een verzameling tekeningen ontstaan in Rubens' atelier* (Rubenshuis, Antwerp, 1993), Ghent, 1993, pp. 16–37.

Huvenne, *Rubenshuis*, 1988
P. Huvenne, 'Het Rubenshuis', *Openbaar Kunstbezit in Vlaanderen*, XVI.4, 1988, pp. 123–168.

Huvenne, *Tekeningen*, 1993
P. Huvenne, 'Tekeningen naar de decoratie van het Rubenshuis / Drawings after the decorations of the Rubens house', in P. Huvenne and I. Kockelbergh, eds, [Exh. Cat.] *Rubens Cantoor: een verzameling tekeningen ontstaan in Rubens' atelier* (Rubenshuis, Antwerp, 1993), Ghent, 1993, pp. 156–163.

Huvenne – Kockelbergh, eds, *Cantoor*, 1993
P. Huvenne and I. Kockelbergh, eds, [Exh. Cat.] *Rubens Cantoor: een verzameling tekeningen ontstaan in Rubens' atelier* [in Dutch and English] (Rubenshuis, Antwerp, 1993), Ghent, 1993.

Imhof, *Aankopen van Rubens*, 2004
D. Imhof, 'Aankopen van Peter Paul Rubens bij Balthasar I Moretus', in P. Delsaerdt, D. Imhof, M. De Schepper et al., eds, [Exh. Cat.] *Een hart voor boeken: Rubens en zijn bibliotheek / La passion des livres: Rubens et sa bibliothèque* (Museum Plantin-Moretus, Antwerp, 2004), Antwerp, 2004, pp. 22–26.

Jacobs, *Amstelkerk*, 1990
J.M.M. Jacobs, "Vitruvius moet wel geacht, maar niet alleen geloofd werden': De Amstelkerk en de architectuur van de 17de eeuw', *Jaarboek Monumentenzorg*, 1990, pp. 48–69.

Jacobs, *Vasari's Vision*, 1984
F.H. Jacobs, 'Vasari's Vision of the History of Painting: Frescoes in the Casa Vasari, Florence', *The Art Bulletin*, LXVI, 1984, pp. 399–416.

Jaffé, *Antwerp Sketchbook*, 1966
M. Jaffé, *Van Dyck's Antwerp Sketchbook*, I–II, London, 1966.

Jaffé, *Rubens and Italy*, 1977
Michael Jaffé, *Rubens and Italy*, Oxford, 1977.

Jaffé et al., *Rubens*, 2005
D. Jaffé, E. McGrath, M. Moore Ede et al., [Exh. Cat.] *Rubens: A Master in the Making* (The National Gallery, London, 2005–2006), London, 2005.

Jakumeit, *Review Rubens – Baroque Passions*, 2005
C. Jakumeit, [Review Symposium] 'Rubens – Baroque Passions (Herzog Anton Ulrichmuseum, Braunschweig, 4 October 2004)', *Kunstchronik*, LVIII, 2005, pp. 331–334.

Janse, *Trap en Trede*, 1995
H. Janse, *Trap en Trede, Houten trappen in Nederland, Een bouwhistorische beschouwing*, Zeist – The Hague, 1995.

Jansen, *Beeldhouwers*, 1940
A. Jansen, 'Documentatie over Antwerpsche Beeldhouwers, 2[de] deel', *Antwerpen's Oudheidkundige Kring*, XVI, 1940, pp. 112–139.

Jansen, *Bijdrage*, 1946
A. Jansen, 'Bijdrage tot de geschiedenis van de Antwerpsche barokbeeldhouwkunst', *Tijdschrift voor Geschiedenis en Folklore*, IX, 1946, pp. 5–63.

Jansen, *O.L.Vrouwkapel*, 1938
A. Jansen, 'De beelden van de O.L. Vrouwkapel in de St Caroluskerk te Antwerpen', *Antwerpen's Oudheidkundige Kring, Jaarboek*, XIV, 1938, pp. 50–58.

Jansen – Van Herck, *Van den Eynde*, 1945
A. Jansen and C. Van Herck, 'De Van den Eynde's, Antwerpsche Bouwmeesters en Beeldhouwers uit de XVIIe eeuw', *Koninklijke Oudheidkundige Kring van Antwerpen, Jaarboek*, XX–XXI, 1944–1945, pp. 5–90.

Jaumain – Balcers, *Bruxelles 1910*, 2010
S. Jaumain and W. Balcers, *Bruxelles 1910, De l'exposition universelle à l'Université*, Brussels, 2010.

Jehee, *Licht*, 2010
J. Jehee, *Tussen lucht en licht. De ontwikkeling van de vensters, kozijnen, ramen en luiken*, Zwolle, 2010.

Jeroense, *Flinck*, 1997
P. Jeroense, 'Govaert Flinck (1615–1660), Eine Künstlerbiografie', *Niederdeutsche Beiträge zur Kunstgeschichte*, 36, 1997, pp. 73–112.

Jonckheere, *Prototypes (CRLB)*, 2016
K. Jonckheere, *Portraits after Existing Prototypes (Corpus Rubenianum Ludwig Burchard*, XIX), London – Turnhout, 2016.

De Jonge, *Travée alternée*, 1986
K. De Jonge, *La travée alternée dans l'architecture italienne de la Renaissance, origines et développement*, unpublished doctoral disertation. K.U.Leuven, I–II, Leuven, 1986.

De Jonge – Ottenheym, eds, *Unity and Discontinuity*, 2007
K. De Jonge and K. Ottenheym, eds, *Unity and Discontinuity. Architectural Relations between the Southern and Northern Low Countries 1530–1700* (*Architectura Moderna*, V), Turnhout, 2007.

De Jongh, *Realisme en Schijnrealisme*, 1971
E. de Jongh, 'Realisme en schijnrealisme in de Hollandse schilderkunst van de zeventiende eeuw', in [Exh. Cat.] *Rembrandt en zijn Tijd*, Brussels, 1971, pp. 143–194.

Jordens, *Forchoudt*, 2010
K. Jordens, *Het management van een zeventiende eeuwse kunstfirma. Case study: de Firma Forchoudt*, unpublished master thesis, University of Ghent, Ghent, 2010.

Joseph – Schwilden, *Fierlants*, 1988
S. Joseph and T. Schwilden, *Edmond Fierlants 1819–1869, Photographies d'art et d'architecture*, Brussels, 1988.

Joyce, *Ancient Paintings*, 1992
H. Joyce, 'Grasping at Shadows: Ancient Paintings in Renaissance and Baroque Rome', *The Art Bulletin*, LXXIV, 1992, pp. 219–246.

Judson, *Passion (CRLB)*, 2000
J.R. Judson, *The Passion of Christ* (*Corpus Rubenianum Ludwig Burchard*, VI), Turnhout – London, 2000.

Judson – Van de Velde, *Title-pages (CRLB)*, 1978
J.R. Judson and C. Van de Velde, *Book Illustrations and Title-pages* (*Corpus Rubenianum Ludwig Burchard*, XXI), I–II, Brussels – London – Philadelphia, PA, 1978.

Junius, *De pictura*, 1637
F. Junius, *De pictura veterum libri tres*, Amsterdam, 1637.

Juntunen, *Mythologische Historien*, 2005
E. Juntunen, *Peter Paul Rubens' bildimplizite Kunsttheorie in ausgewählten mythologischen Historien (1611–1618)*, Petersberg, 2005.

Juvenal–Persius, *Juvenal–Persius*, ed. and trans. Ramsay, 1979
Juvenal and Persius, *Juvenal and Persius*, ed. and trans. G.G. Ramsay (*Loeb Classical Library*), Cambridge, MA – London, 1979.

Juvenal – Persius, *Juvenal – Persius*, trans. Morton Braund, 2004
Juvenal and Persius, *Juvenal and Persius*, ed. and trans. S. Morton Braund (*Loeb Classical Library*), Cambridge, MA, 2004.

Van Kalck, *Rubens and the Brussels Museum*, 2007
M. van Kalck, 'Rubens and the Brussels Museum Before 1880: A Question of Equilibrium Between National Sentiment and "Well-Meaning" Centralization', in J. Vander Auwera and S. van Sprang, eds, [Exh. Cat.] *Rubens: A Genius at Work. The Works of Peter Paul Rubens in the Royal Museums of Fine Arts of Belgium Reconsidered / Rubens: l'atelier du génie. Autour des œuvres du maître aux Musées royaux des Beaux-Arts de Belgique / Rubens: een genie aan het werk. Rondom de Rubenswerken in de Koninklijke Musea voor Schone Kunsten van België* (Musées royaux des Beaux-Arts de Belgique, Brussels, 2007–2008), Tielt, 2007, pp. 18–23.

Kelchtermans, *Portret*, 2019
L. Kelchtermans, *Portret van een jonge vrouw: Minzame dames op hun mooist in de zeventiende eeuw*, Antwerpen, 2019.

Kieser, *Antikes*, 1933
E. Kieser, 'Antikes im Werke des Rubens', *Münchner Jahrbuch der bildenden Kunst*, X, 1933, pp. 110–137.

King, *Artists' Houses*, 2002
C. King, 'Artists' Houses: Mass-Advertising, Artistic Status and Theory in Antwerp c. 1565', in M.-C. Heck et al., eds, *Théorie des arts et création artistique dans l'Europe du Nord du XVIe au début du XVIIIe siècle*, Lille, 2002, pp. 173–189.

Kitlitschka, *Rubens*, 1963
W. Kitlitschka, *Rubens und die Bildhauerei: die Einwirkung der Plastik auf sein Werk und Rubens' Auswirkung auf die Bildhauer des 17. Jahrhunderts* (doctoral dissertation, Universität Wien, 1963), I–II, Vienna, 1963.

Kitlitschka, *Van Mildert*, 1972
W. Kitlitschka, 'Hans van Milderts Stellung innerhalb der niederländischen Plastik des Frühbarock', in *Festschrift für Otto Demus und Otto Pächt* (*Wiener Jahrbuch für Kunstgeschichte*, XXV, 1972), pp. 222–230, figs 145–152.

Kleinert, *Atelierdarstellungen*, 2006
K. Kleinert, *Atelierdarstellungen in der niederländischen Genremalerei des 17. Jahrhunderts – realistischer Abbild oder glaubwürdiger Schein ?*, Petersberg, 2006.

Klinge – Lüdke, eds, *Teniers*, 2005
M. Klinge and D. Lüdke, eds, [Exh. Cat.] *David Teniers der Jüngere, 1610–1690: Alltag und Vergnügen in Flandern* (Staatliche Kunsthalle, Karlsruhe, 2005–2006), Karlsruhe, 2005.

Knaap – Putnam, eds, *Pompa Introitus*, 2013
A.C. Knaap and M.C.J. Putnam, eds, *Art, Music and Spectacle in the Age of Rubens, The Pompa Introitus Ferdinandi*, London, 2013.

Koeleman, *Art Gallery of Rubens*, 2015
F.A. Koeleman, 'Studying the Studio: the Art Gallery of Rubens Depicted ?', *Western European Art in the 17th and 19th Centuries. The Fate of the Classical Tradition: from Pattern to Interpretation*, 2015, pp. 647–654, 877. Published online: <URL: http://poporowapa.midasweb.nl/assets/pdf/koeleman-studying_the_studio.pdf

Koldewijn, *Wanden*, 1985
R.D. Koldewijn, [Exh. Cat.] *Wanden en plafonds, Tekeningen uit de verzameling Lodewijk Houthakker* (Nijmeegs Museum 'Commanderie van Sint-Jan', Nijmegen, 1985), Nijmegen, 1985.

Konrad, *Meisterwerke*, 1928–34
M. Konrad, *Meisterwerke der Skulptur in Flandern und Brabant*, I–X, Berlin, 1928–1934.

De Koomen, *Monsters*, 2003
A. de Koomen, 'Geketende natuur en ontketende verbeelding, Monsters en fabeldieren in de kunst van de renaissance', in J. de Hond, ed., *Monsters en Fabeldieren, 2500 geschiedenis van randgevallen*, Amsterdam – 's-Hertogenbosch, 2003, pp. 59–85.

Kräftner et al., *Rubens in Wien*, 2004
J. Kräftner et al., [Exh. Cat.] *Rubens in Wien: Die Meisterwerke / Rubens in Vienna: The Masterpieces* (Liechtenstein Museum; Kunsthistorisches Museum; Gemäldegalerie der Akademie für Bildende Künste, Vienna, 2004), Vienna, 2004.

Kraitrová, *Mantegna*, 1985
M. Kraitrová, 'Das Haus von Andrea Mantegna in Mantua und von Piero della Francesca in Sansepolcro', in E. Hüttinger,

BIBLIOGRAPHY

ed., *Künstlerhäuser von der Renaissance bis zur Gegenwart*, Zürich, 1985, pp. 51–56.

Krempel, *Petel*, 2007
L. Krempel, [Exh. Cat.] *Georg Petel. 1601/02–1634; Bildhauer im Dreißigjährigen Krieg* (Haus der Kunst, Munich, 2007), Munich, 2007.

Kris – Kurz, *Die Legende*, 1934
E. Kris and O. Kurz, *Die Legende vom Künstler, ein geschichtlicher Versuch*, Vienna, 1934.

Kris – Kurz, *Legend*, 1979
E. Kris and O. Kurz, *Legend, Myth and Magic in the Image of an Artist: a Historical Experiment*, New Haven, CT, 1979.

Laine – Magnusson, eds, *Tessin*, 2002
M. Laine and B. Magnusson, eds, *Travel notes 1673–77 and 1687–88 [a complete edition of Tessin's Travel journals]* (Nicodemus Tessin the Younger: Sources, Works, Collections, III), Stockholm, 2002.

Lammertse – Vergara, *Rubens Sketches*, 2018
F. Lammertse and A. Vergara, [Exh. Cat.] *Rubens. Painter of Sketches / Rubens. Schilder van schetsen* (Museo Nacional del Prado, Madrid, 2018; Museum Boijmans Van Beuningen, Rotterdam, 2018–2019), Madrid, 2018.

De Landtsheer, ed., *Iusti Lipsi Epistolae*, 1991–
J. De Landtsheer, ed., *Iusti Lipsi Epistolae*, Brussels, I–, Brussels, 1991– (ongoing).

Lange – Schnackenburg, eds, *Pan & Syrinx*, 2004
J. Lange and B. Schnackenburg, eds, [Exh. Cat.] *Pan & Syrinx: Eine erotische Jagd. Peter Paul Rubens, Jan Brueghel und ihre Zeitgenossen* (Gemäldegalerie Alte Meister, Museum Schloss Wilhelmshöhe, Staatliche Museen, Kassel; Städelsches Kunstinstitut, Frankfurt am Main, 2004), Kassel, 2004.

De Lattin, *Antwerpsche stadsbeeld*, 1940–1955
A. de Lattin, *Evoluties van het Antwerpsche stadsbeeld* (Geschiedkundige Kronijken, I–IX), Antwerp, 1940–1955.

Laubscher, *Arcus Novus und Arcus Claudii*, 1976
H.P. Laubscher, 'Arcus Novus und Arcus Claudii, zwei Triumphbögen an der Via Lata in Rom', *Nachrichten der Akademie der Wisschenschaften in Göttingen. Philologisch-Historische Klasse*, 1976, pp. 65–108.

Leeflang – Luijten, eds, *Goltzius*, 2003
H. Leeflang and G. Luijten, eds, [Exh. Cat.] *Hendrick Goltzius, Dutch Master (1558–1617). Drawings, Prints and Paintings / Hendrick Goltzius (1558–1617). Tekeningen, prenten en schilderijen* (Rijksmuseum, Amsterdam; Metropolitan Museum of Art, New York; Toledo Museum of Art, Toledo, OH, 2003–2004), Zwolle, 2003.

Lemerle, *Le bucrane*, 1996
F. Lemerle, 'Le bucrane dans la frise dorique à la Renaissance. Un motif Véronais', *Annali di architettura*, 1996, pp. 85–92.

Lemmens, *Atelier*, 1964
G.Th.M. Lemmens, 'De schilder in zijn atelier', in [Exh. Cat.] *Het schildersatelier in de Nederlanden, 1500–1800* (De Waag, Nijmegen, 1964), Nijmegen, 1964, pp. 6–26. Also published in [Exh. Cat.] *De schilder in zijn wereld, van Jan van Eyck tot Van Gogh en Ensor* (Stedelijk Museum Het Prinsenhof, Delft, 1964–1965; Koninklijk Museum voor Schone Kunsten Antwerpen, Antwerp, 1965), Delft – Antwerp, 1964, pp. 14–32.

Lennon, *Victimarii*, 2015
J.J. Lennon, '*Victimarii* in Roman Religion and Society', *Papers of the British School at Rome*, LXXXIII, 2015, pp. 65–89.

Levi, *Cat. Mantua (sculpture)*, 1931
A. Levi, *Sculture Greche e Romane del Palazzo Ducale di Mantova*, Rome, 1931.

Leyssens, *Apostelbeelden*, 1942
I. Leyssens, 'De Apostelbeelden in de St. Romboutskathedraal te Mechelen', *Gentsche Bijdragen tot de Kunstgeschiedenis*, VIII, 1942, pp. 49–64.

Leyssens, *Hercules*, 1948
I. Leyssens, 'Rond een Hercules van Lucas Fayd'Herbe', *Handelingen van de Kon. Kring voor Oudheidkunde, Letteren en Kunst van Mechelen*, LII, 1948, pp. 211–215.

Leyssens, *Van Mildert*, 1941
I. Leyssens, 'Hans van Mildert, 158?–1638', *Gentsche Bijdragen tot de Kunstgeschiedenis*, VII, 1941, pp. 73–136.

Libertus, *Faydherbe*, 1938
M. Libertus, *Lucas Faydherbe, Beeldhouwer en Bouwmeester, 1617–1697*, Antwerp, 1938.

Lind, *Rubens*, 1946
L.R. Lind, 'The Latin Life of Peter Paul Rubens by his Nephew Philip: A Translation', *The Art Quarterly*, IX, 1946, pp. 37–44.

Ling, *Roman Painting*, 1991
R. Ling, *Roman Painting*, Cambridge, 1991.

Lippold, *Antike Gemäldekopien*, 1951
G. Lippold, *Antike Gemäldekopien* (Abhandlungen der Bayerischen Akademie der Wissenschaften, philosophisch-historische Klasse, N.F., XXXIII), Munich, 1951.

Lipsius, *De Constantia*, 1584
J. Lipsius, *De Constantia libri duo, qui alloquium praecipue continent in publicis malis*, Antwerp, 1584.

Lisken-Pruss, *Gonzales Coques*, 2013
M. Lisken-Pruss, *Gonzales Coques (1614–1684), der kleine Van Dyck* (Pictura Nova: Studies in 16th- and 17th-Century Flemish Painting and Drawing, XIII, eds K. Van der Stighelen and H. Vlieghe), Turnhout, 2013.

Lodewyck et al., *Conservation of the Portico*, 2003
W. Lodewyck, N. Mandel and N. Bruneel, *Conservation of the Portico of the Rubenshuis*, integrated project work, KULeuven, Leuven, 2002–2003.

Logan, *Review Rubens*, 1991
A.-M. Logan, '[Review] H. Braham, 'Rubens. Paintings, Drawings, and Prints in the Princes Gate Collection (The Courtauld Gallery, 1988)', *Master Drawings*, XXIX, 1991, pp. 314–315.

Logan, *Rubens as a Teacher*, 2006
A.-M. Logan, 'Rubens as a Teacher: "He may teach his art to his students and others to his liking"', in A. Golahny et al., eds, *In His Milieu. Essays on Netherlandish Art in Memory of John Michael Montias*, Amsterdam, 2006, pp. 247–263.

Logan – Belkin, *Drawings, I*, 2021
A.-M. Logan and K. Belkin, *The Drawings of Peter Paul Rubens. A Critical Catalogue, Volume One (1590–1608)* (Pictura Nova: Studies in the 16th- and 17th- Century Flemish Paintings and Drawing, XXII, eds K. Van der Stighelen and H. Vlieghe), Turnhout, 2021.

Lombaerde, *Antwerp in its Golden Age*, 2001
P. Lombaerde, "Antwerp in its Golden Age: 'one of the largest cities in the Low Countries' and 'one of the best fortified in Europe'", in P. O'Brien et al., eds, *Urban Achievement in Early Modern Europe. Golden Ages in Antwerp, Amsterdam and London*, Cambridge, 2001, pp. 99–127.

Lombaerde, *Distribution*, 2002
P. Lombaerde, 'Distribution and Reception of Rubens's *Palazzi di Genova* in the Southern Netherlands: a Status Questionis', in P. Lombaerde, ed., *The Reception of P.P. Rubens's Palazzi di Genova During the 17th century in Europe: Questions and Problems* (*Architectura Moderna*, I), Turnhout, 2002, pp. 99–120.

Lombaerde, *Painter-Architect*, 2014
P. Lombaerde, 'Painter-Architect or Painter & Architect', in P. Lombaerde, ed., *The Notion of the Painter-Architect in Italy and the Southern Low Countries* (*Architectura Moderna*, XI), Turnhout, 2014, pp. ix–xxiv.

Lombaerde, *Rubens*, 2014
P. Lombaerde, 'Rubens, Architectural Space and Light', in P. Lombaerde, ed., *The Notion of the Painter-Architect in Italy and the Southern Low Countries* (*Architectura Moderna*, XI), Turnhout, 2014, pp. 201–222.

Lombaerde, *Rubens the Architect*, 2011
P. Lombaerde, 'Rubens the Architect', in P. Lombaerde, 'Rubens the Architect', in B. Uppenkamp and B. van Beneden, eds, [Exh. Cat.] *Palazzo Rubens: The Master as Architect / Palazzo Rubens: de meester als architect / Palazzo Rubens: le maître et l'architecture* (Rubenshuis, Antwerp, 2011), Antwerp, 2011, pp. 124–157.

Lombaerde, *Rubens / Vredeman de Vries*, 2018
P. Lombaerde, 'When Rubens Meets Vredeman de Vries: Caryatids, Herms and Terms in the Painted and Decorative Work of P.P. Rubens', in S. Frommel et al., eds, *Bauen mit dem menschlichen Körper. Anthropomorphe Stützen von der Antike bis zur Gegenwart / Construire avec le corps humain. Les ordres anthropomorphes et leurs avatars dans l'art européen de l'antiquité à la fin du XVIe siècle* (*Itinéraires = percorsi*, 4), 2018, II, pp. 117–127.

Lombaerde, *Significance*, 2002
P. Lombaerde, 'The Significance of the Two Volumes of Rubens's Palazzi di Genova', in P. Lombaerde, ed., *The Reception of P.P. Rubens's Palazzi di Genova during the 17th Century in Europe: Questions and Problems*, (*Architectura Moderna*, I), Turnhout, 2002, pp. 51–80.

Lombaerde – Geerts, *Antwerpen verbeeld*, 2015
P. Lombaerde and K. Geerts, [Exh. Cat.] *Antwerpen verbeeld, De gouden eeuw in kaart en prent / Antwerp Portrayed, The Golden Age in Maps and Prints / Anvers imaginé, L'âge d'or en cartes et estampes* (Museum Plantin-Moretus, Antwerp, 2015), Antwerp, 2015.

López-Rey, *Velázquez*, 1979
J. López-Rey, *Velázquez, the Artist as a Maker, with a Catalogue Raisonné of his Extant Works*, Lausanne – Paris, 1979.

Loth, *Alternating Pediments*, 2013
C. Loth, *Alternating Pediments (Classical Comments by Calder Loth)*, published online, 6 January 2013: <URL: https://www.classicist.org/articles/classical-comments-alternating-pediments/

Lucian, *Opera*, trans. Erasmus et al., 1546
Lucian, *Opera, quae quidem extant, omnia, a Graeco sermone in Latinum conversa [...]*, trans. D. Erasmus, P. Melanchthon et al., Paris, 1546.

Lucian, *Opera*, eds Cognatus – Sambucus, 1602
Lucian, *Opera, quae quidem extant, omnia, Graece & Latine, una cum Gilberti Cognati et Ioannis Sambuci annotationibus utilissimis...*, Basel, 1602.

Lucian, *Phalaris etc.*, transl. Harmon, 1913
Lucian, *Phalaris, Hippias or The Bath. Dionysus.Heracles. Amber or the Swans...*, trans. A.M. Harmon (*Loeb Classical Library*, XIV), Cambridge, MA, 1913.

Lunsingh Scheurleer, *Aertsen*, 1947
Th.H. Lunsingh Scheurleer, 'Pieter Aertsen en Joachim Beuckelaer en hun ontleeningen aan Serlio's architectuurprenten', *Oud Holland*, LXII, 1947, pp. 123–134.

Lunsing Scheurleer, *Mauritshuis*, 1979
Th.H. Lunsingh Scheurleer, 'The Mauritshuis as Domus Cosmographica, I', in E. van den Boogaart et al., eds, *Johan Maurits van Nassau-Siegen, 1604–1679. A Humanist Prince in Europe and Brazil. Essays on the Occasion of the Tercentenary of his Death*, The Hague, 1979, pp. 143–189.

Lydakis, *Greek Painting*, 2004
S. Lydakis, *Ancient Greek Painting and Its Echoes in Later Art*, Los Angeles, CA, 2004.

Maclot, *Artists' Houses*, 2018
P. Maclot, 'Artists' Houses and Workshops in 16th century Antwerp: the Cases of Frans & Cornelis Floris', in A. Tacke et al., eds, *Künstlerhäuser im Mittelalter und der Frühen Neuzeit / Artists' Homes in the Middle Ages and the Early Modern Era*, Petersberg, 2018, pp. 115–124.

Maclot, *Portrait Unmasked*, 2014
P. Maclot, 'A Portrait Unmasked: The Iconology of the Birds'-Eye View of Antwerp by Virgilius Bononiensis (1565) as a Source for Topological Research of Private Buildings in Fifteenth- and Sixteenth-Century Antwerp', in K. Lichtert et al., eds, *Portraits of the City. Representing Urban Space in Later Medieval and Early Modern Europe, Studies in European Urban History (1100–1800)*, Turnhout, 2014, pp. 33–47.

Maclot, *Rubenssite*, 2016
P. Maclot, *Bouwhistorisch onderzoek, analyse en waardenstelling van de Rubenssite: het als monument beschermde Rubenshuis [...] en Kolveniershof met Rubenianum [...]*, unpublished report for the Stad Antwerpen, Antwerp, 2016.

Maclot, *Rubenssite*, 2019
P. Maclot, 'De Rubenssite: van pre-industrieel complex tot museale kunstenaarswoning', *M & L, Monumenten, Landschappen en Archeologie*, XXXVIII.4, 2019, pp. 20–33.

De Maere – Wabbes, *Dictionary*, 1994
J. De Maere and M. Wabbes, *Illustrated Dictionary of 17th Century Flemish Painters*, I–III, Brussels, 1994.

Maes – Laenens, *Juristen*, 1977
T. Maes and C. Laenens, [Exh. Cat.] *Juristen en Rechtsleven ten tijde van Rubens* (Gerechtsgebouw, Antwerp, 1977), Antwerp, 1977.

De Maeyer, *Albrecht en Isabella*, 1955
M. De Maeyer, *Albrecht en Isabella en de schilderkunst. Bijdrage tot de geschiedenis van de XVIIe-eeuwse schilderkunst in de Zuidelijke Nederlanden* (*Verhandelingen van de Koninklijke Vlaamse Academie voor Wetenschappen, Letteren en Schone Kunsten van België, Klasse der Schone Kunsten*, IX), Brussels, 1955.

Magurn, ed., *Letters*, 1955
R.S. Magurn, ed., *The Letters of Peter Paul Rubens*, Cambridge, MA, 1955.

Mai – Wettengl, eds, *Wettstreit*, 2002
E. Mai and K. Wettengl, eds, *Wettstreit der Künste, Malerei und Skulptur von Dürer bis Daumier*, Munich – Wolfratshausen – Cologne, 2002.

Van Mander, *Antijcke Schilders*, 1603
K. van Mander, *Het Leven der oude Antijcke doorluchtige Schilders, soo wel Egyptenaren, Griecken als Romeynen*, Alkmaar, 1603 [also printed with *Het Schilder-Boeck*, Haarlem, 1604, fols 62–90v].

Van Mander, *Grondt*, ed. Miedema, 1973
K. van Mander, *Den Grondt der Edel vry Schilder-const: Waer in haer ghestalt, aerdt ende wesen, de leer-lustighe Jeught in verscheyden Deelen in Rijm-dicht wort voor ghedraghen* [Haarlem, 1604], I–II, ed. H. Miedema, Utrecht, 1973 (1st edn 1969).

Van Mander, *Leven*, 1604
K. van Mander, *Het leven der doorluchtige Nederlandtsche en Hooghduytsche schilders* [printed with *Het Schilder-Boeck*], Haarlem, 1604.

Van Mander, *Lives*, ed. Miedema, 1994–99
K. van Mander, *The Lives of the Illustrious Netherlandish and German Painters*, ed. H. Miedema, I–VI, Doornspijk, 1994–1999.

Van Mander, *Schilder-Boeck*, 1604
C. [K] van Mander, *Het Schilder-Boeck, waerin voor eerst de leerlustighe Iueght den gronndt der Edel Vry Schilderconst in verscheyden deelen wort voorghedraghen [...]*, Haarlem, 1604. Available online: *DBNL*, The Hague, <URL: http://www.dbnl.org/tekst/mand001schi01_01/colofon.php>

Van Mander, *Wtlegghingh*, 1604
C. [K] van Mander, *Wtlegghingh op den Metamorphosis Pub. Ouidij Nasonis. Alles streckende tot voordering des vromen en eerlijcken borgherlijcken wandels. Seer dienstich den Schilders, Dichters, en Constbeminders, oock yeghelijck wt leering byeen gebracht en gheraemt* [printed with *Het Schilder-Boeck*], Haarlem, 1604.

Mansfield, *Zeuxis*, 2007,
E. C. Mansfield, *Too beautiful to picture. Zeuxis, myth and mimesis*, Minneapolis, MN – London, 2007.

Mansuelli, *Cat. Florence*, 1958
G.A. Mansuelli, *Galleria degli Uffizi: Le sculture* (*Cataloghi dei musei e gallerie d'Italia*), I, Rome, 1958.

Van Maris, *Rubens*, 2018
B. van Maris, 'Zó katholiek was Rubens nu ook weer niet, Rubens flirtte met esoterie' [interview with Teresa Esposito], *De Standaard*, 16 april 2018, p. D11.

Marnef, *Antwerp*, 1996
G. Marnef, *Antwerp in the Age of Reformation, Underground Protestantism in a Commercial Metropolis, 1550–1577*, Baltimore, MD – London, 1996.

Martin, *Banqueting Hall (CRLB)*, 2005
G. Martin, *The Ceiling Decoration of the Banqueting Hall* (*Corpus Rubenianum Ludwig Burchard*, XV), I–II, London – Turnhout, 2005.

Martin, *Cat. London, NG (Flemish School)*, 1970
G. Martin, *The Flemish School, circa 1600–circa 1900* (*The National Gallery Catalogues*), London, 1970 (repr. 1986).

Martin, *Ceiling Paintings (CRLB)*, 1968
J.R. Martin, *Rubens; the Ceiling Paintings for the Jesuit Church in Antwerp* (*Corpus Rubenianum Ludwig Burchard*, I), Brussels – London – New York, 1968.

Martin, *Pompa (CRLB)*, 1972
J.R. Martin, *The Decorations for the Pompa Introitus Ferdinandi* (*Corpus Rubenianum Ludwig Burchard*, XVI), Brussels – London – New York, 1972.

Martin, *Sweerts*, 1971
G. Martin, 'Sweerts and Rubens', *The Burlington Magazine*, CXIII, 1971, p. 96.

Massing, *Calomnie*, 1990
J.-M. Massing, *Du texte à l'image. La calomnie d'Apelle et son iconographie*, Strasbourg, 1990.

Matsier, *Bedrogen oog*, 2009
N. Matsier, *Het bedrogen oog, De kunst van de trompe-l'oeil*, Amsterdam – Antwerp, 2009.

Maufort, *Duarte*, 2002
D. Maufort, 'Le portrait des Duarte, une famille de musiciens d'Anvers peint par Gonzales Coques conservé au Szépművészeti Múzeum de Budapest', in B. Cardon, ed., *'Als ich can': liber amicorum in Memory of Professor Dr Maurits Smeyers* (*Corpus of Illuminated Manuscripts*, XII), Leuven, 2002, pp. 941–960.

McAllister Johnson, *Prolegomena*, 1969
W. McAllister Johnson, 'Prolegomena to the Images ou Tableaux de platte peinture, with an Excursus on Two Drawings of the School of Fontainebleau', *Gazette des Beaux-Arts*, LXXIII, 1969, pp. 277–304.

McGrath, *Emperor's Mullet*, 2020
E. McGrath, 'Rubens, Snijders and the Emperor's Mullet', *Journal of the Warburg and Courtauld Institutes*, LXXXIII, 2020, pp. 349–358.

McGrath, *History (CRLB)*, 1997
E. McGrath, *Subjects from History* (*Corpus Rubenianum Ludwig Burchard*, XIII.1), I–II, London, 1997.

McGrath, *Musathena*, 1987
E. McGrath, 'Rubens's "Musathena"', *Journal of the Warburg and Courtauld Institutes*, L, 1987, pp. 233–245.

McGrath, *Mythographic Handbooks*, 2009
E. McGrath, 'Artists and Mythographic Handbooks: Some Evidence of Use and Ownership' in R. Duits and F. Quiviger, eds, *Images of the Pagan Gods: Papers of a Conference in Memory of Jean Seznec* (*Warburg Institute Colloquia*, XIV), London, 2009, pp. 389–419.

McGrath, *Pompa*, 1971
E. McGrath, *Rubens' 'Pompa Introitus Ferdinandi' and the Traditions of Civic Pageantry*, unpublished doctoral dissertation, University of London, Warburg Institute, 1971.

McGrath, *Rubens's House*, 1976–78
E. McGrath, 'The Painted Decoration of Rubens's House', *Gentse Bijdragen tot de Kunstgeschiedenis*, XXIV, 1976–1978, pp. 133–146.

McGrath, *Rubens's House*, 1978
E. McGrath, 'The Painted Decoration of Rubens's House', *Journal of the Warburg and Courtauld Institutes*, XLI, 1978, pp. 245–277.

McGrath et al., *Mythological Subjects I (CRLB)*, 2016
E. McGrath, G. Martin, F. Healy, et al., *Mythological Subjects. I. Achilles to the Graces* (*Corpus Rubenianum Ludwig Burchard*, XI.1), I–II, London – Turnhout, 2016.

McHam, *Pliny*, 2013
S.B. McHam, *Pliny and the Artistic Culture of the Italian Renaissance: The Legacy of the Natural History*, London – New Haven, CT, 2013.

Meganck, *Coberger*, 1998
T. Meganck, *De kerkelijke architectuur van Wensel Coberger 1577/61–1634 in het licht van zijn verblijf te Rome* (*Verhandelingen van de Koninklijke Academie voor Wetenschappen, Letteren en Schone Kunsten van België, Klasse der Schone Kunsten*, LX), Brussels, 1998.

Merle du Bourg, *Henri IV Series (CRLB)*, 2017
A. Merle du Bourg, *The Henri IV Series* (*Corpus Rubenianum Ludwig Burchard*, XIV.2), Turnhout – London, 2017.

Merle du Bourg, ed., *Jordaens*, 2013
A. Merle du Bourg, ed., [Exh. Cat.] *Jordaens, 1593–1678* (Petit Palais, Musée des Beaux-Arts de la Ville de Paris, Paris, 2013–2014), Paris, 2013.

Merle du Bourg, *Rubens*, 2004
A. Merle du Bourg, *Peter Paul Rubens et la France, 1600–1640*, Villeneuve d'Ascq, 2004.

Mertens – Stoppie, *Conservatievisie*, 2019
R. Mertens and E. Stoppie, 'Een museale en contextuele conservatievisie. Portiek en paviljoen als 'collectiestukken' van het museum Rubenshuis', *M & L, Monumenten, Landschappen en Archeologie*, XXXVIII.4, 2019, pp. 52–68.

Van der Meulen, *Antique (CRLB)*, 1994
M. Van der Meulen, *Copies after the Antique* (*Corpus Rubenianum Ludwig Burchard*, XXIII), I–III, London, 1994.

Van der Meulen – Schregardus, *Rubens*, 1975
H.M. Van der Meulen – Schregardus, *Petrus Paulus Rubens Antiquarius. Collector and Copyist of Antique Gems* (doctoral dissertation, Rijksuniversiteit Utrecht, 1975), Alphen aan de Rijn, 1975.

Michel, *Rubens*, 1771
J.F.M. Michel, *Histoire de la vie de P.P. Rubens, Chevalier, & Seigneur de Steen, illustrée d'Anecdotes, qui n'ont jamais paru au Public, & de ses tableaux étalés dans les Palais, Églises & Places publiques de l'Europe: & par la Démonstration des Estampes existantes & relatives à ses Ouvrages*, Brussels, 1771.

Michel, *Rubens*, 1774
[J.F.M. Michel], *Historische levensbeschryving van Petrus Paulus Rubbens, ridder, heere van steen &c.: verrykt met veele gewigtige byzonderheden, welken by geen andere schryvers tot heden toe te vinden zyn geweest : nevens eene naauwkeurige opgave zyner schilderyen, berustende in de hoven, kerken, en verdere openbaare gebouwen van Europa, met aanwyzing welke van dezelven in het koper zyn gebragt*, Amsterdam, 1774.

Middelkoop, ed., *Kopstukken*, 2002
N. Middelkoop, ed., [Exh. Cat.] *Kopstukken, Amsterdammers geportretttteerd, 1600–1800* (Amsterdams Historisch Museum, Amsterdam, 2002–2003), Amsterdam, 2002.

Miedema, *Kunst*, 1981
H. Miedema, *Kunst, kunstenaar en kunstwerk bij Karel van Mander. Een analyse van zijn levensbeschrijving*, Alphen aan de Rijn, 1981.

Millen, *Voyage of Maria de'Medici*, 1983
R.F. Millen, 'Rubens and the Voyage of Maria de' Medici from Livorno to Marseilles. Etichetta, Protocol, Diplomacy and Baroque Convention. Essay towards a Study of History of Art', in M. Gregori, ed., *Rubens e Firenze*, Florence, 1983, pp. 113–176.

Millen – Wolf, *Maria de' Medici*, 1989
R.F. Millen and R.E. Wolf, *Heroic Deeds and Mystic Figures: A New Reading of Rubens' Life of Maria de' Medici*, Princeton, NJ, 1989.

Milman, *Architectures peintes*, 1986
M. Milman, *Architectures peintes en trompe-l'œil: Les illusions de la réalité*, Geneva, 1986.

De Mirimonde, *Duel musical*, 1971
A.P. de Mirimonde, 'Á propos de l'iconographie du "Duel musical d'Apollon et de Pan" de P.P. Rubens', *Bulletin des Musées royaux des Beaux-Arts de Belgique / Bulletin der Koninklijke Musea voor Schone Kunsten van België*, XX, 1971, pp. 55–65.

Moffitt, *Sluter's Pleurants*, 2005
J.F. Moffitt, 'Sluter's *Pleurants* and Timanthes' *Tristitia Velata*: Evolution of, and Sources for a Humanist *Topos* of Mourning', *Artibus et Historiae*, XXVI.51, 2005, pp. 73–84.

Mols, *Annotations manuscrites*, n.d.
F.J.J. Mols (1722–1790), *Annotations manuscrites sur Rubens*, MSS in KBR, Brussels (a photocopy in the Rubenianum, Antwerp).

Von Moltke, *Flinck*, 1965
J.W. von Moltke, *Govaert Flinck, 1615–1660*, Amsterdam, 1965.

Monballieu, *Nachtmael*, 1965
A. Monballieu, 'P.P. Rubens en het *Nachtmael* voor St.-Winoksbergen (1611), een niet uitgevoerd schilderij van de meester', *Jaarboek Koninklijk Museum voor Schone Kunsten Antwerpen*, 1965, pp. 183–205.

Montano, *Aggiunta delle Porte*, 1610
G.B. Montano, *Nvova et vltima aggivnta delle porte d'archittetura di Michel Angelo Buonaroti*, Rome, 1610 (convolution with I. Barozzio da Vignola, *Regola delli Cinque Ordini d'Architettura di M. Iacomo Barozzio da Vignola Libro Primo, et originale*, Rome: Anreas Vaccarius, 1607).

Montias, *Art and Auction*, 2002
J.M. Montias, *Art at Auction in 17th Century Amsterdam*, Amsterdam, 2002.

Montias, *Promise*, 2001
J.M. Montias, 'What Happened to Rubens's Promise to Deliver a Painting to Hans Thijsz.?', *Jaarboek Koninklijk Museum voor Schone Kunsten Antwerpen*, 2001, pp. 95–103.

Moortgat, *Rubens's Renovation / Rubenshuis*, 2021
I. Moortgat, 'New Evidence of Rubens's Renovation of his Antwerp House (Rubenshuis) in 1615', *JVDPPP-Journal (Jordaens Van Dyck Panel Paintings Project)*, I, 2021, pp. 72–74.

Moortgat, *Rubens Roof Boarding*, online publication [acc. 18/12/2021]
I. Moortgat, 'Rubens Roof Boarding', in J. Vander Auwera and J. Davies, eds, *Jordaens Van Dyck Panel Paintings Project*.; translation by Justin Davis, see URL: http://jordaensvandyck.org/archive/rubens-roof-boarding-5-january-1621/ [accessed 18 December 2021].

Morford, *Stoic Garden*, 1987
M. Morford, 'The Stoic Garden', *Journal of Garden History*, VII, 1987, pp. 151–175.

Morford, *Stoics*, 1991
M. Morford, *Stoics and Neostoics, Rubens and the Circle of Lipsius*, Princeton, NJ, 1991.

Mount, ed., *Reynolds*, 1996
H. Mount, ed., *Sir Joshua Reynolds, A Journey to Flanders and Holland*, Cambridge, 1996.

Mourits, *Thysius*, 2016
E. Mourits, *Een kamer gevuld met de mooiste boeken, De bibliotheek van Johannes Thysius (1622–1653)*, Nijmegen, 2016.

Van Mulders, *Collaborations Brueghel (CRLB)*, 2016
C. Van Mulders, *Works in Collaboration: Jan Brueghel I & II* (*Corpus Rubenianum Ludwig Burchard*, XXVII.1), Turnhout, 2016.

Van Mulders, *Twelve Busts*, 2008
C. Van Mulders, 'Peter Paul Rubens [...], Twelve Busts of Famous Greek and Roman Philosphers, Poets, Orators and Statesmen', in V. Herremans et al., [Exh. Cat.] *Heads on Shoulders. Portrait Busts in the Low Countries, 1600–1800 /*

BIBLIOGRAPHY

Voorbeeldige busten, Het borstbeeld in de Nederlanden, 1600–1800 (Koninklijk Museum voor Schone Kunsten Antwerpen, Antwerp, 2008), Ghent, 2008, pp. 106–114.

Müller, *Casa Pippi*, 2018
F. Müller, 'Giulio Romanos Mantuaner 'Künstlerhaus' als *summa artistica*. Eigenreferenzialitäten i Architektur und Ausstattung der Casa Pippi (1538–1542)', in A. Tacke et al., eds, *Künstlerhäuser im Mittelalter und der Frühen Neuzeit / Artists' Homes in the Middle Ages and the Early Modern Era*, Petersberg, 2018, pp. 106–114.

Müller, *Casa Zuccari*, 1985
B. Muller, 'Die Casa Zuccari in Florenz und der Palazzo Zuccari in Rom – Künstlerhaus und Haus der Kunst', in E. Hüttinger, ed., *Künstlerhäuser von der Renaissance bis zur Gegenwart*, Zürich, 1985, pp. 101–120.

Muller, *Collector*, 1989
J.M. Muller, *Rubens: The Artist as Collector*, Princeton, NJ, 1989.

Müller, *Holbein*, 1988
C. Müller, *Hans Holbein d.J., Zeichnungen aus dem Kupferstichkabinett der Öffentlichen Kunstsammlung Basel*, Basel, 1988.

Muller, *Moribvs Antiqvis*, 2008
J.M. Muller, 'Moribvs Antiqvis: "according to ancient ways"', in V. Herremans et al., [Exh. Cat.] *Heads on Shoulders: Portrait Busts in the Low Countries, 1600–1800 / Voorbeeldige busten: het borstbeeld in de Nederlanden, 1600–1800* (Koninklijk Museum voor Schone Kunsten Antwerpen, Antwerp, 2008), Ghent, 2008, pp. 13–27.

Muller, *Perseus and Andromeda*, 1981–82
J.M. Muller, The 'Perseus and Andromeda' on Rubens's House', *Simiolus*, XII, 1981–1982, pp. 131–146.

Muller, *Rubens's Collection*, 2004
J.M. Muller, 'Rubens's Collection in History', in K. Belkin and F. Healy, [Exh. Cat.] *A House of Art. Rubens as Collector* (Rubenshuis, Antwerp, 2004), Antwerp – Schoten, 2004, pp. 10–85.

Muller, *Rubens's Emblem*, 1981
J.M. Muller, 'Rubens's Emblem of the Art of Painting', *Journal of the Warburg and Courtauld Institutes*, XLIV, 1981, pp. 221–222.

Muller, *Rubens's Museum*, 1977
J.M. Muller, 'Rubens's Museum of Antique Sculpture: An Introduction', *The Art Bulletin*, LIX, 1977, pp. 571–582.

Muller, *St Jacob's Church*, 2016
J.M. Muller, *St Jacob's Antwerp Art and Counter Reformation in Rubens's Parish Church* (Brill's Studies on Art, Art History, and Intellectual History, XIII), Leiden, 2016.

Muller, *Theory and Practice*, 1982
J.M. Muller, 'Rubens's Theory and Practice of the Imitation of Art', *The Art Bulletin*, LXIV, 1982, pp. 229–247.

Müller Hofstede, *Entwurfszeichnung*, 1967
J. Müller Hofstede, 'Aspekte der Entwurfszeichnung bei Rubens', in *Stil und Überlieferung in der Kunst des Abendlandes*, III: *Theorien und Problemen* (Acts of the International Congress of the History of Art: 21, Bonn, 1964), Berlin, 1967, pp. 114–125.

Müller Hofstede, *Ölskizzen*, 1969
J. Müller Hofstede, 'Neue Ölskizzen von Rubens', *Städel-Jahrbuch*, II, 1969, pp. 189–242.

Müller Hofstede, *Review Burchard – d'Hulst*, 1966
J. Müller Hofstede, [Review] 'L. Burchard and R.-A. d'Hulst, *Rubens Drawings*, I–II (Brussels, 1963)', *Master Drawings*, IV, 1966, pp. 435–454.

Müller Hofstede, *Rubens in Italien*, 1977
J. Müller Hofstede, [Exh. Cat.] *Peter Paul Rubens, 1577–1640*. I, *Rubens in Italien. Gemälde, Ölskizzen, Zeichnungen; Triumph der Eucharistie, Wandteppiche aus dem Kölner Dom*; II, *Maler mit dem Grabstichel, Rubens und die Druckgraphik* (Kunsthalle, Cologne, 1977), Cologne, 1977.

Müller Hofstede, *Ut Pictura Poesis*, 1976–78
J. Müller Hofstede, "Ut Pictura Poesis": Rubens und die humanistische Kunsttheorie', *Gentse Bijdragen tot de Kunstgeschiedenis*, XXIV, 1976–1978, pp. 171–189.

Muls, *De Vos*, 1932
J. Muls, *Cornelis de Vos, schilder van Hulst*, Antwerp, [1932].

Musso, *Painted Architecture*, 2014
S.F. Musso, 'Painting and Painted Architecture in Genoa: what Peter Paul Rubens probably saw', in P. Lombaerde, ed., *The Notion of the Painter-Architect in Italy and the Southern Low Countries* (Architectura Moderna, XI), Turnhout, 2014, pp. 161–182.

Naeye, *De Proost*, 1976
R. Naeye, 'Bartholomeus De Proost, Architect (1815–1869)', *Antwerpen, Tijdschrift der Stad Antwerpen*, XXI, 1976, pp. 217–224.

De Nave, ed., *Around Rubens*, 1991
F. de Nave, ed., [Exh. Cat.] *Around Rubens: Prints and Drawings from the Stedelijk Prentenkabinet / Rondom Rubens: tekeningen en prenten uit eigen verzameling* (Stedelijk Prentenkabinet, Museum Plantin-Moretus, Antwerp, 1991), Antwerp, 1991.

Neerman, *Calumny of Apelles*, 2016
M. Neerman, 'The *Calumny of Apelles* by Maerten de Vos', *The Rubenianum Quarterly*, 2016, 4, pp. 3–4.

Neerman et al., *Calumny of Apelles*, 2018
M. Neerman et al., 'The *Calumny of Apelles*. A Rediscovered Masterpiece by Maerten de Vos', *Bulletin van het Koninklijk Instituut voor het Kunstpatrimonium / Bulletin de l'institut royal du Patrimoine artistique*, XXXV, 2016–2018, pp. 107–137.

Nellen, *Hugo de Groot*, 2007
H. Nellen, *Hugo de Groot, Een leven in strijd om de vrede, 1583–1645*, Amsterdam, 2007.

Neumayr von Ramssla, *Johann Ernst*, 1620
J.W. Neumayr [Neumair] von Ramssla, *Des durchlauchtigen hochgebornen Fürsten und Herrn / Herrn Johann Ernsten des Jüngern / Hertzogen zu Sachsen / Jülich / Cleve und Berg / Landgrafen in Düringen [...] Reise in Franckreich, Engelland und Niederland*, Leipzig, 1620.

Neurdenburg, *Beeldhouwkunst*, 1948
E. Neurdenburg, *De zeventiende eeuwsche beeldhouwkunst in de Noordelijke Nederlanden: Hendrick de Keyser, Artus Quellinus, Rombout Verhulst en tijdgenooten*, Amsterdam, 1948.

Neurdenburg, *Hendrick de Keyzer*, 1930
E. Neurdenburg, *Hendrick de Keyzer, beeldhouwer en bouwmeester in Amsterdam*, Amsterdam, 1930.

Nichols, *Goltzius*, 2013
L.W. Nichols, *The Paintings of Hendrick Goltzius, 1558–1617. A Monograph and Catalogue Raisonné* (Aetas Aurea. Monographs on Dutch & Flemish Painting, XXIII), Doornspijk, 2013.

Van Nierop, *Romeyn de Hooghe*, 2018
H. Van Nierop, *The Life of Romeyn de Hooghe, 1645–1708. Prints, Pamphlets, and Politics in the Dutch Golden Age*, Amsterdam, 2018.

Van Nierop et al., eds, *Romeyn de Hooghe*, 2008
H. van Nierop et al., eds, *Romeyn de Hooghe: De verbeelding van de late Gouden Eeuw*, Zwolle, 2008.

Van den Nieuwenhuizen, *Descente de croix*, 1962
J. Van den Nieuwenhuizen, '[La Descente de croix de Rubens, Étude préalable au traitement]. Histoire matérielle', *Bulletin Institut Royal du Patrimoine Artistique – Koninklijk Instituut van het Kunstpatrimonium*, V, 1962, pp. 27–85.

De Nijn et al., eds, *Faydherbe*, 1997
H. De Nijn, H. Vlieghe, H. Devisscher, eds, [Exh. Cat.] *Lucas Faydherbe, 1617–1697: Mechels beeldhouwer & architect* (Stedelijk Museum Hof van Busleyden, Mechelen, 1997), Mechelen, 1997.

Norris – Popham, *Review Seilern*, 1955
C. Norris and A.E. Popham, [Review] 'A. Seilern, *Flemish Paintings and Drawings at 56 Princes Gate, London SW7* (London, 1955)', *The Burlington Magazine*, XCVII, no. 633, 1955, pp. 396–398 and 403.

Oldenbourg, *Rubens*, 1922
[R. Oldenbourg], *Peter Paul Rubens. Sammlung der von Rudolf Oldenbourg veröffentlichten oder zur Veröffentlichung vorbereiteten Abhandlungen über den Meister*, ed. W. von Bode, Munich – Berlin, 1922.

Onians, *Meaning*, 1988
J. Onians, *Bearers of Meaning, The Classical Orders in Antiquity, the Middle Ages and the Renaissance*, Princeton, NJ, 1988.

Ottenheym, *Architectural Ornament*, 2007
K. Ottenheym, 'Architectura Moderna. The systemization of architectural ornament around 1600', in K. De Jonge and K. Ottenheym, eds, *Unity and Discontinuity. Architectural Relations between the Southern and Northern Low Countries 1530–1700* (*Architectura Moderna*, V), Turnhout, 2007, pp. 111–136.

Ottenheym, *Frederik Hendrik en de bouwkunst*, 1997
K. Ottenheym, '"van Bouw-lust soo beseten". Frederik-Hendrik en de bouwkunst', in M. Keblusek and J. Zijlmans, eds, [Exh. Cat.] *Vorstelijk vertoon. Aan het hof van Frederik Hendrik en Amalia* (Haags Historisch Museum, The Hague, 1997–1998), The Hague – Zwolle, 1997, pp. 105–125.

Ottenheym, *La Vera Simmetria*, 2007
K. Ottenheym, 'La Vera Simmetria conforme le regole degli antichi. Rubens and Huygens on Vitruvius', in K. De Jonge and K. Ottenheym, eds, *Unity and Discontinuity. Architectural Relations between the Southern and Northern Low Countries 1530–1700* (*Architectura Moderna*, V), Turnhout, 2007, 137–161.

Ottenheym, *Mauritshuis*, 2014
K. Ottenheym, 'De architectuur en de bouwgeschiedenis van het Mauritshuis', in Q. Buvelot et al., *Het Mauritshuis, het gebouw*, The Hague – Zwolle, 2014, pp. 39–53.

Ottenheym, *Palazzi di Genova*, 2002
K. Ottenheym, 'Peter Paul Rubens's *Palazzi di Genova* and its Influence on Architecture in the Netherlands', in P. Lombaerde, ed., *The Reception of P.P. Rubens's Palazzi di Genova During the 17th century in Europe: Questions and Problems* (*Architectura Moderna*, I), Turnhout, 2002, pp. 81–98.

Ottenheym, *Rubens en Huygens*, 1997
K. Ottenheym, 'De correspondentie tussen Rubens en Huygens over architectuur (1635–40)', *Bulletin van de Koninklijke Nederlandse Oudheidkundige Bond*, XCVI, 1997, pp. 1–11.

Ottenheym, *Scamozzi*, 2010
K. Ottenheym, *Schoonheid op maat, Vincenzo Scamozzi en de architectuur van de gouden eeuw*, Amsterdam, 2010.

Ovid, *Metamorphoses*, trans. Miller, 1977–84
Ovid, *Metamorphoses*, trans. F.J. Miller, rev. G.P. Goold (*Loeb Classical Library*), I–II, Cambridge, MA – London, 1977–1984.

Palomino, *Museo Pictórico*, 1715–24
A. Palomino de Castro y Velasco, *El museo pictórico y escala óptica*, Madrid, I–II, Madrid, 1715–1724.

Parent, *L'Architecture des Pays-Bas*, 1926
P. Parent, *L'Architecture des Pays-Bas méridionaux: Belgique et Nord de la France aux XVIe, XVIIe et XVIIIe siècles*, Paris, 1926.

Pasena Armani, *Perino del Vaga*, 1987
E. Pasena Armani, *Perino del Vaga. L'annello mancante*, Genoa, 1987.

Pasquier – Martinez, eds, *Praxitèle*, 2007
A. Pasquier and J.-L. Martinez, eds, [Exh. Cat.] *Praxitèle* (Musée du Louvre, Paris, 2007), Paris, 2007.

Penny, *Cat. Ashmolean Museum*, 1992
N. Penny, *Catalogue of European Sculpture in the Ashmolean Museum, 1540 to the Present Day: French and other European Sculpture (Excluding Italian and British)*, I–II, Oxford, 1992.

Philippot et al., *Architecture*, 2003
P. Philippot, D. Coekelberghs, P. Loze et al., *L'architecture religieuse et la sculpture baroques dans les Pays-Bas méridionaux et la principauté de Liège 1600–1770*, Sprimont, 2003.

Philostratus, *Imagines*, trans. Fairbanks, 2000
Philostratus, *Imagines*, [...], transl. A. Fairbanks (*Loeb Classical Library*), Cambridge, MA – London, 2000.

Pignatti, *Veronese*, 1968
T. Pignatti, *Veronese, La Villa di Maser* (*I grandi decoratori*, VIII), Milan, 1968.

De Piles, *Dissertation*, 1681
R. de Piles, *Dissertation sur les Ouvrages des plus fameux Peintres, dédiée à Monseigneur le duc de Richelieu. La vie de Rubens*, Paris, [1681].

Pliny, *Natural History – IX*, trans. Rackham, 1952
Pliny, *Natural History. Volume IX: Books 33–35*, trans. H. Rackham (*Loeb Classical Library*), Cambridge, MA, 1952.

Plomp, *Collecting*, 2005
M.C. Plomp, 'Collecting Rubens's Drawings', in Logan – Plomp, [Exh. Cat.] *Peter Paul Rubens. The Drawings* (Metropolitan Museum of Art, New York, 2005), New Haven, CT – London, 2005, pp. 37–59.

De Poorter, *Eucharist (CRLB)*, 1978
N. De Poorter, *The Eucharist Series* (*Corpus Rubenianum Ludwig Burchard*, II), I–II, Brussels – London – New York, 1978.

De Poorter, *Kolveniers*, 1988
N. De Poorter, 'Rubens "onder de wapenen", De Antwerpse schilders als gildebroeders van de kolveniers in de eerste helft van de 17de eeuw', *Jaarboek Koninklijk Museum voor Schone Kunsten Antwerpen*, 1988, pp. 203–252.

De Poorter et al., *Rubens*, 1990
N. De Poorter with G. Jansen and J. Giltaij, [Exh. Cat.] *Rubens en zijn tijd – Rubens and his Age* (Museum Boymans-van Beuningen, Rotterdam, 1990), Rotterdam, 1990.

Prims, *Cavendish*, 1939
F. Prims, 'Lord Cavendish in het Rubenshuis – Méthode pour dresser les chevaux (1648–1660)', *Antwerpiensia: losse Bijdragen tot de Antwerpsche Geschiedenis*, XIII, 1939 [Antwerp 1940], pp. 197–203.

BIBLIOGRAPHY

Prims, *Hillewerve,* **1932**
F. Prims, 'Hillewerve in het huis van Rubens', in *Antwerpiensia: losse Bijdragen tot de Antwerpsche Geschiedenis*, V, 1931 [Antwerp, 1932], pp. 145–152.

Prims, *Kloosterstraat,* **1927**
F. Prims, 'Rubens in de Kloosterstraat', in *Antwerpiensia: losse Bijdragen tot de Antwerpsche Geschiedenis*, I, 1927, no. 38 [Antwerp, 1928], pp. 215–219).

Prims, *Manège van Cavendish,* **1939**
F. Prims, 'De Manège van Cavendish in het Rubenshuis', *Antwerpiensia: losse Bijdragen tot de Antwerpsche Geschiedenis*, XIII, 1939 [Antwerp 1940], pp. 204–209.

Prims, *Prieel van Rubens,* **1948**
F. Prims, 'Het zomerhuis of prieel van Rubens', in *Antwerpiensia: losse Bijdragen tot de Antwerpsche Geschiedenis*, XVIII, 1947–1948, no. 36, pp. 140–142.

Prims, *Rubenshuis,* **1946**
F. Prims, *Het Rubenshuis, Gids bij de mythologische en humanistische versieringen*, Antwerp, 1946.

Prims, *Van Eycke,* **1939**
F. Prims, 'Van Eycke's "Lof van Antwerpen"', *Antwerpiensia: losse Bijdragen tot de Antwerpsche Geschiedenis*, XIII, 1939 [Antwerp 1940], pp. 223–228.

Prims, *Waalse Kerk,* **1948**
F. Prims, 'Waalse kerk en Rubenshuis', *Antwerpiensia: losse Bijdragen tot de Antwerpsche Geschiedenis*, XVIII, 1947–1948, no. 37, pp. 143–146.

Prinz, *Philosophers,* **1973**
W. Prinz, 'The Four Philosophers by Rubens and the Pseudo-Seneca in Seventeenth-Century Painting', *The Art Bulletin*, LV, 1973, pp. 410–428.

Puget de la Serre, *Histoire curieuse,* **1632**
J. Puget de la Serre, *Histoire curieuse de tout ce qui c'est passé a l'entree de la Reyne, mere du roy très chrestien dans les villes des Pays Bas*, Antwerp, 1632.

Radi, *Disegni de Architettura,*
B. Radi, *Vari disegni de Architettura ornata de porte inventati* [...], Rome, 1619.

Ravelli, *Polidoro,* **1978**
L. Ravelli, *Polidoro da Caravaggio (Monumenta Bergomensia, XLVIII)*, I–II, Bergamo, 1978.

De Reiffenberg, *Rubens,* **1837**
A.F.T. de Reiffenberg, 'Nouvelles recherches sur Pierre-Paul Rubens, contenant une vie inédite de ce grand peintre, par Philippe Rubens, son neveu, avec des notes et des éclaircissements recueillis par le Baron de Reiffenberg', *Nouveaux mémoires de l'Académie Royale des Sciences et Belles-Lettres de Bruxelles*, X, 1837, pp. 3–21.

Renger, *Altäre für Bayern,* **1990**
K. Renger, [Exh. Cat.] *Peter Paul Rubens. Altäre für Bayern* (Alte Pinakothek, Bayerische Staatsgemäldesammlungen, Munich, 1990–1991), Munich, 1990.

Renger – Denk, *Cat. Munich (Flämische Malerei),* **2002**
K. Renger, with C. Denk, *Flämische Malerei des Barock in der Alten Pinakothek*, Munich – Cologne, 2002.

Richardson – Stevens, *Soane,* **1999**
M. Richardson and M.A. Stevens, eds., [Exh. Cat.] *John Soane, Architect:Master of Space and Light* (Royal Academy, London, 1999), London, 1999.

Van Riet – Kockelbergh, *Faydherbe,* **1997**
S. Van Riet and I. Kockelbergh, 'Lucas Faydherbe als beeldhouwer', in H. De Nijn et al., eds, [Exh. Cat.] *Lucas Faydherbe, 1617–1697: Mechels beeldhouwer & architect* (Stedelijk Museum Hof van Busleyden, Mechelen, 1997), Mechelen, 1997, pp. 32–69.

Ripa, *Iconologia,* **1603**
C. Ripa, *Iconologia*, Rome, 1603.

Ripa, *Iconologia,* **ed. Pers, 1644**
[C. Ripa], *Iconologia, of uytbeeldingen des Verstands: van Cesare Ripa van Perugien, Ridder van SS. Mauritius en Lazzaro. Waer in Verscheiden afbeeldingen van Deughden, Ondeughden, Genegentheden, Menschlijcke Hertztochten, Konsten, Leeringen… uyt het Italiaens vertaelt door D.P. Pers*, Amsterdam, 1644.

La Rocca, *Arcus et area Claudii,* **1994**
E. La Rocca, 'Arcus et arae Claudii', in V.M. Strocka, ed., *Die Regierungszeit des Kaiser Claudius: Umbruch oder Episode*, Mainz am Rhein, 1994, pp. 267–299.

Van Rooijen-Buchwaldt – de Jong, *Pallas,* **1994**
M.J.H. van Rooijen-Buchwaldt and E. de Jong, *De fonteijn van Pallas, Een geschenk van Amsterdam aan Johan Maurits*, Amsterdam, 1994.

Roosens, *Le Roy,* **1999**
B. Roosens, 'La famille anversoise Le Roy: des marchands de poudre à canon devenus chevalier (XVIe–XVIIe siècle). Recherches autour de quelques portraits d'Antoon van Dyck', *Jaarboek Koninklijk Museum voor Schone Kunsten Antwerpen*, 1999, pp. 138–157.

Rooses, *Afdoening,* **1910**
M. Rooses, 'De afdoening van het Kruis, Uit het rekeningboek der Antwerpsche Kolveniersgilde', *Rubens-Bulletijn*, V, 1910, pp. 230–233.

Rooses, *Afrekeninghen,* **1910**
M. Rooses, 'Afrekeninghen aengaende de kinderen van wylen heer Albert Rubens', *Rubens-Bulletijn*, V, 1910, pp. 63–68.

Rooses, ed., *Albertus Rubens,* **1897**
M. Rooses, ed., 'Staet ende inventaris van den Sterffhuyse van Mynheer Albertus Rubens ende vrouwe Clara del Monte', *Rubens-Bulletijn*, V, 1897, pp. 18–59.

Rooses, ed., *Boek gehouden,* **1878**
M. Rooses, ed., *Boek gehouden door Jan Moretus II als deken der St. Lucasgilde (1616–1617)*, Antwerp, 1878.

Rooses, *Huis van Rubens,* **1910**
M. Rooses, 'Het huis van Rubens heropgebouwd in de wereldtentoonstelling te Brussel in 1910', *De Vlaamsche Gids*, 1910, pp. 193–207 [pp. 5–19 in repaginated reprint].

Rooses, *Leven,* **1903**
M. Rooses, *Rubens' leven en werken,* Amsterdam – Antwerp – Ghent, 1903.

Rooses, *Maison,* **1888**
M. Rooses, 'La maison de Rubens', *Rubens-Bulletijn*, III, 1888, pp. 217–237 [cf. an undated reprint exists which is repaginated pp. 5–25].

Rooses, *Œuvre,* **1886–92**
M. Rooses, *L'Œuvre de P.P. Rubens. Histoire et description de ses tableaux et dessins*, I–V, Antwerp, 1886–1892.

Rooses, *Reizigers,* **1898**
M. Rooses, 'De vreemde reizigers Rubens of zijn huis bezoekende', *Rubens-Bulletijn*, V, 1898 (1907), pp. 221–229.

Rooses, *Rubens,* **1904**
M. Rooses, *Rubens*, Philadelphia, PA – London, 1904.

Rooses, ed., *Sterfhuis Isabella Brant*, 1896
M. Rooses, ed., 'Staat van goederen in het Sterfhuis van Isabella Brant', *Rubens-Bulletijn*, IV, 1896, pp. 154–188.

Rooses – Ruelens, eds, *Correspondance*, 1887–1909
M. Rooses and C. Ruelens, eds, *Correspondance de Rubens et documents épistolaires concernant sa vie et ses œuvres*, I–VI, Antwerp, 1887–1909.

Roscoe, *Belgium*, 1841
T. Roscoe, *Belgium in a Picturesque Tour*, London, 1841.

Rosenthal, *Occasio*, 2000
L. Rosenthal, 'Seizing Opportunity: Rubens's Occasio and the Violence of Allegory', *Jaarboek Koninklijk Museum voor Schone Kunsten Antwerpen*, 2000, pp. 185–207.

Rosenthal, *Rubens*, 2005
L. Rosenthal, *Gender, Politics, and Allegory in the Art of Rubens*, Cambridge, MA, 2006.

Rott, *Palazzi (CRLB)*, 2002
H.W. Rott, *Palazzi di Genova. Architectural Drawings and Engravings* (Corpus Rubenianum Ludwig Burchard, XXII, Architecture and Sculpture, 1), I–II, London – Turnhout, 2002.

Rowlands, *Rubens Drawings*, 1977
J. Rowlands, [Exh. Cat.] *Rubens Drawings and Sketches* (The British Museum, Department of Prints and Drawings, London, 1977), London, 1977.

Le Roy, *Notitia Marchionatus*, 1678
J. Le Roy, *Notitia Marchionatus sacri Romani Imperii hoc est Urbis et agri Antverpiensis oppidorum, dominiorum, monasteriorum, castellorumque sub eo*, Amsterdam, 1678.

Van Royen, *Familiecorrespondentie*, 1942
R. Van Royen, 'Een familiecorrespondentie van omstreeks 1600', *Leidsch Jaarboekje (Jaarboekje voor Geschiedenis en Oudheidkunde van Leiden en Rijnland)*, XXXIV, 1942, pp. 124–150.

Rubens, *De Re Vestiaria*, 1665
A. Rubens ['Albertus Rubenius Petri Pauli f.'], *De Re Vestiaria Veterum, pracipue de lato clavo libri duo, et alia eiusdem Opuscula posthuma ...*, Antwerp, 1665.

Rubens, *Electorum Libri*, 1608
[P. Rubens], *Philippi Rvbeni[i] Electorum Libri II: In quibus antiqui Ritus, Emendationes, Censuræ. Eivsdem ad Iustum Lipsium Poëmatia*, Antwerp, 1608.

Ruelens, *Rubens*, 1883
C. Ruelens, 'La vie de Rubens, par Roger de Piles', *Rubens-Bulletijn*, II, 1883, pp. 157–175.

Van Ruyssevelt – Somers, *Kreitz*, 1998
A. van Ruyssevelt and Marc Somers, *Willy Kreitz, 1903–1982: Klassiek en modernistisch beeldhouwer*, Antwerp, 1998.

Ruyten, *Opzoekingswerken Rubenshuis*, 1954
T. Ruyten, *Nota's aangaande opzoekingswerken, welke de wederopbouw van het Rubenshuis voorafgingen*, unpublished note in typescript, Rubenshuis, Antwerp, 1954.

Sabbe, *Andromeda-sage*, 1927
M. Sabbe, 'De Andromeda-sage als politieke allegorie', in *Album opgedragen aan Prof. Dr. J. Vercoullie, door ambtgenooten, oud-leerlingen en vereerders [...]*, Brussels, 1927, pp. 235–239.

Sabbe, *Geestesleven te Antwerpen*, 1927
M. Sabbe, 'Het geestesleven te Antwerpen in Rubens' tijd', in F. Prims et al., *Rubens en zijne eeuw*, Brussels, 1927, pp. 61–172.

Sabbe, *Geestesleven te Antwerpen*, 1927a
M. Sabbe, *Het geestesleven te Antwerpen in Rubens' tijd*, Brussels, 1927.

Sagittarius, *Ulysses Saxonicus*, 1621
T. Sagittarius, *Ulysses Saxonicus seu Iter quod illustrissimus [...] Johannes–Ernestus dux Saxoniae [...] per Germaniam, Galliam, Angliam, & Belgium, Anno 1613 magno cum fructu instituit, et felicissime absolvit [...]*, Wroclaw, 1621.

Van der Sanden, *Oud Konst-Tooneel*, [1760–75]
J. van der Sanden, *Oud Konst-Tooneel van Antwerpen of historische denkschriften, academische instellingen, de voornaemste Konstenaeren en oefeninghe der nederdutsche Rhetorijke in de Belgische Provinciën*, I–III, MS in the Felixarchief, Antwerp (Privilegiekamer, PK # 173).

Sandrart, *Teutsche Academie*, 1675–80
J. von Sandrart, *L'Academia Todesca della Architectura, Scultura & Pittura: oder Teutsche Academie der Edlen Bau-, Bild- und Mahlerey-Künste*, I–II, Nürnberg etc., 1675–80.

T'Sas, *Catalogue*, 1797
N.J. T'Sas, *Catalogue de la rare et nombreuse collection d'estampes et de desseins qui composoient le cabinet de feu M. Pierre Wouters, en son vivant Prêtre, Chanoine de l'Église Collégiale de S. Gomer, à Lierre en Brabant, Trésorier et Bibliothécaire de Sa Majesté Apostolique, etc. [...]*, Brussels, 1797.

Scamozzi, *Idea*, 1615
V. Scamozzi, *L'idea della architettura universale, de Vinzenzo Scamozzi, architetto veneto, divisa in X Libri*, I–VI, Venice, 1615.

Schama, *Rembrandt*, 1999
S. Schama, *Rembrandt's Eyes*, New York, 1999.

Scheller, *Rockox*, 1978
R. Scheller, *Nicolaas Rockox als oudheidkundige*, Antwerp, 1978.

De Schepper, ed., *Rubens' Bibliotheek*, 2004
M. De Schepper, ed., [Exh. Cat.] *Een hart voor boeken, Rubens en zijn bibliotheek / La passion des livres, Rubens et sa bibliothèque* (Museum Plantin-Moretus, Antwerp, 2004), Antwerp, 2004.

Scholten, *Quellinus*, 2010
F. Scholten, *Artus Quellinus, Sculptor of Amsterdam*, Amsterdam, 2010.

Scholten, *Werkplaats-academie*, 2004
F. Scholten, 'Rubens' werkplaats-academie of *de ghemeynschap die onse Consten van Schildry ende Belthouwery t'samen hebben*', in J. de Jong et al., eds, *Rubens and the Netherlands* (Netherlands Yearbook for History of Art, LV) / *Rubens en de Nederlanden* (Nederlands Kunsthistorisch Jaarboek, LV), Zwolle, 2004, pp. 34–53.

Schoonbaert – Cardyn-Oomen, eds, *Cat. Antwerpen (19th and 20th Cent.)*, 1981
L. Schoonbaert and D. Cardyn-Oomen, eds, *Tekeningen, aquarellen en prenten 19de en 20ste eeuw* [Museum voor Schone Kunsten, Antwerpen], Antwerp, 1981.

Schoy, *Influence italienne*, 1879
A. Schoy, *Histoire de l'influence italienne sur l'architecture dans les Pays-Bas*, Brussels, 1879.

Schoy, *Rubens*, 1878
A. Schoy, *Pierre-Paul Rubens (Les grands architectes de la Renaissance aux Pays-Bas)*, Brussels, 1878.

Schütte, *Fassadenmalerei*, 1992
U. Schütte, 'Gemälde an der Fassade, Die deutschen Architekturtraktate und die Fassadenmalerei zwischen 1500 und 1800', *Münchner Jahrbuch der bildenden Kunst*, XLIII, 1992, pp. 113–132.

Schwartz, *Rembrandt*, 2006
G. Schwartz, *De Grote Rembrandt*, Zwolle, 2006.

BIBLIOGRAPHY

Schwarz, *Künstlerhaus*, 1990
H.-P. Schwarz, *Das Künstlerhaus, Anmerkungen zur Sozialgeschichte des Genies*, Braunschweig, 1990.

Schweikhart, *Fassadenmalerei in Verona*, 1973
G. Schweikhart, *Fassadenmalerei in Verona vom 14. bis zum 20. Jahrhundert* (Italienische Forschungen, 3. Folge, VII), Munich, 1973.

Scott, *Perseus and Andromeda*, 1988
J.B. Scott, 'The Meaning of Perseus and Andromeda in the Farnese Gallery and on the Rubens House', *Journal of the Warburg and Courtauld Institutes*, LI, 1988, pp. 250–260.

Seilern, *Cat. London, Princes Gate*, 1955
A. Seilern, *Catalogue of Flemish Paintings & Drawings at 56 Princes Gate, London SW7*, London, 1955.

Seilern, *Corrigenda and Addenda*, 1971
A. Seilern, *Corrigenda & Addenda to the Catalogue of the Paintings & Drawings at 56, Princes Gate, London SW7*, 1971.

Seneca, *Opera*, 1615
[L.A. Seneca], *L. Annæi Senecæ Philosophi Opera, Qvæ Exstant Omnia. Editio secunda, atque ab ultimâ Lipsi[i] manu*, Antwerp, 1615.

Serlio, *Architecturen*, transl. Coecke van Aelst, 1606
S. Serlio, *Van de architecturen vijf boecken Sebastiani Serlii, Overgeset uyt d'Italiaense in de Nederduytsche sprake door Pieter Coecke van Aelst [...]*, transl. P. Coecke van Aelst, Amsterdam, 1606 (convolution of the translation of Serlio's five books).

Serlio, *Extraordinario libro*, 1551
S. Serlio, *Extraordinario libro di architettvra [...]Nel quale si dimostrano trenta porte di opera Rustica mista con diuersi oridini; Et venti di opera dilicata*, Lyon, 1551.

Serlio, *Livre extraordinaire*, 1551
S. Serlio, *Livre extraordinaire de architecture [...]Auquel sont demonstrees trente Portes Rustiques meslees de divers ordres. Et vingt autres d'oeuvre delicate en diverses especes*, Lyon, 1551.

Serlio, *Terzo libro /antiquita*, 1540
S. Serlio, *Il terzo libro di Sabastiano Serlio bolognese, nel qual si figurano, e descrivono le antiqvita di Roma, e le altre che sono in Italia, e fvori d'Italia*, Venice, 1540 (1st edn).

Serlio, *Quatro libro /Regole generali*, 1537
S. Serlio, *Regole generali di Architettura sopra le cinque maniere [...], IV*, Venice, 1537 (1st edn).

De Sevin, *Pindus Charitatis*, s.d.
F.D. de Sevin, *Pindus Charitatis, sive Horae subsecivae*, s.l., s.d.[1675–1695]. Online publication: <URL: https://books.google.be/books?vid = GENT900000136037&printsec = frontcover#v = onepage&q&f = false

Shearman, *Raphael's Cartoons*, 1972
J. Shearman, *Raphael's Cartoons in the Collection of Her Majesty the Queen and the Tapestries for the Sistine Chapel*, London, 1972.

Silver, *Massys*, 1984
L. Silver, *The Paintings of Quinten Massys with Catalogue raisonné*, Oxford, 1984.

Simon, *Götter*, 1990
E. Simon, *Die Götter der Römer*, Munich, 1990.

Von Simson, *Rubens*, 1996
O. von Simson, *Peter Paul Rubens (1577–1640). Humanist, Maler und Diplomat* (Berliner Schriften zur Kunst. Herausgegeben vom Kunsthistorischen Institut der Freien Universität Berlin, VIII), Mainz, 1996.

Slothouwer, *Paleizen*, 1945
D.F. Slothouwer, *De paleizen van Frederik Hendrik*, Leiden, 1945.

Sluijter, *Andromeda*, 2009
E.J. Sluijter, 'Rembrandt, Rubens and Classical Mythology: The Case of Andromeda', in C. Van de Velde, ed., *Classical Mythology in the Netherlands in the Age of Renaissance and Baroque. Proceedings of the International Conference organized, Antwerp, 19–21 May 2005 / La mythologie classique aux temps de la Renaissance et du Baroque dans les Pays-Bas. Actes du Colloque international, Anvers, 19–21 mai 2005*, Leuven – Paris – Walpole, MA, 2009, pp. 25–66.

Sluijter, *Fabulen*, 2000
E.J. Sluijter, *De 'heydensche fabulen' in de schilderkunst van de Gouden Eeuw: Schilderijen met verhalende onderwerpen uit de klassieke mythologie in de noordelijke Nederlanden, circa 1590–1670*, Leiden, 2000.

Sluijter, *Rembrandt / Female Nude*, 2006
E.J. Sluijter, *Rembrandt and the Female Nude*, Amsterdam, 2006.

Smith, *Princesse de Toscane*, 1991
M. Smith, 'Princesse de Toscane', in [Exh. Cat.] M.-N. Baudouin-Matuszek et al., *Marie de Médicis et le Palais du Luxembourg* (Musée du Luxembourg, Paris, 1991–1992; Fondation Septentrion, Marcq-en-Barœul, 1992), Paris, 1991, pp. 37–97.

Snaet, *Glory of God*, 2007
J. Snaet, 'For the Greater Glory of God: Religious Architecture in the Low Countries 1560–1700', in K. De Jonge and K. Ottenheym, eds, *Unity and Discontinuity. Architectural Relations between the Southern and Northern Low Countries 1530–1700* (Architectura Moderna, V), Turnhout, 2007, pp. 251–298.

Snaet, *Reformatie versus contrareformatie*, 2008
J. Snaet, *Reformatie versus contrareformatie: De religieuze architectuur in de Noordelijke en Zuidelijke Nederlanden gedurende de 16de en 17de eeuw*, unpublished doctoral dissertation, KULeuven, Leuven, 2008.

Snaet, *Tempels*, 1999
J. Snaet, 'De eerste protestantse tempels in de Nederlanden. Een onderzoek naar vorm en perceptie', *Bulletin van de Koninklijke Nederlandse Oudheidkundige Bond*, XCVIII, 1999, pp. 45–58.

Speth-Holterhoff, *Cabinets*, 1957
S. Speth-Holterhoff, *Les peintres flamands de cabinets d'amateurs au XVIIe siècle*, Paris – Brussels, 1957.

Spicer, *Elbow*, 1991
J. Spicer, 'The Renaissance elbow,' in J. Bremmer and H. Roodenburg, eds, *A Cultural History of Gesture from Antiquity to the Present Day*, Cambridge, 1991, pp. 84–128.

De Staelen, *Rubens*, 2014
C. De Staelen, 'Rubens: The ingenious master as an architect ?, in P. Lombaerde, ed., *The Notion of the Painter-Architect in Italy and the Southern Low Countries* (Architectura Moderna, XI), Turnhout, 2014, pp. 237–264.

Stechow, *Classical Tradition*, 1968
W. Stechow, *Rubens and the Classical Tradition* (Martin Classical Lectures, XXII), Cambridge, MA, 1968.

Steppe, *Koordoksaal*, 1952
J.K. Steppe, *Het koordoksaal in de Nederlanden* (Verhandelingen van de Koninklijke Vlaamse Academie voor Wetenschappen, Letteren en Schone Kunsten van België, Klasse der Schone Kunsten, VII), Brussels, 1952.

Stiegemann, ed., *Rubens*, 2020
C. Stiegemann, ed., [Exh. Cat.] *Peter Paul Rubens und der Barock im Norden* (Erzbischöfliches Diözesanmuseum, Paderborn, 2020), Petersberg, 2020.

Van der Stighelen, *Andries Snellinck*, 1989
K. Van der Stighelen, 'De (atelier-)bedrijvigheid van Andries Snellinck (1587–1653) en Co', *Jaarboek Koninklijk Museum voor Schone Kunsten Antwerpen*, 1989, pp. 303–341.

Van der Stighelen, *Cornelis de Vos*, 1990
K. Van der Stighelen, *De Portretten van Cornelis de Vos (1584/5–1651): Een kritische catalogus* (Verhandelingen van de Koninklijke Academie voor Wetenschappen, Letteren en Schone Kunsten van België, Klasse der Kunsten, 51), Brussels, 1990.

Van der Stighelen, *Zelfbeeld*, 2000
K.Van der Stighelen, 'Van zelfbeeld tot ezel: kunstenaarsalaam op zestiende- en zeventiende-eeuwse zelfportretten', in H. Vlieghe, A. Balis and C. Van de Velde, eds, *Concept, Design and Execution in Flemish Painting (1550–1700)*, Turnhout, 2000, pp. 233–260.

Van der Stighelen – Vlieghe, *Portraits Unidentified Sitters* (*CRLB*), 2021
K. Van der Stighelen and H. Vlieghe, *Portraits of Unidentified and Newly Identifed Sitters Painted in Antwerp* (Corpus Rubenianum Ludwig Burchard, XIX.3), London – Turnhout, 2021.

Stokroos, *Fonteinen*, 2005
M. Stokroos, *Fonteinen in Nederland, Historische watervoerende monumenten*, Zutphen, 2005.

Strauss – Van der Meulen, *Rembrandt*, 1979
W.L. Strauss and M. van der Meulen, *The Rembrandt Documents*, New York, 1979.

De Strobel, ed., *Sistine Chapel / Tapestries*, 2020
A.M. De Strobel, ed., *Leo X and Raphael in the Sistine Chapel: the Tapestries of the Acts of the Apostles*, I–II, Vatican City, 2020.

Stumpel, *Spiegelingen*, 2006
J. Stumpel, 'Spiegelingen in het atelier', in M. Haverman et al., eds, *Ateliergeheimen, over de werkplaats van de Nederlandse kunstenaar van 1200 tot heden*, Lochem – Amsterdam, 2006.

Stutz, *Residenz*, 1985
Z. Stutz, 'Die Residenz des Malerfürsten Rubens in Antwerpen und das vornehme Bürgerhaus Rembrandts in Amsterdam', in E. Hüttinger, ed., *Künstlerhäuser von der Renaissance bis zur Gegenwart*, Zürich, 1985, pp. 139–152.

Van Suchtelen – Van Beneden, *Room for Art*, 2009
A. van Suchtelen and B. van Beneden, [Exh. Cat.] *Room for Art in Seventeenth-Century Antwerp / Kamers vol kunst in zeventiende eeuws Antwerpen* (Rubenshuis, Antwerp, 2009–2010; Mauritshuis, The Hague, 2010), Zwolle, 2009.

Svenningsen, *Rubens Cantoor*, 2013
J. Svenningsen, 'The Classification of Drawings in the so-called Rubens' Cantoor', *Master Drawings*, LI, 3, 2013, pp. 349–359.

Swillens, *Van Campen*, 1961
P. Swillens, *Jacob van Campen, schilder en bouwmeester, 1595–1657*, Assen, 1961.

Terwen, *Johan Maurits*, 1979
J.J. Terwen, 'The Buildings of Johan Maurits van Nassau', in E. van den Boogaart et al., eds, *Johan Maurits van Nassau-Siegen, 1604–1679. A Humanist Prince in Europe and Brazil. Essays on the Occasion of the Tercentenary of his Death*, The Hague, 1979, pp. 55–143.

Tessin, *Studieresor*, ed. Sirén, 1914
N. Tessin, O. Sirén, ed., *Studieresor i Danmark, Tyskland, Holland, Frankrike och Italien*. anteckningar, bref och ritningar [1687], Stockholm, 1914.

Thijs, *Raemvelt*, 1993
A.K.L. Thijs, 'Op en om het "Raemvelt". Techniek en terminologie van de lakenbereiding te Antwerpen', in P. Catteeuw and F. Hellemans, eds, *In verscheidenheid. Liber Amicorum prof. dr. em. Robert Van Passen*, Aartrijke, 1993, pp. 301–309.

Thuillier – Foucart, *Galerie Médicis*, 1969
J. Thuillier and J. Foucart, *Rubens, La Galerie Médicis au Palais du Luxembourg*, Milan – Paris, [1969].

Thys, *Historiek der straten*, 1893
A. Thys, *Historiek der straten en openbare plaatsen van Antwerpen*, 2nd ed., Antwerp, 1893 [reprint 1873].

Thys, *Historique*, 1873
A. Thys, *Historique des rues et places publiques de la ville d'Anvers*, Antwerp, 1873.

Tijs, *Atlas*, 2007
R. Tijs, *Antwerpen: atlas van een stad in ontwikkeling*, Tielt, 2007.

Tijs, *Herdersgrot*, 2002
R. Tijs, 'De herdersgrot met fontein in de patio van het oorspronkelijke huis van Rubens te Antwerpen', *Brabom* (Berichten en Rapporten over het Antwerps Bodemonderzoek en Monumentenzorg), V, 2002, pp. 115–138.

Tijs, *Hirtengrotte*, 2002
R. Tijs, 'Über die Hirtengrotte in Rubens' Garten: Der Einfluss der italienischen Renaissance auf nördliche Gartenkonzepte', *Die Gartenkunst*, XIV, 2002, 1, pp. 9–18.

Tijs, *Historisch portret*, 2001
R. Tijs, *Antwerpen: historisch portret van een stad*, Tielt, 2001.

Tijs, *Renaissance- en barokarchitectuur*, 1999
R. Tijs, *Renaissance- en barokarchitectuur in België, Vitruvius' erfenis en de ontwikkeling van de bouwkunst in de Zuidelijke Nederlanden van renaissance tot barok*, Tielt, 1999.

Tijs, *Rubens*, 2004
R. Tijs, *De andere Rubens, Activiteiten – Interesses – Leefwereld*, Leuven, 2004.

Tijs, *Rubens en Jordaens*, 1984
R. Tijs, *P.P. Rubens en J. Jordaens: Barok in eigen Huis: een architectuurhistorische studie over groei, verval en restauratie van twee 17de-eeuwse kunstenaarswoningen te Antwerpen*, Antwerp, 1984.

Timmermans, *Patronen van patronage*, 2008
B. Timmermans, *Patronen van patronage in het zeventiende-eeuwse Antwerpen: een elite als actor binnen een kunstwereld* (Studies Stadsgeschiedenis, III), Amsterdam, 2008.

Toulier, *Villa Médicis*, I, 1989
B. Toulier, *La Villa Médicis. I: Documentation et description*, ed. A. Chastel, Rome, 1989.

Trofimova, ed., *Alexander*, 2010
A. Trofimova, ed., [Exh. Cat] *The Immortal Alexander the Great. The Myth, the Reality, his Journey, his Legacy / De Onsterfelijke Alexander de Grote. De Mythe, de Werkelijkheid, zijn Reis, zijn Erfenis* (Hermitage Amsterdam, Amsterdam, 2010–2011), Amsterdam, 2010.

Van Tyghem, *Bouwwerf*, 1966
F. van Tyghem, *Op en om de Middeleeuwse bouwwerf, De gereedschappen en toestellen gebruikt bij het bouwen van de vroege middeleeuwen tot omstreeks 1600 [...]* (Verhandelingen van de

Koninklijke Vlaamse Academie voor Wetenschappen, Letteren en Schone Kunsten van België, Klasse der Schone Kunsten, XXVIII), Brussels, 1966.

Upmark, *Besuch,* **1900**
G. Upmark, 'Ein Besuch in Holland, 1687, aus den Reiseschilderungen des schwedischen Architecten Nicodemus Tessin d.J.', *Oud-Holland,* XVIII, 1900, pp. 117–128, 144–152, 199–210.

Uppenkamp, *Rubens's palazzetto,* **2018**
B. Uppenkamp, 'Rubens's *palazzetto* in Antwerp', in A. Tacke et al., eds, *Künstlerhäuser im Mittelalter und der Frühen Neuzeit / Artists' Homes in the Middle Ages and the Early Modern Era* (*Artifex, Quellen und Studien zur Künstlersozialgeschichte / Sources and Studies in the Social History of the Artist*), Petersberg, 2018, pp. 218–232.

Uppenkamp – Van Beneden, *Architectural Symbolism,* **2011**
B. Uppenkamp and B. van Beneden, 'Rubens and Architectural Symbolism', in B. Uppenkamp and B. van Beneden, [Exh. Cat.] *Palazzo Rubens: The Master as Architect / Palazzo Rubens: de meester als architect / Palazzo Rubens: le maître et l'architecture* (Rubenshuis, Antwerp, 2011), Antwerp, 2011, pp. 76–122.

Uppenkamp – Van Beneden, *Palazzo Rubens,* **2011**
B. Uppenkamp and B. van Beneden, [Exh. Cat.] *Palazzo Rubens: The Master as Architect / Palazzo Rubens: de meester als architect / Palazzo Rubens: le maître et l'architecture* (Rubenshuis, Antwerp, 2011), Antwerp, 2011.

Uppenkamp – Van Beneden, *Vera simmetria,* **2011**
B. Uppenkamp and B. van Beneden, '"La vera simmetria". Rubens's Italian Examples', in B. Uppenkamp and B. van Beneden, [Exh. Cat.] *Palazzo Rubens: The Master as Architect / Palazzo Rubens: de meester als architect / Palazzo Rubens: le maître et l'architecture* (Rubenshuis, Antwerp, 2011), Antwerp, 2011, pp. 34–74.

Vaenius, *Emblemata Horatiana,* **1607**
O. Vaenius (Van Veen), *Q. Horatii Flacci Emblemata,* Antwerp, 1607.

Varshavskaya, *Rubens,* **1975**
M. Varshavskaya, *Kartiny Rubensa v Ermitazhe* [*Paintings by Rubens in the Hermitage*], Leningrad, 1975.

Van der Veen, *Studeerkamers,* **2000**
J. van der Veen, 'Eenvoudig en stil: Studeerkamers in zeventiende-eeuwse woningen, voornamelijk te Amsterdam, Deventer en Leiden', in J. de Jong et al., eds, *Wooncultuur in de Nederlanden 1500–1800* (*Nederlands Kunsthistorisch Jaarboek,* LI, 2000), Zwolle, pp. 138–171.

Van de Velde, *Floris,* **1975**
C. Van de Velde, *Frans Floris (1519/20–1570). Leven en Werken* (*Verhandelingen van de Koninklijke Vlaamse Academie voor Wetenschappen, Letteren en Schone Kunsten van België, Klasse der Schone Kunsten,* XXX), I–II, Brussels, 1975.

Van de Velde, *Rubens's Letters,* **2011**
C. Van de Velde, 'Rubens's Letters', *The Rubenianum Quarterly,* 2011, 4, pp. 3–4.

Van de Velde, *L'itinéraire italien,* **1978–79**
C. Van de Velde, 'L'itinéraire italien de Rubens', *Bulletin de l'Institut Historique Belge de Rome,* XLVIII–XLIX, 1978–1979, pp. 239–259.

Van de Velde, *Painted Decoration,* **1985**
C. Van de Velde, 'The Painted Decoration of Floris's House', in G. Cavalli-Björkman, ed., *Netherlandish Mannerism. Papers Given at a Symposium in Nationalmuseum Stockholm, September 21–22, 1984,* Stockholm, 1985, pp. 127–134.

Van de Velde, *Rubens' Brieven,* **2006**
C. Van de Velde, *Rubens' brieven in het Nederlands,* in K. Van der Stighelen, ed., *Munuscula Amicorum. Contributions on Rubens and His Colleagues in Honour of Hans Vlieghe* (*Pictura Nova,* X), I–II, Turnhout, 2006, I, pp. 147–183.

Van de Velde, *Rubens' Hemelvaart,* **1975**
C. Van de Velde, 'Rubens' Hemelvaart van Maria in de kathedraal te Antwerpen', *Jaarboek Koninklijk Museum voor Schone Kunsten Antwerpen,* 1975, pp. 245–277.

Veldman, *Leerrijke reeksen,* **1986**
I.M. Veldman, [Exh. Cat.] *Leerrijke reeksen van Maarten van Heemskerck* (Frans Halsmuseum, Haarlem, 1986), The Hague – Haarlem, 1986.

Vène, *Bibliographia Serliana,* **2007**
M. Vène, *Bibliographia Serliana, Catalogue des éditions imprimées des livres du traité d'architecture de Sebastiano Serlio (1537–1681),* Paris, 2007.

Venuti – Amaduzzi, *Vetera Monumenta,* **1774–79**
R. Venuti and J.C. Amaduzzi, *Vetera Monumenta quae in Hortis Caelimontanis et in aedibus Matthaeiorum adservantur [...],* I – III, Rome, 1774–1779.

Vercoullie, *Van der Sanden,* **1913**
J. Vercoullie, 'Sanden (Jacques van der)', in *Biographie nationale de Belgique,* XXI, Brussels, 1912–1913, cols 310–311.

Vergara – Lammertse, *Young Van Dyck,* **2012**
A. Vergara and F. Lammertse, eds, [Exh. Cat.] *El Joven Van Dyck / The Young Van Dyck* (Madrid, Museo Nacional del Prado, 2012–2013), Madrid, 2012.

Verhelst, *Maagdenhuis,* **1996**
D. Verhelst, *Tot eerlick onderhoudt van meyskens cleene. Geschiedenis van het Maagdenhuis van Antwerpen,* Antwerp, 1996.

Vermeulen, *Bouwstijlen Nederlanden,* **n.d.**
F.A.J.Vermeulen, *ABC van de bouwstijlen in de Nederlanden,* Amsterdam, 2nd ed., n.d. [c. 1960].

Vermeylen, *Antwerp Beckons,* **2004**
F. Vermeylen, 'Antwerp Beckons. The Reasons for Rubens' Return to the Netherlands in 1608', in J. de Jong et al., eds, *Rubens and the Netherlands* (*Netherlands Yearbook for History of Art,* LV) / *Rubens en de Nederlanden* (*Nederlands Kunsthistorisch Jaarboek,* LV), Zwolle, 2004, pp. 16–33.

Vervaet et al., *Rubens,* **1990**
J. Vervaet et al., *P.P. Rubens: catalogus schilderijen, olieverfschetsen, Koninklijk Museum voor Schone Kunsten Antwerpen,* Antwerp, 1990.

Vey, *Van Dyck,* **1962**
H. Vey, *Die Zeichnungen Anton Van Dycks* (*Monographien des 'Nationaal Centrum voor de Plastische Kunsten van de XVIde en XVIIde eeuw',* 1), I–II, Brussels, 1962.

Vignola, *Cinque Ordini,* **1563**
I. Barozzio da Vignola, *Regola delli cinque ordini d'Architettura,* Rome, 1563.

Vignola, *Porte d'Architettura di Michel Angelo,* **1602**
I. Barozzio da Vignola, *Nuova et Ultima Aggiunta delle Porte d'Architettura di Michel Angelo Buonaroti Fiorentino Pittore Scultore et Architetto Excellmo,* Rome, 1602.

Vitruvius, *Ten Books,* **trans. Morgan, 1960**
Vitruvius, *The Ten Books on Architecture,* trans. M.H. Morgan, New York, 1960 (reprint of 1914 edn).

Vlieghe, *Faydherbe,* **1997**
H. Vlieghe, 'Lucas Faydherbe en Rubens', in H. De Nijn, H. Vlieghe and H. Devisscher, eds, [Exh. Cat.] *Lucas Faydherbe, 1617–1697: Mechels beeldhouwer & architect* (Stedelijk Museum Hof van Busleyden, Mechelen, 1997), Mechelen, 1997, pp. 24–27.

Vlieghe, *Portraits (CRLB),* **1987**
H. Vlieghe, *Rubens. Portraits of Identified Sitters Painted in Antwerp* (Corpus Rubenianum Ludwig Burchard, XIX, 2), London, 1987.

Vlieghe, *Saints (CRLB),* **1972–73**
H. Vlieghe, *Saints* (Corpus Rubenianum Ludwig Burchard, VIII), I–II, Brussels – London – New York, 1972–1973.

Voet, *Golden Compasses,* **1969**
L. Voet, *The Golden Compasses. A History and Evaluation of the Printing and Publishing Activities of the Officina Plantiniana at Antwerp,* I, Amsterdam, 1969.

Voet et al., *Antwerpen,* **1978**
L. Voet et al., *De stad Antwerpen van de Romeinse tijd tot de 17de eeuw. Topografische studie rond het plan van Virgilius Bononiensis, 1565,* Brussels, 1978.

De Vos, *Jacques Francart,* **1998**
A. De Vos, *Jacques Francart, Premier livre d'Architecture (1617): studie van een Zuid-Nederlands modelboek met poortgebouwen* (Verhandelingen van de Koninklijke Academie voor Wetenschappen, Letteren en Schone Kunsten van België, Klasse der Schone Kunsten, LX), Brussels, 1998.

V.S
C.G. Voorhelm Schneevoogt, *Catalogue des estampes gravées d'apres P.P. Rubens, avec l'indication des collections ou se trouvent les tableaux et les gravures,* Haarlem, 1873.

Van Vyve, *Guide,* **1854**
J. Van Vyve, *Guide dans la ville et les environs d'Anvers. Description des monuments, objets d'Art et antiquités précédée d'un notice historique,* Antwerp, 1854.

Waagen, *Treasures,* **1854**
[G.F.] Waagen, *Treasures of Art in Great Britain. Being an Account of the Chief Collections of Paintings, Drawings, Sculptures, Illuminated Mss., etc., etc.,* I–III, London, 1854.

Warnke, *Chimären,* **1993**
M. Warnke, *Chimären der Phantasie,* in C. Brink and W. Hornbostel, eds, [Exh. Cat.] *Pegasus und die Künste* (Museum für Kunst und Gewerbe, Hamburg, 1993), Munich, 1993, pp. 61–69.

Warnke, *Rubens,* **1977**
M. Warnke, *Peter Paul Rubens: Leben und Werk* (DuMont Kunst-Taschenbücher, LI), Cologne, 1977.

Watteeuw, *Domestic Staff,* **2015**
B. Watteeuw, 'Household Names? Domestic staff in Rubens's Home', in B. van Beneden, ed., [Exh. Cat.] *Rubens in Private: The Master Portrays his Family / Rubens privé: de meester portretteert zijn familie* (Rubenshuis, Antwerp, 2015), Brussels, 2015, pp. 54–75.

Watteeuw, *Material Girl,* **2019**
B. Watteeuw, 'Material Girl. Helena Fourment Wearing a Huyck', in A.D. Newman and L. Nijkamp, eds, *Undressing Rubens. Fashion and Painting in Seventeenth-Century Antwerp,* London – Turnhout, 2019, pp. 183–223.

Vande Weghe, *Antwerpse straatnamen,* **1977**
R. Vande Weghe, *Geschiedenis van de Antwerpse straatnamen,* Antwerp, 1977.

Westfehling, *Zeichnungen Rubens,* **2001**
U. Westfehling, 'Drei verschollene Zeichnungen von Peter Paul Rubens', *Wallraf-Richartz-Jahrbuch,* LXII, 2001, pp. 171–222.

Wethey, *Titian,* **1969–75**
H.E. Wethey, *The Paintings of Titian: Complete Edition,* I–III, London, 1969–1975.

Wheelock et al., *Van Dyck,* **1990**
A.K. Wheelock, S.J. Barnes, J.S. Held et al., [Exh. Cat.] *Anthony van Dyck* (National Gallery of Art, Washington, 1990–1991), Washington, 1990.

White, *Rubens,* **1987**
C. White, *Peter Paul Rubens, Man and Artist,* New Haven, CT – London, 1987.

White, *Van Dyck,* **2021**
C. White, *Anthony van Dyck and the Art of Portraiture,* London, 2021.

Wilmers, *Schut,* **1996**
G. Wilmers, *Cornelis Schut (1597–1655). A Flemish Painter of the High Baroque* (Pictura Nova: Studies in 16th- and 17th-Century Flemish Painting and Drawing, I), Turnhout, 1996.

Winner, *Rubens' Götterrat,* **1997**
M. Winner, 'Rubens' "Götterrat" als Friedensbild. Dichtung und Malerei von Peter Paul Rubens', *Münchner Jahrbuch der bildenden Kunst,* XLVIII, no. 3, 1997, pp. 113–134.

Wirth, *Häuser,* **1985**
L. Wirth, 'Die Häuser von Raffael in Rom und von Giulio Romano in Rom und Mantua', in E. Hüttinger, ed., *Künstlerhäuser von der Renaissance bis zur Gegenwart,* Zürich, 1985, pp. 57–68.

De Wit, *Grand Staircase,* **2016**
A. de Wit, 'Grand Staircase and joinery work on the Lange Vijverberg, The Hague (The Netherlands) in light of documents', in P. Fraiture et al, eds, *Between Carpentry and Joinery, Wood Finishing Work in European Medieval and Modern Architecture* (Scientia Artis, XII), Brussels, 2016, pp. 240–253.

Wood, *Copies, Raphael (CRLB),* **2010**
J. Wood, *Copies and Adaptations from Renaissance and Earlier Artists. Italian Artists. I. Raphael and his School* (Corpus Rubenianum Ludwig Burchard, XXVI.2), I–II, London – Turnhout, 2010.

Wood, *Copies, Titian (CRLB),* **2010**
J. Wood, *Copies and Adaptations from Renaissance and Later Artists. Italian Artists. II. Titian and North Italian Art* (Corpus Rubenianum Ludwig Burchard, XXVI.2), I–II, London – Turnhout, 2010.

Wood, *Drawings,* **1990**
J. Wood, 'Padre Resta's Flemish Drawings. Van Diepenbeeck, Van Thulden, Rubens, and the School of Fontainebleau', *Master Drawings,* XXVIII, 1990, pp. 3–53.

Wood, ed., *Lives,* **2005**
J. Wood, ed., *The Lives of Rubens by Giovanni Baglione, Joachim von Sandrart, Roger de Piles,* London, 2005.

Woollett, *Rubens and Brueghel,* **2006**
A.T. Woollett, 'Two Celebrated Painters: The Collaborative Ventures of Rubens and Brueghel, ca. 1598–1625', in A.T. Woollett and A. Van Suchtelen, [Exh. Cat.] *Rubens and Brueghel: A Working Friendship / Rubens & Brueghel: een artistieke vriendschap* (The J. Paul Getty Museum, Los Angeles; Mauritshuis, The Hague, 2006–2007), Zwolle, 2006, pp. 1–41.

Worsley, *Cavalier,* **2007**
L. Worsley, *Cavalier, A Tale of Chivalry, Passion and Great Houses*, London, 2007.

Worsley, *Inigo Jones,* **2007**
G. Worsley, *Inigo Jones and the European Classicist Tradition*, New Haven, CT – London, 2007.

Worsley – Addyman, *Riding Houses,* **2002**
L. Worsley and T. Addyman, 'Riding Houses and Horses: William Cavendish's Architecture for the Art of Horsemanship', *Architectural History, Journal of the Society of Architectural Historians of Great Britain*, XLV, 2002, pp. 194–229.

Worsley et al., *Horsemanship,* **2006**
L. Worsley et al., 'Horsemanship', in B. van Beneden and N. De Poorter, eds, [Exh. Cat.] *Royalist Refugees: William and Margaret Cavendish in the Rubens House 1848–1660* (Antwerp, Rubenshuis, 2006), Antwerp, 2006, pp. 37–54.

Wouk, *Façade of Floris,* **2014**
E. Wouk, '"Humanae Societati Necessaria": The Painted Façade of the House Of Frans Floris' in P. Lombaerde, ed., *The Notion of the Painter –Architect in Italy and the Southern Low Countries* (*Architectura Moderna,* XI), Turnhout, 2014, pp. 89–125.

Wouk, *Frans Floris,* **2018**
E. Wouk, *Frans Floris (1519/20–1570): Imagining a Northern Renaissance*, Leiden, 2018.

Zimmermann, *Rubenshaus,* **2004**
P.S. Zimmermann, 'Das Rubenshaus in Antwerpen im Verhältnis zu dem Stichwerk "Palazzi di Genova"', in M. Droste and A. Hoffmann, eds, *Wohnformen und Lebenswelten im interkulturellen Vergleich*, Frankfurt a. M. et al., 2004, pp. 161–175.

Zorach et al., *Virtual Tourist,* **2008**
R. Zorach et al., *The Virtual Tourist in Renaissance Rome, Printing and Collecting the Speculum Romanae Magnificentiae*, Chicago, 2008.

Exhibitions

Amsterdam, 2011–12
Rubens, Van Dyck & Jordaens: Flemish Painters from the Hermitage / Rubens, Van Dyck & Jordaens, Vlaamse meesters uit de Hermitage, Hermitage Amsterdam, Amsterdam, 2011–2012.

Antwerp, 1956
Tekeningen van P.P. Rubens, Rubenshuis, Antwerp, 1956.

Antwerp, 1958
Herinneringen aan P.P. Rubens, Rubenshuis, Antwerp, 1958.

Antwerp, 1971
Rubens en zijn tijd. Tekeningen uit Belgische verzamelingen. Tentoonstelling naar aanleiding van het 25-jarig bestaan van het Rubenshuis als museum, Rubenshuis, Antwerp, 1971.

Antwerp, 1991
Around Rubens. Prints and Drawings from the Stedelijk Prentenkabinet / Rondom Rubens: Tekeningen en prenten uit eigen verzameling, Museum Plantin-Moretus en het Stedelijk Prentenkabinet, Antwerp, 1991.

Antwerp, 1993a
Rubens Cantoor. Een verzameling tekeningen onstaan in Rubens' atelier, Rubenshuis, Antwerp, 1993.

Antwerp, 2008
Heads on Shoulders. Portrait Busts in the Low Countries, 1600–1800 / Voorbeeldige Busten. Het borstbeeld in de Nederlanden, 1600–1800, Koninklijk Museum voor Schone Kunsten Antwerpen, Antwerp, 2008.

Antwerp, 2011
Palazzo Rubens: The Master as Architect / Palazzo Rubens: de meester als architect / Palazzo Rubens: le maître et l'architecture, Rubenshuis, Antwerp, 2011.

Antwerp, 2015
Rubens in Private: The Master Portrays his Family / Rubens privé: de meester portretteert zijn familie, Rubenshuis, Antwerp, 2015.

Antwerp – London, 1999
Antoon Van Dyck:1599–1641/ Anthony van Dyck: 1599–1641 / Antoine van Dyck: 1599 1641, Koninklijk Museum voor Schone Kunsten, Antwerp; Royal Academy of Arts, Antwerp – London, 1999.

Braunschweig, 2004
Peter Paul Rubens. Barocke Leidenschaften, Herzog Anton Ulrich-Museum, Braunschweig, 2004.

Cologne, 2011
Aus der Graphischen Sammlung, Wallraf-Richartz-Museum, Cologne, 2011. [without catalogue]

Cologne, 2018
Rubens & co. Drawings of Masters from Flanders, Wallraf-Richartz-Museum, Cologne, 2018. [without catalogue]

London, 1988–89
Rubens: Paintings, Drawings, Prints in the Princes Gate Collection, Courtauld Institute Galleries, London, 1988–1989.

Ottawa, 1980
The Young Van Dyck / Le jeune Van Dyck, National Gallery of Canada, Ottowa, 1980.

Paris, 1981
Antoon Van Dyck et son iconographie: eaux-fortes, gravures et dessins de la foundation Custodia, collection Frits Lugt, Institut néerlandais, Paris, 1981.

Vienna, 2004b
Rubens in Wien. Die Meisterwerke, Liechtenstein Museum, Vienna; Kunsthistorisches Museum, Vienna; Gemäldegalerie der Akademie der Bildenden Künste in Wien, Vienna, 2004.

EXPLANATIONS

BNF: Bibliothèque national de France, Paris

DAMS: website of the collection of the museum and heritage institutions of Antwerp

KBR: Koninlijke Bibliotheek / Bibliothèque royale, Brussels

KB.DK: Det Kongelige Bibliotek, Copenhagen

Index I: Collections

This index lists, as far as their present whereabouts are known, all works catalogued. Copies, apart from prints, have also been included. These works are listed alphabetically according to place. The number of the catalogue entry is given first, followed by Copy numbers where relevant, by references to pages in Volume I and references to figures (in italics), in Volume II. Works the present whereabouts of which are not known can be found in Index II by subject matter.

ANTWERP, CENTRAAL DEPOT MUSEA – STAD ANTWERPEN

After ? Hans van Mildert after Rubens, plaster cast, positive:
Caryatid (Sphinx), **No. 35, Copy 2** I: 409–410; II: *figs 184–185*

After ? Hans van Mildert after Rubens, plaster cast, positive:
Pediment with a Niche, Flanked by Two Eagles Holding a Fruit Garland, **No. 27, Copy** I: 401

After ? Hans van Mildert after Rubens, plaster cast, negative:
Pediment with a Niche, Flanked by Two Eagles Holding a Fruit Garland, **No. 27, Copy** I: 401

After ? Hans van Mildert after a design by Rubens, plaster cast, negative:
Keystone with the Head of Medusa and a Thunderbolt, **No. 25, Copy** I: 398

After ? Hans van Mildert after a design by Rubens, plaster cast, positive:
Keystone with the Head of Medusa and a Thunderbolt, **No. 25, Copy** I: 398; II: *fig. 145*

After ? Hans van Mildert after Rubens, plaster cast, negative:
Female Satyr Facing Left, **No. 33, Copy** I: 407

After ? Hans van Mildert after Rubens, plaster cast, positive:
Female Satyr Facing Left, **No. 33, Copy** I: 407

After ? Hans van Mildert after Rubens, plaster cast, negative:
Male Satyr Facing Left, **No. 32, Copy** I: 407

After ? Hans van Mildert after Rubens, plaster cast, positive:
Male Satyr Facing Left, **No. 32, Copy** I: 407

After ? Hans van Mildert after Rubens, plaster cast, negative:
Male Satyr Facing Right, **No. 30, Copy** I: 405

Anonymous artist after a design by Rubens, (architectural) sculpture :
Scallop, **No. 23** I: 321, 341, 393–395, 424 n. 1; II: *fig. 131*

ANTWERP, PLANTIN-MORETUS MUSEUM

Rubens, drawing:
Architectural Study of a Window Surround and other Elements, **No. 7a** I: 58, 118, 137, 144, 173, 346–347, 370; II: *fig. 54*

ANTWERP, RUBENSHUIS

Anonymous artist, statue :
Bacchus, **No. 38** I: 299, 306, 335 n. 53, 409, 417–420, 423; II: *figs 201–203*

? Hans van Mildert after Rubens, sculpture / high relief:
Bucrania, **No. 29** I: 258, 397, 404–405; II: *figs 165–166*

Anonymous 18th-century artist (?) after a sculpture after a design by Rubens, plaster cast:
Bust of a Faun, **No. 1, Copy** I: 147, 170, 277, 332, 339, 394; II: *fig. 35*

20th-century sculptor after ? Hans van Mildert after Rubens, relief
Dolphin (left), **No. 26 (left)** I: 259, 400–401; II: *fig. 149*

? Hans van Mildert after Rubens, relief:
Dolphin (right), **No. 26 (right)** 142, 251, 259, 397, 400–401; II: *fig. 150*

? Hans van Mildert after Rubens, relief:
Pediment with a Niche, Flanked by Two Eagles Holding a Fruit Garland, **No. 27** I: 251, 261, 344 n. 6, 397, 401–402; II: *fig. 153*

After a design by Rubens, architecture:
Garden Pavilion, **No. 34** I: 83 n. 101, 295–319 (Chapter X), 408–409; II: *figs 177–178*

Frans Claessens after ? Hans van Mildert after Rubens, sculptures:
Caryatids Left and Right (Sphinxes), **No. 35**, **Copy 1** I: 409–410; II: *figs 184–185*

? Hans van Mildert after Rubens, statue:
Youth with a Cornucopia, **No. 36** I: 91, 280 n. 86, 299, 314, 315, 328, 409, 410–414; II: *fig. 187*

Anonymous seventeenth-century artist after Rubens (?), statue:
Hercules, **No. 40** I: 299, 315, 324, 330, 331, 332, 335, 393, 401, 409, 420, 421–425; II: *fig. 211*

After ? Hans van Mildert after Rubens, *plaster cast*:
Hercules, **No. 40, Copy** I: 421; II: *fig. 214*

229

INDEX I: COLLECTIONS

Anonymous artist after a design by Rubens, (architectural) sculpture:
Head of Hercules, **No. 23** I: 321, 341, 393–395, 424 n. 1; II: *fig. 131*

? Hans van Mildert after a design by Rubens, architectural-sculptural element:
Keystone with the Head of Medusa and a Thunderbolt, **No. 25** I: 259, 285, 392 n. 3, 397, 398–400; II: *fig. 144*

After a design by Rubens, architecture:
Portico, **No. 24** I: 83 n. 101, 249–293 (Chapter IX), 295, 395–398, 400, 401, 402, 404, 405, 407; II: *fig. 138*

? Hans van Mildert after Rubens, relief:
Ram's Heads Ending in a Volute and a Snake's Head, **No. 28 (left)** I: 261, 285, 300 n. 16, 397, 402–404, 405 n. 6; II: *fig. 158*

? Hans van Mildert after Rubens, relief:
Ram's Heads Ending in a Volute and a Snake's Head, **No. 28 (right)** I: 261, 285, 300 n. 16, 397, 402–404, 405 n.6; II: *fig. 161*

? Hans van Mildert after Rubens, relief:
Female Satyr Facing Left, **No. 33** I: 407; II: *fig. 176*

? Hans van Mildert after Rubens, relief:
Female Satyr Seen from Behind, Facing Left, **No. 31** I: 405–406; II: *fig. 173*

? Hans van Mildert after Rubens, relief:
Male Satyr Facing Left, **No. 32** I: 407; II: *fig. 175*

? Hans van Mildert after Rubens, relief:
Male Satyr Facing Right, **No. 30** I: 251, 405, 406, 407; II: *fig. 171*

BUDAPEST, SZÉPMŰVÉSZETI MÚZEUM, COLLECTION OF PRINTS AND DRAWINGS

After Rubens, drawing:
The Sacrifice of Iphigenia, **No. 11, Copy 2** I: 355; II: *fig. 72*

COLOGNE, WALLRAF-RICHARTZ-MUSEUM & FONDATION CORBOUD, GRAPHISCHE SAMMLUNG, ON LOAN FROM A PRIVATE COLLECTION

Rubens, drawing:
The Sacrifice of an Ox, **No. 10a** I: 58, 137, 173, 352, 354, 364; II: *fig. 65*

COPENHAGEN, STATENS MUSEUM FOR KUNST, KONGELIGE KOBBERSTIKSAMLING

Willem Panneels after Rubens, drawing:
Alexander with the Thunderbolt, **No. 12, Copy** I: 59, 85 n. 109, 167, 359; II: *fig. 84*

Attributed to Willem Panneels after Rubens, drawing:
Andromeda Liberated by Perseus, **No. 18, Copy** I: 59, 377; II: *fig. 112*

Willem Panneels after Rubens, drawing
The Sacrifice of Iphigenia, **No. 11, Copy 1** I: 59, 85 n. 109, 355, 356, 403; II: *figs 71, 75, 77*

Willem Panneels, drawing:
Female Satyr Seen from Behind, Facing Left, **No. 31, Copy 1** I: 59, 406; II: *fig. 174*

DUNDEE, THE MCMANUS / DUNDEE'S ART GALLERY & MUSEUM

Anonymous 17th-century Flemish silversmith after Rubens, silver plaque:
The Calumny of Apelles, **No. 13a, Copy 1** I: 363

LONDON, THE COURTAULD GALLERY

Rubens, drawing:
Architectural Studies and Figure Studies for an Entombment, **No. 13b** I: 18, 58, 125, 137, 144 n. 17, 173, 347, 363, 368, 369–370; II: *fig. 97*

Rubens, drawing:
The Calumny of Apelles, **No. 13a** I: 58, 85 n. 109, 137, 173, 363–369; II: *fig. 96*

PARIS, FONDATION CUSTODIA

Anthony van Dyck after Rubens, drawing:

The Portico of Rubens's House, Antwerp, **No. 24, Copy 1** I: 58, 270, 295, 396; II: *fig. 139*

Index II: Subjects

This index lists in alphabetical order by title of the principal subject all works catalogued. Under each title are gathered all known representations, listed in the same order as in the catalogue, these include works executed after designs by Rubens and works by Rubens himself. The number of the catalogue entry is given first, followed by Copy or print numbers where relevant, by references to pages in Volume I and references to figures (in italics) in Volume II.

ALEXANDER WITH THE THUNDERBOLT, NO. 12

Mural painting after a design by Rubens (Antwerp, Rubens's House, formerly on north façade of the studio, lost), **No. 12** I: 144–145, 359–362, 363; II: *figs 82–83*

Willem Panneels after Rubens, drawing (Copenhagen, Statens Museum for Kunst, Kongelige Kobberstiksamling), **No. 12, Copy** I: 59, 85 n. 109, 167, 359; II: *fig. 84*

ANDROMEDA LIBERATED BY PERSEUS, NO. 18

Mural painting after a design by Rubens (Antwerp, Rubens's House, formerly on east façade (facing the courtyard) of the studio wing, lost), **No. 18** I: 152, 174, 175, 176 n. 21, 178, 180, 285, 344 n. 5, 375, 377–387, 399, 400 n. 9; II: *figs 107, 110*

Attributed to Willem Panneels after Rubens, drawing (Copenhagen, Statens Museum for Kunst, Kongelige Kobberstiksamling), **No. 18, Copy** I: 59, 377; II: *fig. 112*

THE 'ANTIQUARIUM', NO. 20

After a design by Rubens, architecture (Antwerp, Rubens's House, lost), **No. 20** I: 92, 96, 111, 147, 154, 200, 201, 232, 233 n. 11, 238, 241, 244, 246, 247 n. 49, 389–391, 392, 395 n. 5; II: *fig. 127*

THE NORTH WALL OF THE 'ANTIQUARIUM', NO. 22

After a design by Rubens, architecture (Antwerp, Rubens's House, lost), **No. 22** I: 147 n. 27, 238, 242, 244, 390, 392–393; II: *fig. 127*

THE TRIUMPH OF APOLLO, NO. 9

Mural painting after a design by Rubens (Antwerp, Rubens's House, formerly on the east or garden façade of the studio, lost), **No. 9** I: 144–145, 174 n. 16, 348–350, 354 n. 2, 369 n. 16, 401 n. 1; II: *fig. 60*

ARCHITECTURAL STUDIES AND FIGURE STUDIES FOR AN ENTOMBMENT, NO. 13B

Rubens, drawing (London, The Courtauld Gallery),
No. 13b I: 18, 58, 125, 137, 144 n. 17, 173, 347, 363, 368, 369–370; II: *fig. 97*

ARCHITECTURAL STUDY OF A WINDOW SURROUND AND OTHER ELEMENTS, NO. 7A

Rubens, drawing (Antwerp, Museum Plantin-Moretus), **No. 7a** I: 58, 118, 137, 144, 173, 346–347, 370; II: *fig. 54*

BUNDLE OF ATTRIBUTES, NO. R3

Anonymous seventeenth-century artist, painted or in relief (formerly Antwerp, Rubens's House, in the spandrel on the side of the garden pavilion, lost), **No. R3** I: 306, 431–432; II: *fig. 233*

BACCHUS, NO. 38

Anonymous artist, statue (Antwerp, Rubenshuis, garden pavilion), **No. 38** I: 299, 306, 335 n. 53, 409, 417–420, 423; II: *figs 201–203*

BUCRANIA, NO. 29

? Hans van Mildert after Rubens, sculpture / high relief (Antwerp, Rubenshuis, portico), **No. 29 (left)** I: 258, 397, 404–405; II: *fig. 165*

? Hans van Mildert after Rubens, sculpture / high relief (Antwerp, Rubenshuis, portico), **No. 29 (right)** I: 258, 397, 404–405; II: *fig. 166*

CERES, NO. R4

Anonymous artist, statue (formerly (until c. 1938) Antwerp, Rubenshuis, garden pavilion; whereabouts unknown), **No. R4** I: 299, 311–313, 414, 415, 417 n. 2, 432–433; II: *fig. 235*

FOUR BUSTS IN NICHES, INCLUDING A FAUN NO. 1

Sculptures after a design by Rubens, possibly carved in the round, or executed in plaster or stucco (Antwerp, Rubens's House, formerly on the north façade of the studio, lost), **No. 1** I: 146 n. 20, 145–149, 339–340, 341; II: *figs 16–18, 27, 33–34*

INDEX II: SUBJECTS

Anonymous 18th-century artist (?) after a sculpture after a design by Rubens, *Bust of a Faun*, plaster cast (Antwerp, Rubenshuis), **No. 1, Copy** I: 147, 170, 277, 332, 339, 394; II: *fig. 35*

BUST IN A NICHE WITH A SCALLOP, FLANKED BY CORNUCOPIAS NO. 2

Sculpture or mural painting after a design by Rubens, possibly sculpted in the round, or executed in stone or stucco, or painted in *trompe-l'oeil* (Antwerp, Rubens's House, formerly on the north façade of the studio, lost), **No. 2** I: 141, 145–149, 150, 340–341, 394, 409; II: *figs 16–18, 27, 36–37*

THE CALUMNY OF APELLES, NO. 13

Mural painting after a design by Rubens (Antwerp, Rubens's House, formerly on the north façade of the studio, lost), **No. 13** I: 63, 144–145, 176, 349, 362–363, 364, 370; II: *figs 90–91*

THE CALUMNY OF APELLES, NO. 13A

Rubens, drawing (London, The Courtauld Gallery), **No. 13a** I: 58, 85 n. 109, 137, 173, 363–369; II: *fig. 96*

Anonymous 17th-century Flemish silversmith after Rubens, silver plaque (Dundee, The McManus / Dundee's Art Gallery & Museum), **No. 13a, Copy 1** I: 363

Anonymous German artist after Rubens, copper plaque (whereabouts unknown), **No. 13a, Copy 2** I: 364

CARYATIDS LEFT AND RIGHT (SPHINXES?), NO. 35

? Hans van Mildert after Rubens, sculptures (formerly Antwerp, Rubenshuis, garden pavilion, lost), **No. 35** I: 297, 328, 409–410, 418, 421; II: Cf. *figs 184–185*

Frans Claessens after ? Hans van Mildert after Rubens, sculptures (Antwerp, Rubenshuis, garden pavilion), **No. 35, Copy 1** I: 409–410; II: *figs 184–185*

After ? Hans van Mildert after Rubens, plaster cast (of one caryatid), positive (Antwerp, Centraal Depot Musea – Stad Antwerpen), **No. 35, Copy 2 (positive)** I: 410

A CHARIOT RACE (THE LOWERING OF THE CLOTH), NO. 8

Mural painting after a design by Rubens (Antwerp, Rubens's House, formerly on the east or garden façade of the studio, lost), **No. 8** I: 144–145, 347–348, 351, 375 n. 2 ; II: *fig. 57*

THE CUPOLA OF THE 'ANTIQUARIUM', NO. 21

After a design by Rubens, architecture (Antwerp, Rubens's House, lost), **No. 21** I: 111, 241, 390, 391–392, 400 n. 7, 403 n.1; II: *fig. 127*

DOLPHINS, NO. 26

20th-century sculptor after ? Hans van Mildert after Rubens, *Dolphin (left)*, relief (Antwerp, Rubenshuis, portico), **No. 26 (left)** I: 259, 400–401; II: *fig. 149*

? Hans van Mildert after Rubens, *Dolphin (right)*, relief (Antwerp, Rubenshuis, portico), **No. 26 (right)** I: 142, 251, 259, 397, 400–401; II: *fig. 150*

PEDIMENT WITH A NICHE, FLANKED BY TWO EAGLES HOLDING A FRUIT GARLAND, NO. 27

? Hans van Mildert after Rubens, relief (Antwerp, Rubenshuis, portico), **No. 27** I: 251, 261, 344 n. 6, 397, 401–402; II: *fig. 153*

After ? Hans van Mildert after Rubens, plaster cast, postive (Antwerp, Centraal Depot Musea – Stad Antwerpen), **No. 27, Copy (positive)** I: 401

After ? Hans van Mildert after Rubens, plaster cast, negative (Antwerp, Centraal Depot Musea – Stad Antwerpen), **No. 27, Copy (negative)** I: 401

FLORA FARNESE, NO. 6

Mural painting or relief after a design by Rubens (Antwerp, Rubens's House, formerly on the east or garden façade of the studio wing, lost), **No. 6** I: 156, 344–355; II: *fig. 47*

FOUNTAIN WITH A PUTTO (CUPID) ON A DOLPHIN, NO. 41

Anonymous artist, fountain (? formerly Antwerp, Rubens's House, in the garden, lost, if ever existed), **No. 41** I: 115, 259 n. 27, 425–428; II: *fig. 218*

GARDEN PAVILION, NO. 34

After a design by Rubens, architecture (Antwerp, Rubenshuis), **No. 34** I: 83 n. 101, 295–319 (Chapter X), 408–409; II: *figs 177–178*

HEAD OF HERCULES UNDER A SCALLOP AND GARLANDS, NO. 23

After a design by Rubens, *Fruit Garlands Suspended from Lion Heads*, (architectural) sculpture (lost), **No. 23** I: 321, 341, 393–395, 424 n. 1; II: *fig. 131*

INDEX II: SUBJECTS

YOUTH WITH A CORNUCOPIA (GENIUS LOCI?), NO. 36

? Hans van Mildert after Rubens, statue (Antwerp, Rubenshuis, garden pavilion), **No. 36** I: 91, 280 n. 86, 299, 314, 315, 328, 409, 410–414; II: *fig. 187*

HERCULES, NO. 40

Anonymous seventeenth-century artist after Rubens (?), statue (Antwerp, Rubenshuis, garden pavilion), **No. 40** I: 299, 315, 324, 330, 331, 332, 335, 393, 401, 409, 420, 421–425; II: *fig. 211*

After ? Hans Van Mildert after Rubens, plaster cast (Antwerp, Rubenshuis), **No. 40, Copy** I: 421; II: *fig. 214*

BUST OF HERCULES, NO. 39

? After Rubens, sculpture (? formerly Antwerp, Rubens's House, garden pavilion), **No. 39** I: 285, 302, 303, 394, 420, 422, 423; II: *fig. 210*

THE DRUNKEN HERCULES, NO. 15

Mural painting after a design by Rubens (Antwerp, Rubens's House, formerly on north façade of the studio, lost), **No. 15** I: 144–145, 174, 176, 370, 373–375; II: *fig. 101*

HEAD OF HERCULES UNDER A SCALLOP AND GARLANDS, NO. 23

After a design by Rubens, *Head of Hercules*, (architectural) sculpture (Antwerp, Rubenshuis), **No. 23** I: 321, 341, 393–395, 424 n. 1; II: *fig. 131*

FOUR UNIDENTIFIED HERM BUSTS, NO. 3

Sculpture or mural paintings after a design by Rubens, possibly sculpted in the round, or executed in stone or stucco, or painted in *trompe-l'oeil* (Antwerp, Rubens's House, formerly on the north façade of the studio, lost), **No. 3** I: 145–149, 341–342; II: *figs 17–18, 27, 37–38*

HERMES BELVEDERE, NO. 5

Mural painting or relief after a design by Rubens (Antwerp, Rubens's House, formerly on the east or garden façade of the studio, lost), **No. 5** I: 156, 343–344, 345, 379; II: *fig. 44*

SIX HERMS, NO. 4

Sculpture or mural paintings after a design by Rubens, possibly sculpted in the round, or executed in stone or stucco, or painted in *trompe-l'oeil* (Antwerp, Rubens's House, formerly on the north façade of the studio, lost), **No. 4** I: 70 n. 69, 144–145, 162 n. 62, 169, 321 n. 2, 341 n. 1, 342–343; II: *figs 17–18, 27, 37–38*

YOUTHFULL HERO WITH A LANCE AND CHARIOT, NO. 16

Mural painting after a design by Rubens (Antwerp, Rubens's House, formerly on east façade (facing the courtyard) of the studio, lost), **No. 16** I: 144–145, 176, 375; II: *fig. 106*

THE SACRIFICE OF IPHIGENIA, NO. 11

Mural painting after a design by Rubens (Antwerp, Rubens's House, formerly on north façade of the studio, lost), **No. 11** I: 144–145, 176 n. 21, 193 n. 79, 352, 355–359, 360, 363, 403; II: *figs 69–70*

Willem Panneels after Rubens, drawing (Copenhagen, Statens Museum for Kunst, Kongelige Kobberstiksamling), **No. 11, Copy 1** I: 59, 85 n. 109, 355, 356, 403; II: *figs 71, 75, 77*

After Rubens, drawing (Budapest, Szépművészeti Múzeum, Collection of Prints and Drawings), **No. 11, Copy 2** I: 355; II: *fig. 72*

After Rubens, drawing (whereabouts unknown), **No. 11, Copy 3** I: 355; II: *fig. 73*

LOGGIA WITH A FIGURE AND ANIMALS, NO. 17

Mural painting after a design by Rubens (Antwerp, Rubens's House, formerly on the east façade (facing the courtyard) of the studio, lost), **No. 17** I: 96 n. 22, 183–184, 375, 376–377; II: *fig. 107*

KEYSTONE WITH THE HEAD OF MEDUSA AND A THUNDERBOLT, NO. 25

? Hans van Mildert after a design by Rubens, architectural-sculptural element (Antwerp, Rubenshuis, central arch of the portico), **No. 25** I: 259, 285, 392 n. 3, 397, 398–400; II: *fig. 144*

After ? Hans van Mildert after a design by Rubens, plaster cast, negative (Antwerp, Centraal Depot Musea – Stad Antwerpen), **No. 25, Copy (negative)** I: 398

After ? Hans van Mildert after a design by Rubens, plaster cast, positive (Antwerp, Rubenshuis), **No. 25, Copy (positive)** I: 398; II: *fig. 145*

MINERVA, NO. R2

Anonymous seventeenth-century artist, statue (formerly Antwerp, Rubens's House, on top

INDEX II: SUBJECTS

of the portico, lost), **No. R2** I: 281, 324, 384, 397, 429, 430–431; II: *figs 227, 231*

? Pictura , No. R1

Anonymous seventeenth-century artist, statue (formerly Antwerp, Rubens's House, on top of the portico, lost), **No. R1** I: 281, 284, 324, 384, 397, 404 n. 7, 428–430; II: *figs 227–228*

Portico, No. 24

After a design by Rubens, architecture (Antwerp, Rubenshuis), **No. 24** I: 249–293 (Chapter IX), 395– 398

Anthony van Dyck after Rubens, drawing (Paris, Fondation Custodia), **No. 24, Copy 1** I: 58, 270, 295, 396; II: *fig. 139*

? Anthony van Dyck after Rubens, painting (whereabouts unknown), **No. 24, Copy 2** I: 396

Sculpted details, plaster casts **No. 24, Copy 3**: I: 396 and see under Nos 25, 27, 30–33

Ram's Heads Ending in a Volute and a Snake's Head, No. 28

? Hans van Mildert after Rubens, relief (Antwerp, Rubenshuis, portico), **No. 28 (left)** I: 261, 285, 300 n. 16, 397, 402–404, 405 n. 6; II: *fig. 158*

? Hans van Mildert after Rubens, relief (Antwerp, Rubenshuis, portico), **No.28 (right)** I: 261, 285, 300 n. 16, 397, 402–404, 405 n.6; II: *fig. 161*

The Sacrifice of an ox, No. 10

Mural painting after a design by Rubens (Antwerp, Rubens's House, formerly on the east or garden façade of the studio, lost), **No. 10** I: 144–145, 176, 179 n. 31, 350–353, 354, 358 n. 6, 404 n. 2; II: *fig. 64*

The Sacrifice of an ox, No. 10A

Rubens, drawing (Private Collection, on loan to the Wallraf-Richartz-Museum & Fondation Corboud, Graphische Sammlung, Cologne), **No. 10a** I: 58, 137, 173, 352, 354, 364; *II: fig. 65*

Female Satyr Facing Left, No. 33

? Hans van Mildert after Rubens, relief (Antwerp, Rubenshuis, portico), **No. 33** I: 407; II: *fig. 176*

After ? Hans van Mildert after Rubens, plaster cast, negative (Antwerp, Centraal Depot Musea – Stad Antwerpen), **No. 33, Copy (negative)** I: 407

After ? Hans van Mildert after Rubens, plaster cast, positive (Antwerp, Centraal Depot Musea – Stad Antwerpen), **No. 33, Copy (positive)** I: 407

Female Satyr Seen from Behind, Facing Left, No. 31

? Hans van Mildert after Rubens, relief (Antwerp, Rubenshuis, portico), **No. 31** I: 405–406; II: *fig. 173*

Willem Panneels, drawing (Copenhagen, Statens Museum for Kunst, Kongelige Kobberstiksamling), **No. 31, Copy 1** I: 59, 406 ; II: *fig. 174*

After ? Hans van Mildert after Rubens, plaster cast, negative (Antwerp, Centraal Depot Musea – Stad Antwerpen), **No. 31, Copy 2 (negative)** I: 406

Male Satyr Facing Left, No. 32

? Hans van Mildert after Rubens, relief (Antwerp, Rubenshuis, portico), **No. 32** I: 407; II: *fig. 175*

After ? Hans van Mildert after Rubens, plaster cast, negative (Antwerp, Centraal Depot Musea –Stad Antwerpen), **No. 32, Copy (negative)** I: 407

After ? Hans van Mildert after Rubens, plaster cast, positive (Antwerp, Centraal Depot Musea – Stad Antwerpen), **No. 32, Copy (positive)** I: 407

Male Satyr Facing Right, No. 30

? Hans van Mildert after Rubens, relief (Antwerp, Rubenshuis, portico), **No. 30** I: 251, 405, 406, 407; II: *fig. 171*

After ? Hans van Mildert after Rubens, plaster cast, negative (Antwerp, Centraal Depot Musea – Stad Antwerpen), **No. 30, Copy (negative)** I: 405

Head of Hercules under a Scallop and Garlands, No. 23

After a design by Rubens, *Scallop*, (architectural) sculpture (Antwerp Centraal Depot Musea – Stad Antwerpen), **No. 23** I: 321, 341, 393–395, 424 n. 1; II: *fig. 131*

Staircase, No. 19

After Hans van Mildert after a design by Rubens, joinery (Antwerp, Rubens's House, lost), **No. 19** I: 54 n. 15, 119 n. 5, 125 n. 29, 126, 184,

INDEX II: SUBJECTS

202, 203 n. 3, 204, 327, 387–388, 389, 405 n. 2; II: *fig. 124*

DESIGN FOR THE STAIRCASE IN RUBENS'S HOUSE, NO. 19A

Rubens, drawing (whereabouts unknown, probably lost), **No. 19a** I: 388, 389

VENUS (AND CUPID), NO. 37

Anonymous artist, sculpture (formerly Antwerp, Rubenshuis, garden pavilion, lost), **No. 37** I: 59, 306, 326, 409, 414–417; II: *figs 195–197*

WINDOW SURROUND, NO. 7

Architecture, probably bluestone (or painted in *trompe-l'oeil*?) (Antwerp, Rubens's House, formerly on the façades of the studio, lost), **No. 7** I: 63 n. 48, 143–144, 345–346, 347; II: *fig. 52*

ZEUXIS AND THE MAIDENS OF CROTON, NO. 14

Mural painting after a design by Rubens (Antwerp, Rubens's House, formerly on north façade of the studio, lost), **No. 14** I: 144–145, 370–372; II: *fig. 98*

235

Index III: Other Works by or after Rubens Mentioned in the Text

The following abbreviations are used throughout this index: **C** – cartoon; **D** – drawing; **E** – engraving, etching or woodcut; **P** – painting; **S** – oil sketch; **Sc** – sculpture; **T** – tapestry

OLD TESTAMENT

Abraham and Melchizedek **P** (Caen, Musée des Beaux-Arts) I: 382; II: *fig. 119*
Bathsheba Receiving David's Letter **P** (Dresden, Staatliche Kunstsammlungen, Gemäldegalerie Alte Meister) I: 427
The Flight of Lot and His Family from Sodom **P** (Paris, Musée du Louvre): I: 269; II: 52, *appendix III.21*
Judith Beheading Holofernes **P** (Braunschweig, Herzog Anton Ulrich-Museum) I: 39
Susanna and the Elders **P** (Madrid, Real Academia de Bellas Artes de San Fernando) I: 426, 427; II: 48, *fig. 222*
Susanna and the Elders **P** after Rubens (St Petersburg, The State Hermitage Museum) I: 426; II: 53, *appendix III.22*
    E by Christoffel Jegher I: 426; II: *fig. 225*
Susanna and the Elders **P** (Munich, Bayerische Staatsgemäldesammlungen, Alte Pinakothek) I: 107 n. 37

NEW TESTAMENT AND RELATED SUBJECTS

The Triptych of the Adoration of the Magi **PP** (Mechelen, Church of St John the Baptist and St John the Evangelist) I: 134
The Adoration of the Magi **P** (Madrid, Museo Nacional del Prado) I: 120 n. 10, 130
An Angel **P** (Flint, MI, Flint Institue of Arts) I: 283 n. 95
Ecce Homo **P** (St Petersburgh, The State Hermitage Collection) I: 350 n. 14
The Triptych of the Elevation of the Cross **PP** (Antwerp, Cathedral of Our Lady) I: 120 n. 10, 130; II: 32
    The Elevation of the Cross I: 283 n. 95
The Triptych of the Descent from the Cross **PP** (Antwerp, Cathedral of Our Lady) I: 24 n. 9, 52, 120 n. 10, 124, 130, *text ill. 55*, 131 n. 46; II: 31, 33, 34
    The Descent from the Cross (centre panel) I: 132
The Entombment **D** (Amsterdam, Rijksprentenkabinet) I: 370 n. 1
The Lamentation with St Francis **P** (Brussels, Musées royaux des Beaux-Arts de Belgique) I: 356; II: *fig. 74*
The Triptych of the Resurrection of Christ ('The Moretus Triptych') **PP** (Antwerp, Cathedral of Our Lady) I: 119 n. 5
The Supper at Emmaus **P** (Madrid, Museo Nacional del Prado) I: 300, 322, 409; II: 54, *appendix III.25*
The Assumption of the Virgin **P** (Vienna, Kunsthistorisches Museum) I: 133
    D Copy by Willem Panneels after Rubens (Budapest, Szépművészeti Múzeum, Print Room) I: 268, *text ill. 118*
The Assumption of the Virgin **S** (lost) I: 268
The Last Judgement ('Great') **P** (Munich, Bayerische Staatsgemäldesammlunge, Alte Pinakothek) I: 134–135

THE HOLY TRINITY, THE LIFE OF THE VIRGIN, MADONNAS, THE HOLY FAMILY

The Education of the Virgin **P** (Antwerp, Koninklijk Museum voor Schone Kunsten Antwerpen) I: 66 n. 55
The Assumption of the Virgin: see New Testament and Related Subjects
Upper Part of an Altar Dedicated to the Virgin Mary **S** (Antwerp, Rubenshuis) I: 403; II: *fig. 163*

SAINTS

The Martyrdom of St Catherine of Alexandria **P** (Lille, Musée des Beaux-Arts) I: 356
The Miracles of St Francis Xavier **P** (Vienna, Kunsthistorisches Museum) I: 225 n. 72
The Miracles of St Ignatius of Loyola **P** (Vienna, Kunsthistorisches Museum) I: 225 n. 72
St Teresa of Avila Interceding for Bernardino de Mendoza **P** (Antwerp, Koninklijk Museum voor Schone Kunsten Antwerpen) I: 66 n. 55

OTHER RELIGIOUS SUBJECTS

The Ceiling Paintings for the Jesuit Church in Antwerp **PP** (destroyed) I: 220 nn. 57 and 59, 328
    Abraham and Melchizedek **S** (Paris, Musée du Louvre) I: 398

INDEX III: OTHER WORKS BY OR AFTER RUBENS MENTIONED IN THE TEXT

The Eucharist Series **TT** (Madrid, Convent of the Descalzas Reales) I: 111, 190 n. 68
    Angels Playing Music I: 111
    Angels Playing Music I: 111
    The Eucharist Overcoming Pagan Sacrifices
        S (Madrid, Museo Nacional del Prado) I: 353
    King David Playing the Harp I: 111 n. 46

MYTHOLOGY

Achilles Discovered among the Daughters of Lycomedes **P** Studio (Madrid, Museo Nacional del Prado) I: 180, 400 n. 9
The Achilles Series **TT** I: 343 n. 1
Achilles Discovered among the Daughters of Lycomedes **T** various locations I: 372 n. 4
The Decorations for the Torre de la Parada **PP** I: 282 n. 94, 334, 350 n. 7, 378
    Cupid on a Dolphin **S** (Brussels, Musées royaux des Beaux-Arts de Belgique) I: 426, 428 n. 3
    Jupiter and Lycaon **P** by Jan Cossiers after Rubens (Madrid, Museo Nacional del Prado) I: 399, 400 n. 6
    Mercury **P** (Madrid, Museo Nacional del Prado) I: 282 n. 94
    Musical Contest between Apollo and Marsyas (formerly The Judgment of Midas) **P** by Jacques Jordaens after Rubens (Madrid, Museo Nacional del Prado) I: 350 n. 7
        S (Brussels, Musées royaux des Beaux-Arts de Belgique) I: 350 n. 7
    Perseus and Andromeda **S** (whereabouts unknown) I: 378, 385 n. 6
    Vulcan Forging the Thunderbolt for Jupiter **P** (Madrid, Museo Nacional del Prado) I: 399, 400 n. 6
Andromeda Chained to the Rock **P** (Berlin, Staatliche Museen zu Berlin, Gemäldegalerie Alte Meister) I: 378
Andromeda Liberated by Perseus **P** (St Petersburg, The State Hermitage Museum) I: 378; II: *figs 111, 116, 120*
    E by Pierre François Tardieu I: 380
Andromeda Liberated by Perseus **P** (Berlin, Staatliche Museen zu Berlin, Gemäldegalerie Alte Meister) I: 378; II: *fig. 113*
Andromeda Liberated by Perseus **P** begun by Rubens, completed by Jacques Jordaens (Madrid, Museo Nacional del Prado) I: 378
The Bath of Diana, fragment of a *Diana and Actaeon* **P** studio of Rubens (Amersfoort, Rijksdienst voor Cultureel Erfgoed, on loan to the Museum Boijmans Van Beuningen, Rotterdam) I: 427
The Discovery of Erichtonius by the Daughters of Cecrops **P** (Vaduz – Vienna, Liechtenstein, The Princely Collections) I: 382, 394, 426; II: *figs 117, 137*
The Discovery of Erichtonius by the Daughters of Cecrops **S** Stockholm, Nationalmuseum I: 301, 322, 426, 427, *text ill. 138*; II: 53, *appendix III.23*; *fig. 226*
    Study for Aglauros Opening the Basket **D** (Antwerp, Museum Plantin-Moretus, Prentenkabinet) I: 346, 347
Ganymede Welcomed into Heaven **P** Vaduz, Fürstlich Schwarzenberg'sche Kunststiftung, on permanent loan to Vaduz – Vienna, Liechtenstein, The Princely Collections I: 402; II: *fig. 156*
The Drunken Hercules: see Allegory
Head of Hercules with a Snub Nose **D** after an unidentified (16th-century?) model (London, The British Museum) I: 420; II: *fig. 209*
Head of Medusa: see Copies after the Antique
The Head of Medusa **P** with Frans Snijders (Vienna, Kunsthistorisches Museum) I: 399
Mercury: see under Architecture and Sculpture
The Judgement of Paris **P** (Madrid, Museo Nacional del Prado) I: 371, 419, 420 n. 9
The Judgement of Paris **P** (London, The National Gallery) I: 371
Prometheus Bound **P** (Philadelphia, Philadelphia Museum of Art) I: 180, 384 n. 4
Venus: see under Architecture and Sculpture
Venus with Ceres and Bacchus (Sine Cerere et Baccho friget Venus): see Allegory

ALLEGORY

Homage to Ceres **S** with Frans Snijders (St Petersburg, The State Hermitage Museum) I: 118, 143 n. 14, 152, 265, 268, 269, 315, 382, 415, 433 n. 4; II: 48, *figs 23, 121*
Cimon and Iphigenia **P** with Frans Snijders (Vienna, Kunsthistorisches Museum) I:
    S (Longniddry (Scotland), Gosford House, Collection of the Earl of Wemyss and March) I: 427, 428; II: *fig. 223*
Hercules Overcoming Discord (Hercules Victor Discordiae) **S** (Amsterdam, Instituut Collectie Nederland. On long-term loan to Rotterdam, Museum Boijmans Van Beuningen) I: 332, 423
The Drunken Hercules **P** (Dresden, Staatliche Kunstsammlungen, Gemäldegalerie Alte Meister) I: 174 n. 16, 373; II: *fig. 105*
The Coronation of a Hero **P** (Munich, Bayerische Staatsgemäldesammlungen, Alte Pinakothek) I: 374
Honor and Virtue **S** (USA, Private Collection) I: 412, 413–414 n. 10
Honos and Virtus **D** (Antwerp, Museum Plantin-Moretus) I: 328, 411; II: *fig. 191*
Nature Adorned: see Works in Collaboration: With J. Brueghel I
The Horrors of War **P** (Florence, Palazzo Pitti, Galleria Palatina ed Apartamenti Reali) I: 188 n. 59, 367, 369 nn. 14, 18

237

INDEX III: OTHER WORKS BY OR AFTER RUBENS MENTIONED IN THE TEXT

Roma Triumphans (The Triumph of Rome) **S** The Hague, Royal Picture Gallery Mauritshuis I: 361, 362 n. 9

Roma Triumphans (The Triumph of Rome) **D** Follower of Rubens (Vienna, Albertina) I: 362 n. 9

Venus with Ceres and Bacchus (Sine Cerere et Baccho friget Venus) **P** (Kassel, Museumslandschaft Hessen Kassel, Gemäldegalerie Alte Meister) I: 432

Victory Crowning a Hero **P** (Kassel, Museumslandschaft Hessen Kassel, Gemäldegalerie Alte Meister) I: 174 n. 16, 349, 350 n. 12

Sketches for a Figure of Victory **DD** (recto and verso) (Darmstadt, Hessisches Landesmuseum) I: 350, 354; II: *figs 62–63*

Youthful and Fertile Love (Venus Frigida) **P** (Brussels, Musées royaux des Beaux-Arts de Belgique) I: 416

HISTORY

Alexander and Roxana **P** ? Rubens or Studio (Jerusalem, Israel Museum) I: 362 n. 10, 385 n. 17, 386 n. 37

Triumph of Alexander **D** (Berlin, Staatliche Museen zu Berlin, Kupferstichkabinett) I: 361

The Decius Mus Series **TT I:** 127, 134, 137, 179, 352; II: 35
    PP (Vaduz – Vienna, Liechtenstein, The Princely Collections) I: 72 n. 72, 134, 135, 137, 179, 180 n. 35, 263, 353, 358 n. 6, 399, *text ill. 56*
    The Interpretation of the Victim I: 352, 353 n. 17, 358 n. 7, 403 n. 9; II: *fig. 78*
    The Death of Decius Mus I: 210, 399, 400 n. 4
    The Obsequies of Decius Mus I: 399, 400 n. 9, 403 n. 5; II: *fig. 148*

The Emperors Series **PP**: see Portraits

The Henri IV Series **PP** I: 412, 413 n. 10

Horatius Cocles Defending the Sublician Bridge **S** Rubens, retouched by anon. artist (Vaduz – Vienna, Liechtenstein, The Princely Collections) I: 413–414 n. 10

The Medici Series **PP** (Paris, Musée du Louvre)
    The Birth of Maria de' Medici I: 289, 398
    Henri IV Consigns the Regency to Maria de' Medici I: 409; II: 51, *appendix III.18, fig. 24*
        S (Munich, Bayerische Staatsgemäldesammlungen, Alte Pinakothek): I: 289, 296, 300, 409, *text ill. 135*; II: 51, *appendix III.19, fig. 93*
    The Departure of Maria de' Medici from Paris (presumably lost)
        S (Munich, Bayerische Staatsgemäldesammlungen, Alte Pinakothek) I: 365, *text ill. 135*; II: *fig. 93*
    The Flight from the Chateau of Blois
        S (Munich, Bayerische Staatsgemäldesammlungen, Alte Pinakothek) I: 289; II: 52, *appendix III.20, fig. 24*

The Ceiling Decoration of the Banqueting Hall **PP** (London, Whitehall, Banqueting House) I: 412

The Duke of Buckingham Ascending Triumphant to the Temple of Virtue and Honour I: 412, 413 n. 10

The 'Pompa Introitus Ferdinandi' **PP** I: 264–265, 293, 326, 328, 334, 366, 412
    The Stage of Welcome I: 329, 403, 412, 413
        The Statue of Good Hope (Spes) **E** by T. van Thulden I: 329, 345; II: *fig. 50*
        Pedestal with Ram's Heads **E** by T. van Thulden I: 403; II: *fig. 164*
        Genius of the City of Antwerp **E** by T. van Thulden I: 412; II: *fig. 192*
    The Arch of Philip I: 266, 283 n. 95
        Jupiter and Juno **P** Studio of Rubens (Antwerp, Private Collection) I: 283 n. 95
    The Portico of the Emperors **EE** I: 145, 326, 432
        Frederick III and Albert II, with Mars Ultor and Ceres **E** by T. van Thulden I: 146, *text ill. 62*
    Juno **E** by T. Van Thulden I: 145 n. 18
    The Stage of Isabella I: 266, 297 n. 5
        E by T. van Thulden I: 297, *text ill. 136*
    The Arch of Ferdinand I: 412
        The Front Face of the Arch of Ferdinand **P** after Rubens (Antwerp, Rubenshuis) I: 265
        E by T. van Thulden I: 412, 414 n. 11
        The Rear Face of the Arch of Ferdinand **S** St Petersburg (The State Hermitage Museum) I: 412
        E by T. van Thulden I: 412, 414 n. 11; II: *fig. 192*
    The Temple of Janus I: 366
        S (St Petersburg, The State Hermitage Museum) I: 369 n. 10
        E by T. van Thulden I: 369 n. 10
    The Stage of Mercury I: 266
    The Arch of the Mint I: 266
    The Arch at St Michael's I: 266

St Ambrose and Theodosius **P** with A. van Dyck (Vienna, Kunsthistorisches Museum) I: 269; II: 49, *appendix III.14*
    P Copy by A. van Dyck (London, The National Gallery) I: 269; II: *appendix III.15*

The Fortitude of Scaevola **P** (formerly Madrid, Real Alcázar, destroyed) I: 322 n. 5
    P Studio (Budapest, Szépművészeti Múzeum) I: 322
    D Copy (detail), probably by Willem Paneels (Copenhagen, Statens Museum for Kunst, Kongelige Kobberstiksamling) I: 322, 323, *text ill. 150*

GENRE SCENES

The Garden of Love **P** (Madrid, Museo Nacional del Prado) I: 292, *text ill. 134*, 304; II: 54, *appendix III.24*
Dancing Peasants and Mythological Figures **P** (Madrid, Museo Nacional del Prado) I: 317, 318, *text ill. 146*

LANDSCAPES

Stormy Landscape with Philemon and Baucis **P** (Vienna, Kunsthistorisches Museum) I: 282 n. 94
The Park of a Castle **P** (Vienna, Kunsthistorisches Museum) I: 62 n. 44
The Castle Grounds at Ekeren **P** After Rubens (Antwerp, Rubenshuis) I: 62 n. 44

HUNTING SCENES

Alexander's Lion Hunt **P** whereabouts unknown I: 362 n. 10
Wolf Hunt **P** whereabouts unknown I: 133; II: 35

PORTRAITS

Anne of Austria, Queen of France **P** (Madrid, Museo Nacional del Prado) I: 342, 343 n. 5
Anne of Austria, Queen of France **P** after Rubens (whereabouts unknown, formerly in New York, The Metropolitan Museum of Art) I: 343 n. 5
The Emperor Series **PP** I: 243, 399
   Caligula **P** (Stuttgart, Staatsgalerie) I: 399, 400 n. 5
   Trajan **P** (Stuttgart, Staatsgalerie) I: 399, 400 n. 5
Helena Fourment with her Son Frans (?) Rubens ('Hélène Fourment au carrosse') **P** (Paris, Musée du Louvre I: 60, 138, 139, 155, 158, 159, 167, 175, 205, 275, 342, 346; II: 37, 45, *appendix III.7, figs 21, 31, 55*
Caspar Gevartius **P** (Antwerp, Museum voor Schone Kunsten Antwerpen) I: 276
Martina Plantin **P** (Antwerp, Museum Plantin-Moretus) I: 119 n. 5
Peter Paul Rubens, Philip Rubens, Justus Lipsius and Joannes Woverius ('The Four Philosophers') **P** (Florence, Palazzo Pitti) I: 394; II: *fig. 134*
Peter Paul Rubens with his Wife Helena Fourment and his Son Nicolaas Rubens ('The Walk in the Garden') **P** ? Rubens and Studio (Munich, Bayerische Staatsgemäldesammlungen, Alte Pinakothek) I: 60, 62 n. 44, 107, 108, 115, 161 n. 56, 275, 297, 298, 299 n. 15, 301, 302, 303, 304, 305, 309, 311, 312, 323, 324, 331, 394, 408, 410, 411, 414, 415, 417, 418, 419, 420, 422, 423, 425, 426, 427, 431; II: 37, 45, *appendix III.6, figs 25, 182, 205, 210, 218*
Peter Paul Rubens with his Wife Helena Fourment and one of their Daughters **P** (New York, The Metropolitan Museum of Art) I: 62 n. 47
Seneca and Nero **S** (whereabouts unknown) I: 263 n. 40

BOOK ILLUSTRATIONS AND TITLE-PAGES

F. d' Aguilón, *Opticorum libri sex…*(1613)
   Title-Page **E** by T. Galle I: 402 n. 4
J. De Bie, *Nomismata Imperatorum Romanorum aurea, argentea, aerea* (1617)
   Title- Page **E** by M. Lasne I: 399, 400 n. 4
H. Goltzius, *Romanae et Graecae Antiquitatis Monumenta* (1645)
   Title- Page **E** by C. Galle I I: 362 n. 9
F. Haraeus, *Annales Ducum seu principum Brabantiae* (1623)
   Title-Page **E** by L. Vorsterman I: 366
      D (London, The Royal Collection Trust) I: 366, 369 n. 10
J. Hemelaers and J. de Bie, *Imperatorum Romanorum numismata aurea* (1615) I: 265
   Title- Page **E** by J. de Bie I: 265, 362 n. 12
J. Lipsius, *L.Annaei Senecae Philosophi Opera quae extant omnia* (1615) I: 118, 148, 181 n. 37
   The Bust of Seneca **E** by C. Galle I I: 118, 148, 181 n. 37, 339, *text ill. 63*
S. Pietrasanta, *De Symbolis Heroicis Libri IX* (1634)
   D after Rubens (Paris, Fondation Custodia) I: 429, 430
   E by C. Galle I I: 430 n. 6
Ph. Rubens, *Electorum Libri II* (1608) **EE** I: 181 n. 37, 345, 362 n. 5, 404
   Iconismus apicis in lapide clivi capitolini **E** by C. Galle I I: 404; II: *fig. 169*
   Iconismus circensium et missionis mappae (Illustration of Circus Racing and the Lowering of the Cloth) **E** by C. Galle I I: 348; II: *fig. 59*
   Iconismus Duplicis Statue Tunicatae (Two Statues Wearing a Tunica) **E** by C. Galle I I: 345, 362 n. 5; II: *fig. 49*
Ph. Rubens, *S. Asterii Amaseae Homiliae* (1615)
   Vignette with the *Portrait of Philip Rubens* **E** by C. Galle I I: 395 n. 6
Printer's Device for the Plantin Press **D** (Antwerp, Plantin-Moretus Museum) I: 297 n. 5, 404 n. 4

ARCHITECTURE AND SCULPTURE

High Altar of the Kapellekerk in Brussels, after a design by Rubens **Sc** by Hans van Mildert (Sint-Joost-ten-Node (Brussels), Church of St Judoc) I: 327
High Altar for the Jesuit Church of Antwerp, after a design by Rubens **Sc** (Antwerp, Church of St Carolus Borromeus) I: 328, 403 n. 4
The Cupola for the Apse in the Antwerp Jesuit Church,

possibly after a design by Rubens **Sc** Antwerp, Church of St Carolus Borromeus I: 391; II: *figs 129, 162*
High Altar of the Abbey of St Michael's, after a design by Rubens **Sc** probably by Hans van Mildert (lost) I: 328
Design for the High Altar for the Church of the Calced Carmelites in Antwerp **D** (New York, The Metropolitan Museum of Art) I: 329
Mercury, after a design by Rubens **Sc** possibly by Artus Quellinus I (St Petersburg, The State Hermitage Museum) I: 333, 334, *text ill. 154*
Design for a Sepulchral Monument for J. Richardot (1540–1609) **D** (Amsterdam, Rijksprentenkabinet) I: 394
Head of a Sphinx **D** ? Rubens or retouched by him (Mougins, Musée d'Art Classique de Mougins) I: 410 n. 2; II: *fig. 186*
Susanna and the Elders
    Sc basin by Theodoor Rogiers I (Antwerp, Rubenshuis) I: 428
Venus, after a design by Rubens **Sc** possibly by Artus Quellinus I (St Petersburg, The State Hermitage Museum) I: 334
The Triumph of the Sea-Born Venus, after a design by Rubens
    Sc salt cellar by G. Petel (Stockholm, Swedish Royal Collections, Husgerådkammern) I: 417 n. 12
Hermathena **D** (London, The British Museum, Department of Prints and Drawings) I: 283

COPIES AFTER THE ANTIQUE

The Abduction of Proserpina **D** ? Rubens (Antwerp, Rubenshuis) I: 362 n. 3
Centaur Tormented by Cupid **D** (Cologne, Wallraf-Richartz-Museum & Fondation Corboud) I: 350; II: *fig. 61*
The Capitoline Eagle **D** (Washington, National Gallery of Art) I: 402 n. 5
The Mattei Eagle **D** Copy by W. Panneels after Rubens (Copenhagen, Statens Museum for Kunst, Kongelige Kobberstiksammling) I: 402
The Mattei Eagle **D** another Copy by W. Panneels after Rubens (Copenhagen, Statens Museum for Kunst, Kongelige Kobberstiksammling) I: 402
A Dancing Faun and Standing Silenus with a Dish **D** after Rubens (Copenhagen, Statens Museum for Kunst, Kongelige Kobberstiksammling) I: 373, 374 n. 4
Resting Faun **D** after Rubens (Copenhagen, Statens Museum for Kunst, Kongelige Kobberstiksammling) I: 419, 420 n. 7
Head of Medusa **D** (New York, The Morgan Library & Museum) I: 398; II: *fig. 146*

Drunken Silenus with Faun and Maenad **D** (Dresden, Staatliche Kunstsammlungen, Kupferstichkabinett) I: 373, 374 n. 3
Herm Bust of Sophocles **E** by Paulus Pontius I: 341; II: *fig. 40*

COPIES AND ADAPTATIONS

After German and Netherlandish Artist
The Count and the Death **D** after Hans Holbein II (Antwerp, Museum Plantin-Moretus, Stedelijk Prentenkabinet) I: 263 n. 40
The Sacrifice to Venus **P** partly after Adam Elsheimer (London, The Courtauld Gallery) I: 367; II: *fig. 95*

After Italian Artists
The Castration of Uranus **D** after P. da Caravaggio, retouched by Rubens (Antwerp, Private Collection) I: 192 n. 76
Two Trophies of Arms **D** after P. da Caravaggio, retouched by Rubens (St Petersburg, The State Hermitage Museum I: 192 n. 76
Vase with a Trophy of Chain Mail and Sword **D** after P. da Caravaggio, retouched by Rubens (Paris, Musée du Louvre) I: 192 n. 76
The Rape of the Sabine Women with a Vase and a Hexonagal Sword **D** after P. da Caravaggio, retouched by Rubens (Toronto, Art Gallery of Ontario) I: 192 n. 76
The Continence of Scipio **D** after P. da Caravaggio, retouched by Rubens (Paris, Musée du Louvre) I: 192 n. 76
A Standing Robed Man, called Democritus, but more properly Socrates **D** after P. da Caravaggio, retouched by Rubens (Lattner Family Collection) I: 192 n. 76
A Man Leading a Horse **D** after P. da Caravaggio, retouched by Rubens (London, The British Museum) I: 192 n. 76
A Crowd of Nine Worshippers with a Votive Offering before a Priest **D** after P. da Caravaggio, retouched by Rubens (Paris, Musée du Louvre) I: 192 n. 76
Apollo Killing Two of the Sons of Niobe **D** after P. da Caravaggio, retouched by Rubens (Paris, Musée du Louvre) I: 192 n. 76
Perseus Showing the Head of Medusa to Phineus and his Companions **D** after P. da Caravaggio, retouched by Rubens (Paris, Musée du Louvre) I:192 n. 75, 193 n. 79, 356
A Sea-Battle **D** after P. da Caravaggio, retouched by Rubens (Weimar, Klassik Stiftung Weimar) I: 192 n. 78
The Rape of Europa **P** after Titian (Madrid, Museo Nacional del Prado) I: 428 n. 3

INDEX III: OTHER WORKS BY OR AFTER RUBENS MENTIONED IN THE TEXT

THEORETICAL NOTEBOOK

Theoretical Notebook **DD** (lost, apart from a few surviving pages) I: 120–121, 283, 291 n. 120, 420 n. 7
MS Chatsworth, Copy **DD** attr. to A. van Dyck (known as 'Van Dyck's Antwerp Sketchbook') (Chatsworth, The Devonshire Collection) I: 425 n. 8
    Columna Tùscana, fol. 74v **D** after S. Serlio I: 121 n. 13
MS Johnson, Copy **DD** (London, The Courtauld Gallery) I: 283
MS de Ganay, Copy DD (Brussels, King Baudouin Foundation, on loan to the Rubenshuis, Antwerp)
    De Figuris Humanis I: 425 n. 8
    De figurae humanae statibus I: 420 n. 7

WORKS IN COLLABORATION

With J. Brueghel I
Nature Adorned **P** (Glasgow, Kelvingrove Art Gallery and Museum) I: 406

With A. van Dyck
St Ambrose and Theodosius **P** (Vienna, Kunsthistorisches Museum): see History

With F. Snijders
Cimon and Iphigenia **P** (Vienna, Kunsthistorisches Museum): see Allegory
The Emperor's Mullet **P** (Vienna, Kunsthistorisches Museum) I: 269; II: 50, *appendix III.17*
Homage to Ceres **P** (St Petersburg, The State Hermitage Museum): see Allegory
The Head of Medusa **P** (Vienna, Kunsthistorisches Museum): see Mythology

Index IV: Names and Places

Proper, abstract and compound names listed here are of historical and fictional personages, personifications, symbols and historical concepts, authors and titles of their books (up to 1800), titles and localities of works not by Rubens, and of previous owners of works catalogued.

Aarschot, Duke of I: 133
Achilles Tatius I: 176 n. 21, 383, 384 (nn. 1, 4)
   Leucippe and Clitophon I: 378, 384–385 nn. 4, 6, 15
Aelius Caesar (Lucius Ceionus Commodus) I: 271 n. 75
Aerdenbodeghem, Peter van II: 13–14
Aertsen, Pieter I: 316 n. 49
Agrigento I: 370
Aguilón SJ, François d'(Franciscus Aguilonius)
   Opticorum libri sex I: 14, 402 n. 4
Albert, Archduke of Austria I: 34, 133, 325 n. 11
Alberti, Leon Battista I: 358 n. 9, 372 n. 3
   De Pictura (1540) I: 368 n. 1
Aldobrandini Wedding (Roman fresco), Rome, Musei Vaticani I: 178, 372 n. 5
Alexander the Great, King of Macedonia I: 55 n. 18, 59, 238, 360, 361, 362 (nn. 9, 10, 13), 386 (nn. 27, 37)
Alva (Alba), Fernando Álvarez de Toledo y Pimentel, 3rd Duke of I: 26, 382
Amaduzzi, Johannes Christophorus
   (with Rudolfino Venuti) *Vetera Monumenta* (1774–1779) I: 374 n. 1; II: *fig. 104*
Amersfoort
   Rijksdienst voor Cultureel Erfgoed II: 60
Ammanati, Bartolomeo
   Courtyard (architecture), Palazzo Pitti, Florence I: 288 n. 112, 289, *text ill. 131*
   Garden portal with inscribed tablets (architecture), Rome, Villa Medici I: 262, *text ill. 113*
Amsterdam II: 5, 6, 24, 32, 33, 34 n. 49, 36, 38, 89, 121 n. 16, 198, 248, 286 n. 107, 355, 400 n. 3
   Amstelkerk I: 29 n. 27
   Breestraat
      Rembrandthuis I: 40
   City of I: 278 n. 78
   Felix Meritis Society I: 248
   Keizersgracht
      'Felix Meritis' (Building) I: 248
   Leliegracht
      House of Govaert Flinck I: 247
   Paleis op de Dam (Royal Palace, formerly Town Hall) I: 282 n. 94, 332, 333, 335, 404 n. 6, 420 n. 4, 425 n.10, 432 n. 1, *text ill. 153*
   Rijksmuseum I: 193 n. 83, 194, 248 n. 57, *text ill. 76*
   Rijksprentenkabinet I: 370 n. 1, 394
   Stadsarchief II: 5
   Town Hall: see Paleis op de Dam
Andriessens, Godevriet II: 8
Angelrot, Balthasar I:196

Antinous Belvedere: see *Hermes Belvedere*
Antiphilus I: 180
Antwerp I:
   Abbey of St Michael I: 23, 26, 129, 266, 328; II: 32
   Ambtmanstraat
      'Salvator' (house) I: 307 n. 29
   Arenbergstraat I: 119, 197, 214; II: 10, 34
      House of Frans Floris (demolished) I: *text ill. 81*
   'The Botanic Sanctuary' hotel: see St Elizabeth Hospital
   Carmelite Order (Brothers of the Blessed Virgin Mary of Mount Carmel) I: 88
   Cathedral of Our Lady I: 24 n. 9, 37, 52, 87, 120 n 10, 124, 130–133, 268 n. 58, 327 n. 21, *text ill. 55*; II: 8–9, 33–34
      Chapter of the Cathedral of Our Lady (Antwerp) I: 37 nn. 59–60
   Centraal Depot Musea – Stad Antwerpen I: 251 n. 10, 393, 398, 401, 405–407, 410 ; II: *figs 136, 145*; see also Index I
   Church of St Andrew (St Andrieskerk) I: 118
   Church of St Augustine I: 265, 297, *text ill. 115*; II: 34
   Church of St Carolus Borromeus: see Jesuit Church
   Church of the Calced Carmelites (destroyed) I: 329
   Church of the Discalced Carmelites I: 66, 95, 96, *text ill. 32*
   Church of the Dominicans: see Church of St Paul
   Church of St James (St Jacobskerk) I: 87, 88, 118, 329; II: 35
      Tombstone of Hendrik Hillewerve and Margareta Goos I: 97 n. 23
   Church of St Paul
      Tomb of Ambrosius Capello I: 265 n. 46
   Church of St Walburga I: 130; II: 20, 21, 32
   Church of St Willibrord (Berchem)
      Tomb of Anna Maria van Berchem I: 265 n. 46
   City of I: 35, 42, 76, 82, 83, 84, 412; II: 12
   FelixArchief (Stadsarchief Antwerp) I: 24, 29 n. 25, 37 n. 60, 65, 78 n. 84, 81, 82 n. 97, 83, 84 n. 105, 154 n.39, 204, 208, 235, 252, 255, 307, 394 n. 1, *text ills 13, 22–23, 82, 85, 98, 104, 110*; II: *figs 2, 131*
      Door with a *Head of Hercules under a Scallop, and Garlands* of Rubens's House (photograph) II: 6, 8, 9, 10, 13, 14, 15, 17, 18, 20, 22, 27, 28, 29, 68, *fig. 131*
   Guild of the Arquebusiers: see Kolveniersgilde
   Guild of the Mercers: I: 327 n. 21
   Guild of St Luke I: 89, 119; II: 10, 34
   Herentals canal I: 24

242

INDEX IV: NAMES AND PLACES

Hof van Descalsos: see Discalced Carmelites
Hoogstraat
   Mercator Orteliushuis I: 225 n. 74
Hopland I: 24 n. 8, 25, 35, 41, 46, 47, 65, 72, 80, 95, 106, 108, 214, 227; II: 14, 15, 17, 19, 20, 27, 28, 36, 38
   'Breda' (house) I: 45; II: 14, 36
   'Huybrechtssens house' II: 14
   'De Witte Roos' (house) I: 45; II: 15, 16, 19
House of Cornelis van Dalem (lost) I: 284
Jesuit Church (Church of St Carolus Borromeus) I: 13, 14, 18, 58, 61 n. 42, 63 n. 49, 120, 133, 134, 158, 199, 220, 224, 225 n. 72, 266, 273 n. 66, 316 n. 45, 326 n. 13, 327 n. 21, 328, 391, 392 n. 3, 398, 399, 401, 403, 410, 432 n. 1; II: *figs 129, 152*
Jodenstraat
   'De Sterre' (house) II: 19
Jordaens's House I: 199, 200, 224, 264, 267 n. 54, *text ill. 114*
Kipdorp I: 26, 61 n. 42
Kolveniersgilde (Gilde van St Christoffel) I: 24, 25, 35, 41, 48, 65, 123, 124, 130, 296, 303; II: 33
Kolveniershof I: 16, 24, 29, 65, 80, 94, 97, 106, 122, 123, 250 n. 7, 296, 302, 310, 421; II: 7, 8, 9, 33
Kolveniersstraat I: 24, 41, 80
Koninklijk Museum voor Schone Kunsten Antwerpen I: 66 n. 55, 199 n. 99, 305 n.22; II: 64
Korte Nieuwstraat
   'Drie Gulden Coppen' (house) I: 32 n. 38
   Sint-Annagodshuis I: 32 n. 38
Lammekensraamveld I: 25, 35, 41, 42, 65; II: 5, 14, 15, 16, 19
Lange Gasthuisstraat II: 28
Lange Nieuwstraat
   'De Meerminne' (house) I: 52 n. 10
Maagdenhuis Museum I: 326 n.13
Meir I: 25, 50, 64 n. 51, 67 n. 59, 74, 80, 100, 159
   'Het Hoefijzer'(house) I: 214
   Osterrieth House I: 308 n. 29
   Sint-Arnoldus House ('Sint-Arnout' or 'Maison de Rubens') I: 25–28, 27, 80, *text ills 1–2*; II: 32
Melkmarkt
   'De Gouden Schoen' (house), now hotel 'De Gulde Schoen' I: 225 n. 74
De Munt I: 54 n. 15
Museum Plantin-Moretus I: 23 n. 2, 40 n. 75, 42, 43, 65, 144, 328, 411, 413, *text ills 152, 155*; II: 42; see also Index I
   Plantin-Moretus Archief I: 23 n. 2; II: 10, 12
   Stedelijk Prentenkabinet I: 255, 256, text ills 4–6, 12, 111, 152, 346; II: 42, 43, 66, *figs 1, 54, 191*
      Anonymous 17th-Century Artist, *Palazzetto Viewed from the Garden* (drawing) I: 255, *text ill. 111*
   Plantin-Moretus Printing house (Officina Plantiniana) I: 55 n. 17, 120, 245 n. 41, 263 n. 39, 297 n. 5, 324, 334, 335, 404, 413 n. 8; see also Index I
'Round Temple': see Walloon Church
Rubens's House (see also Architectural and decorative terms; see 'Contents' for the components, the wings, the façades, etc.)
   Antichambre I: 77, 203, 204, 235, 393; II: 31
   'Antiquarium', later Hillewerve's chapel I: 16, 18, 19, 61, 75, 105, 111, 112, 128, 200, 216, 219, 227, 228, 229–248, 389–393, 394; *text ills 99, 101, 102, 103*; II: 35, 36, 37, 44, 46, *figs 127, 128, 130*
   Art Gallery I: 100 n. 27, 230–232, *text ill. 97*
   Bedroom (Hillewerve's) I: 89, 97, 112–113, 212, 213, 215, *text ills 47, 90*
   Cantoor I: 18, 58–59, 100 n. 28, 172 n. 10, 225–228, 357, 381, 416; II: 37
   Cellars I: 43, 44, 137, 203, *text ill. 8*
   Chapel (Hillewerve's) I: 75, 77, 89, 92, 96, 97, 105, 110–112, 147 n. 27, 154, 200, 232, 233 n. 10, 234, 235, 236, 238, 239, 240, 240, 241, 242, 243, 246, 324, 389, 390, 391, 392, *text ill. 102*, II: 26, 31, 39, *fig. 127*
   Coach House (Wagon House) I: 75, 102, 103, 158, 206, 207, *text ill. 37*; II: 27
   Courtyard I: 43, 44, 62, 92, 94–95, 100–101, 103, 113–116, 117, 126, 132, 168, 173, 175, 182–185, 229, 230, 249, 252, 284, *text ills 8, 34, 36, 44, 48, 49, 50, 104*; II: 39, 42, 43, 62, 64, 66, 67, 137, 138; II: *appendix III.1, 2, 40, 44, 47, 48, 49; figs 4, 10, 11, 16, 17*
   Dormer I: 99, 101, 102, 139, 185, 212 n. 31, 213, 217 n. 47, 230, 275, 297, 409
   Fireplace I: 70, 71, 110, 112, 205, 206, 207, 212, 321, *text ill. 19*; II: 56, *appendix III.28a–29*
   Fountain I: 304, 324, 425–428
      Fountain with Bagpiper I: 114–115, 324, 339, 340 n. 2, *text ill. 50*
   Gallery: see Architectural and decorative terms
   Garden I: 34, 47, 48, 60, 62 n. 44, 67, 69, 75 n. 78, 79, 93, 94, 95, 96, 97, 102, 103, 106–108, 115, 127, 215, 263, 264, 292, 301, 302, 315, 424, 426, *text ills 13, 17, 27, 31, 37, 39, 40, 41, 42, 43*; II: 21, 23, 34, 37, *appendix III.2, 6, 10, 26; figs 4, 8, 18, 25*
   Garden pavilion: I: 295–319, see also Chapter X and Index II, Nos 34–40, *text ill. 22*; II: 37, 38, *appendix III.2, 3, 6, 10, 18, 25, 26, 34, 36a, 37, 41, 42, 46, 50, 51, 53; figs 177–182*
   Kitchen I: 35, 43, 100
   Lying Dog (sculpture) I: 116; II: 66
   Mezzanine I: 69, 157, 186, 202, 203–204
   'Museum' (Elegantissimum), ('mouseion') I: 225, 227–228, 233; II: 10
   Passageway from the Wapper to the garden I: 102–104, 109 n. 43, 158, 160, 206, 207, 221, 228 n. 94, *text ills 38– 86*
   Passageway from the garden to the Hopland I:

41, 45
Pergola (latticed) I: 95, 106, 214 n. 33, *text ills 31, 40*
Portico: 83 n. 101, 249–293 (Chapter IX), 295, 395–398, 400, 401, 402, 404, 405, 407; II: *fig. 138*; see also Index II, Nos 24–33, R1–R4
Roof I: 15, 49, 50, 57, 65, 99, 101, 102, 104, 124–125, 132, 137, 138–139, 154, 158, 160, 185, 201, 207, 212 n. 31, 213, 217–218, 219, 230, 231 n. 6, 252; II: 13–14, 34, 35
Shutters ('blaffeturen') I: 57, 132, 157, 203, 209; II: 19
Stables I: 46 n. 89, 68, 69, 75, 95, 96, 97, 103, 108–109, 117, 160, 343, *text ills 37, 42–43*
Staircase I: 17, 54 n. 15, 77, 122, 125–126, 133, 134, 137, 151, 184–185, 197 n. 90, 201–203, 204, 222, 223 n. 67, 230; II: 10–11, 35, *figs 124–126*
'Studiolo Secreto' I: 18, 50, 225, 227–228; II: 14, 36
Vases (free-standing) I: 75, 106, *text ills 27, 41*; II: 27, 28
Walkways (covered) I: 94, 95, 106–107, 214 n. 33, *text ills 31, 39*
Wash house I: 75, 103, 206
Water pump I: 98, 99, 113, *text ill. 48*
Weathervane I: 99, 138, 160, 275
Winch or Windlass I: 222–225
The large workshop on the ground floor / later a 'Salon' I: 110, 204–205, 212, 223
The upstairs studio (or so-called 'Pupils' studio') I: 211–217, 220, 222, *text ill. 91*
Rubenshuis (Museum) I: 16, 30, 31 n. 35, 32 n. 44, 37 n. 60, 41, 62 (nn. 42, 44), 82, 83, 84 n. 105, 85, 88 n. 5, 116 n. 56, 148, 149, 153, 172, 202 n. 2, 205, 206, 216, 220, 222 n. 65, 231, 232, 236, 240, 241, 249, 276 n. 75, 282 n. 92, 308, 309, 321 n. 1, 331 n. 40; II: 5, 6, 9, 13, 20, 22, 23, 24, 25, 42, 43, 55, 57, 62, 64, 65, 67; see also Index I
Anonymous artist, *Bust of Cicero* (plaster) I: 308, 309, *text ill. 141*
Anonymous artist, *Head of a Woman (Niobe?)* (plaster) I: 308, 309, *text ill. 142*
Anonymous 17th-century artist, *Hercules* (No. 40; statue) I: 299, 324, 330, 331, 335, 393, 421–425; II; *fig. 211*
Anonymous artist, *Bacchus* (No. 38, statue) I: 299, 306, 335 n. 53, 409, 417–420; II: *figs 201–203*
Schuttershofstraat
'House St Quinten' I: 199
Sint-Michielsstraat (now Kloosterstraat) I: 23, 26, 118, 129, 131; II: 32, 33, 34
St Elizabeth Hospital (now 'The Botanic Sanctuary' hotel) I: 326 n. 15
St Michael's Abbey I: 23, 26, 129, 266, 328; II: 7, 32
Studiebureau Lode De Clercq I: 340 n. 3

Tapissierspand I: 51
Town Hall I: 130, 316 n. 50
State Chamber (Staatsiekamer, later Statenkamer) I: 376
Vaart (canal) I: 24, 159
Vaartstraat: see Wapper
Museum Vleeshuis I: 116 n. 56
Vrijdagmarkt I: 72; II: 18
Walloon Church (Waelekerck) I: 28–31, 42, 64
Wapper (sometimes Vaartstraat) I: 17, 23–48, 51, 52, 54, 55, 57, 60, 62, 64 n. 51, 68 n. 62, 69, 72, 73, 75, 80, 84 n. 105, 88, 93, 94, 95, 96, 98, 99, 101, 102–104, 105, 108, 109 n. 43, 118, 119, 122, 125, 128, 129, 132, 133, 134, 137, 138, 139, 140, 151, 154, 158, 159, 160, 161, 163, 184, 185, 187, 188 n. 57, 201, 203, 204, 206, 207, 208, 212, 220 n. 60, 225, 227 n. 88, 228, 229, 249, 269, 295, 329, 387, 393, 396, 409, *text ills 9, 30, 38, 86*; II: 5, 6, 10, 11, 15, 16, 17, 18, 19, 20, 23, 24, 27, 28, 32, 33, 34, 35, 36, 37, 38
Zwartzustersstraat II: 11
Antwerp – Beveren, Rijksarchief I: 26 n. 16
Apelles I: 52, 55 n. 18, 150, 177 n. 23, 179, 180, 181, 182, 238, 361, 362 n. 13, 362 n. 9, 364, 365, 366, 369 n. 16, 372 n. 9, 383; II: 12, 26
Alexander Holding a Thunderbolt (painting), lost I: 361
The Calumny of Apelles (painting), lost I: 176, 363, 364, 365, 366, 367, 368 n. 1, 369 n. 12
The Triumph of Alexander the Great (painting), lost I: 176
Apollo Belvedere (sculpture), Rome, Musei Vaticani I: 416
Ara of Cleomenes (Roman altar), Florence, Museo Archeologico Nazionale di FirenzeI: 357; II: *fig. 81*
Ara Pacis Augustae (Roman altar), Rome, Museo dell'Ara Pacis I: 353 n. 8
Architectural and decorative terms (see also Antwerp, Rubens's house)
Aegicranium (ram's skull) I: 297, 300, 302, 303, 403, 404, 405 n. 6
'Antiquarium': see Antwerp, Rubens's house
Arcade: see Gallery
Arch I: 19, 62, 64, 67, 74, 78, 79, 91, 105, 106, 110, 111, 151, 157, 159, 163, 183, 184, 185, 186 n. 48, 206, 229, 241, 249, 250 n. 5, 251, 252, 253, 254, 255, 256, 257, 258, 259, 260, 262, 264, 265, 266, 267, 268, 269, 270, 272, 287, 288 n. 111, 289, 293, 295, 296, 297, 298, 300, 302, 304, 316, 317, 322 n. 6, 326, 339, 345 n. 7, 351, 360, 361, 387, 394, 395, 397, 398, 401, 405, 406, 407, 408 n. 2, 409, 412, 414 n. 17, 424
Geniculated I: 118 n. 1, 142, 148, 259, 264, 265–267, 268, 269, 272, 285, 286, 293, 297, 339, 397, 398
'Syrian' I: 317
With concave corners I: 264–265, 267 n. 56
Architrave I: 157, 161, 183, 193, 194, 195, 196, 200, 203, 206, 207, 259, 260, 261, 269, 270, 289

244

INDEX IV: NAMES AND PLACES

n. 115, 296, 297, 300, 304, 316, 318, 398, 404, 409
Bacon motif ('speklagen') I: 101, 105
Baluster I: 112, 151, 183, 261, 300, 307, 387, 388,
Balustrade I: 96, 111, 183, 199 n. 97, 250 n. 5, 253, 255, 256, 260, 261, 271, 272, 274, 275, 278, 279, 280, 281, 299, 300, 303, 305, 318, 376, 377 n. 5, 388, 404, 426, 430
Barrel vault I: 210, 238, 239, 242, 390, 392, 394
Bossed (surface) I: 118 n. 1, 142, 148, 152, 153, 268, 269, 287, 292
Brazier I: 19, 139, 143, 275, 305, 346, 347
Bucranium I: 139, 258, 260, 300 n. 16, 397, 403, 404
Bust: see Antwerp, Rubens's house
Caisson I: 183
Caryatid I: 19, 69, 70, 109, 251 n. 12, 297, 300, 321, 328, 331, 342, 343, 409, 410
Corinthian Order I: 74, 143 n. 12, 183, 376
Column I: 62, 63, 67, 74, 96, 141, 142, 151, 159, 160, 184, 185, 193, 217 n. 43, 250, 256, 257, 258, 259, 260, 261, 267, 269, 270, 287, 291, 292, 293, 296, 297, 298, 299, 300, 302, 303, 306, 309, 310, 316, 318, 369, 376, 397, 404, 409, 414, 418, 419, 422, 432; II: 50
  Banded I: 118 n. 1, 153, 155, 268, 270, 289, 397
  Engaged I: 140, 147, 151, 153, 170, 258, 259, 268, 269, 397
  Half I: 140, 169, 257, 260, 287, 288 n. 112, 290, 291, 293, 397, 398
  Square I: 298, 304
Consoles I: 139, 427
Cornice I: 62, 138, 140, 141, 151, 156, 160, 171, 190, 193, 243 n. 36, 248, 258, 297, 298, 404
Cornucopia I: 139, 141, 145, 171, 280 n. 86, 299, 302, 305, 309, 311 n. 35, 312, 315, 328, 331, 341, 394, 409, 411, 412, 413, 414 (nn. 11, 15)
'Crosettes': see 'Ears'
Cupola I: 211, 212, 213, 214, 215, 216, 217, 218, 219, 220, 224, 232, 233, 237, 238, 239, 240, 241, 242, 245, 246, 247, 390, 391, 392, 403
'*Diaeta*' I: 51, 153, 156, 352, 383
Dome I: 18, 96, 97, 105, 106, 111, 113, 210, 216, 217, 218, 219, 231, 233, 234, 240, 241, 244, 245, 246, 247, 248, 273 n. 68, 390, 391
Doric Order I: 118 n. 1, 141, 142, 151, 153, 160, 257, 258, 259, 267, 268, 269, 270, 287, 288, 291, 293, 297, 298, 397, 398, 400, 403, 404
'Ears' ('Crossettes') I: 143, 144, 157, 210, 346, 347
Eave I: 62, 138–140, 160, 193,
Entablature I: 141, 142, 196, 256, 297, 302, 407
Festoon: see Garland
Finial I: 99, 139, 275
Gallery (ground floor) / arcade (see also Loggia: raised Gallery) I: 184–185
Garland I: 19, 142, 144, 241, 261, 286, 298, 299, 300, 302, 303, 313, 315, 321, 322, 346, 388, 391, 393, 394, 401, 402, 420, 421, 422, 424 n. 1, 432 n. 1
Grotto I: 114, 115,

Grotesques I: 241, 391
Guttae I: 142, 256, 258, 259, 297, 397, 398, 404
Herm I: 19, 70, 144, 145, 148, 149, 151, 152, 156, 162, 169, 171, 172 (nn. 11, 12), 182, 183, 193, 292, 301, 321, 326, 342, 343, 347, 432, 433 n. 4
'Herm bust' I: 141, 149, 150, 171, 174, 341
Hood moulding (eyebrow like) I: 297, 300, 301, 302, 409
Ionic Order I: 67, 297, 298, 342, 409, 410
Lantern I: 67, 106, 217, 218, 231, 240, 245, 316 n. 45, 391
Lex horti I: 262, 263
Loggia (raised Gallery) I: 17, 96 n. 22, 151, 162, 168, 169, 173, 183, 184, 186, 190, 199, 241, 266, 275 n. 74, 300, 316, 317, 318, 319, 376, 383
Manège I: 68 n. 64, 70, 216, 237 n. 19
Metope I: 258, 300, 404
Modillion I: 62, 102, 139, 160, 297,
Niche I: 90, 91, 101, 106, 109, 111, 115, 118, 141, 142, 145, 146, 147, 148, 149, 150, 156, 161, 164, 169, 170, 189, 194, 198, 200, 210, 228, 232, 234, 236, 238, 240, 241, 242, 243, 246, 255, 257, 260, 261, 262, 264, 265, 266, 268, 275, 276, 277, 278, 293, 297, 298, 299, 300, 302, 303, 304, 305, 306, 307, 308, 309, 310, 311, 312, 313, 314, 315, 318, 321, 322, 323, 328, 330 n. 33, 331, 332, 339, 340, 341, 390, 392, 394, 395, 397, 401, 402, 409, 410, 411, 412, 413, 420, 421, 423, 425 n. 12, 431, 433 n. 1
Oculus I: 18, 111, 113, 142, 151, 171, 185, 205, 209, 211, 218, 233, 245, 246, 297, 301, 390, 91, 395
Pediment I: 19, 145, 150, 152, 161 n. 58, 163, 169, 171, 182, 193, 194, 250, 257, 268, 269, 271, 272, 274, 275, 286, 293, 297, 305, 317, 341, 346, 397, 403, 410
  Alternating (segmental and triangular) I: 141, 143, 144, 151, 162
  Broken I: 260, 261 n. 30, 347, 398, 401, 409
  Open-topped I: 144
Piano nobile I: 142, 153, 181, 204 n. 9, 246
Pilasters I: 111, 151, 153, 159, 171, 194, 195, 200, 236, 241, 242, 250, 254, 257, 298, 369, 388, 390, 392, 397
Quoins I: 19, 118 n. 1, 143, 152, 171, 269, 287, 342
Riding House I: 67, 68, 69, 204 n. 8, 216
Rosettes I: 258, 269, 297, 397, 404
Rustica I: 142, 148, 152, 153, 163, 256, 260, 287, 288, 289, 290 n. 116, 291, 292, 339, 397
Serliana I: 19, 259–260, 269, 292 n. 127, 293, 295, 296, 298, 301, 307, 316–319, 397, 401, 409
Shell motif I: 111, 141, 145, 151, 210, 261, 296 n. 4, 303, 321, 322, 341, 392, 393, 394, 395, 397
Sphere (crowning) I: 138, 139, 160, 271, 272, 274, 275, 302, 347,
Stepped gable I: 41, 46, 47, 69, 95, 99, 101, 102, 108, 109, 159
Tondo I: 87, 94, 297
Triglyph I: 141, 151, 297, 300

245

INDEX IV: NAMES AND PLACES

Tuscan Order I: 258, 290, 291 n. 120
Tympanum I: 141, 144, 157, 182, 261, 401
Vase (façade motif) I: 143, 145, 156, 171 n. 9, 182, 260, 342, 346, 347
Volute I: 111, 113, 141, 171, 260, 261, 297, 300, 302, 303, 305, 306, 340, 346, 375, 393, 394, 397, 398, 402, 403, 404, 410
Arezzo
   Casa Vasari I: 181, 200, 342, 357, 359 n. 12, 371, 372 n; 9; II: *fig. 79*
Aristides I: 347, 348 n. 3
Armitstead, George I: 363
Arquebusiers: see Kolveniersgilde
Arquennes I: 122, 250 n. 7, 395
Asia I: 360
Athenion I: 180
Augsburg I: 197
Aulis I: 356, 357, 358 n. 2
   Port I: 355
Austria, Maria Maddalena of, Grand Duchess of Tuscany I: 289 n. 114
Averbeke, Émile van I: 30 n. 32, 55 n. 20, 57 n. 25, 83, 84, 85, 115 n. 52, 143 n. 11, 154, 172, 207 n. 18, 217 n. 43, 225 n. 73, 236, 240, 253, 254, 255, 279, 283 n. 95, 430, 431 n. 1
   The South Façade of the Studio Wing (blueprint), Antwerp, FelixArchief I: 208, *text ill. 85*
   The Reconstruction of the South Wing of the Rubenshuis (intersection of the studio wing) (blueprint), Antwerp, FelixArchief I: 204, *text ill. 82*; II:
   The Reconstruction of the East Wing of the Rubenshuis (intersection south-north) (blueprint), Antwerp, FelixArchief I: 155, 235, *text ill. 98*; II:
   Garden Façade of the Rubenshuis (drawing), Antwerp, Rubenshuis Archive I: 155 n. 42
   Plan of the First Floor of the Rubenshuis (blueprint), Antwerp, Rubenshuis Archive I: 154 n. 39; II: *fig. 5*
Avesnes (France) I: 395, 410, 417, 420 (nn. 1, 3), 421, 424 n. 1
Aylesbury I:
   Discover Bucks Museum (formerly Buckinghamshire County Museum)
      Anonymous seventeenth-century artist, *View of the Courtyard of Rubens's House* (painting) I: 15, 19, 61–63, 92 n. 16, 138, 139, 141, 142 n. 9, 143 n. 14, 145, 149, 150, 159, 161 n. 58, 170, 171, 174, 175, 184, 257, 273, 275, 276, 278, 280, 339, 340, 341, 342, 346, 347, 355, 356, 358, 359, 360, 362, 363, 396; II: 39, 43, *appendix III.3; figs 16, 27, 37, 42, 52, 70, 83, 91, 141*

Bacher, Andries (also Backer or Backaert) I: 32, 33, 35, 36, 38, 39; II: 6, 7, 8, 33
Baellieur, Cornelis de I:
   A Collector's Cabinet with the Figure of Pictura ('Il *Gabinetto di Rubens'*) (painting, attributed to), Schloss Rohrau, Graf Harrach'sche Familiensammlung I: 210, 211, *text ill. 88*; II: 58, *appendix III.32*
Interior of a Picture Gallery (painting, formerly attributed to), Florence, Palazzo Pitti, Galleria Palatina ed Appartamenti Reali) I: 391
Baldinucci, Filippo
   Notizie de' professori del disegno (1702) I: 75, 168, 169, 172 n. 10, 173, 183, 186, 187, 247 n. 54, 376, 380; II: 24, 40, *appendix I.32*
Balen, Hendrick van I: 52 n. 10
Balen, Jan van I: 215, 247
   Bathing Women (painting, attributed to), Amersfoort, Rijksdienst voor het cultureel erfgoed I: 271, 280; II: 60, *appendix III.35*
Basan, François I:
   Catalogue des estampes gravées d'après P.P. Rubens (1767) I: 169; II: 28, 29, 30, 41, *appendix I.41*
Basel I: 368 n. 3
   House 'Zum Tanz' I: 196, 197 n. 90, *text ill. 80*
   Kunstmuseum Basel I: 196, 197 n. 90
Bassano, Jacopo I: 55
Baudius, Dominicus I: 181 n. 37,
Bayonne I: 32 n. 39
Bellori, Giovanni Pietro I:
   Le Vite de' Pittori, Scultori e Architetti moderni (1672) I: 51, 74, 232 n. 8, 233, 234, 390; II: 22, 39, *appendix I.28*
Berchem, Anna Maria van I: 265 n. 46
Berlin I: 270
   Kaiser-Friedrich-Museum II: 50
   Staatliche Museen zu Berlin I: 174, 246 n. 47, 378, 380, 381, 382, 385 (nn. 13, 26)
      Gemäldegalerie Alte Meister I: 385 n. 11
         Anonymous seventeenth-century artist, *Portrait of a Couple in a Garden* (painting) I: 15, 60, 71, 272, 275, 281, 283, 299 n. 15, 304, 308, 309, 312, 403, 408, 410, 411, 414, 418, 419, 421, 422, 423, 424 n. 1; II: 38, 47, *appendix III.10; figs 22, 167, 181, 208, 212, 230*
      Kupferstichkabinett I: II: 56, 361, 362 n. 11
Besançon
   Bibliothèque municipale
      Collection Chifflet II: 15
Bettinelli, Saverio I: 191 n. 61
Beuckelaer, Joachim I: 316 n. 49
Beyerlick, Laurens I: 181 n. 38
Bie, Jacques [Jacob] de I: 38 n. 63, 51 n. 6, 129; II: 33
   Imperatorum Romanorum Numismata aurea (1615) I: 362 n. 12
      Title-Page (engraving) I: 265
   Imago Iovis cum fulmine (engraving) I: 361; II: *fig. 87*
Blaeu, Joan I: 286
   Map of Antwerp (1649) (engraving) I: 65, *text ill. 12*
Bleeckvelt / bleeckhoff / bleyckhove I: 23, 34, 42, 104 n. 32; II: 5, 6, 7, 15, 16

INDEX IV: NAMES AND PLACES

Blommaert, Victor I: 240 n. 29, 270 n. 63
   Rubenshuis, Antwerp (drawing), Antwerp – Beveren, Rijksarchief, Archief Provincie Antwerpen, Fonds Blommaert I: 142 n. 7
Blomme, Henri I: 84
Bocchi, Achille I: 404 n. 5
Boeck, Michiel De II: 16
Bokhoven
   Church of St Anthony Abbot I: 425 n. 11
Bolsover Castle (UK) I: 67, 68, *text ill. 15*
Boni di Pellizuoli, Donato de'
   Gates of the City Walls, Antwerp I: 290
Bononiensis, Virgilius
   Map of Antwerp (woodcut, 1565) I: 24, 40, 43, 47 n. 42, 99, 100; II: *fig. 1*
Bonte, M.
   Cross-sections of the Portico (blueprint), Antwerp, FelixArchief I: 255, *text ill. 110*
Borghese, Scipione, Cardinal I: 350, 373
Borghese Vase: see Paris, Musée du Louvre
Borromini, Francesco I:
   Façade of the Collegio di Propaganda Fidei, Rome I: 264 n. 43
   Façade of the Oratorio di S. Filippo, Rome I: 264 n. 43
De Bosschaert (de Pret) family I: 76, 78 n. 82, 168, 233; II: 29
Bosschaert de Pret, Charles-Jean de I: 78; II: 40
Bosschaert de Pret, Charles-Nicolas de I: 78; II: 40
Bossche, Abraham van den: II: 13, 124, 125
Bossche (Bosch), Bastiaen van den I: 122, 125; II: 19
Botticelli, Sandro
   The Calumny of Apelles (painting), Florence, Le Gallerie degli Uffize I: 364, 368 n. 5
Boudaen, Hans II: 6
Bourges I: 267 n. 56
Brant, Isabella I: 23, 45, 55, 56, 61 (nn. 40, 41), 118, 181 n. 37, 271, 280; II: 16, 32, 36, 44
Brant, Jan I: 23, 27, 52 n. 10, 129, 130, 131, 132 n. 51, 226; II: 32, 33, 34
Brant, Herman van den I:; II: 23
Braun, Adolphe
   The Garden Pavilion of Rubens's House (photograph) I: 82, 307, 408, 413 n. 3, 433 n. 2; II: 69, *appendix III.53*
Braun, Georg
(with Frans Hogenberg) *Civitates orbis terrarium* (1572–1617) I: 43, *text ill. 7*
Braunschweig
   Herzog Anton-Ulrich-Museum I: 39
Braunschweig-Wolfenbüttel, Heinrich Julius von, Duke I: 32
Brecht
   Kempuseum (formerly Kempisch Museum) I: 89 n. 10
Breda I: 54, 386 n. 40
   Palace I: 316 n. 50
Bredenbach, Johanna II: 8
Bree, Mathieu Ignace van
   Rubens Surrounded by his Colleagues in the Garden Pavilion (painting), Weimar, Klassik Stiftung Weimar I: 306, 307, 421; II: 63, *appendix III.41*
Brée, Philippe van
   The Farewell of Van Dyck in the Courtyard of Rubens's House, (painting), Antwerp, Rubenshuis I: 274 n. 68, 398; II: 62, *appendix III.40*
   Rubens Painting in his Garden (painting), Brussels, Musées royaux des Beaux-Arts de Belgique I: 306, 307, 311, 418, 419, 432; II: 63, *appendix III.42; fig. 236*
Bremen
   Kunsthalle Bremen
      Anonymous (Dutch or Flemish?) artist, *Interior of a Sculptor's Workshop* (drawing) I: 209
Brimeu, Marie de I: 31
Broechem
   Church of Our Lady I: 116 n. 57
Broechoven van Bergeyck, Jan-Baptist van I: 56; II: 38
Brosse, Salomon de I: 249 n. 2, 270 n. 63
   The façades of the Palais du Luxembourg, Paris (architecture) I: 289
Brueghel, Jan I I: 51, 132 n. 48
Brueghel, Jan II I:
   Allegory of Painting / Allegory of Pictura (painting), The Netherlands, Private Collection I: 210, 211, *text ill. 89*; II: 58, *appendix III.33*
   Allegory of Painting / Allegory of Pictura (painting, probably by), Private Collection II: 58, *appendix III.33*
   Nature Adorned (painting with Rubens), Glasgow, Kelvingrove Art Gallery and Museum I: 406
Bruhl, Heinrich de, Comte I: 380, 385 n. 25; II: 30
Bruijningh, Jan Fransen II: 30
Brussels I: 34, 55 n. 17, 56, 58, 75, 82, 88, 89, 134, 274; II: 35, 38, 39, 40
   Béguinage
      Church of St John the Baptist I: 265 n. 46
   Church of St Augustine I: 297 n. 6
   Church of St Michael (now Cathedral of St Michael and St Gudula) I: 89
   Church of Notre-Dame du Sablon (Onze-Lieve-Vrouw-ter-Zavelkerk)
      Thurn und Taxis Chapel I: 265 n. 46
   Coudenberg Palace I: 133, 326 n. 12
   Sint-Joost-ten-Node (Saint-Josse-ten-Noode)
      Church of St Judoc I: 327 n. 20
   Kapellekerk I: 327
   KBR (Koninklijke Bibliotheek van België / Bibliothèque royale de Belgique/ Royal Library) I: 76, 77, 198
   KIK–IRPA (Koninklijk Instituut voor het Kunstpatrimonium / Institut royale du Patrimoine artistique) I: 340
   King Baudouin Foundation I: 331 n. 40
   Musées royaux des Beaux-Arts de Belgique I: 307, 356, 358 n. 4, 390, 416, 418, 432; II: 63
   World Exhibition 1910 I: 84, 282 n. 92

INDEX IV: NAMES AND PLACES

Bucephalus I: 360, 361
Buckingham, Duke of I: 45 n. 83, 87 n. 3, 415, 417 n.10, 427, 428 (nn. 10, 11)
Budapest
    Szépművészeti Múzeum I: 74, 268, 322, 355, 357, 358, 359 (nn. 17, 18), 403 n. 2; see also Index I
Bulliau, Jasper (Jaspar, Gaspar) I: 122, 125, 126, 202, 387, 388, 389; II: 10, 11, 35
Burchard, Ludwig I: 85, 115 n. 52

Cadiz I: 76 n. 79
Caen I: 267 n. 56
    Musée des Beaux-Arts I: 382, 420 n. 1
Caers, Christoffel I: 35; II: 6, 7, *appendix I.2*
Caers, Hendrick I: 35 n. 53
Caesar: see Julius Caesar
Caligula I: 399
Cambridge
    The Fitzwilliam Museum I: 376
Campen, Jacob van
    Plans for the Huis ten Bosch, The Hague I: 247
    Plans for the Mauritshuis, The Hague (drawing by Pieter Post), The Hague, Koninklijke Bibliotheek / Nationale Bibliotheek van Nederland I: 218, 247, *text ill. 92*
Canelle Adrien
    Rubens, his Family and Visitors in the Courtyard of his House (lithograph) II: 67, *appendix III.49*
Capitoline or Medici Venus: see Rome, Musei Capitolini
Caravaggio, Polidoro da I: 152 n. 38, 192, 193
Cardon, Forcy I: 326
Carleton, Dudley I: 50, 55, 122, 126, 127 n. 34, 133, 187, 188, 237, 270, 390, 427; II: 11, 35
Carpentras
    Carmelite Convent I: 267
Cartari, Vincenzo
    Imagini (Images) (1556) I: 365, 368 n. 4, 369 n. 9, 414 n. 14; II: *fig. 94*
        Genio buono (woodcut engraving) I: 411, 412, 413 n. 6; II: *fig. 194*
Castiglione, Baldassare I: 372 n. 3
Cattaneo, Franco I: 134; II: 35
Caus, Salomon de
    Les raisons des forces mouvantes (1615) I: 115
Cavendish, Margaret I: 66–72, *text ill. 14*; II: 38, 39, 47, 56
    Natures Pictures (1656) II: 38, 56
    Sociable Letters (1664) I: 71, 72 n. 70
Cavendish, William, 1st Duke of Newcastle I: 66–72, 95, 101 n. 29, 108, 204 n. 8, 216, 284, 343, 422, *text ill. 14*; II: 38, 39, 47, 56
    La méthode nouvelle (1658) I: 67, 69, 70; II: 38
    New Method (1667) I: 68 n. 63
Ceres Palliata (statue), Rome, Villa Borghese I: 433 n. 4
Champmol I: 358 n. 9
Chantilly
    Musée Condé I:
        Roman, *Candelabrum Base* (sculpture): I: 193 n. 83,

358 n. 7; II: *fig. 80*
Charles I, King of England, Scotland and Ireland I: 71
Charles II, King of England, Scotland and Ireland I: 66; II: 39
Chaumont I: 264 n. 43
Chifflet, Jean-Jacques
    De linteis sepulchralibus Christi [...] (1624) I: 54 n. 16; II: 15
Chifflet, Philippe
    Diary ('Diaire') I: 54, 233
Choul, Guillaume du
    Discours de la religion des anciens Romains (1556) I: 353 nn. 2, 7, 354 n. 1, 413 n. 6
    A Roman Sacrifice (woodcut) I: 352, 353 n. 11, 354; II: *fig. 68*
Christian IV, King of Danmark I: 53 n. 11
Christie's London (auctioneer) I: 63 n. 49
    Elegant Company in a Garden (painting after David Teniers II) II: 59, *appendix III.34*
Christie's New York (auctioneer)
    Anonymous 17th-century artist, *Bathsheba Bathing* (painting) II: 61, *appendix III.38*
Cicero I: 283, 308, 309, 356
    De Inventione I: 370, 371, 372 n. 1
    De natura deorum I: 176 n. 21
    De Oratore I: 358 n. 8
Claessens, Frans I: 410 n. 1
    Caryatids Left and Right (Sphinxes?) (sculptures), Antwerp, Rubenshuis I: 409, 410 n. 1, 421; see also Index II, No. 35, Copy 1
Cleemput, Anna-Catharina van I: 90 n. 10
Cleves
    Museum Kurhaus Kleve I: 278 n. 78
Clouwet, Petrus
    William Cavendish and his Family Seated in Front of a Fireplace [in Rubens's House] (engraving after Abraham van Diepenbeeck) I: 71, *text ill. 19*; II: 56, *appendix III.28a; fig. III.28b*
Cobergher, Wenzel
    St Augustine's Church, Antwerp I: 265, 266, 297, *text ill. 115*; II: 34
Cock, Hieronymus
    Bird's-eye View of Antwerp (engraving, 1557) I: 42, *text ill. 4*
Coecke van Aelst, Pieter
    Van de architecturen vijf boecken Sebastiani Serlii (1539) I: 121 n. 16, 316
Cognatus, Gilbertus I: 368 n. 3
Colnaghi, P&D, & Co (dealer) I: 363
Cologne I: 26, 30; II: 32
    Wallraf-Richartz-Museum & Fondation Corboud I: 350, 354; see also Index I
Commodus I: 422, 423, 424 n. 7
Conti, Natale
    Mythologia I: 374
Coop, Aert I: 40
Coop (Cop or Coops), Nicolaes I: 34, 39, 40; II: 5, 6
Coop, Nicolaes II I: 34 n. 51

Copenhagen I: 53; II: 35
   Det Kongelige Bibliothek II: 227
   Statens Museum for Kunst
      Kongelige Kobberstiksamling I: 59, 322 n. 5, 323, 344 n. 4, 355, 359, 374 n. 4, 377, 386 n. 27, 406, 416, 417 n. 16, 420 n. 7, 424 n. 7; II: *fig. 46, 71, 84, 100, 112, 174, 200–201*; see also Index I
Coques, Gonzales I: 47, 8
   Portrait of the Duarte Family (painting), Leipzig, Museum der Bildenden Künste I: 74 n. 77
   Portrait of the Duarte Family (painting), Budapest, Szépművészeti Múzeum I: 74, n. 75
   Portrait of Maria Agnes van Eycke as St Agnes (painting), London, The National Gallery I: 73, 74, 105, 229, 273, 276, 278, 396, *text ills 20, 95, 123*; II: 39, 47, *appendix III.11*
Corpus Christi, Feast of I: 53
Corr, Erin I: 80
   The Courtyard of Rubens's House (engraving after Nicaise de Keyser) II: 64, *appendix III.44*
   The Portico of Rubens's House (engraving after Nicaise de Keyser and J. Stordiau) I: 80, 82, 273; II: 65, a*ppendix III.45*
   The Garden Pavilion of Rubens's House (engraving with Jozef Linnig after Nicaise de Keyser and J. Stordiau); I: 80, 307, 413 n. 3; II: 65, *appendix III.46*
Cort, Cornelis
   The Calumny of Apelles (engraving after Federico Zuccaro) I: 364; II: *fig. 92*
Cortona, Pietro da I: 293
Corvers, notary II: 28
Cossiers, Jan I: 209 n. 23, 215, 247
   Jupiter and Lycaon (painting after Rubens), Madrid, Museo Nacional del Prado I: 399
Cosway, Richard I: 43
Cotrone (Italy): see Croton
Crayer(e), Francho(e)ys de II: 9, 34
Croes, Jacques (Jacob or Jan) van I: 89 n. 8, 427
   Façade of Frans Floris's House (drawing), Brussels, KBR I: 197, 198, *text ill. 81*; II:
   View of the Courtyard of Rubens's House (1684) (etching by Jacob Harrewijn): see Jacob Harrewijn I: 17, 63, 89, 90, 91, 92, 357, 363; II: 42, *appendix III.1; fig. 17*
   View of Rubens's House and Garden (1692) (etching by Jacob Harrewijn): see Jacob Harrewijn I: 17, 63, 89, 90, 91, 92, 184, 357, 363, 385 n. 26, 427; II: 43, *appendix III.2; fig. 18*
Croton (Cotrone) (Italy) I: 370
   The Temple of Hera (Juno) Lacinia I: 372 n. 2
Croton, The Five Maidens of I: 370, 371
Croÿ, Charles de, Duke of Aarschot I: 32 n. 37
Cupid I: 61, 85, 200, 254, 256, 257, 271, 275, 276, 280, 303, 326, 330, 350, 378, 379, 382, 385 n. 5, 386 n. 37, 394, 395, 401, 409, 414, 415, 416, 417, 425, 426, 427, 428; II: 45, 46, 48, 53, 60

Danzig I: 53 n. 11
Darmstadt
   Hessisches Landesmuseum I: 350, 354
Deckers, Edward
   Minerva (statue), Antwerp, Rubenshuis I: 282
   Mercury (statue), Antwerp, Rubenshuis I: 282
Deckers, Maria I: 7
Delen, Dirk van
   Courtyard of Rubens's House, at Antwerp, with Figures Seated at a Table; a Garden in the background (painting, attributed to), whereabouts unknown I: 62
Delfontaine, Jean I: 122, 140 n. 6, 250 n. 7
Democritus I: 149 n. 34
Demosthenes I: 149 n. 34, 228
Descamps, Jean-Baptiste
   La vie des peintres flamands, allemands et hollandois (1753–1764) I: 220 n. 56, 243 n. 36, 248
Descartes, René I: 66
Deurne (near Antwerp) I: 90 n. 10
Diepenbeeck, Abraham van I: 359 n. 17
   Courbette de côté à gauche (engraving by Lucas Vorsterman) II I: 67, 70, *text ill. 18*
   'Fontainebleau Sketchbook' (album of drawings, designs attributed to), various locations I: 359 n. 17
   William and Margaret Cavendish Watching while William's Sons Charles and Henry are Demonstrating a Courbette and a Ballotade (engraving, after) I: 67, *text ill. 14*
   William Cavendish and his Family Seated in Front of a Fireplace in Rubens's House (drawing), London, The British Museum II: 56, *appendix III.28a; fig. III.28a*
   William Cavendish and his Family Seated in Front of a Fireplace in Rubens's House (drawing), Staatliche Museen zu Berlin, Kupferstichkabinett I: 321; II: 56, *appendix III.29*
   William Cavendish and his Family Seated in Front of a Fireplace in Rubens's House (engraving by Petrus Clouwet) I: 70, 71, 321, 343, *text ill. 19*; II: 56, *appendix III.28b*
Dionysius of Halicarnassus
   Opera
      De priscis scriptoribus censura I: 372 n. 2
Dioscuri, the (Castor and Pollux) I: 361
Dominici, Bernardo *de*
   Vite de' pittori, scultori, ed architetti napoletani (III, 1742) I: 53 n. 12
Dresden
   Staatliche Kunstsammlungen
      Gemäldegalerie Alte Meister I: 174 n. 16, 373, 374, 375 n. 10, 406, 427
      Kupferstichkabinett I: 373
Duarte family I: 67 n. 59
Duarte, Gaspar I: 74
Duffel

INDEX IV: NAMES AND PLACES

Church of St Martin I: 265 n. 46
Dundee (Scotland)
   The McManus / Dundee's Art Gallery & Museum; I: 363; see also Index I
Dupuy, Pierre I: 50 n.3, 193 n. 80
Dyck, Anthony van I: 19, 87 n. 3, 127, 151, 220, 247, 271 n. 68, 397, 398; II: 36, 48, 62
   St Ambrose and Theodosius (painting with Rubens), Vienna, Kunsthistorisches Museum I: 269; II: 49, *appendix III.14*
   St Ambrose and Theodosius (painting, Copy after Rubens), London, The National Gallery I: 127, 269; II: *appendix III.15*
   St John the Evangelist and St John the Baptist (painting), Berlin, Kaiser-Friedrich-Museum (lost) I: 127, 270; II: 50, *appendix III.16*
   St Martin Dividing his Cloak (painting), Zaventem, Church of St Martin I: 269, 398
   The Fish Market (The Emperor's Mullet) (painting with Rubens's studio and Frans Snijders), Vienna, Kunsthistorisches Museum I: 269; II: 50, *appendix III.17*
   Portrait of Caterina Balbi (?) (painting), Genoa, Palazzo Reale I: 427
   Portrait of Isabella Brant (painting), Washington, DC, National Gallery of Art I: 60, 256, 257, 271, 276, 280, 395, 430; II: 44, *appendix III.5; fig. 19*
   Portrait of Maarten Ryckaert (painting),Madrid, Museo Nacional del Prado I: 46 n. 87
   Portrait of Maria Stappaert (?) and her Son (painting), London, The National Gallery I: 61 n. 41
   Architectural Study of Rubens's Portico (drawing; No. 24, Copy), Paris, Fondation Custodia I: 58, 295, 396; II: *fig. 139*
   The Portico of Rubens's House (painting, Copy ? van Dyck after Rubens), whereabouts unknown I: 270, 396
   MS Chatsworth (drawings after Rubens's Theoretical Notebook, attr. to) (also known as 'Van Dyck's Antwerp Sketchbook'), Chatsworth, The Devonshire Collection I: 121 n. 13, 425 n. 8

Egyptian Mummy I: 54, 233; II: 15, 36
Ehrenberg, Wilhelm Schubert van I: 63 n. 49, 392 n. 3
   The Interior of the Antwerp Jesuit Church (painting), Antwerp, Rubenshuis I: 62 n. 42
Ekeren I: 62 n. 44
   Hof van Ursele II: 17, 36
Elewijt
   Het Steen I: 50; II: 37
Ephesus
   Temple of Artemis (Diana) I: 361
Esbroeck, Victor Van
   Amphitrite (statue), Antwerp, Rubenshuis I: 43
   Neptune (statue), Antwerp, Rubenshuis I: 43
Euanthes
   Diptych with *Andromada Chained to a Rock* and *Prometheus Bound* (painting), lost I: 180, 378
Euripides
   Iphigenia in Aulis I: 355, 357, 358 n. 2, 359 n. 11, 384 n. 1
Everaerts, Hendrik II: 11
Eycke, family I: 66, 72 n. 72, 74, 88, 93, 431
Eycke, Giovanni Battista van I: 72 n. 72
Eycke, Jacomo (also Jacob) the Younger van I: 72, 74, 87, 102, 104, 284; II: 20, 39
Eycke, Joanna van I: 88; II: 24, 25, 39
Eycke, Joseph van I: 88; II: 24, 25, 39
Eycke, Maria Agnes van I: 73, 74, 105, 229, 273, 276, 396; II: 39, 47
Eycke, Teresia van I: 88; II: 24, 25, 39
Eynde, Huibrecht van den
   Faustina Group (statue), Antwerp, Maagdenhuis Museum I: 326

Falconeto, Giovanni Maria
   Frescoes, Verona, Casa Trevisani-Lonardi, Façade (photograph) I: 191 n. 72, 192, *text ill. 75*
Farnese Hermes (statue), London, The British Museum I: 344 n.2
Faydherbe, Jan Lucas I: 423
Faydherbe, Lucas I: 18, 50, 215, 221, 244 n. 37, 310, 311, 325, 326, 330–332, 339, 340, 418, 419, 421; II: 37, 38
   Maria Mater Dolorosa (statue), Mechelen, Beguinage Church I: 330, 331 n. 39
   Cupid and Psyche Asleep on a Bed (statuette), St Petersburg, The State Hermitage Museum I: 330
   Hercules (bust), London, Victoria and Albert Museum I: 331
   Hercules (bust), Brussels, King Baudouin Foundation, on loan to the Rubenshuis I: 331
   Hercules (statue), formerly house of Jan Lucas Faydherbe, lost I: 332, 423; II: 17, *fig. 213*
Feldt, Cornelis: see Cornelis Velt
Ferdinand, Cardinal-Infante of Spain, Governor of the Spanish Netherlands I: 55
Ferdinando II, Grand Duke of Tuscany I: 188
Ferrara
   Palazzo d'Este I: 402 n. 3
Fierlants, Edmond I: 116, 274 n. 69, *text ill. 53*
   Rubens's Garden Pavilion (photograph), Antwerp, FelixArchief I: 81, 82, 307, 408, 411, 413 n. 3, 418, 432, 433 n. 2, *text ill. 22*; II: 68, *appendix III.51; figs 189, 235*
   The Portico of Rubens's House (photograph) Antwerp, FelixArchief I: 81, 82, 274, 339, 340, 396, *text ill. 23*; II: 68, *appendix III.52; figs 53, 125*
Flinck, Govaert I: 243 n. 36, 247, 248; II: 38
Flora Farnese (sculpture), Naples, Museo Archeologico Nazionale di Napoli I: 152, 344, 345; II: *fig. 48*
Florence I: 287, 288
   Casa Buonarotti I: 286, *text ill. 128*
   Casa Vasari I: 181, 200, 371, 372 n. 9

Casa Zuccari I: 200
Le Gallerie degli Uffize I: 354, 367
   Roman, *Mercury* (statue) I: 419, 420 n. 8
   Roman, *A Roman Sacrifice* (sarcophagus relief) I: 351, 353 n. 6
   Roman, *A Roman Sacrifice* (relief) I: 351, 353 n. 7
   Museo Archeologico Nazionale di Firenze II: *fig. 81*
   Palazzo Pitti I: 188 n. 59, 260 n. 29, 288, 289, 391, 394, *text ill. 131*; II: *fig. 134*
Floris (de Vriendt), Cornelis
   Choir Screen of the Cathedral, Tournai I: 316 n. 50
Floris (de Vriendt), Frans I: 89 n. 8, 181, 189, 197, 198, 214
Floris, Jan-Baptist II: 29
Florus II: 19
Fontainebleau I: 267 n. 57, 359 n. 17
Forchondt (Forchoudt), Guilliam I: 76
Forchondt (Forchoudt), Justus (Justo) I: 76
Fornenbergh, Alexander van
   Den Antwerpschen Protheus[…] (1658) I: 199
Fourment, Helena I: 55, 56, 57, 62, 72, 138, 160, 299 n. 15, 301, 329, 372, 417 n. 5; II: 18, 37, 38, 39, 45, 55
Francart, Jacques I: 297
   Church of St Augustine, Brussels I: 297 n. 6
   Le premier livre d'architecture (1617) I: 121, 143, 275 n. 74, 297
France I: 29, 54 n.15, 267; II: 37, 59, 227
Francken, Frans I II: 58
Francken, Frans II II: 58
   Encyclopaedic Still Life with a Cabinet (painting), London, Syon House, Collection of the Duke of Northumberland I: 390, 391
   Interior of a Picture Gallery (painting), Salisbury, Wilton House, Collection of the Earl of Pembroke I: 390
   'Salon de Rubens' (painting with Cornelis de Vos), Stockholm, Nationalmuseum I: 61
Frascati
   Villa Aldobrandini I: 261 n. 30
Frederik Hendrik, Prince of Orange I: 332, 333 n. 44
Freudian interpretation I: 372 n. 3
Fruytiers, Philip
   The Four Eldest Children of Peter Paul Rubens and Helena Fourment, with a Maid and Helena Fourment (?) (gouache), London, The Royal Collection Trust I: 60, 298, 304, 409; II: 55, *appendix III.26*
   Portrait of a Lady with Maid and Three Children (gouache), Antwerp, Koninklijk Museum voor Schone Kunsten Antwerpen I: 305 n. 22
   Portrait of an Unknown Family in a Garden (gouache), whereabouts unknown I: 305 n. 22

Gaasbeek
   Castle I: 428 n. 9; II: 16, 20
Galle, Cornelis I

Bust of Seneca (engraving after Rubens) I: 148 n. 31, 149, *text ill. 63*
Iconismus apicis in lapide clivi capitolini ('Illustration of the Pointed Helmet on the Relief on the Capitoline Hill') (engraving after Rubens) I: 404; II: *fig. 169*
Iconismus circensium et missionis mappae ('Illustration of Circus Racing and the Lowering of the Cloth') (engraving after Rubens) I: 348; II: *fig. 59*
Iconismus Duplicis Statue Tunicatae ('Two Statues Wearing a Tunica') (engraving after Rubens) I: 345; II: *fig. 49*
Title-Page for S. Pietrasanta, *De Symbolis Heroicis Libri IX* (engraving) I: 430 n. 6
Galle, Cornelis II
   Bust of Philip Rubens, in a niche (engraving after Rubens) I: 394
Gatchina Venus (Roman sculpture after a Greek original), St Petersburg, The State Hermitage Museum I: 426; II: *fig. 219*
Gazette van Antwerpen I: 75 n. 78; II: 28, 40
Geest, Cornelis van der I: 54 n. 15, 416, 417 n. 15, 426
Genoa I: 162–163, 165, 186 n. 47, 193–196
   Palazzo Cattaneo Adorno I: 194
   Palazzo del Principe Andrea Doria I:193, 194, *text ill. 76*
   Palazzo Gambaro I: 196, *text ill. 79*
   Palazzo Interiano Pallavicino I:194, 195, *text ills 77–78*
   Palazzo Reale I: 427
   Villa Grimaldi 'Fortezza' (Palazzo D) I: 195
   Villa Spinola di San Pietro (Palazzo C) I: 195 n. 86
Gerbier, Balthasar I: 55 n. 17
   Eer ende Claght-Dicht Ter Eeren van den lofweerdighen constrijcken ende Gheleerden Henricus Goltius I: 386 n. 36
Gevaerts (Gevartius), Jan Gaspar I: 228, 276; II: 20
   Pompa Introitus honori Serenissimi Principis Ferdinandi (1641 or 1642) I: 64, 345 n. 7, 362 (nn. 9, 10), 372, 412, 414 (nn. 11, 16, 17), 430 n. 4
Ghent
   Cathedral of St Bavo I: 325 n. 11
   Calvinist 'temple' I: 29 n. 24, 30, *text ill. 3*
Gheringh, Anton I: 63
   Interior of the Antwerp Jesuit Church (painting, formerly attributed to Wilhelm Schubert von Ehrenberg), Brussels, Musée d'Ixelles I: 63 n. 49
   Elegant Figures in a Baroque Interior (painting), whereabouts unknown I: 63 n. 49
   Interior of an Italian Church (painting), whereabouts unknown I: 63 n. 49
Giambologna
   Bagpiper (statuette, attributed to), Cambridge, The Fitzwilliam Museum I: 115
Gielis, Franchoys I: 25–28, 31, 32, 33, 34, 41; II: 7, 14
Gielis, Magdalena II: 7
Gielis, Martha I: 31; II: 7

Gladstone, William Ewart I: 363
God I: 372 n. 8, 400 n. 13
Goeree, Willem
    Inleydinge tot de algemeene Teyken-Konst […] I: 209
Golnitzius (Golnitz/ Göllnitz), Abraham I: 53 n. 11
    Ulysses Belgico-Gallicus (1631) I: 53 n. 11
Goltzius, Hendrik I: 386 n. 36
    Hercules and Caucus (painting), The Hague, Mauritshuis, on loan to the Frans Hals Museum, Haarlem I: 424, 425 n. 18
    Mercury As Painter (painting), The Hague, Mauritshuis, on loan to the Frans Hals Museum, Haarlem I: 281, 284 n. 98
    Minerva (painting), The Hague, Mauritshuis, on loan to the Frans Hals Museum, Haarlem I: 281, 284 n. 98
    The Triumph of Virtue over the Enemies of the Arts I: 384
    Romanae et Graecae Antiquitatis Monumenta (1645) I: 362 n. 9
Gonzaga, Vincenzo I, Duke of Mantua I: 191, 287, 288
Goos, Margareta I: 87, 88 n. 4, 97
Go(o)ris, Harmen (Herman) II: 6
Göttingen
    University
        Anonymous, *Rubens and his Son (Albert?)*, (on loan to Antwerp, Rubenshuis, since 2006) II: 55, *appendix III.27*
Grand, Jan Le I: 181 n. 40
Grotius, Hugo I: 53
Gruytere, Jan de (Janus Gruterus) I: 126, 127 n. 32; II: 12, 35
Guyot, Toussaint I: 56 n. 23; II: 18

Haarlem
    Frans Hals Museum I: 200 n. 100, 281 n. 87
    Guild of St Luke I: 218 n. 49
Habsburg, House of I: 274 n. 70
Hadrian (Publius Aelius Traianus Hadrianus) I: 276
Haecht, Tobias van I: 119
Haecht, Willem van I: 231
    The Studio of Apelles (*Apelles Painting Campaspe*) (painting), The Hague, Mauritshuis I: 60, 238, 239, 240, 241, 242, 243, 247, 275 n. 71, 389, 390, 391, 392, 394, *text ill. 100*; II: 37, 46, *appendix III.8*; *figs 128, 130, 135*
    A Picture Gallery (painting), Isle of Bute (Scotland), Mount Stuart, Collection of the Marquess of Bute I: 57, 151, 322, 417 n. 14, *text ill. 151*; II: *appendix III.31*
    The Art Gallery of Cornelis van der Geest (painting), Antwerp, Rubenshuis I: 386 n. 27, 416, 417 n.15, 426; II: 57, *appendix III.30*; *figs 199, 224*
Haeften, Johnny van (dealer) II: 59
Haer, Frans van den: see Haraeus, Franciscus
Haghe, Louis
    Sketches in Belgium and Germany
        The Visit of Maria de' Medici to Rubens (lithograph) II: 66, *appendix III.48*
Halberstadt I: 32
Hanikaert, Peeter I: 17
Haraeus, Franciscus (Frans van den Haer)
    Annales Ducum seu principum Brabantiae (1623) I: 366
Harrewijn, Frans I: 90 n. 10; II: 42, 43
Harrewijn, Jacob I: passim
    View of the Courtyard of Rubens's House (1684) (etching after Jacques van Croes) I: Chapter III and passim, *text ills 25, 27, 29, 34, 44–45, 48, 50–51, 58, 94, 122, 124*; II: *appendix III.1*; *figs 17, 28, 33–34, 36,38, 43, 53, 69, 82, 90, 98, 101, 142, 151, 168, 180, 227–228, 231*
    View of Rubens's House and Garden (1692) (etching after Jacques van Croes) I: Chapter III and passim, *text ills 9, 17, 24, 26, 28, 30–33, 35–37, 39–42, 46–47, 52, 57, 61, 66, 68, 90, 102, 139*; II: *appendix III.1*; *figs 18, 26, 29–30, 32, 39, 41, 44, 47, 51, 57, 60, 64, 106–107, 110, 122, 124, 127, 183, 188, 195, 206, 233*
Harrewijn, Jacob-Gerard I: 90 n. 10
Heemskerck, Maarten van
    Casa degli Omenoni, Milan (drawing), Berlin, Staatliche Museen zu Berlin I: 246 n. 47
    The Cycle of the Vicissitudes of Human Affairs (*Circulus vicissitudinis rerum humanarum*) (engravings, after) I: 369 n. 13
    Envy Bringing Forth War (engraving, after) I: 369 n. 13
Heidelberg
    University
        Universitätsbibliothek Heidelberg I: 127 n. 32; II: 12
Heinsius, Daniel I: 181 n. 37
Helman, Constantia II: 20
Hemelaers, Jan
Imperatorum Romanorum Numismata aurea (1615) I: 265, 362 n. 12
Hendrickx, Tanneke I: 45; II: 15, 16
Henri IV, King of France I: 288, 289, 296, 300, 409, 412, 413 n. 10; II: 51
Herck, Eugène Van I: 28
Hercules Farnese (sculpture), Naples, Museo Archeologico Nazionale I: 332, 393, 416, 422, 423; II: *fig. 216*
Hermes Belvedere (sculpture), Rome, Musei Vaticani I: 152, 333, 334, 345, 379; II: *figs 44, 45, 46*
Herstraten, Jaspar [Kaspar] van (de) I: 387, 389; II: 10, 11
Heurck, Émile Van I: 89 n. 10
Heyden, Petrus (Pieter) van der
    View on the City of Antwerp (engraving after Lambert van Noort, 1569) I: 42, 64, *text ill. 5*
Hillewerve, Cornelia I: 72–74, 87, 88, 385 n. 16; II: 22, 24, 25, 39, 40
Hillewerve, Cornelis I: 87
Hillewerve, family II: 47
Hillewerve, Franciscus I: 87, 88
Hillewerve, Frederik I: 87 n. 1

Hillewerve, Hendrik I: 17, 68 n. 62, 74, 75, 76, 87, 88, 89, 90, 91, 92, 93, 94, 96, 97, 98, 102, 105, 106, 107, 108, 110, 112, 113, 115, 116, 117, 147 n. 27, 153, 154, 158, 167, 186, 199, 200, 205, 211, 212, 213, 214, 215, 217, 232, 233 n. 10, 234, 236, 238, 240, 241, 242, 246, 256, 273, 277, 278, 279, 281, 282, 283, 284, 299 n. 15, 305, 306, 314, 315, 324, 343, 363, 379, 380, 381, 385 n. 16, 389, 390, 391, 392, 415, 416, 424, 425, 427, 428 n. 13, 429, 430, 431, *text ills 24, 29, 47, 90, 102*; II: 22, 23, 24, 25, 26, 39, 40, 42
Hippocrates I: 228
Hoefnagel, Joris
   Panoramic View of Antwerp (engraving, 1574) I: 30 n. 29, 42, 43, 64, *text ill. 7*
Hoefnagels, Antoine I: 251 n.10
Hoens, Hendrick I: see Hendrik Hoons
Hogenberg, Frans
   Map of Antwerp with the Citadel and the Head (etching, 1572) I: 42, *text ill. 6*
   (with Georg Braun) *Civitates orbis terrarium* (1572–1617) I: 42, 43, *text ill. 7*
Holbein, Hans II I: 197
   Façade (Tanzgässlein) of the House 'Zum Tanz', Basel (drawing), Basel, Kunstmuseum Basel I: 196, 263 n. 40, *text ill. 80*
   Façade of the Hertensteinhaus, Lucerne (drawing), Basel, Kunstmuseum Basel, Kupferstichkabinett I: 197 n.90
Homer I: 149 n. 34
   Iliad I: 358 n. 2
Honselersdijk
   Palace Honselaarsdijk I: 333
Hooghe, Romeyn de
   Schouburgh der Nederlandse veranderingen (1674) I: Title-Page I: 429, 430 n. 5
Hoon, Peter II: 7
Hoons (Hoens), Hendrik I: 27, 35; II: 7, 23
The Horse Tamer: see Rome, Quirinal
Houbraken, Arnold
   Groote Schouburgh (1719) I: 243 n. 36, 247 n. 54, 248
Hove, Geeraert Van II: 16
Huybrechts, Marcus II: 14, 16
Huygens, Constantijn I: 67, 160; II: 38
Huysmans, Camille I: 83, 282
Hyginus I:
   Fabulae I: 349, 350 n. 3, 384 n. 1

Iconoclastic Fury I: 29
Immerzeel, Engelbert van I: 425 n. 11
India, Bernardino I: 191 n. 72
Isabella Clara Eugenia, Infanta of Spain I: 54, 168, 187, 188, 233, 297, 380, 386 n. 40, 390, 412; II: 15, 34, 36, 37
Isle of Bute (Scotland): see Mount Stuart

James II, King of England, Scotland and Ireland I: 66; II: 39

Janssens, Cornelis I: 226
Janssens, Hiëronymus I: 304; II: 60
Jegher, Christoffel
   Susanna and the Elders (woodcut) II: 53, *fig. 225*
Jerusalem
   Temple of Solomon I: 29
Jones, Inigo
   Banqueting House, London I: 143 n. 13
Jordaens, Jacques (Jacob) I: 16, 199, 224, 265, 353 n. 19, 376
   Andromeda Liberated by Perseus (painting begun by Rubens, completed by Jordaens), Madrid, Museo Nacional del Prado) I: 378
   Musical Contest between Apollo and Marsyas (formerly The Judgment of Midas) (painting after Rubens), Madrid, Museo Nacional del Prado I: 350 n. 7
   Cupid and Psyche (painting), Madrid, Museo Nacional del Prado I: 61, 271, 303, 394, 395, 409, 426, 428; II: 46, *appendix III.9; figs 20, 159, 179, 220*
   The Story of Cupid and Psyche (ceiling paintings from the Jordaens House), Antwerp, The Phoebus Foundation I: 200 n. 100
   The Discovery of Erichtonius by the Daughters of Cecrops (painting), Vienna, Kunsthistorisches Museum I: 427, 428
   Figures in an Architectural Setting (drawing), Brussels, KBR I: 377 n. 5
   A Company Making Music in a Loggia (drawing), Cambridge, Fitzwilliam Museum I: 199; II: *fig. 109*
   A Company Making Music in a Loggia (drawing), whereabouts unknown I: 377–378 n. 5
   Scenes of the Country Life (tapestry series), Vienna, Kunsthistorisches Museum I: 377 n. 5
   Signs of the Zodiac (ceiling paintings from the Jordaens House), Paris, Palais du Luxembourg, Bibliothèque du Sénat I: 200 n. 100
   Maid Carrying a Dish, in a Loggia (drawing), Besançon, Musée des Beaux-Arts I: 377 n. 5
   A Maidservant with a Basket of Fruit and Two Lovers (painting), Glasgow, Kelvingrove Art Gallery and Museum I: 199 n. 99
   A Maidservant with a Basket of Fruit and Two Lovers (painting), Antwerp, Koninklijk Museum voor Schone Kunsten Antwerpen I: 199 n. 99
   Self-portrait with Family (painting), Madrid, Museo Nacional del Prado I: 426, 427
   Wall Decoration (drawing), Washington, National Gallery of Art I: 266
Julius II, Pope I: 422
Julius III, Pope I: 318
Julius Caesar I: 149 n. 34, 348 n. 4
Junius, Franciscus
   De pictura (1637) I: 176 n. 21, 179, 181; II: 37
Juvenal (Decimus Iunius Iuvenalis)

Satires (Satyrae) I: 260, 261–262, 263, 270 n. 63, 397, 399, 405, 406, 424, 425 n. 15

Kaers, Hendrick: see Caers, Hendrick
Kassel
   Museumslandschaft Hessen Kassel
      Gemäldegalerie Alte Meister I: 174, 349, 350, 432, 433 n. 4
Kew
   The National Archives II: 11
Keyser, Hendrick de
   Architectura Moderna oft Bouwinge van onsen tyt (1631) I: 267 n. 55
Keyser, Nicaise de
   Studies of Details of the Portico (drawing), Antwerp, Koninklijk Museum voor Schone Kunsten Antwerpen I: 274, 277; II: 64, *appendix III.43*
   The Courtyard of Rubens's House (engraving by Erin Corr) I: 273; II: 64, *appendix III.44*
   The Portico of Rubens's House (design with J. Stordiau, engraving by Erin Corr), Antwerp, Rubenshuis I: 80, 82, 251, 273, 277; II: 65, *appendix III.45*
   The Garden Pavilion of Rubens's House (design with J. Stordiau, engraving by Erin Corr and Jozef Linnig), Antwerp, Rubenshuis I: 80, 307, 413 n. 3; II: 65, *appendix III.46*
Königsberg I: 32 n. 39
Kolveniers (Antwerp Guild of Arquebusiers): see Antwerp
Kreitz, Willy
   Venus (statue), Antwerp, Rubenhuis I: 312; II: *fig. 177*
Kroměříž
   Archbishop's Palace
      Archdiosan Museum I: 428; II: 62

La Flèche
   Collège des Jésuites I: 264 n. 43, 267, *text ill. 117*
Lafreri, Antonio
   Speculum Romanae Magnificentiae (c. 1568) I: 121–122, 285, 361
      Roma victrix (engraving after Nicolas Béatrizet) I: 361; II: *fig. 89*
Langius, Carolus I: 263
Lede (Belgium) I: 395
Leenaerts, Fernandt II: 17
Leiden I: 32, 39, 263 n. 39
   Rijksmuseum van Oudheden
      Anonymous Roman artist after Alkamenes, *Hecate Triformis* (statue) I: 241 n. 32
   University I: 53; II: 35
      Universiteitsbibliotheek
         Bibliotheca Thysiana I: 31, 32 n. 42
Lelie, Adriaan de
   Drawing Gallery of the Felix Meritis Society (painting), Amsterdam, Rijksmuseum I: 248
Leonardo da Vinci I: 224
Leoni, Leone I: 246

Leopold Wilhelm, Archduke of Austria I: 87 n. 3
Letter, Thomas de I: 75; II: 27, 28, 40
Leuven
   Groot Begijnhof I: 113, 142 n. 8
   Town hall I: 225 n. 75
lex horti I: 262, 263
Leys, Henri I: 82 n. 97
Liberal Arts I: 181
Lier
   Church of St Gommarus I: 58 n. 30, 225 n. 75
Linden, Lodewijck van II: 7
Lindos I: 374
Linnig, Jozef
   The Garden Pavilion of Rubens's House (engraving with E. Corr after N. de Keyser and J. Stordiau) I: 80, 307, 413 n. 3; II: 65, *appendix III.46*
   The Courtyard of Rubens's House (engraving after the Harrewijn print of 1684) II: 66, *appendix III.47*
Lipsius, Justus I: 399
   De Constantia (1584) I: 263
   Twee boecken vande stantvasticheyt (1584) I: 263 n. 39
   Epistolae I: 227
   L. Annaei Senecae Opera Quae Extant Omnia (1615) I: 118, 148, 181 n. 37, 339, 413 n. 6, *text ill. 63*
Lomazzo, Gian Paolo I: 189, n. 75, 358 n. 9
   Trattato (1584) I: 147 n. 24
Lombardo, Antonio
   Relief with Inscription and Eagles (relief), Vaduz–Vienna, Liechtenstein, The Princely Collections I: 401, 402; II: *fig. 155*
London I: 32 n. 39, 50 n. 3, 59, 62, 63 n. 49, 71, 85, 248, 363, 364, 386 n. 29, 396; II: 43, 59, 66
   Banqueting House: I: 143 n. 13, 413 n. 10
   The British Museum I: 344 n. 2, 420; II: 56, *fig. 209*
   The Courtauld Gallery (formerly The Courtauld Institute of Art) I: 363, 367, 369; see also Index I
   The National Gallery I: 61 n. 41, 73, 269, 272 n. 65, *text ill. 20*; II: 39, 47, 49
      Anonymous 17th-century painter, *Portrait of a Young Man* (painting) I: 272, *text ill. 119*
   The Royal Collection Trust II: 55
   Sir John Soane's Museum I: 248 n. 58
   Syon House I: 390–391
   Victoria and Albert Museum I: 191, 331 n. 40
      (?) After Georg Petel, *Venus and Cupid* (bronze statuette) I: 416
Longniddry (Scotland), Gosford House, The Earl of Wemyss and March I: 427
Los Angeles
   Los Angeles County Museum of Art
      Roman, *A Roman Sacrifice* (sarcophagus relief) I: 353 n. 6
Losson, François Antoine
   Cadastral Map of Antwerp (print, 1846) I: 24, 27 n. 19, 35 n. 54, 42, 79–80; II: *fig. 2*

INDEX IV: NAMES AND PLACES

Lucas, Jan I: 332
Lucas, J. Th. II: 29
Lucas, Margaret: see Cavendish, Margaret
Lucerne I: 197 n. 90
    Hertensteinhaus (demolished) I: 197 n. 90
Lucian I: 368 n. 2
    Opera, quae quidem extant, omnia I: 176 n. 21, 363, 364, 365, 367, 368 (nn. 1, 3, 4), 369 n. 18
Lunden, Guillaume II: 20
Lutherans I: 29
Lysippus
    Alexander The Great (statue), lost I: 361

Madrid I: 59; II: 37
    Academia de Bellas Artes de San Fernando I: 427
    Museo Nacional del Prado I: 46 n. 87, 120 n. 10, 130 n. 41, 271, 292, 300, 303, 304 n. 21, 317, 318, 343 n. 5, 378, 385 n. 11, 395, 399, 400 n. 9, 409, 419, 420 n. 9, 426, 427, 428; II: 46, 48, 54
    Torre de la Parada I: 282 n. 94, 334, 350 n. 7, 378, 399, 426
Male, Jan Baptista van II: 11
Mander, Karel van I: 424
    Het Leven der oude Antijcke doorluchtige Schilders [...] (1603) I: 176 n. 21, 189 n. 63, 197, 198, 372 n. 3
    Het Schilder-boeck (1604) I: 189
Mantegna, Andrea I: 177, 246
Mantua I: 163, 191, 192, 287, 317
    Chiesa Sant'Orsola I: 264 n. 43
    House of Giulio Romano I: 163, 164, 200, 284, 403 n. 6
    House of Mantegna I: 246
    Palazzo Ducale I: 287, 317
        Roman, *Proserpina sarcophagus* (sarcophagus relief) I: 361; II: *fig. 86*
        Roman, *A Roman Sacrifice* (sarcophagus relief) I: 351; II: *fig. 66*
    Palazzo Te I: 287, 288, 317
    Porta della Cittadella: I: 288
Marcus Aurelius (Marcus Aurelius Antoninus) I: 149 n. 34, 228, 276
Mariën, M. I: 346
Marsyas (river in Phrygia) I: 349, 350
Mary (The Virgin) I: 111
Mary Magdalen I: 356, 358 n. 4
Maser
    Villa Barbaro Mattei I: 376
Massangis (France) I: 395, 410
Matthew, Tobie I: 133; II: 35
Maturino da Firenze I: 192
    Frescoes (with Polidoro da Caravaggio), Rome, Façade of Palazzo Milesi I: 192
    Ovid's Metamorphoses (frescoes, with Polidoro da Caravaggio), Rome, façades of Casino del Bufalo I: 192
Mechelen I: 31, 330, 331
    Beguinage Church I: 330
    Bruul I: 425 n. 12
    Cathedral of St Rumboldt I: 325 n. 10
    Church of St John the Baptist and St John the Evangelist I: 134
    House of Jan Lucas Faydherbe I: 332, 423
    Leermarkt I: 425 n. 12
Medici, Maria de', Queen of France I: 54 n. 15, 55, 288, 289, 296, 300, 322, 365, 398, 409; II: 37, 51, 52, 66, *figs 24, 93*
Medici, Ferdinando II de', Grand Duke of Tuscany I: 188
Mentmore (Buckinghamshire)
    Mentmore Towers I: 321, 322
Metrodorus of Athens
    The Triumph of Lucius Aemilius Paulus (painting), lost I: 55 n. 18
Metsys, Quinten I: 199
    Paintings for a room in his house ('St Quinten'), Antwerp, Schuttershofstraat (lost) I: 199, 376
Meuse (river) I: 263
Michel, J.F.M.
    Histoire de la vie de P.P. Rubens (1771) I: 79 n. 85, 222
Michelangelo Buonarotti I: 122, 266, 293
    Façade of the Palazzo Farnese, Rome (architecture, completion) I: 143 n. 13
    Study for the Porta Pia (drawing), Florence, Casa Buonarotti I: 286, *text ill. 128*
    Porta Pia, Rome (architecture) I: 265, 285, 286
Milan
    Casa degli Omenoni I: 246
    Cathedral I: 269
Mildert, Hans van (also Johannes or Jan) I: 18, 122, 125, 126 n. 30, 244, 249, 325, 327–329, 330, 387, 418, 421; II: 19, 37
    Decorations for the Pompa Introitus Ferdinandi I: 326, 328, 329; II: *fig. 50*
    Emperors (statues for the *Pompa Introitus Ferdinandi*), destroyed in the fire at the Brussels Coudenberg Palace in 1731 I: 326 n. 12
    Honos (sculpture after a design by Rubens, attributed to), Antwerp, Museum Plantin-Moretus I: 328, 411, 412, 413 n. 8, *text ill. 152*
    Virtus (sculpture after Rubens, possibly by), Antwerp, Museum Plantin-Moretus I: 411, 412, 413 n. 8
    Youth with a Cornucopia (Genius Loci?) (No. 36; sculpture, after a design by Rubens, attributed to), Antwerp, Rubenshuis, garden pavilion I: 328, 410–414; II: *fig. 187*
    Bucrania (No. 29; architectural sculpture after a design by Rubens, possibly by), Antwerp, Rubenshuis, portico I: 327; II: *figs 165–166*
    Left Caryatid (Sphinx?) (No. 35; sculpture after a design by Rubens, attributed to), formerly Antwerp, Rubenshuis, garden pavilion, lost I: 328, 409–410; II: *fig. 184*
    Right Caryatid (Sphinx?) (No. 35; sculpture after a design by Rubens, attributed to), formerly Antwerp, Rubenshuis, garden pavilion, lost

I: 328, 409–410; II: *fig. 185*
Dolphin (left) (No. 26; modern relief after Hans van Mildert after a design by Rubens, original lost), Antwerp, Rubenshuis, portico I: 327, 400–401
Dolphin (right) (No. 26; relief after a design by Rubens, original possibly by), Antwerp, Rubenshuis, portico I: 327, 400–401; II: *fig. 150*
High Altar of the Church of the Calced Carmelites, Antwerp (architectural-sculptural surround after a design by Rubens), destroyed I: 329
High Altar of the Jesuit Church of Antwerp (architectural sculptural surround, after Rubens and Huyssens, attributed to), Antwerp, Church of St Carolus Borromeus I: 328
High Altar of the Kapellekerk, Brussels (architectural-sculptural surround after a design by Rubens), Brussels, Sint-Josse-ten-Node I: 327
High Altar of the St John's Cathedral,'s-Hertogenbosch (architectural-sculptural surround), whereabouts unknown, presumably lost I: 327
Keystone with the Head of Medusa (architectural sculpture after a design by Rubens, possibly by), Antwerp, Rubenshuis, portico I: 398–400; II: *fig. 144*
Pediment with a Niche Surrounded by Two Eagles Holding a Fruit Garland (No. 27; architectural sculpture after a design by Rubens, possibly by), Antwerp, Rubenshuis, portico I: 327, 401–402; II: *figs 153, 157*
Ram's Head Ending in a Volute and a Snake's Head (architectural sculpture after a design by Rubens, possibly by; No. 28), Antwerp, Rubenshuis, portico I: 327, 402–404; II: *fig. 157*
Female Satyr Seen from Behind, Facing Left (No. 31; architectural sculpture after a design by Rubens, possibly by), Antwerp, Rubenshuis I: 327, 405–406; II: *fig. 173*
Female Satyr Facing Left (No. 33; architectural sculpture after a design by Rubens, possibly by), Antwerp, Rubenshuis I: 327, 407–408; II: *fig. 176*
Male Satyr Facing Right (No. 30; architectural sculpture after a design by Rubens, attributed to), Antwerp, Rubenshuis I: 327, 405; II: *fig. 171*
Male Satyr Facing Left (No. 32; architectural sculpture after a design by Rubens, possibly by), Antwerp, Rubenshuis I: 327, 407; II: *fig. 175*
Sculptures Crowning the High Altar for St Michael's Abbey, Antwerp (sculpture after a design by Rubens, attributed to), Zundert (The Netherlands), Church of St Trudo I: 328

Staircase (joinery after Rubens), formerly in Antwerp, Rubens's House, lost I: 126, 184, 202, 387–389; II: 10–11, 35, *fig. 124*
Mildert, Jan van I: 329
Mildert, Johannes van I: 329
Mildert, Peter [Paul] van I: 327
Mildert, widow of Hans van I: 329; II: 19
Moens, Hendrick II: 20
Mols, François I: 40, 76, 234
 Annotations manuscrites sur Rubens (c. 1763) I: 78, 124 n. 25, 168, 169,172, 175, 186, 188 n. 57, 213, 234, 250, 310, 380, 381, 385 n. 26; II: 20–21
 KBR, MS 5724 (*Vie de Rubens, Notes et remarques*); MS 5726 (*Rubeniana, tome 2*) I: 77; II 30–31
  Plan of Rubens's House I: 17, 68 n. 62, 76–78, 82, 93, 94, 97, 98, 103, 105, 109, 111, 113, 151 n. 37, 154, 185, 186, 201, 202, 203, 204, 212, 213, 214, 217, 218, 222, 228, 230 n. 2, 234, 235, 236, 385 n. 26, 387, 388, 389, 390, *text ill.21*; II: 41, 44, *appendix I.43*; *figs 3, 125–126*
Momper, Joos de II I: 119, 226
Monogrammist TG
 Façade of Frans Floris's House Series (8 engravings) *Pictura, Sculptura and Architectura* (?) I: 197, 198 n. 93
Monte, Deodaat del I: 226
Montmorency, Helena de I: 425 n. 11
Mooson, Petrus Domenicus II: 28
Moretus, Albert I: 53 n. 11
Moretus, Balthazar I I: 128, 263 n. 39; II: 12, 34, 35
 Preface to J. Lipsius's, *L.A. Senecae Opera Quae Extant Omnia* (1615) I: 148, 181 n. 37; II: 10
 Journal (1613–1640) I: 121, 122
Moretus, Balthazar III I: 53 n. 11, 88
Moretus, Jan I I: 23, 119 n. 5, 263 n. 39; II: 31
Moretus, widow of Jan I: 119 n. 5; II: 10
Mortel, Pauwel van de I: 326
Mount Stuart (Isle of Bute (Scotland))
 Collection of the Marquess of Bute I:322 n. 6, 417 n. 14; II: 57
Moy, Clara de I: 23, 27, 129; II: 32
Mucius Scaevola I: 322, 403 n. 2
Munich
 Bayerische Staatsgemäldesammlungen
  Alte Pinakothek I: 60, 107, 134, 135, 161 n. 56, 296, 300, 301, 302, 303, 306, 365, 374, 48, 410, 414, 418, 420, 425; II: 37, 45, 51, 52
Musson, Matthijs I: 87 n. 3
Mythological Characters
 Achilles I: 180, 343 n. 1, 355, 357, 359 n. 11, 372 n. 4, 375 n. 2, 400 n. 9
 Adonis I: 375 n. 2
 Agamemnon, King of Mycenae I: 355, 356, 357, 358, 359 n. 13
 Ajax I: 356, 357
 Amor I: 115, 312, 313, 314
 Andromeda I: 17, 59, 92, 152, 168, 169, 174, 175, 176,

178, 180, 182, 186, 188, 190, 285, 344 n. 5, 375, 377, 378–387, 399; II: 24, 30
Apollo I: 156 n. 44, 174 n. 16, 175, 181, 348–350, 354, 361, 369 n. 16, 384, 401 n. 1, 416, 420 n. 4, 431
Bacchante (*Maenad*) I: 277, 307, 340, 373, 374 (nn. 2, 3), 433 n. 1
Bacchus I: 299, 302, 303, 306, 309, 310, 311 n. 35, 312, 313, 315, 331, 335 n. 53, 343, 344, 373, 374, 409, 412, 417 n. 15, 417–420, 423, 424, 432
Bellerophon I: 375 n. 2, 385 n. 7
Calchas I: 356
Callisto I: 370 n. 1, 428; II: 62
Cerberus I: 361
Ceres I: 118, 143 n. 14, 146, 152, 265, 268, 269, 299, 310, 311, 312, 313, 314, 315, 382, 409, 412, 414, 415, 417, 423, 432, 433
Chimera I: 385 n. 7
Cupid I: 61, 85, 200, 254, 256, 257, 271, 275, 276, 280, 303, 326, 330, 350, 378, 379, 382, 385 n. 5, 386 n. 37, 394, 395, 401, 414, 415, 416, 417, 425, 426, 427, 428; II: 45, 46, 48, 53, 60
Diana I: 156 n. 44, 355, 359 n. 13, 361, 372 n. 9, 427; II: 61
Euridice I: 179
Faun I: 146, 147, 148, 277, 307, 332, 339, 340, 349, 350 n. 7, 373, 374, 394, 419
Flora I: 152, 344, 345
Gorgon I: 379, 398, 399
Helen of Troy I: 370
Hercules I: 174 n. 16, 176, 177 n. 25, 197, 285, 299, 302, 303, 304, 307, 309, 310, 311, 312, 313, 314, 315, 319, 321, 323, 324, 330, 331, 332, 334, 335 n. 53, 341, 370, 373–375, 384, 393–395, 404, 406, 409, 412, 414 n. 11, 416, 421–425; II: 47, 63
Hermathena I: 281 n. 88, 283
Hermes: see Mercury
Hesperides I: 422, 423
Hippocrene I: 384
Hippolytus I: 375 n. 2
Iphigenia I: 176, 177 n. 25, 181, 193 n. 79, 352, 355–359, 360, 363, 403, 426, 427
Janus I: 365, 366, 414 n. 11
Juno I: 145 n. 18, 283 n. 95, 372 n. 2, 417 n. 5
Jupiter I: 283 n. 95, 360, 361, 399, 40 n. 9, 425 n. 10
Liber I: 315
Lycaon I: 399
Lycomedes I: 180, 372 n. 4, 375 n. 2, 400 n. 9
Mars I: 146, 332, 333, 425 n. 10
Marsyas I: 349, 350
Medusa I: 19, 192 n. 75, 193 n. 79, 241, 251, 257, 259, 281, 285, 289 n. 115, 356, 377, 378, 379, 382, 384, 397, 398, 399, 400 (nn. 3, 9), 430
Melanthius I: 375 n. 3
Meleager I: 375 n. 2
Menelaus I: 356, 357
Mercury (Hermes) I: 92, 152, 197, 261, 266, 272, 281, 282, 283, 284, 285 n. 104, 333, 334, 343–344, 355, 366, 369 n. 11, 376, 379, 384, 387 n. 50,

397, 403, 404 n. 6, 419, 420 n. 4, 424, 425 n. 18, 428–430, 431
Midas I: 348, 349, 350 n. 7, 365
Minerva (Athena) I: 257, 261, 277, 278, 279, 280, 281, 282, 283, 284, 285 n. 104, 333, 340, 366, 369 (nn. 11, 14), 384, 387 n. 50, 397, 424, 429, 430–431, 433 n. 1
Muses I: 227, 384
Nemean lion I: 421
Orpheus I: 179
Pan I: 148 n. 28
Paris I: 370, 371, 419, 420 n. 9
Pegasus I: 377, 378, 379, 380, 381, 384, 385 (nn. 7, 26), 399
Perseus I: 17, 59, 152, 168, 174, 175, 176, 178, 182, 186, 188, 190, 192, 193 n. 79, 285, 344 n. 5, 356, 375, 377–387, 398, 399
Pluto I: 347, 361
Proetus I: 375 n. 2
Prometheus I: 180, 378, 384 n. 4
Proserpina I: 347, 361, 362 n. 3
Satyr I: 19, 59, 90, 148, 251, 257, 260, 261, 262, 263, 271, 272, 310, 327, 331, 339, 349, 350, 373, 374, 395, 397, 400, 405, 406, 407, 408 n. 2; II: 64
Silenus I: 59, 148, 339, 373, 374 (nn. 3, 4)
Telephus I: 422
Tmolus I: 348, 349
Ulysses I: 356, 357
Venus I: 180, 299, 302, 303, 304, 306, 309, 310, 311, 312, 313, 314, 315, 324, 326, 331, 333, 334, 367, 369 n. 17, 374 n. 2, 375 n. 2, 382, 401, 409, 414–417, 424, 426, 428 n. 4, 431, 432; II: 57

Naples I:
  Museo Archeologico Nazionale di Napoli
    Roman, *Amor Riding a Dolphin* (statue) I: 426, 428 n. 5; II: *fig. 221*
    Roman, *Andromeda* (relief) I: 383, 386 n. 42
    Roman, *Andromeda* (relief) I: 383, 386 n. 42
    Roman, *Flora Farnese* (statue): I: 344, 345 n. 2; II: *fig. 48*
    Roman, *Genius* (statue) I: 412, 414 n. 15; II: *fig. 193*
    Roman, *Hercules Farnese* (statue) I: 422, 424 n. 6; II: *fig. 216*
    Roman, *The Sacrifice of Iphigenia* (fresco after ? Timanthes) I: 357
    Roman, *Perseus and Andromeda* (painting) I: 386 n. 42
Nassau-Siegen, Johan Maurits van I: 278 n. 78
Nealkes I: 375 n. 3
Neuburg
  Jesuit Church I: 134
Neumay(e)r von Ramssla, Johann Wilhelm
  Des durchlauchtigen hochgebornen Fürsten und Herrn / Herrn Johann Ernsten des Jüngern / Hertzogen zu Sachsen / Jülich / Cleve und Berg / Landgrafen in Düringen […] *Reise in Franckreich, Engelland und Niederland* (1620)

INDEX IV: NAMES AND PLACES

I: 52, 54, 120 n. 9; II: 12, 34
Neve, Sebastiaan de
   Saints (statues), Antwerp, Jesuit Church, Chapel of Our Lady I: 326
New York I: 305 n. 22; II: 61
   The Metropolitan Museum of Art I: 62, 133 n. 53, 343 n. 5, 388 n. 3
   The Morgan Library & Museum II: *fig. 147*
Nicias
   Andromeda (painting), lost I: 178, 180, 383
Nieulandt, Adriaen van
   Title-Page for C. Ripa, *Iconologia* (1644) I: 429
Nole, family de I: 325
   Apostles (statues), Mechelen, Cathedral of St Rumbold I: 325 n. 10
Nole, Andries de I: 325
Nole, Jan (or Hans) de I: 325
Nole, Robrecht de I: 325
Nonnius, Ludovicus I: 228
   The Arch of the Portuguese (invention), from the decoration for the Entry of the Cardinal-Infante I: 345 n. 7
Noort, Lambert van
   View on the City of Antwerp (engraving by Petrus Van der Heyden) I: *text ill. 5*
Norbertines I: 26, 129
Nuremberg I: 197

Obernkirchen (Germany) I: 395
Opstal, Gerard van I: 244, 329
Orme, Philibert de l'
   L'Architecture I: 121, 267 n. 57
Ottley, William Young I: 386 n. 29
Ovid
   Metamorphoses I: 192, 348, 349, 350 (nn. 1, 2), 378, 384 (nn. 1, 2), 385 (nn. 6, 8, 10, 15), 387 n. 48
Oxford
   Ashmolean Museum I: 415, 416, 417 (nn. 9, 18); II: *figs 197–198*
   Worcester College
      Unknown French architect, *Fountain with Giants* (drawing) I: 292 n. 128

Palladio, Andrea I: 121, 143, 346, 404 n. 1
   Basilica (architecture), Vicenza I: 317, *text ill. 144*
Palliata as Ceres: see *Ceres Palliata*
Palomino y Velasco, Acisclo Antonio
   El museo pictórico y escala óptica (1715–24) I: 187 n. 52
   Frontispiece I: 429, 430 n. 5; II: *fig. 229*
Panneels, Willem I: 17, 19, 58–59, 172 n. 10, 173, 225, 344, 357, 359, 361 n. 1; II: 36, 37
   The Assumption of the Virgin (drawing after Rubens, attributed to), Budapest, Szépművészeti Múzeum, Print Room I: 268, *text ill. 118*
   Andromeda Liberated by Perseus (drawing after ? Rubens, attributed to), Copenhagen, Statens Museum for Kunst, Kongelige Kobberstiksamling I: 59, 381; II: *fig. 112*
   Three Studies of the Cupid Embracing a Goose (drawing after Rubens), Copenhagen, Statens Museum for Kunst, Kongelige Kobberstiksamling I: 428 n. 8
   Study of the Hermes Belvedere (drawing after Rubens), Copenhagen, Statens Museum for Kunst, Kongelige Kobberstiksamling I: 343, 344 n. 4; II: *fig. 46*
   Study of the Hermes Belvedere (drawing after Rubens),Copenhagen, Statens Museum for Kunst, Kongelige Kobberstiksamling I: 343
   The Sacrifice of Iphigenia (drawing after Rubens; No. 11, Copy 1), Copenhagen, Statens Museum for Kunst, Kongelige Kobberstiksamling I: 59, 355, 356, 358; II: *figs 71, 75, 77*
   Alexander with the Thunderbolt (drawing after Rubens; No. 12, Copy), Copenhagen, Statens Museum for Kunst, Kongelige Kobberstiksamling I: 59, 167, 169, 359, 360; II: *fig. 84*
   Venus and Cupid (drawing), Copenhagen, Statens Museum for Kunst, Kongelige Kobberstiksamling I: 416, 417 n. 16; II: *fig. 200*
   Venus and Cupid (drawing), Copenhagen, Statens Museum for Kunst, Kongelige Kobberstiksamling I: 416, 417 n. 16; II: *fig. 201*
   Top of Lars Porsenna's Throne (drawing, attributed to), Copenhagen, Statens Museum for Kunst, Kongelige Kobberstiksamling I: 322
   Niche with Scallop and Bust (drawing, attributed to), Copenhagen, Statens Museum for Kunst, Kongelige Kobberstiksamling I: 322, 323, *text ill. 150*
   Eagle with Spread Wings (drawing after Rubens, attributed to), Copenhagen, Statens Museum for Kunst, Kongelige Kobberstiksammling I: 402 n. 5
   Two Studies of Eagle with Spread Wings (drawing after Rubens, attributed to), Copenhagen, Statens Museum for Kunst, Kongelige Kobberstiksammling I: 402 n. 5
   Female Satyr Seen from Behind, Facing Left (drawing), Copenhagen, Statens Museum for Kunst, Kongelige Kobberstiksamling I: 59, 406; II: *fig. 174*
   Study of a Cuirass (drawing after Rubens?, attributed to), Copenhagen, Statens Museum for Kunst, Kongelige Kobberstiksamling I: 386 n. 27
Paris I: 53, 62 n. 64, 66, 249 n. 2, 267 (nn. 56, 57), 270 n. 63, 287, 289 n. 14
   Bibliothèque nationale de France II: 67
   Fondation Custodia I: 266, 270, 396; see also Index I; Anonymous 17th-century artist, *Sepulchral Monument of a Young Nobleman* (drawing) I: 266

INDEX IV: NAMES AND PLACES

Musée du Louvre ; II: 37, 45, 51, 52, 59, 60, 62, 67, 192 n. 75, 269, 346, 365, 368 n. 3, 398
   Attic, *Borghese Vase* (sculpture) I: 373, 374 n. 2; II: *figs 102–103*
   Roman, *Centaur Tormented by Cupid* (sculpture) I: 350
   Roman, *Faun with Pipes* (statue) I: 419
   Palais du Luxembourg I: 123 n. 21, 200 n. 100, 267 n. 57, 288, 289, 300, *text ill. 132*
Parma, Margaret of I: 29, 42
Parrhasius I: 188, 357, 374, 375 n. 11
   Priest with a Boy (painting), lost I: 176
Pausias
   The Sacrifice of an Ox ('immolatio boum') (formerly in Rome, Pompey's portico, lost) I: 176, 177 n. 25, 352, 353 (nn. 16, 17, 18), 354
Pearce, Edward
   Staircase from a House in England (sculpture), New York, The Metropolitan Museum of Art I: 388 n. 3
Peeters, Balthasar I: 16
Peiresc, Nicolas-Claude Fabri de I: 50, 179, 188, 277; II: 14, 36
Perino del Vaga
   The North Façade of the Palazzo Doria, Genoa (drawing), Chantilly, Musée Condé I: 193
   The North Façade of the Palazzo Doria, Genoa (drawing), Amsterdam, Rijksmuseum I: 193, 194, *text ill. 76*
Persijn, Reinier van
   After Adriaen van Nieulandt, Title-Page to C. Ripa, *Iconologia* (1644) I: 430 n. 3
Personifications
   Abundantia I: 314, 411
   Bonus Eventus I: 414 n. 17
   Calumnia (Calumny) I: 63, 176, 177, 349, 362–369, 370
   Conspirancy: see Treachery
   Constancy I: 275 n. 72
   Deceit (Deception) I: 364, 365, 368 n. 7
   Detractio I: 369 (n. 13)
   Diligence: 198 n. 93
   Earth's fertility (Ops) I: 314, 410, 413 n. 4, 423, 424
   Envy: see Invidia
   Fame I: 197, 210
   Fertility I: 148 n. 29, 314, 412
   Furor I: 365, 366, 369 n. 9
   Furor Poetico I: 284, 429, 430 n. 2
   Genius Loci I: 314, 410, 411, 412, 414 n. 17; II: *fig. 192*
   Hatred I: 364, 365
   Honos (Honour) I: 280, 314, 315, 328, 410–414
   Hope: see Spes
   Ignorantia I: 349
   Imaginatione (Fantasy) I: 429, 430 (nn. 2, 5), 284
   Innocence I: 365, 366, 367, 369 n. 17
   Inspiration (Mercury) I: 197, 261, 272, 281, 282, 283, 284, 285 n. 104, 333, 343, 366, 376, 384, 387 n.50, 397, 403, 419, 420 n. 4, 424, 428, 429, 430, 431, 432 n. 2
   Intrigue: see Treachery
   Ira: see Furor
   Invidia I: 364, 365, 366, 369 n. 13, 374
   Jealousy: see Invidia
   Justice I: 197
   Labour (Hercules) I: 197, 198 n. 93, 315, 374, 412, 423, 424
   Minerva: see Wisdom
   Pictura I: 181,198, 210, 211, 282, 284, 428, 429, 430 (nn. 4, 5)
   Poenitentia (Repentance) I: 366
   Poetry I: 198 n. 93, 384
   Protector of cornfields (Hercules) I: 314
   Prudentia I: 431
   Rage: see Hatred
   Rome I: 361, 362 n. 9
   Skill (Usus): 198 n. 93
   Spes I: 329, 345,
   Suspicion I: 364, 365
   Treachery I: 364
   Truth: see Veritas
   Veritas (Truth) I: 366
   Victory I: 171 n. 16, 348, 349, 350, 354, 360, 374, 377, 378, 381, 383
   Virtus I: 275 n. 72, 384, 411, 413, 414 n. 11
   Wisdom (Minerva) I: 275 n. 72, 280, 283, 366, 369 n. 14
Petel, Georg I: 244 n. 37, 415, 417; II: 36
   The Triumph of the Sea-Born Venus (ivory sculpture after Rubens), Stockholm, Swedish Royal Collections, Husgerådkammern I: 416, 417 n. 12
   Venus and Cupid (ivory statuette), Oxford, Ashmolean Museum I: 306, 326, 415, 416, 417 n. 9; II: *figs 197–198*
Petrarch, Francesco (Petrarca) I: 372 n. 3
Philadelphia
   Philadelphia Museum of Art I: 384 n. 4
Phillips London (auctioneer) I: 386 n. 29
Philostratus I:
   Eikones or *Imagines* I: 383, 384 (nn. 1, 3)
      Andromeda Liberated by Cupid (engraving) I: 176, 178 n. 26, 378, 385 (nn. 5, 9, 15); II: *fig. 115*
Pieters, Anthoni de II: 24
Piles, Roger de I: ; II: 23, 39
   Dissertation sur les Ouvrages des plus fameux Peintres, dédiée à Monseigneur le duc de Richelieu. La vie de Rubens (1681) I: 44 n. 82, 51 n. 8, 75, 108, 163, 234, 237, 245, 389, 390
Pio da Carpi, Rodolfo I: 401
Pius IV, Pope I: 265, 285
Plantin, Christopher I: 119 n. 5
Plantin, Martina I: 118, 119 n. 5, 133; II: 10, 34
Plato I: 149 n. 34, 372 n. 8
Pliny the Elder (Gaius Plinius Secundus)
   Natural History (*Naturalis Historia*) I: 55 n. 18, 116 n. 55, 147, 176, 177, 178, 179, 181, 188, 238,

345 n. 4, 347, 348 n. 3, 349, 350 n. 4, 352, 353 n. 16, 354, 356, 357, 358 n. 8, 359 (nn. 12, 16), 361, 362 (nn. 8, 9), 368 n. 1, 370, 372 (nn. 2, 3, 9), 374, 375 (nn. 9, 11), 383, 386 n. 41
Pluijm, Cornelis II: 7
Plutarch
   Vitae Parallelae I: 361, 362 n. 9, 375 n. 3
Polidoro da Caravaggio I: 192
   The Façade of Palazzo Gaddi, Rome (drawing by an anonymous sixteenth-century painter), Vienna, Albertina I: 192
   The Façade of Palazzo Milese, Rome (frescoes) I: 192
   Ovid's Metamorphoses (frescoes, with Maturino da Firenze), Rome, decorating the façades of Casino del Bufalo I: 192
   Perseus Showing the Head of Medusa to Phineus and his Companions (fresco), Rome, Museo di Roma, Palazzo Braschi I: 356
   Rape of the Sabine Women (fresco, with Maturino da Firenze), Rome, façade of Palazzo Ricci-Sacchetti I: 152 n.38
Pompa Introitus Ferdinandi (Antwerp, 1635) I: 64, 65, 380, 412
Pompeii I: 178, 179, 357, 383
Pontius, Paulus
   Herm Bust of Sophocles (engraving after Rubens) II: *fig. 40*
Poperinge I: 32
Pordenone, Giovanni Antonio
   Frescoes, Genoa, Palazzo del Principe Andrea Doria, façade (destroyed) I: 193
   Façade of Palazzo d'Anna, Venice (drawing), London, Victoria and Albert Museum I: 191, *text ill. 74*
Porsenna, Lars, Etruscan King I: 322
Post, Pieter
   North-South Cross-Section of the Mauritshuis, The Hague (drawing after Jacob van Campen), The Hague, Koninklijke Bibliotheek / Nationale Bibliotheek van Nederland I: 218, *text ill. 92*
Prague I: 181, 197, 342
Praxiteles I: 343, 344, n. 2, 345 n. 4, 419, 420 n. 7
Preti, Mattia I: 53
Princen, Gielis I: 19
Prussia I: 32
'Pseudo-Seneca' (Roman bust), formerly in the collection of P.P. Rubens, lost I: 147, 148, 149 n. 32, 150, 322, 323, 340, 341
Pudicitia Mattei (plaster cast after the Roman original in the Musei Vaticani, Rome) I: 371; II: *fig. 100*
Puget de la Serre, Jean
   Histoire curieuse de tout ce qui c'est passé a l'entree de la Reyne, mere du roy très chrestien dans les villes des Pays Bas (1632) I: 54 n. 15, 55, 181 n. 38
Pypelinckx, Dionys I: 35 n. 53
Pypelinckx, Hendrik I: 25
Pypelinckx, Maria I: 25, 26, 27, 34, 35 n. 54, 127 n. 32, 129; II: 32
Pypelinckx, Susanna I: 27, 35 n. 54; II: 32

Quellinus, Artus I I: 18, 326, 332–335, 419, 420 n. 4, 423, 425 n. 10
   Statues and Reliefs for the Amsterdam Town Hall (with assistants)
     Apollo (sculpture), Amsterdam, Paleis op de Dam I: 332
     Jupiter (sculpture), Amsterdam, Paleis op de Dam I: 332, 425 n. 10
     Mars (sculpture), Amsterdam, Paleis op de Dam I: 332, 425 n. 10
     Mercury (sculpture), Amsterdam, Paleis op de Dam I: 282 n. 94, 332, 333, 404 n. 6; II: *text ill. 153*
   Statues for the Steps of Honselaarsdijk Palace, lost I: 333
   Statues for the Gardens of Nieuburch Palace, Rijswijk, lost I: 333
   Labore et Constantia (relief), Antwerp, Museum Plantin-Moretus I: 334, 335, *text ill. 155*
   Mercury (statuette after Rubens, attributed to), St Petersburg, The State Hermitage Museum I: 333, 334; II: *text ill. 154*
   Minerva (marble fountain), Cleves, Museum Kurhaus Kleve I: 278 n. 78
   Venus (statuette after Rubens, attributed to), St Petersburg, The State Hermitage Museum I: 334
   Engelbert van Immerzeel and Helena de Montmorency (Tomb), Bokhoven-near 's Hertogenbosch, Church of St Anthony Abbot I: 425 n. 12
Quellinus, Catharina I: 334
Quellinus, Erasmus I
   Paintings for the Pompa Introitus Ferdinandi (after Rubens) I: 326, 334
   Paintings for the Torre de la Parada (after Rubens) I: 334
   Wooden Pulpit, Antwerp, Chapel of St Elizabeth's Hospital (now part of 'The Botanic Sanctuary' hotel) I: 326 n. 15
Quellinus, Erasmus II I: 226
Quellinus, Hubertus
   Decorative Elements (bundles of attributes) after the Sculptural Decoration of the Town Hall of Amsterdam (engraving after Artus Quellinus I) I: 431; II: *fig. 234*
Quintilian I:
   Institutio Oratoria I: 356, 358 n. 8

raamveld or *raamhof* I: 23, 25, 31, 41
Radi, Bernardino
   Disegni de Architettura (1619) I: 275 n. 74
Raes, Jan I
   The History of Decius Mus (tapestries after Rubens) I: 134; II: 35
Raet, Marie de I: 116 n. 57
Raphael (of Urbino) (Rafaello Sanzio) I: 383

INDEX IV: NAMES AND PLACES

The Acts of the Apostles (tapestries) I: 352
  The Sacrifice at Lystra I:
    (cartoon by Raphael and his Assistants)
      London, The Royal Collection, on loan to the
        Victoria and Albert Museum I: 352, 353 n. 12
Rembrandt Harmensz. van Rijn I: 40
  Panorama near Bloemendael Showing the Saxenburg
    Estate (etching) I: 40 n. 73
Reuflet, A.J. Noël
  Primitief Kadasterplan 201, Antwerpen sectie C (1824),
    Antwerp, Kadasterarchief I: 80 (nn. 91, 92)
Reynolds, Joshua I: 124 n. 25
Rijn, Titus van I: 40 n. 74
Rijswijk
  Palais Nieuburch I: 333
Ripa, Cesare
  Iconologia (1603) I: 284, 429, 430 (nn. 2, 3)
Rockox, Nicolaas I: 226–228; II: 30
Rogiers, Theodoor I
  Susanna and the Elders (silver decoration of a basin
    after Rubens), Antwerp, Rubenshuis I: 428
Rohrau (Lower Austria)
  Schloss Rohrau, Graf Harrach'se
    Familiensammlung I: 210
Rokeghem, Lieven van I: 26 n. 16
Romano, Giulio I: 163, 200, 284, 285 n. 104, 403 n. 6
  Design for a Loggia with Rustic Portal (drawing),
    Vienna, Albertina, Grafische Sammlung
    I: 317, 318, *text ill. 145*
  Palazzo Ducale, Mantua I: 287, 317
  Palazzo Te, Mantua I: 287, 288, *text ill. 129*
    Study for the Palazzo Te (drawing), Vienna,
      Albertina I: 288, *text ill. 130*
    Study for the Palazzo Te (drawing), Stockholm,
      Nationalmuseum I: 288
  Porta della Citadella, Mantua I: 288
Rome I: 88, 126, 148, 163–165, 178, 192, 197, 200, 245,
  276, 318, 343, 344, 348 n. 4, 349, 350, 352, 356,
  361, 373, 402, 425 n. 8; II: 10, 22, 23, 26
  Arch of Constantine
    Roman, *The Sacrifice to Apollo* (relief) I: 361; II:
      fig. 85
  Borgho Vecchio I: 361
  Casa Sassi I: 246
  Casino del Bufalo I: 192
  Collegio di Propaganda Fide I: 364 n. 43
  Fondazione Torlonia
    Roman, *Resting Faun* (statue) I: 419; II: *fig. 207*
  Forum Boarum
    Arch of the Argentarii I: 351
  Musei Capitolini
    Roman, *Adromeda Liberated by Perseus* (relief) I:
      386 n. 42
    Roman, *Resting Faun* (statue) I: 420 n. 7
  Musei Vaticani I: 344 n. 2
    Roman, *Eagle with Spread Wings* (statue) I: 402 n. 5
    Roman, *Hercules ('Commodus')* (statue) I: 422, 424
      n. 7; II: *fig. 217*

  Roman, *The Lowering of the Cloth* (relief) I: 348; II:
    fig. 58
  Capitoline or Medici Venus (statue after an original
    of Praxiteles) I: 428 n. 4
  Museo dell' Ara Pacis I: 353 n. 8
  Museo Nazionale delle Terme I: 428 n. 8
    Roman, *Child Embracing a Goose* (statue) I: 426
  Oratorio di S. Filippo Neri I: 264 n. 43
  Palazzo Barberini I: 348 n. 4
  Palazzo Borghese I: 160 n. 53, 161 n. 57, 183 n. 43
  Palazzo Braschi I: 192 n. 75
  Palazzo Cesi I: 361
  Palazzo dei Conservatori
    Roman, *Barbarian Kings* (statues) I: 361; II: *fig. 88*
    Roman, *Marcus Aurelius Sacrificing before the*
      Capitoline Temple (relief) I: 356; II: *fig. 76*
    Roman, *Sacrificial Scene* (relief) I: 351
  Palazzo del Quirinale I: 160 n. 53
  Palazzo di Venezia I: 183 n. 43
  Palazzo Farnese I: 143 n. 13, 160 n. 53, 161 n. 57, 183,
    text ill. 73, 344, 345, 356, 424 n. 6, 426
  Palazzo Gaddi I: 192
  Palazzo Mattei di Giove I: 147 n. 26, 164, 165, *text ill.*
    71, 179, 403 n. 2
  Palazzo Milesi I: 192
  Palazzo Pallavicini Rospigliosi
    Casino dell' Aurora
      The Abduction of Proserpina (sarcophagus relief)
        I: 362 n. 3
  Palazzo Ricci-Sacchetti I: 152 n. 38
  Palazzo Zuccari I: 200 n. 102
  Pantheon I: 18, 219, 233–234, 241, 244–46, 390–391
  Pompey's Portico I: 352, 356
  Porta Maggiore I: 288 n. 111
  Porta Pia I: 121, 161 n. 57, 265, 267, 275 n. 74, 285–
    287, *text ill. 126*, 291, 401, 402 n. 2
  Portico of Philip I: 372 n. 2
  Quirinal
    Roman, *The Horse Tamer* (statue): I: 379, 381; II:
      fig. 123
  Vatican
    Belvedere I: 344 n. 2, 420 n. 8, 422
  Villa Borghese (Galleria Borghese) I: 433 n. 4
  Villa Carpi I: 401, 402 n. 2
  Villa Giulia I: 140 n. 53, 275 n. 74, 290, 318, 319, *text*
    ill. 148
  Villa Madama I: 241, 414 n. 15
  Villa Medici I: 262, *text ill. 113, 147*
    Garden façade I: 144, 160 n. 53, 161 n. 57, 163, 179,
      180, *text ill. 72*, 318, 347, 353 (nn. 6, 7), 398; II:
      figs 56, 146
    Roman, *A Roman Sacrifice* (relief) I: 351, 353 n. 8;
      II: *fig. 67*
    Loggia di Cleopatra I: 318, 319, *text ill. 147*
    Loggia del Bosco (or del Grotto) I: 318
Rotschild, Mayer de I: 322 n. 3
Rotterdam
  Museum Boijmans Van Beuningen I: 332, 423, 427

INDEX IV: NAMES AND PLACES

Staircase from a house in The Hague (architectural sculpture) I: 388 n. 3
Rouen I: 267 n. 56
Roy, Peter Le II: 14
Roy, Philippe le I: 116 n. 57
Rubens, Albert I: 50, 55, 56, 57, 72
Rubens, Blandina I: 26; II: 32
Rubens, Clara Serena I: 118; II: 33
Rubens, Constantia Albertina I: 72
Rubens, Franciscus II: 20
Rubens, Isabella Helena I: 72
Rubens, Jan I: 26
Rubens, Nicolaas I: 50, 55, 56, 57, 72, 78 n. 82, 118 n. 3, 301
Rubens, Philip (brother of Peter Paul) I: 26, 127 n. 32, 129, 181 n. 37, 191 n. 71, 386 n. 38, 394; II: 32
   Electorum libri II I: 344–245, 348, 362 n. 5, 404 n. 3; II: 32
   Ad Petrum Paullum Rubenium navigantem I: 181 n. 37
Rubens, Philip (nephew of Peter Paul) I: 72 n. 71, 75; II: 17, 20
   Vita Petri Pauli Rubenii I: 23, 44, 50, 51, 108, 129, 153, 156, 163, 212 n. 30, 234, 353 n. 18, 390; II: 20–21, 29, 39
Rudolf II, Holy Roman Emperor I: 197
Ryckaert, David II I: 46; II: 19, 38
Ryckaert, David III I: 46 n. 87
Ryckaert, Maarten I: 46 n. 87
Ryckius, Justus I: 181 n. 37
Ryckmans, Nicolaes
   Façade of the Palazzo Interiano Pallavicino (Palazzo G) (engraving in *Palazzi di Genova* (*Palazzi Antichi*), 1st series, 1622) I: 195, *text ill. 77*
   Façade of the Palazzo Gambaro (without the painted decorations) (engraving in *Palazzi di Genova* (*Palazzi Moderni*), 2nd series, after 1622, figura 6) I: 196, *text ill. 79*

Sadeler, Aegidius
   Hermathene (etching after Hans von Aachen) I: 281 n. 88
   Frontispiece for *Vestigi della antichita di Roma* […], engraving (1606) I: 342, 343 n. 4
Sagittarius, Thomas
   Ulysses Saxonicus seu Iter quod illustrissimus [...] Johannes–Ernestus dux Saxoniae [...] per Germaniam, Galliam, Angliam, & Belgium, Anno 1613 magno cum fructu instituit, et felicissime absolvit [...] (1621) I: 52
Saints
   Bavo I: 56 n. 22, 325 n. 11
   Joseph I: 111, 240 n. 27, 242, 324
   Madonna I: 111, 189, 324, 403
Sambucus, Ioannes I: 368 n. 3
Sanden, Jacob(us) van der
   Oud Konst-Tooneel van Antwerpen (1760–75) I: 77, 78, 168, 169, 212, 213, 214, 217, 250 n. 5, 310; II: 29, *appendix I.42*, 40, 41
Sandrart, Joachim von
   L'Academia Todesca della Architectura, Scultura & Pittura: oder Teutsche Academie der Edlen Bau-, Bild- und Mahlerey-Künste (1675–80) I: 74, 108 n. 38, 208 n. 19, 209 n. 22, 234, 237, 333, 389; II: 22, *appendix I.29*, 39
Sanmichele, Michele
   Fortezza di Sant'Andrea, Venice I: 290 n. 117
   Porta Nuova, Verona I: 290 n. 117
   Porta Palio, Verona I: 290 n. 117
Sansovino, Jacopo
   Zecca, Venice I: 290 n. 117
Santvoort, Godevaert van I: 37 n. 60; II: 9
Saphyrus I: 227 n. 90
Savonnières I: 410
Scaevola: see Mucius Scaevola
Scamozzi, Vincenzo I: 143, 346, 404 n. 1
   L'idea della architettura universal (1615) I: 121, 208, 245
Scheldt I: 34, 130, 401 n. 2
Schets, Koenraad I: 31
Schottius I: 53
Schut, Cornelis I: 215, 247
Schweig, Louis I: 82 n. 96
   Rubens's Garden Pavilion (stereoscopic photograph), Antwerp, Museum aan de Stroom I: 82, 307, 408, 432, 433 n. 2; II: *appendix III.50*
   Rubens's Garden Pavilion (photographic print), Paris, Bibliothèque nationale de France II: 67
Seilern, Antoine, Count I: 363, 364, 365, 367, 370 n. 1
Seneca (Lucius Annaeus Seneca) I: 119, 147, 148, 149 (nn. 32, 34), 150, 151, 227, 233, 322, 323, 339, 341, 394, 401, 402, 413 n. 6; II: 10, 57
Serlio, Sebastiano I: 121, 178, 189; II: 34
   Extraordinario libro di architettvra [...] (1551) I: 275 n. 74, 292
   Livre extraordinaire (1551) I: 292 n. 127
   Regole generali di architettura (1537) I: 120, 189–190, 290–291, 316, 317, 380
      The Five Orders (engraving) I: 290, *text ill. 133*
      A Façade (engraving) I: 316, *text ill. 143*
   Tutte l'opere d'architettura et prospetiva (1540) I: 244-245
   Van de architecturen vijf boecken Sebastiani Serlii (1616) I: 121 n. 16, 316
Sevin, Franciscus Desiderius de
   Pindus Charitatis [1675–1695] I: 89, 97, 111, 232, 245; II: 26, *appendix I.36*, 40
The Drunken Silenus (ancient sculpture), formerly in the collection of Cyriacus Mattei, Rome, now lost
   E I: 373, 374 n. 1; II: *fig. 104*
Sint-Joost-ten-Node (Saint-Josse-ten-Noode): see Brussels
Sluter, Claus
   Pleurants (sculpture), Dijon, Musée des Beaux-Arts I: 358 n. 9
Smekens (family) I: 48

Smekens, Hans I: 45; II: 15, 16, 17, 19
Smits, Syke II: 16
Smits, Weduwe I: 17
Snaet, Joris
  Reconstruction of a Protestant Temple in Ghent (drawing), Private Collection I: 29 n. 27, 30, *text ill. 3*
Snellinckx, Andries
  The Park of a Castle (painting after Rubens), whereabouts unknown I: 62 n. 43
Snellinckx, widow of Andries I: 61–62
Snijders, Frans
  Homage to Ceres (painting with Rubens), St Petersburg, The State Hermitage Museum I: 118, 143 n. 14, 152, 265, 268, 269, 315, 382, 415, 433 n. 4; II: 48, *appendix III.13; fig. 23*
  Cimon and Iphigenia (painting with Rubens), Vienna, Kunsthistorisches Museum I: 426, 427
  The Fish Market (The Emperor's Mullet) (painting with Rubens's studio, with Anthony van Dyck identified as the principal executant), Vienna, Kunsthistorisches Museum I: 269; II: 50, *appendix III.17*
Soane, John I: 248
Soane's House, now Sir John Soanes's Museum: see London
Socrates I: 149 n. 34
Sophocles I: 149 n. 34, 384 n. 1
Sotheby's London (auctioneer) I: 364
Sotheby's Monaco (auctioneer) I: 386 n. 29; II: 61
Sotheby's New York (auctioneer) I: 305 n. 22
Spain
  Private Collection
    Anonymous 17th-century painter of the *Bathsheba Bathing* (painting) I: 271, 426; II: 61, *appendix III.38*
Sperling, Otto I: 20, 53–54, 213–214, 215, 217, 218, 219, 220, 221, 244; II: 21, 35
  Selvbiografi (1602–1673) I: 53–54, 213–214, 215, 217, 218, 219, 220, 221, 244; II: 21, 35
Spranger, Bartholomeus I: 181, 197, 198, 350 n. 9
Staben, Hendrik
  Archdukes Albrecht and Isabella Visiting a Picture Gallery (painting), Brussels, Musées royaux de Beaux-Arts de Belgique I: 390
  Archdukes Albrecht and Isabella Visiting a Picture Gallery (painting), Beloeil, Castle I: 390
Staetmasse (Inventory of Rubens's Estate) I: 46, 56–57, 68 n. 62, 108, 222, 233, 244, 329, 393; II: 18–19, 38
Stappaert, Maria I: 61 n. 41
Steencruyse, Michiel van I: 75; II: 27, 40
Stockholm I: 32 n. 39
  Nationalmuseum I: 61, 288, 301, 427; II: 53
  Riksarkivet II: 25
  Swedish Royal Collections I: 417 n. 12
Stordiau, J.
  The Portico of Rubens's House (designed with Nicaise de Keyser, engraving by Erin Corr) I: 80; II: 65, *appendix III.45*
  The Garden Pavilion of Rubens's House (designed with Nicaise de Keyser, engraving by Erin Corr and Jozef Linnig) I: 80, 307; II: 65, *appendix III.46*
St Petersburg
  The State Hermitage Museum I: 118, 143 n. 14, 174, 228, 239, 268, 315, 330, 333, 334, 350 n. 14, 378, 379, 380, 381, 382, 383, 385 (nn. 11, 13), 415, 426, 433 n. 4
    Roman, *Perseus and Andromeda* (cameo) I: 386 n. 42
    Anonymous 17th-century artist, *Portrait of Rubens and his Son (Albert?)* (painting) I: 241; II: *appendix III.27*
    Anonymous 17th-century artist after ? Rubens, *Architectural Sketchbook* (album of pen sketches) I: 272, 273, *text ills 120–121*
Stuart, Henry, Duke of Gloucester I: 66; II: 39
Stuart, Mary, widow of William II, Prince of Orange I: 66; II: 39
Suermondt, Barthold II: 56
Sustermans, Justus I: 168 n. 5, 188
Sweerts, François (Franciscus Sweertius) I: 120 n. 9, 123, 126, 127, 134, 220 n. 56; II: 12, 35
Switzerland I: 197

Tardieu, Pierre-François
  Andromeda Liberated by Perseus (etching and engraving after Rubens) I: 380; II: 30, *fig. 114*
Teniers, David II II: 61
  Elegant Company in a Garden (painting), Antwerp, The Phoebus Foundation I: 107, 303, 305, 409, 410, 411, 426; II: 59, *appendix III.34; fig. 190*
Tessin, Nicodemus I: 74–75, 167, 172; II: 40
  Studieresor i Danmark, Tyskland, Holland, Frankrike och Italien I: 75; II: 25
The Hague I: 66, 90 n. 10, 122, 388 n. 3, 389, 391, 392; II: 37
  Huis ten Bosch
    Oranjezaal I: 247
  Huygenshuis (demolished) I: 160; II: 38
  Mauritshuis I: 218, *text ill. 100*, 238, 361; II: 46
Thovion, Clara de I: 25–26
Thulden, Theodoor van
  'Fontainebleau Sketchbook' (album of drawings, designs attributed to), various locations I: 359 n.17
  Map of Antwerp with the Joyous Entry of Cardinal-Infante Ferdinand (etching and engraving) I: 64
  The Stage of Welcome (etching after Rubens) I: 403, 412
    The Statue of Good Hope I: 329, 345; II: *fig. 50*
    Pedestal with ram's heads I: 403; II: *fig. 164*
    Genius of the City of Antwerp I: 412, 413; II: *fig. 192*
  Portico of the Emperors (etching after Rubens) I: 145,

146, *text ill. 62*
The Stage of Isabella (etching after Rubens) I: 266, 297, *text ill. 136*
The Arch of Ferdinand (Rear Face) (etching after Rubens) I: 412
Thys (Thisius) family I: 31–33, 36, 37, 38, 39, 45
Thys, Anthony I: 38; II: 7
Thys, Christoffel I: 31–33, 40; II: 7
Thys, François I: 40; II: 7
Thys, Hans (Johan(nes)) I: 32, 33, 34, 38, 39, 40, 129, 388; II: 5–6, 7, 33
Thys, Hans II I: 38, 39 n. 66
Thys, Magdalena (see also Andries Bacher) I: 32, 33, 35; II: 6, 7
Memoriael I: 32 n. 42
Timanthes I: 179
The Sacrifice of Iphigenia (painting), lost I: 176, 177 n. 25, 181, 356, 358 n. 9, 359 n. 13
Titian (Tiziano Vecellio) I:
Ecce Homo (painting), Vienna, Kunsthistorisches Museum I: 87 n. 3
The Rape of Europa (painting), Boston, MA, Isabella Stewart Gardner Museum I: 428 n. 3
Tournai
Cathedral I: 316 n. 50
Trajan I: 399
Trojan War I: 355, 358 n. 2
Trumbull, William I: 61 n. 61; II: 35
Twelve Years' Truce I: 33–34, 130 n. 42; II: 32

Utrecht I: 32
Uxbridge (Buckinghamshire)
Denham Court II: 43
Uylenburgh (art dealer) I: 248 n. 56
Uylenburgh, Saskia van I: 40 n. 75

Vaduz – Vienna
Liechtenstein, The Princely Collections: see Vienna
Vaga, Perino del
Frescoes, Genoa, Palazzo del Principe Andrea Doria, Façade (destroyed) I: 193
Design for the North Façade of the Palazzo Doria, Genoa (drawing), Amsterdam, Rijksmuseum I: 193 n. 18, 194 (*text ill. 76*)
Design for a Façade of the Palazzo Doria, Genoa (drawing), Chantilly, Musée Condé I: 193 n. 18
Valerius Maximus
Memorabilia I: 356, 358 n. 8
Vasari, Giorgio I: 173 n. 14, 181, 182, 189, 200, 358 n. 9
Lives (Vite) I: 189
Timanthes Painting the 'Sacrifice of Iphigenia' (fresco), Arezzo, Casa Vasari I: 181, 357, 359 n. 12; II: *fig. 79*
Zeuxis and the Maidens of Croton (fresco), Arezzo, Casa Vasari I: 181, 371, 372 n. 9
Vascosan, Michel de I: 368 n. 3
Vecquemans, F. II: 18

Veen, Otto van (Vaenius) I: 345
Emblemata Horatiana (1607)
Man between Hope and Fear I: 345 n. 6
Zeuxis and the Maidens of Croton (oil sketch), whereabouts unknown I: 372; II: *fig. 99*
Velázquez, Diego
Landscape (painting), Madrid, Museo Nacional del Prado I: 318 n. 54
Landscape (another painting), Madrid, Museo Nacional del Prado I: 318 n. 54
Veldenaar or Veldener, Jenin I: 326
Velt, Cornelis II: 6
Venice I: 32 n. 39, 120, 121 n. 15, 245 n. 39, 290 n. 117, 292 n. 127, 316; II: 12
Palazzo d'Anna I: 191
Venus Pudica (sculpture), Rome, Musei Capitolini I: 382
Venuti, Rudolfino
(with J.C. Amaduzzi) *Vetera Monumenta* (1774–1779) I : 373, 374 n. 1; II: *fig. 104*
Verbiest, Pieter
Bird's-eye View of Antwerp from the West (engraving, c. 1650) I: 65, *text ill. 13*
The Siege of Antwerp by Prince Maurice of Orange in 1605 (engraving, 1628) I: 64, *text ill. 10*
Verona I: 191
Casa Trevisani-Lonardi I: 191
City gates I: 290 n. 117
Veronese, Paolo
Loggia with a Lady and her Maid (fresco), Maser, Villa Barbaro I: 376; II: *fig. 108*
Verreycken, Godefridus I: 37 (nn. 59, 60); II: 7, 9
Viani, Antonio Maria
Chiesa Sant'Orsola, Mantua I: 264 n. 43
Vicenza
Basilica I: 316, 371, *text ill. 144*
Vienna
Albertina I: 192 (n. 77), 288, 317, 381
Anonymous 16th-century artist, *The Façade of Palazzo Gaddi, Rome* (drawing after Polidoro da Caravaggio) I: 192 n. 77
Anonymous 17th-century artist, *Pegasus* (drawing) I: 381, 386 n. 28
Kunsthistorisches Museum I: 62 n. 44, 87 n. 3, 133, 225 n. 72, 269, 282 n. 94, 374 n. 2, 399, 426, 427; II: 49, 50
Liechtenstein Museum (The Princely Collections) / Liechtenstein collection I: 382, 394, 399, 401, 402 n. 3, 403 (nn. 2, 5)
Vienne (France) I: 267 n. 56
Vigenère, Blaise de I: 384 n. 3
Vignola, Giacomo Barozzi da I: 121, 290, 404 n. 1
Entrance of the Villa Giulia, Rome I:
Regola delli Cinque ordini d'architettura (1563) I: 122, 401; II: *fig. 170*
Porte d'architettura di Michel Angelo (addendum from 1602 onwards) (engraving) I: 286, *text ill. 127*

Garden Portal of the Villa Carpi in Rome (engraving) I: 401; II: *fig. 154*
Le due regole della prospettiva pratica (1611) I: 286 n. 107
Vinck, Catherina de I: 78 n. 82
Virgil (Publius Vergilius Maro)
   Aeneid I: 365, 369 n. 8
Virtues I: 194, 384, 411–412, 413 n. 10
Vitruvius I: 147, 165, 208, 244, 245
   De architectura libri decem (1567) I: 121; II: 34
   De architectura libri decem (1586) I: 121; II: 34
Voet, Alexander I I: 270, 396
Vorsterman, Lucas I
   Bust of Seneca (engraving after Rubens and his Studio) I: 146
Vorsterman, Lucas II
   Courbette de côté à gauche (engraving after Abraham van Diepenbeeck) I: 70, *text ill. 18*
Vorsterman, Otto II: 14
Vos, Andries de II: 9
Vos, Cornelis de
   'Le Salon de Rubens' (painting with Frans Francken II), Stockholm, Nationalmuseum I: 61
   A Young Painter Behind a Balustrade, whereabouts unknown I: 209, *text ill. 87*
Vos, Maarten de
   The Calumny of Apelles (painting), Private Collection I: 364, 368 n. 5
Vos, Simon de II: 61
Vrancx, Sebastiaan I: 119, 392 n. 3
Vredeman de Vries, Hans
   Mural paintings in the State Chamber of the Antwerp Town Hall (lost) I: 376
      19th-century copies on paper, Antwerp, FelixArchief I: 376

Walle, Benedictus van de I: 61
'Walloon Calvinists' I: 29, 42
Washington, DC
   National Gallery of Art I: 266, 267 n. 54, 271, 395; II: Andrew W. Mellon Collection I: 44

Weimar
   Klassik Stiftung Weimar I: 306, 421; II: 63
Welbeck Abbey I: 68
Werff, Adriaen van der
   The Introduction to the Temple of Fine Arts (oilsketch), Munich, Bayerische Staatsgemäldesammlungen, Alte Pinakothek I: 429, 430 n. 5
Wildens, Jan I: 61, 226
Wildens, Jeremias I: 226
William I, Prince of Orange I: 382, 386 n. 39
William II, Prince of Orange I: 66
Wolley, John I: 55
Wouters, Frans
   The Discovery of Callisto's Pregnancy (painting), Kromeriz, Archbishop's Palace I: 427–428; II: 62, *appendix III.39*
Wouters, Pierre I: 58
Wouwer, Jan van den (Joannes Woveriuis) I: 128, 191 n. 71; II: 12, 35

Yper, Carel van
   Painted Façades in Ypres (lost) I: 198 n. 95
Ypres I: 198 n. 95

Zaltbommel
   Loevestein Castle I: 53
Zaventem
   Church of St Martin I: 269, 398
Zeuxis I: 176, 177 (n. 23), 178 (n. 25), 181, 182, 188, 370–372
   Marsyas Bound (painting), formerly Rome, 'Shrine of Concord' I: 349, 350 n.5
Zuccaro (Zuccari), Federico I: 200, 364, 365, 366, 368 n. 6
   The Calumny of Apelles (painting), lost I: ; II: *fig. 92*
Zuiderzee (now IJsselmeer) I: 38; II: 33

Sources of Photographs

COVER VOL. I
© Collectie Stad Antwerpen, Rubenshuis: photo Bart Huysmans & Michel Wuyts

COVER VOL. II
© Courtauld Institute

AMSTERDAM
© C. Messier (Wikimedia: CC BY-SA 4.0): Text ill. 153
© Rijksmuseum (Public Domain CC0): Text ills 11, 62, 63, 76, 77, 136; Figs 17, 40, 49, 50, 59, 92, 164, 169, 192, 234

ANTWERP
© Ans Brys: Text ill. 55
© Brecht Vanoppen: Text ills 43, 86, 91, 114; Figs 11, 14, 15, 129, 162, 171, 173, 175, 176, 178
© Collectie Stad Antwerpen, Mas: Appendix III.50; Fig. 235
© Collectie Stad Antwerpen, Museum Plantin-Moretus: Text ills 4, 5, 6, 7, 9, 12, 17, 24, 25, 26, 27, 28, 29, 30, 31, 32, 33, 34, 39, 40, 41, 42, 44, 45, 46, 47, 48, 50, 51, 52, 57, 58, 61, 66, 68, 90, 94, 102, 122, 124, 139, 152; Appendix III.1, 2, 47; Figs 1, 18, 26, 28, 29, 30, 32, 33, 34, 36, 38, 39, 41, 43, 44, 47, 51, 53, 54, 57, 60, 64, 69, 82, 90, 98, 101, 106, 107, 110, 114, 122, 124, 127, 142, 151, 153, 168, 180, 183, 184, 185, 187, 188, 191, 195, 206, 225, 227, 228, 231, 233
© Collectie Stad Antwerpen, Rubenshuis: Text ills 49, 64, 67, 93, 96, 97, 99, 142; Appendix III.30, 40, 44, 45, 46, 49; Fig. 133, 144, 145, 163, 165, 166, 199, 214, 215, 224
  / photo Bart Huysmans & Michel Wuyts: Fig. 10
  / photo Michel Wuyts: Fig. 12
© Dtonic: Text ills 65, 108, 109, 112, 137; Figs 138, 140, 149, 150, 157, 158, 161, 177, 202, 203, 204, 211
© FelixArchief, Stadsarchief Antwerpen: Text ills 1, 8, 13, 16, 22, 23, 53, 59, 60, 69, 82, 84, 85, 98, 104, 105, 106, 107, 110; Appendix III.51, 52; Figs 2, 4, 5, 13, 131, 132, 143, 160, 189
© Foto Peter Maes: Text ill. 10
© FrDr (Wikimedia: CC BY-SA 4.0): Text ill. 155
© Helena Busses: Fig. 213
© Joris Snaet: Text ill. 3
© Koninklijk Museum voor Schone Kunsten Antwerpen
© Lode De Clercq: Fig. 136
© Nolde16 (Wikimedia: CC BY-SA 4.0): Text ill. 115
© Rubenianum: Text ills 2, 54, 75, 81, 87, 89, 111, 118, 120, 121, 130, 135, 150, 151, 154; Appendix III.16, 17, 19, 22, 25, 26, 31, 33, 36a, 36b, 37, 38, 39, 41; Figs 6, 7, 8, 9, 58, 61, 62, 63, 68, 72, 73, 87, 94, 95, 99, 104, 105, 109, 119, 134, 152, 154, 186, 194, 207
© The Phoebus Foundation: Appendix III.34; Fig. 190

AREZZO
© MB_Photo / Alamy Stock Photo: Fig. 79

AYLESBURY
© Buckinghamshire County Museum (CC BY 4.0): Appendix III.3 ; Figs 16, 27, 37, 42, 52, 70, 83, 91, 141

BASEL
© Public Domain (Basel, Kunstmuseum): Text ill. 80

BERLIN
© bpk / Gemäldegalerie, SMB / Jörg P. Anders: Appendix III.10, 29; Figs 22, 113, 167, 181, 208, 212 , 230

BRUSSELS
© KBR: Text ill. 21; Appendix III.4, 42, 43; Figs 3, 125, 126
© KIK–IRPA: Text ills 38, 83, 101, 125, 141; Figs 35, 172, 236

BUDAPEST
© SzépművészetiMúzeum / Museum of Fine Arts, 2022: Fig. 72

CHANTILLY
© RMN-Grand Palais (domaine de Chantilly) / René-Gabriel Ojeda: Fig. 80

CHESTERFIELD
© David Dixon (Geograph.org.uk: CC BY SA 2.0): Text ill. 15

COLOGNE
© Wallraf-Richartz-Museum & Fondation Corboud, Graphische Sammlung. Foto: Dieter Bongartz: Fig. 65

COPENHAGEN
© SMK Open (Public Domain CC0): Figs 71, 75, 77, 84, 100, 112, 174, 200, 201
© SMK Photo / Jakob Skou-Hansen: Fig. 46

FLORENCE
© 2021. Photo Scala, Florence - courtesy of the Ministero Beni e Att. Culturali e del Turismo: Fig. 81
© Sailko (Wikimedia: CC-BY-2.5): Text ill. 131

267

SOURCES OF PHOTOGRAPHS

GENUA
© Public Domain (Wikimedia): Text ill. 78

LA FLÈCHE (FRANCE)
© Selbymay (Wikimedia: CC BY-SA 3.0): Text ill. 117

LONDON
© Courtauld Institute: Figs 96, 97
© Sailko (Wikimedia: CC BY 3.0): Appendix III.15
© The British Museum / Trustees of the British Museum: Text ills 19, 73; Appendix III.28a, 28b; Fig. 209
© The National Gallery, London: Text ills 20, 95, 119, 123; Appendix III.11
© Victoria and Albert Museum, London: Text ill. 74

LONGNIDDRY
© Gosford House, East Lothian, The Earl of Wemyss and March: Fig. 223

MADRID
© Museo Nacional del Prado: Text ills 134, 146; Appendix III.9, 24; Figs 20, 159, 179, 220

MANTUA
© Alessio Ferrarini: Fig. 86
© Geobia (Wikimedia: CC-BY-SA-4.0): Text ill. 70
© Ivan Vdovin / Alamy Stock Photo: Fig. 66
© Marcok (Wikimedia: CC-BY-SA 3.0): Text ill. 129

MENTMORE (UK)
© Courtauld Institute of Art: Text ill. 149

MUNICH
© bpk | Bayerische Staatsgemäldesammlungen: Appendix III.6; Figs 25, 93, 182, 196, 205, 210, 218

NAPLES
© Sailko (Wikimedia: CC BY-SA 3.0): Fig. 193
© Su concessione del Ministero dei Beni e delle Attività Culturali – Museo Archeologico Nazionali di Napoli: Figs 48, 216, 221

NEW YORK
© The Morgan Library & Museum: Fig. 147

OXFORD
© Ashmolean Museum: Figs 197, 198

PARIS
© 1987 RMN-Grand Palais (musée du Louvre) / Daniel Arnaudet: Appendix III.21
© Faxa (Wikimedia: CC BY-SA 3.0): Text ill. 132
© RMN Grand Palais (musée du Louvre) / Franck Raux: Appendix III.7; Figs 21, 31, 55
© RMN-Grand Palais (musée du Louvre) / Hervé Lewandowski: Figs 102, 103
© RMN Grand Palais (musée du Louvre) / René-Gabriel Ojeda / Thierry Le Mage: Appendix III.20
© RMN Grand Palais (musée du Louvre) / Thierry Le Mage: Appendix III.18; Fig. 24

RIJSWIJK (THE NETHERLANDS)
© Rijksdienst voor het Cultureel Erfgoed (Wikimedia: CC BY-SA 4.0): Appendix III.35

ROHRAU (LOWER AUSTRIA)
© Graf Harrach'sche Familiensammlung: Text ill. 88; Appendix III.32

ROME
© AGF Srl / Alamy Stock Photo: Text ill. 72; Fig. 56
© CCCP (Wikimedia: CC BY-SA 2.5 CA): Fig. 88
© Dietmar Rabich / Wikimedia Commons / "Rome (IT), Porta Pia -- 2013 -- 3341" / CC BY-SA 4.0: Text ill. 126
© Hans Meyer-Veden: Text ill. 113
© Jean-Pierre Dalbéra (Flickr: CC BY 2.0): Fig. 67
© Jean-Pol Grandmont (Wikimedia: CC BY-SA 3.0): Fig: 217
© Luca Verzulli (CC BY-NC-SA 2.0): Text ill.71
© Matthias Kabel (Wikimedia: CC BY-SA 3.0): Fig. 76
© Miguel Hermoso Cuesta (Wikimedia: CC BY-SA 3.0): Fig. 45
© 2021. Photo Scala, Florence – courtesy of the Ministero Beni e Att. Culturali e del Turismo: Fig. 85
© Sailko (Wikimedia: CC BY-3.0): Text ill. 148; Figs 123, 146
© Wikimedia Commons | Magnus Manske: Text ill. 147

STOCKHOLM
© Nationalmuseum (Public Domain): Text ill. 138; Appendix III.23; Fig. 226

ST PETERSBURG
© The State Hermitage Museum. Photo by Alexander Lavrentyev: Fig. 219
© The State Hermitage Museum. Photo by Vladimir Terebenin, Leonard Kheifets: Appendix III.13, 27; Figs 23, 111, 116, 118, 120, 121

THE HAGUE
© Mauritshuis, The Hague: Text ills 100, 103; Appendix III.8; Figs 128, 130, 135
© Rijksdienst voor het Cultureel Erfgoed (Wikimedia: CC BY-SA 4.0): Text ill. 92

VADUZ –VIENNA
© Liechtenstein, The Princely Collections, Vaduz–Vienna, : Text ill. 56; Figs 78, 117, 137, 148, 156
© LIECHTENSTEIN, The Princely Collections, Vaduz–Vienna / Scala, Florence: Fig. 155

SOURCES OF PHOTOGRAPHS

VICENZA
© Zairon (Wikimedia: CC BY-SA 4.0): Text ill. 144

VIENNA
© Albertina, Vienna: Text ill. 145
© KHM-Museumsverband: Appendix III.14

WASHINGTON, DC
© National Gallery of Art: Text ill. 116; Appendix III.5; Figs 19, 232

CORPUS RUBENIANUM LUDWIG BURCHARD

PATRON
HSH Prince Hans-Adam II von und zu Liechtenstein

Rubenianum Fund

BOARD
Thomas Leysen (Chairman)
Jérémie Leroy, Nils Büttner, Michel Ceuterick, Gregory Martin, Ben van Beneden

BENEFACTORS
Fonds Baillet Latour
The Colnaghi Foundation
Fonds Léon Courtin-Marcelle Bouché, managed by the King Baudouin Foundation
The Klesch Collection
Catherine Lewis Foundation / Schorr Collection
The Samuel H. Kress Foundation
The Michael Marks Charitable Trust
vzw Natuurbehoud Pater David
Broere Charitable Foundation
The Hans K. Rausing Trust

Allaert-d'Hulst family
Arnout Balis
Joris Brantegem
Annette Bühler
Michel Ceuterick
Herman De Bode
Georges De Jonckheere
Eijk and Rose-Marie de Mol van Otterloo
Dr Willem Dreesmann
Antoine Friling
Bob Haboldt
Gaëtan and Bénédicte Hannecart
Jules-André Hayen

Fiona Healy
Steven Heinz
Willem Jan and Karin Hoogsteder
Baroness Paul Janssen
David Koetser
David Kowitz
Eric Le Jeune
Bettina Leysen
Thomas and Nancy Leysen
Stichting Liedts-Meessen
Elizabeth McGrath
Pierre Macharis
Patrick Maselis

Otto Naumann
Natan Saban
Cliff Schorer
Léon Seynaeve
Vic and Lea Swerts
Daniel Thierry
Michel Thoulouze
Tomasso, UK
Johnny Van Haeften
Eric Verbeeck
Juan Miguel Villar Mir
Matthew and Susan Weatherbie
Mark Weiss

DONORS
Patricia Annicq
Bijl-Van Urk Master Paintings
Ingrid Ceusters
Manny and Brigitta Davidson
Jean-Marie De Coster
Baron Bertrand de Giey
Koen De Groeve
Joseph de Gruyter
Philip de Haseth-Möller
Ann Dejonckheere
Jan De Maere
Michel Demoortel
Elisabeth de Rothschild
Bernard Descheemaeker
François de Visscher
Eric Dorhout Mees
Count Ghislain d'Ursel
Jacqueline Gillion
Alice Goldet

Dov Gottesman
Fergus and Olivia Hall
Stéphane Holvoet
Horsch and Huebscher
Christophe Janet
Baron Daniel Janssen
Baron Paul-Emmanuel Janssen
Jean-Louis and Martine Juliard-Reynaers
Gijs Keij
Cécile Kruyfhooft
Christian Levett
Christian and Brigitte Leysen
Sabina Leysen
Anne Leysen-Ahlers
Sergey Litvin
Anne-Marie Logan
Gregory Martin
Filip Moerman
Baron Jean-Albert Moorkens

Philip Mould
Jan Muller
Klaas Muller
Simon and Elena Mumford
Marnix Neerman
Paulson Family Foundation
Joseph and Jane Roussel
Eric Speeckaert
Alexander Thijs and Joop Scheffer
Eric Turquin
Rafael Valls
Lieve Vandeputte
Philippe Van de Vyvere
Guido Vanherpe
Jeannot Van Hool
Tijo and Christine van Marle
Rijnhard and Elsbeth van Tets
Axel Vervoordt
Morris Zukerman

CORPORATE BENEFACTORS
Thomas Agnew's & Co.
BASF Antwerpen NV
Belfius Bank
Bernaerts NV
Biront NV
Christie's

Crop's NV
Dorotheum
Groupe Bruxelles Lambert SA
KBC Group NV
Koller Auctions Ltd
Lazard Frères
Lhoist SA

Matthiesen Ltd
Noortman Master Paintings
Rosy Blue NV
Sibelco – SCR NV
Sotheby's
Telenet NV

and a number of donors and benefactors who wish to remain anonymous